Women in
Jamaican Music

ALSO BY HEATHER AUGUSTYN

*Don Drummond: The Genius and Tragedy
of the World's Greatest Trombonist* (McFarland, 2013)

Ska: An Oral History (McFarland, 2010)

Women in Jamaican Music

HEATHER AUGUSTYN

McFarland & Company, Inc., Publishers
Jefferson, North Carolina

LIBRARY OF CONGRESS CATALOGUING-IN-PUBLICATION DATA

Names: Augustyn, Heather, 1972– author.
Title: Women in Jamaican music / Heather Augustyn.
Description: Jefferson : McFarland & Company, Inc., Publishers, 2020. | Includes bibliographical references and index.
Identifiers: LCCN 2020017422 | ISBN 9781476680958 (paperback) | ISBN 9781476639598 (ebook)
Subjects: LCSH: Women musicians—Jamaica. | Popular music—Jamaica—History and criticism.
Classification: LCC ML82 .A85 2020 | DDC 781.64082/097292—dc23
LC record available at https://lccn.loc.gov/2020017422

BRITISH LIBRARY CATALOGUING DATA ARE AVAILABLE

**ISBN (print) 978-1-4766-8095-8
ISBN (ebook) 978-1-4766-3959-8**

© 2020 Heather Augustyn. All rights reserved

No part of this book may be reproduced or transmitted in any form or by any means, electronic or mechanical, including photocopying or recording, or by any information storage and retrieval system, without permission in writing from the publisher.

Front cover images © 2020 Shutterstock

Printed in the United States of America

*McFarland & Company, Inc., Publishers
Box 611, Jefferson, North Carolina 28640
www.mcfarlandpub.com*

For Ron, Sid, and Frank

Acknowledgments

Thank you to all of the women who have trusted me with your stories and opened up to me about your personal lives, your sacrifices, and your successes. It has been an absolute honor. I have deeply enjoyed our conversations and connecting with you. To the families of those pioneering women who have died: Thank you for helping me to preserve and celebrate your grandmothers, mothers, aunts, sisters, wives, and friends. Together we will make certain that as the decades go by, these legends are always recognized for their contributions to culture.

To my family for supporting my constant attachment to my computer so that I could complete this work, and for indulging my frequent conversations and discussions about any number of topics related to Jamaican music. You are my sounding board and my heart.

To historian extraordinaire Roberto Moore for your expertise, support, and friendship. To mento expert Daniel Neely for your help in locating information on obscure women in obscure articles in your impressive archives. To Chris Flanagan for allowing me to benefit from his decade-long quest and his generous assistance. To John Vaccaro for a bounty of articles on Millie Small. To my editor Charlie Perdue at McFarland for cultivating my work and for understanding the significance of Jamaican music to global culture.

To my teachers, Carol Biel, Barbara Funke, Robert Kelly, James Ballowe, and Kevin Stein. You all gave me the foundation and the passion. To my superiors and colleagues at Purdue Northwest. You always champion my scholarship and I am humbled.

For my fellow skamrades: Thank you for reading my work and engaging in dialogue. May this book only deepen your knowledge and appreciation of ska, folk, mento, jazz, rocksteady, reggae, dub, and dancehall and all other forms, since Jamaican music is like the River Nile, which has made fertile the lands that surround it, for other genres, other musicians, other enthusiasts to grow.

Contents

Acknowledgments vii
Introduction 1

ONE: Women in Jamaican Folk Traditions 3
TWO: Orchestra and Band Leaders and Instrumentalists 10
THREE: Mento and Calypso 34
FOUR: Jazz 43
FIVE: Ska 56
SIX: Blue Beat 75
SEVEN: Rocksteady 88
EIGHT: Reggae 98
NINE: Dancehall 131
TEN: Dance 137
ELEVEN: Champions 147
TWELVE: Studio 162
THIRTEEN: Mothers and Wives 170
FOURTEEN: Female Representation in Song Lyrics 191

Chapter Notes 203
Bibliography 209
Index 211

Introduction

In their article "Playing Like a Girl: The Problems with Reception of Women in Music," authors Carrie Leigh Page and Dana Reason propose that the lack of women in music is a matter of reception. The authors suggest that reception falls into three categories: "Receipt—Getting the music to an audience, which involves access; Response—Having an audience react to the music and form judgments about its worth; Admission—Allowing the work to be part of a collective group, canon, or curriculum."[1] It is the first two steps that I examine in this book, by providing the history of individual women's "receipt," or getting their music to their audience; and the "response" of that audience through discussion of their residencies, bookings, performances, recordings, and media coverage. It is the third step that I hope to provide with the publication of this book: allowing these women "admission" into the canon. In writing the histories of the women contained within this book, it is my wish that their contributions will be allowed reception not only into the Jamaican musical canon but into the canon of music history as a whole.

Bob Marley historian Roger Steffens once told me there have been over 500 books written about Bob Marley. I don't doubt it. Bob Marley is so ubiquitous that one can find his pensive countenance accompanied by some lyrical quotations, be they biblical or that of Marcus Garvey, on garment racks inside the most rural Walmarts of America. Travel to Sao Paulo, Valencia, Johannesburg, Osaka, Mumbai, a youth hostel in Reykjavik, a café in Cartagena, and the visage is there, from Jamaica with love. Imagine walking into Dubuque, Iowa, and seeing a nicely distressed t-shirt with the face of Marcia Griffiths or red, green, and gold music headphones with a package boasting the name of Hortense Ellis. Seems ridiculous. But why should it not be so? Women like Griffiths and Ellis and Rickards and Graydon and dozens of others have not been allowed "receipt" of their music, therefore no "response," and therefore, no "admission"—into the libraries or to the opportunity to commodify their brand on bags of coffee and packets of rolling papers, since that is the way modern society measures success.

There is no justice I seek for these women, for that can never be attained. This book comes too late for that. Nor am I so arrogant as to assume that one writer could ever wave a magic pen and achieve fairness and balance after centuries of struggle. Instead I wish to expose and lay bare the reality of what these women must have had to endure in order to achieve what they did in comparison to their male counterparts. Some were able to make a living at their craft. Some worked at desk jobs or as nurses or in real estate or telemarketing or other "normal jobs" at the same time as performing at night, singing in clubs, traveling to all points on the island or to all corners of the globe. Others left their talent behind for good, because they were tired of being exploited, tired of being propositioned, tired of leaving their children at night when no one else was there to provide care. Men rarely had to make such choices. To write this book alone, I had to take time away from my own children, time that will never return to me—but thankfully, I had the support and means to follow my work through to fruition with little compromise to the necessities of living that eliminate choice from the equation. This book is dedicated to the women who had to make these same choices, and the women whose names will never be known because a choice never existed.

Understand that this book—the women whose stories I tell and the body of work I address—is neither comprehensive nor complete. The wealth of music and musicians is so deep that for every example there is likely a counterexample or a reinforcing example. Nor is this book a catalog of every woman who has contributed to Jamaican music, though it may seem like that in the chapters on the early years, because there were so few. When the 1980s and 1990s came around, there were more women who were finally allowed space in the music industry since they had been empowered by those who blazed the trail before them. Any omission of a particular woman does not in any way diminish her career, impact on others, or importance. This book is not an encyclopedia, rather a collection of narrative biographies.

Moving forward, what can we all do to right the wrongs of history regarding women in Jamaican music? First, we can write more books on them. Bob Marley, as wonderful and worthy as he is of canonical treatment, has already been given his due. Other talented musicians whose words are similarly inspiring, speak to the human condition, and empower and uplift, including women, are ready for their time in the spotlight, so pick up a pen and write the half that has never been told. Second, we can listen to the music these women were able to produce for us. Receive their sacrifice. Receive their art. Sing along. Third, we can spread the word. Introduce someone else to the music of Patsy Todd or Doreen Shaffer. Buy your friend a vinyl, CD, or non-pirated and non-streaming copy of these women's work. Hand off your headphones or play their songs at your next deejay session. Let us recognize these women for their contributions to a musical culture which has been historically male. Let us not allow women in Jamaican music to continue languishing in obscurity. These women are not mere subjects in a history book. Even if they are long gone from this earth, they existed, and through their creativity and music, they live on forever.

CHAPTER ONE

Women in Jamaican Folk Traditions

Though it might be appropriate to begin a chapter on women in Jamaican folk traditions with a folk tale involving a female character, one would be hard pressed to find such a character. The Jamaican Anansi stories, rooted in African culture, feature characters with titles like Bredda Lion, Bredda Snake, Bredda Rabbit, Bredda Bull, Bredda Dog, Bro Scopion, and of course, Bredda Anansi. Anansi stories were tales of resistance, passed through oral tradition to give hope to slaves and the oppressed. For women, who were largely absent from the tales—save for Bredda Anansi's wife, who helped him and put up with his antics—any hope received from these tales of resistance was limited.

In one tale, though, "Anansi and the Yam Hills,"[1] one female character does provide a sense of empowerment over those who try to oppress her. The oppressor in this story, Bredda Anansi himself, has learned the spell of an evil witch named "Five" and used it to trick shoppers in the vegetable market so he can steal their purchases for his hungry family. When the unsuspecting shopper says the word "five," the name of the witch who cast this spell, they disappear, thus leaving their yams for the taking. Mrs. Guinea Fowl, however, is too wise, and she tricks Bredda Anansi in return, forcing him to say the word "five," after which he disappears. It is a tale that portrays women as astute, intelligent, and ultimately clever, and portrays the male as sneaky, devious, and desiring of a shortcut, even if his intention—to feed his hungry family—is good.

This story reveals the struggle that many women in Jamaican culture have had to endure and the strengths they had to employ. They had to be intelligent and clever, and as a result, they were powerful. Though women in Jamaican folk tales and folk traditions may be few in number, they are significant in magnitude.

Nanny of the Maroons

Jamaican culture is filled with such moralistic tales as are found in Anansi stories, folk stories, myth, literature, and song. One key figure in Jamaican history and culture, also a mythical figure, is Nanny of the Maroons. Step out of the baggage claim at the Norman Manley Airport in Kingston, Jamaica, and one is greeted by her likeness—a massive papier-mâché head atop a large puppet-like torso next to other national heroes:

Samuel Sharpe, George William Gordon, Alexander Bustamante, Paul Bogle, Marcus Mosiah Garvey, and Norman Manley himself. Nanny is the stuff of myth, but she was most definitely a real woman who is worthy of the title of national hero.

Most of what we know of Queen Nanny comes from two sources: the British colonizers and slavers, whom she was fighting, and the oral tradition of the Maroons, her people. Historians have been able to research and corroborate many of these stories, so that we know proof positive that she existed and was a fierce leader and warrior for the Maroons. The Maroons were a community of people with origins in the Ashanti, Akan, Twi, and Fanti tribes of modern-day Ghana. Their language is—or was, since few still speak the ancestral tongue—Koromantee, sometimes spelled Coromantie.[2] The tribes were brought to Jamaica as slaves of the Spanish. When the British invaded Jamaica, the Spaniards fled to other areas of the Caribbean, mostly to Cuba. Because the slaves were already familiar with the terrain, and the British were not, many of these slaves used this to their advantage, rebelling and fleeing into the mountains, where they set up their own communities. Many slaves had already escaped from their Spanish kidnappers, who referred to them as the Cimarrons, meaning untamed or wild. This is the origin of the name Maroons. The Maroons are further identified according to their individual settlements in Jamaica—the Leeward Maroons and the Windward Maroons. Nanny was a member of the latter community. It is not surprising that she was allowed to rise to her potential, as women in general were important to the Maroon communities. They were considered leaders, agricultural providers, givers of life, and warriors.

To understand the tremendous power and character of the Maroon people, author Karla Gottlieb attempts to put this into perspective:

> The story of the Maroons is unique in history. How several hundred escaped slaves—without uniforms, without guns and ammunition except those they were able to steal or to obtain covertly, without any steady source of food, and without secure living conditions—could fend off the best soldiers of an empire that had an almost endless supply of sophisticated heavy artillery including portable swivel guns, a seemingly endless supply of new soldiers, as well as a wealth of material resources, is a historical feat that probably could never be duplicated.[3]

The Maroons did have many advantages, however, that the oppressors did not: knowledge of the terrain, which aided in both a clandestine existence and military strategy; and a shared heritage and customs, including reverence for ancestors and the practice of obeah, or "science." Obeah is still very much a part of the Jamaican culture today and guides the actions of those who believe. The word "obeah" is derived from the Ashanti Obayifo or Obeye, which means witch or wizard.[4] It is a system of both protection and destruction through belief in the supernatural.

The Maroons were also able to communicate with one another across long mountainous regions through the use of the abeng, the Akan word for horn:

> To the Maroons of Jamaica, the abeng is a cow horn with a hole drilled on one end which, when blown, produces a variety of sounds, used for communication.... The abeng was like the African talking drum, and was used to carry a vast amount of information through various sounds, over long distances. A hornblower could inform the others, for instance, about the direction of approach of the British[,] the number of people in their regiment, how they were armed, etc. The message would be transmitted through a relay system until it reached town ... without the enemy being able to understand what was being said. It was a major element that helped determine the victory of the Maroons over the British.[5]

Nanny was a warrior leader in these efforts to protect and defend her people. According to Gottlieb, there were three aspects to Nanny's leadership of her people that ensured

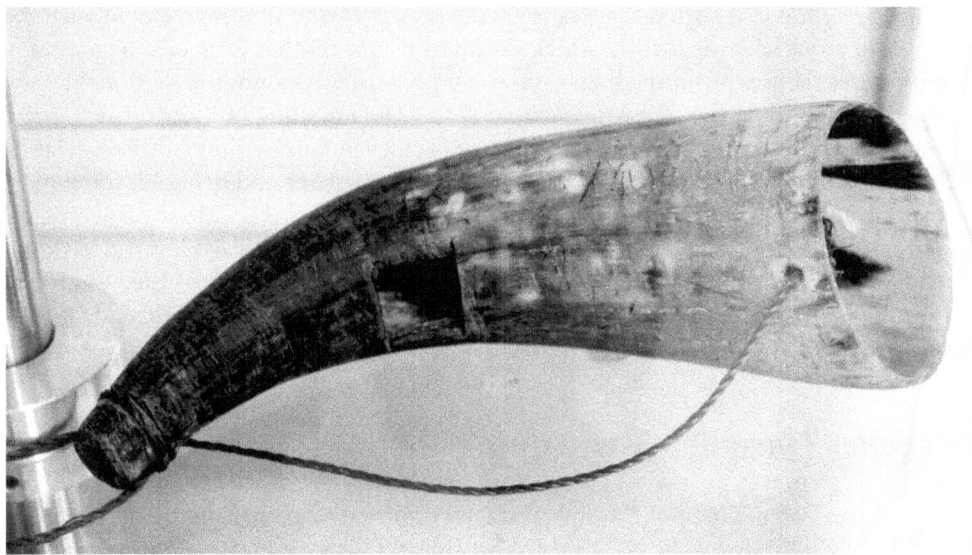

An abeng on display at the National Institute of Jamaica in Kingston (photograph by Heather Augustyn).

their victory over the British, "her use of the abeng, her development of the art of camouflage, and her contribution to the development of guerilla warfare in general."[6] Additionally, she was said to have been master of obeah. The legends of Nanny's abilities feature her catching the bullets of the British in her buttocks, while others show her abilities to boil a large pot of water, Nanny's Pot, without the aid of fire, so that when the British inspected it in amazement, they fainted and fell inside to their deaths. Though these feats are not possible, they do speak to the power of her legend and her association with obeah. Despite the fact that Nanny never actually fought in combat, her strategies were crucial. In addition to her use of the abeng and association with obeah, she is known for her "art of camouflage," as Gottlieb points out. This art involved using the terrain's natural vegetation to adorn the warrior's body: "While the British came crashing through the forests and jungles dressed in heavy black boots and bright red coats, the Maroons were able to camouflage themselves as trees while moving through the forest making very little noise."[7] Nanny's warriors could stand still as trees for hours, undetected by the British soldiers, who died by these literal branches of the military.

Who precisely was Nanny of the Maroons? It is hard to determine her exact ancestry, as records are sparse and somewhat contradictory. Her real name is not known, and she has always been referred to as "Nanny," a combination of the Ashanti words "nana," a title for a spiritual leader or chief, and "ni," meaning first mother. Nanny is the anglicized version of nanani, according to Gottlieb.[8] She has been described through the oral tradition as "a small, wiry woman with piercing eyes."[9] Nanny's reign as leader of the Windward Maroons lasted from about 1728 to 1740. Historical accounts show that Nanny was given land in 1740 as part of the Windward Maroon Land Grant, since she was leader of her people. This is significant because the British only deeded land to white settlers, so this shows that she was revered and respected. It came only in the form of a truce, not a treaty: "Her spirit of freedom was so great that in 1739, when Quao signed the second Treaty (the first was signed by Cudjoe for the Leeward Maroons a few months earlier) with the British, it is reported that Nanny was very angry and in disagreement with the principle of peace with the British, which she knew meant another form of subjugation."[10] The 500 acres she was given she then gave to her people in the founding of Moore Town, which was established the following year, in 1741. "The founding of Moore Town, then, is seen as one of the most significant of her many achievements," writes Gottlieb. "Nanny is a supreme folk heroine; people all over Jamaica know of her and her achievements in her role as 'the mother of us all.'"[11] Her monument/grave marker in Moore Town reads, "Nanny of the Maroons, national hero of Jamaica. Beneath this place known as Bump Grave, lies the body of Nanny, indomitable and skilled chieftainess of the Windward Maroons who founded this town."[12] Her profile also appears on the Jamaican $500 banknote, and she was officially named a national hero in 1976.

Imogene "Queenie" Kennedy

The obeah component of Nanny's character and resulting myth stems from African traditions that were also carried on in revivalist cultures. These revivalist cultures, Kumina Pukkumina (sometimes spelled Pocomania), Zion, and others, blended the religions of the European oppressors with the African Myalism, a religious practice involving good and bad spirits in the supernatural world that impacted life in the temporal world. These spirits, both good (myal) and bad (obeah), were manipulated by humans through rituals and celebrations. Nanny was able to do so, it is said, through her abilities, as were many other female leaders of revivalist communities, including Imogene Kennedy, known early on as Sister B and later as Queenie, an African Kumina queen. Kennedy was born in the village of Dalvey, St. Thomas, in eastern Jamaica. The date of her birth is not known; even she didn't know it, according to Olive Lewin.[13] Her father died when Imogene was very young, and she was close to her mother and grandmother. Because her mother worked to support the family, Queenie's grandparents largely took care of the children. Her grandmother helped to shape Queenie's connection to her community and her spirituality by teaching her the language and stories of her African ancestors. According to one newspaper account, "She had been quoted in interviews as saying that her spiritual initiation occurred at the age of seven, with the commencement of a trance-like state which lasted for 21-day period."[14] In her teenage years her spiritual journey was influenced by two men, Man Parker and his father Ole Parker, who were drummers in the Kumina yard next door to Imogene. The drum was and is more than a mere instrument. It was a connection to the values and practices of the African ancestors and a way to communicate through the spirit of the drummer. As such, Man Parker and Ole Parker were also leaders in the Kumina community, serving as guides and givers to those in spiritual need. Though Imogene's mother was a Baptist and disapproved of her daughter's commiserating with the Kumina people, her punishments did not have an effect. Imogene still attended the Kumina meetings.

Though she can't recall when exactly she moved from St. Thomas to Kingston, it was sometime in the 1930s when Imogene became part of the Kumina people in the city. Her community came to her to help with their troubles and she was soon recognized as a leader. She married Clinton Kennedy, and Lewin writes that Imogene "conducted herself in keeping with the ancestral 'rules' concerning marriage and family life," which was difficult at times because Clinton frequently strayed from the marital relationship.[15] Imogene had one daughter of her own but she cared for many others.

In the 1950s, Imogene, by then known as Queenie, worked with Edward Seaga on his student research, culminating in a recording of folk music for the Smithsonian Folkways. They developed a lifelong friendship, which brought Queenie into the fold for many cultural events and festivals where she demonstrated Kumina song, dance, and ceremony. She appeared on television and performed at the Smithsonian Festival of American Folklife in Washington, D.C., in the summer of 1975. But according to Lewin, Queenie's reach was much deeper than merely bringing knowledge of the Kumina culture to mass audiences: she was a leader and a healer to her people. Among the factors Lewin attributes to Queenie's importance are "her work as a healer/therapist not only among the Kumina 'nation' but also to people beyond it. In a small country like Jamaica, the news of her ability to heal many different types of illness travelled far and fast along the still efficient 'bush telegraph.' Her success generated confidence and enhanced her ability to lead." Lewin also noted "her competence and absolute authority at rituals and ceremonies which identified her as someone with tremendous drive and power to lead."[16]

Imogene "Queenie" Kennedy died on March 10, 1998. The Jamaica Cultural Development Commission has created an award for outstanding performing arts in her name to honor her contributions to Jamaican culture.

Louise "Miss Lou" Bennett-Coverley

Another woman crucial to Jamaican culture and celebratory of folklore is Louise Simone Bennett, who was born on September 7, 1919, in Kingston to father Cornelius Augustus Bennett, a bakery owner, and Kerene Robinson, a skilled dressmaker. Her father died one year after a mysterious incident at his bakery. Newspaper headlines carried the details of the strange event, in which a batch of bread at his bakery made hundreds of people sick and caused the death of one woman. The origin of the contamination was arsenic in the salt, found postmortem and through a laboratory investigation. Cornelius's business never recovered, and he died one year after the incident at the age of 47 from a heart condition. Louise was just seven years old.

Louise first fell in love with Jamaican folklore and culture through the tales of her grandmother, Mimi. Mimi,

Louise Bennett-Coverley in her traditional costume, entertaining an audience at Senecca College in Toronto in 1989 (copyright The Gleaner Company [Media] Limited).

one of eleven children, was still young when slavery was abolished. When Mimi moved from Kingston back to her home community in St. Mary, Louise frequently visited and stayed with her grandmother. It was on one of these visits, at the age of 10, that Louise witnessed a Dinki Mini, which would prove to be a transformative experience. The Dinki Mini is a ritual performed after one's death and according to Bennett herself, it is "an old tribal custom for banishing grief. No sadness is allowed at the Dinki; gaiety and jollity prevail. People sing their loudest, laugh their loudest and dance with exaggerated abandon. Many of our old Jamaican folk-games and mento-dance and songs generate the mood of the Dinki."[17] Author and historian Mervyn Morris says that this experience was meaningful for Bennett, whose own performances are "often confronting hardship with laughter."[18]

Bennett attended a number of exceptional schools as a child and also read the work of Jamaican poet Claude McKay, whose work was written in the Jamaican dialect. This too was a transformative experience, and Bennett began writing poetry of her own in the same vein. She continued to write most of her poetry in Jamaican dialect, accompanying it with an English translation. Bennett received her first award for this unique art form in 1936, which encouraged her to continue. In addition to pursuing poetry, she found the dramatic arts to her liking. She began writing her own plays as well as acting in other productions, including the play *Hot Chocolate* with dancer Daisy Riley and *Upheaval* with Eric Coverley. The costume she wore in *Hot Chocolate* was designed and made by her mother, the dressmaker, and became part of Louise's wardrobe for many performances since it was evocative of a traditional market woman.

Bennett published her first book of poetry in 1942 and read some of her work on ZQI, the first radio station in Jamaica. Through her writing and performances she began to make a name for herself. This didn't, however, result in success with the *Daily Gleaner*, as Bennett had hoped to write a column for the newspaper but was rejected. It was only after the managing director of the newspaper saw Bennett perform at a private dinner that her talent won him over. He invited her to write a column, "Jamaica in Dialect," each Sunday, paying her half a guinea per column. She was soon recognized as a folklorist and wrote poems for special occasions as an informal poet laureate of sorts.

In 1945, Bennett was awarded a scholarship to attend the Royal Academy of Dramatic Art to study acting. While in London she hosted Caribbean Carnival, a half-hour radio show on BBC, and she was hired as a resident artist. She returned home to Jamaica in 1948 and taught at her alma mater, Excelsior, and continued to write poetry and plays. Two years later she was appointed Island Supervisor for the Women's Federation, traveling around the country but finding it difficult to earn a living. Therefore, Bennett returned to London to work for the BBC, this time hosting an hour-long radio show, *West Indian Guest Night*. In 1953, Bennett decided that her vagabond shoes were longing to stray, and she moved to New York City at the urging of her aunt. However, she was unable to find work that realized her talents, though she did teach folk music to Irving Burgie and Harry Belafonte.

In New York Bennett met back up with Eric Coverley, with whom she had acted in a number of productions over the years. The two wrote and produced shows for a small theater in Harlem, and they became close socially. In 1954 they were married in a ceremony at St. Martin's Episcopal Church in Harlem which was attended by family and friends. They were loving partners professionally and privately for the rest of their days.

In 1955 the couple moved back to Jamaica and Louise began recording for Radio Jamaica. In 1959, Bennett began her wildly popular *Lou and Ranny* radio show with Ranny Williams, and *Our Gang*. These were comedy shows, many times performed live at local theaters, and ran until 1964 when JBC workers went on strike and Bennett resigned. She also worked as a drama officer for the Jamaica Social Welfare Commission during this time, helping to develop new talent. She continued to write books of poetry and about Anansi, as well and acted in a number of Pantomime performances through the Little Theatre Movement (LTM), known in Jamaica as Pantomime. "She was integral to the development of the Jamaican Pantomime: she and Ranny Williams were focal personalities in the show for many years and Louise wrote some half-a-dozen scripts after 1949 when she collaborated with Noel Vaz on Busha Bluebear, one of the first distinctively Jamaican Pantomimes," wrote Morris.[19] Morris says that she performed in nearly every Pantomime from 1955, when she and Eric Coverley returned to Jamaica, until 1975.

Many people in Jamaica today remember Louise Bennett fondly and with a sense of nostalgia because they grew up with her as host of the JBC-TV show *Ring Ding*. The children's show was broadcast for a half hour every Saturday morning from 1968 to 1980. It featured Miss Lou with a cast and audience of children singing, dancing, and telling stories. She also appeared on screen in the United States in 1986, cast as a cook in a tourist hotel in the movie *Club Paradise,* starring Robin Williams and Peter O'Toole. She was a consummate performer of all Jamaican art forms, celebrating the culture and language of the folk.

In 1987, both Louise and Eric Coverley moved to Toronto, Canada, in search of better health care for Eric, who was in need of cardiac surgery. They lived the rest of their days in Toronto, though they returned to Jamaica from time to time for performances and to visit friends and family. Eric Coverley died in August 2002 and Miss Lou died on July 26, 2006, at the age of 86. She is interred in National Heroes' Park in Kingston, Jamaica. Her work is remembered for its sense of humor and optimism, despite the heavy social topics that were addressed. "I like to tell stories," Bennett once said, "And I found that I had the gift of laughter."[20]

CHAPTER TWO

Orchestra and Band Leaders and Instrumentalists

Throughout the 1900s in Jamaica, when women were chained by the expectations of culture, gender, class, and race, as they were in most countries throughout the world, how is it that some women were able to break those chains, a few of them pushing forward to lead groups of men in a field that was known virtually only to men? It is astonishing on many levels, yet that is precisely what Leila Wilson, Ivy Graydon, and Janet Enright did. Others, such as Adina Edwards and members of the all-female ska band The Carnations, also went against the grain to follow their inner identity—yet few know their stories.

Leila Wilson

Leila Wilson was born Leila Doris Mossop on March 12, 1902, to father Adolphus Phillipson Mossop and mother Ella Louis Phillips in Montego Bay, Jamaica. Her father, also known as A.P. Mossop, managed the J.E. Kerr and Co. hardware store. "The firm's business included an ironmongery managed by Mr. Mossop whose two daughters Mimi and Leila both became renowned musicians," stated newspaper accounts of the "Early Montego Bay Lay-Out,"[1] or town plan. Leila was the youngest child in a family of five girls and two boys.

When Leila was 19, she sailed to New York City via the S.S. *Zacapa*, and according to Ellis Island manifests, she came to stay with her father. It is not known why her father was residing in New York City, but it may have been due to business, as the hardware store owner at the time, Harry Kerr, started a shipping agency in the city. It was here in New York City that Leila married George Hastings Wilson, a Jamaican who had come to the United States in 1920 to study dentistry at Howard University in Washington, D.C. It is not known how he and Leila met each other or were acquainted, but they were married on July 17, 1922. The *Daily Gleaner* reported the nuptials: "MOSSOP—WILSON—On the 17th July at New York City, Leila Doris the youngest daughter of Mr. and Mrs. A.P. Mossop, Montego Bay, Jamaica, to George Hastings, son of Mr. and Mrs. Arthur E. Wilson of Hopewell Pen, Manchester, Jamaica."[2] They returned to Jamaica in 1931 to raise their son, Warren "Buddy" Wilson, who was born in the United States in 1923. George set his sights on starting his own dental practice.[3]

Just a few months after returning home, before he could even begin his career, George became ill and quickly grew weaker and weaker. On April 8, 1932, George died of a gastric ulcer and asthenia. Leila was left on her own to raise her son. Afraid that playing the piano wouldn't pay the bills, she opened up a dress shop to sell garments to tourists. But her passion was piano, so that very same year, Leila started her own band, The Moderniques. She was the first woman band leader in Jamaica. Mapletoft Poulle, renowned musician and composer of Jamaica's national anthem, recalls, "As a youngster I had the privilege of meeting her [Leila] through my late dear friend Johnnie Lopez, and I think that her enthusiasm for playing infected me considerably. I used to play the piano at the home of my uncle, the late Ernest Rae, and he told me that Mrs. Leila Wilson used to play in the theatres for the silent pictures in the United States of America. When I asked him how he knew this, he said because he had actually seen her performing there."[4]

Leila Wilson performed regularly in Montego Bay and periodically in Kingston. She garnered ample media coverage in the *Daily Gleaner* in 1937 when she performed at the Lido Club, and publicity was positive. Performing with the pianist leader of the Royal Jamaicans, Milton McPherson, Leila Wilson was noted as creating a "sensation at the Coronation Ball," where she promised to "sing and entertain in a delightful manner."[5] The very next day the newspaper also promoted the event. "Music Galore and Two Star Dance Pianists at The Lido Tonight," read the headline:

> There will be music galore at the Lido tonight. Two pianos, two pianists, two soloists and the nine-piece Royal Jamaicans will be on the floor for tonight's pre-holiday dance. Never before in the history of Jamaica's night life have two star dance pianists been engaged on one night for duet turns on two pianos. This will all materialize tonight at the enterprising Lido when the Royal Jamaicans' wizard pianist leader and Mrs. Leila Wilson of Moderniques' fame of Montego Bay appear in numbers on two pianos, arranged specially for the occasion. It will be a sparkling midnight floor show for not only will Lidoites be treated with special duet numbers, but Mrs. Wilson, who has made a name for herself in imitating famous musicians across the seas on the piano, and is also an entertaining singer, will be heard to advantage.[6]

The review of the show was positive: "The enthusiastic audience showed its approval and appreciation of those snappy interpretations of modern jazz ... the playing of the couple was marvelous and that is why there were so many encores. More than six in number they were. And Mrs. Wilson's imitation of that dashing English pianist, Charlie Kuhn, whose fame is known in the wide world was a revelation."[7]

The following year in 1938, Leila Wilson presented *La Petite Revue* at the Arcadien Theatre in Falmouth. She was billed as "Miss Leila Wilson, talented pianist of Montego Bay, and her company."[8] They had previously performed the show at the Strand Theatre in Montego Bay. The theme of the show was "The Sky's the Limit." The year after that, in 1939, Leila performed at an event that was held to raise funds for the restoration of the Montego Bay Parish Church. "The Moderniques Orchestra with Mrs. Leila Wilson at the piano supplied the music and there was not one dull number in their repertoire," stated the newspaper accounts.[9]

It was at the Hotel Casa Blanca that Leila Wilson was able to fully establish herself, earning a residency there that would last for 16 years. During some years she performed three nights a week. This did not prevent her from performing elsewhere throughout the island, including at the Carib Theatre in 1943 with George Moxey, who was billed as the "King of the Ivories"; Wilson was billed as the "Queen of the Ivories."[10] Sometimes she performed with her band The Moderniques, sometimes with a string quartette, sometimes a trio, sometimes with "native accompaniment,"[11] sometimes as "Leila Wilson and the Boys,"[12] and sometimes as "Leila Wilson and her Sunset Orchestra."[13] She led a number of virtuoso musicians, including clarinetist Bertie King, who would go on to lead his own orchestra.

Leila Wilson performed in 1946 for a very special night of entertainment. The pool at the Myrtle Bank Hotel was turned into a scene right out of an Esther Williams film for the "Aquacade" affair, named after one of Williams' popular shows. The event, featuring decorations like a "mermaid's cove," hosted dignitaries from all over the island to support victims of genocide in World War II: "Hundreds are expected at the Myrtle Bank Hotel tomorrow evening when Stanley Motta and his energetic helpers present the seasons most outstanding entertainment, the Aquacade Ball in aid of displaced Jewish persons of Europe. Milton Macpherson of Springfield club fame and Leila Wilson one time leader of Montego Bay's Casa Blanca orchestra will be on hand that evening to provide the music for the many who will 'trip the light fantastic' in the Caribbean Ballroom."[14]

Understand that this sort of coverage for a female piano player in this era speaks volumes about her talent; now understand that this musician rarely performed in Kingston, and her talent speaks even louder. Mapletoft Poulle says:

> I have often thought that had Mrs. Leila Wilson resided in Kingston she would have had more publicity than any of us who live up here, but be that as it may, she was fortunate in being at the right place at the right time, and that is at Montego Bay during the '40s, '50s and '60s when the tourists really came to Jamaica, and I believe that she is probably better known by the tourists who came to Montego Bay than by Jamaicans who live outside of Montego Bay.... She is one of the truly great unsung musicians of this country, and I would venture to say that single-handed she has maintained the very high standard in the orchestras with which she has been associated over these many, many years.[15]

Leila Wilson continued to perform well into her 70s. At the Richmond Hill Inn in Montego Bay in 1977, Leila Wilson was still performing piano for tourists and guests alongside Trenton Spence on tenor sax, Everal Castell on bass and vocals, and Fred White on drums. They played "Blue Moon," "Stardust Melody," and "Robin's Nest." Wilson talked to the audience, connected, and shared her soul through the ivories and conversation. When journalist Ken Jones asked her if at age 75 she had any plans to give up music, her answer was simple and clear: "I guess music will have to give me up."[16] Leila Wilson died in 1996. Her son, Buddy, raised solely by Wilson as a single mother, became a successful surgeon and senior medical officer at St. Ann's Bay Hospital, where he served for over 30 years. Dr. Warren Wilson died in 2002. The emergency and outpatient building at St. Ann's Bay Hospital was named in his honor.[17]

Ivy Graydon

Ivy May Graydon was born on February 17, 1913, to Arnold Graydon, a white British sea captain, and her mother, Angelina, a black Jamaican. Because of her father's relative wealth and status, she was able to attend Immaculate Conception High School. It was at this time, as a young teenager, that she learned to play the piano, though that was not with her family's blessing. Her granddaughter Aldene Shillingford says, "Grandma Ivy was strong willed from a very young age. While at Immaculate her mother had given her money

Pianist and orchestra leader Ivy Graydon in the 1950s (courtesy Aldene Shillingford).

to pay for sewing classes, but Miss Ivy was certain that she did not want to sew. Instead she took the money and paid for the love of her life—music. She learnt to play the piano. It was only when she got an invitation from the Leper's Home to play at their concert (her first assignment) that her parents found out about music classes."[18]

During her time at school she performed for a number of events, including closing exercises at her school, where she was awarded a prize for piano in July of 1924 for playing "The Norwegian Dance." She was just 11 years old. She won another prize for piano the following year, awarded by her school, as well as a prize in science. When she was 15 years old, she performed on a program for the Jamaica United Brotherhood, where her performance was given high accolades in the *Daily Gleaner* on September 1, 1927: "Miss Ivy Graydon was the able accompanist for every item of the programme. She is undoubtedly an accomplished musician with a lot of skill and ability, for which attribute she must be heartedly congratulated." It was not the first time she had performed for the organization, having played piano at an officer installation the year prior.

On October 14, 1928, she was married to Sydney Fitzgerald Gilmore. The marriage record features an exclamation point after Gilmore's listed occupation, which Shillingford explains. "She married Sydney Gilmore from Guyana. Ivy met Sydney when the Barnum and Bailey Circus visited Jamaica. Sydney was a flying trapeze artist and the two fell in love," she says.[19] The occupation on the marriage record was listed as "acrobat"![20]

The Ivy Graydon Orchestra, led by Ivy Graydon at the piano; others unidentified (courtesy Aldene Shillingford).

Ivy Graydon had two children, Dudley Graydon and Gloria Gilmore. Though she was just 16 years old when she had her first child, this did not stop Ivy from continuing her public music performances. Ivy Graydon performed a pianoforte solo at a prestigious event held by the Knights of St. John. Her name is listed as an invitee along with local bishops and priests.[21] Ivy and Sydney had a second child, Gloria, in 1931. The couple, however, were divorced in 1935. What is not uncommon is the reason for that divorce. Sydney was an alcoholic and was extremely abusive, threatening to murder Ivy on a number of occasions with an ice pick and by throwing her in the sea, according to court records.[22] What is uncommon, though, is that Ivy frequently sought medical attention for her injuries. She had Sydney Gilmore arrested for assault and filed a petition for divorce, and she sought and won custody of the two children. Many of their fights stemmed from the fact that Ivy was the breadwinner in the household and she refused to give Sydney money for alcohol. Ivy's father, Arnold, housed the couple or paid their rent, but after their divorce, she was on her own. Arnold Dudley Graydon died in 1937. Newspapers covered the large public funeral as crowds mourned the naval official's passing. He had served as superintendent of the Sailor's Home, and the Alpha Boys Choir performed at the ceremonies.[23] Ivy's mother died nine years later.

A number of musicians in the 1920s and 1930s were able to find work performing in the orchestra pits to accompany silent films before "talkies" came into existence, and in Jamaica they were no exception. Shillingford confirms that Ivy too performed to accompany silent film at a cinema on Cross Roads called simply "Movies Theatre."[24] But her vision to perform for audiences soon extended to being more than just an accompanist, and she formed her own group of musicians, the Ivy Graydon Orchestra. "It started out first as a three-piece band playing dinner music at the Myrtle Bank Hotel," says Ivy's daughter Gloria Phillipps. "It was a piano, a drum, and a violin. Then she caught on to other musicians as time went by and they invited her to form her own orchestra."[25]

Shillingford adds, "People began to hear about her and she eventually formed an orchestra which she led with eleven men in the early 40s. A lot of men admired her for what she was doing, but my grandmother's upbringing also had a lot to do with who she became. I thought she was a feminist because I think it's her survival that assisted her, because of what Jamaica was like in those days."[26] In addition to working as a musician, Graydon also worked as a civilian clerk with the British Army stationed in Jamaica at Up Park Camp, a position that her father's connections likely helped to secure. It provided much need stability and financial support for Ivy, who never remarried until much later in life, and it provided the discipline that she was accustomed to as the daughter of a military father.

"She was a disciplinarian with a capital D," says Shillingford. "Her army experience was not wasted. She was most feared. Her grandchildren have expressed that they have a good idea of what the men in her band went through. Ivy May was not very demonstrative and seemed to find it difficult to express affection like so many others of her generation. In fact, not many people got close to her. We knew her as a stern grandmother. You do not cross her path. She was a stickler for being on time, for good manners, for good posture, and for knowing your place."[27] Ivy demanded that same level of discipline with her band members, and as a result of that and their skill, they became successful throughout Kingston.

By the mid–1940s, Ivy Graydon and Her Orchestra received top billing at places such as the St. Mary Country Club, the U.S.O. Club, the Windsor Hotel, the Morant Bay Tennis Club, the Chinese Athletic Club, the Silver Slipper Club, the Glass Bucket, the Silver Seas Hotel, the Lucas Cricket Club, and the Bournemouth Beach Club. They were booked for carnivals, holiday festivals, and school alumni and association dances. They performed almost every week of the year from the late 1940s through the early 1960s. "She played at clubs, but her focus was on the North Coast. Every weekend she was on the North Coast," says Gloria Phillipps. "And then she had a contract at the Holy Rosary Church in Kingston where every Christmas they would play on Christmas night and it was called the White Christmas Ball. Then besides the White Christmas Ball and the North Coast, she was contracted to play dinner music on Sunday afternoons from six until ten at the Myrtle Bank Hotel." Ivy Graydon employed a number of fine musicians for her orchestra. "I remember the O'Brien brothers, Baby [sometimes called Babe, alto saxophone] and Captain [sometimes called Chappy, saxophone and clarinet] O'Brien, and there was a trumpeter called Murphy," says Phillipps. Other musicians included drummer Donald Jarrett, vocalist Boysie Grant, Iggy Fong Yen and Roy Edwards on trumpet, and a number of other musicians who circulated in and out of the orchestra over the years.

One musician in particular, though, was near and dear to Ivy's heart. Her own son, Dudley, performed saxophone for his mother's band. Ivy's daughter Gloria says she too was encouraged to play music by her mother, but instead she became involved in the music in a different way. Phillipps says, "She wanted me to do the piano like herself. When I went to music lessons, the teacher made the mistake one time of rapping my fingers with a stick, and that was the end of it. And I went to my mother and said I'm not going back there. But I was still doing it in a way because in those days you couldn't get the scores, the music sheets, for different instruments, so she had a friend that would read those and I could sit down and write the accompanying music for all the different instruments. I was good. I could really comprehend for all instruments. Even her friend that had another orchestra, I would help him when I was a little girl."

Phillipps says that when she was a child, she also remembers her mother's band rehearsing in their family home. "Eventually, after my grandparents died, and she changed residence and bought a piano, they would rehearse on a Thursday afternoon. That was the only time I could hear the band playing because we were not allowed to go to night clubs at that time. The trumpeter, two saxophone players, the guy that play the bass, and the drummer and the guitar, they would all come and rehearse on a Thursday afternoon at about six o'clock and rehearse until about 9:30. It was in the week because they are always busy on the weekends. It was a little jazz, ballroom music, and also the semi-classics," says Phillipps.

Ivy Graydon's impact on Jamaican music extends beyond her piano, beyond the stage. In the early 1950s, Graydon spearheaded an effort to organize musicians into a union, for better treatment, better pay, and better standards. As esteemed music journalist Hartley Neita wrote in the *Star* on October 3, 1952, "a musician is as much a professional in his own sphere as a doctor or a lawyer is in his." One assumes he also meant "her" own sphere, as Graydon opened her home to meetings where musicians from various orchestras met to prepare to join forces with other well-established professional unions in order to have bargaining power. Neita explained the need: "Most of Jamaica's musicians are freelancers. Only the Glass Bucket and Colony Clubs in Kingston employ regular bands to play every night. Bournemouth and Sugar Hill Clubs also have their own troupe of regulars, but they only play there twice or thrice weekly—and for what? All the other bands are usually occupied only one night per week on the average. Because of the timidity of bandleaders, dance promoters are charged only £30 or so for an average ten-piece band. Out of this £30 the bandleader has to provide transportation, hire a piano and microphone, buy drinks and supper for his men and sometimes even advertise the dance to ensure that enough patrons attend so that the promoter can find the money to pay him and his men. Shocking, huh?" He argued that there was a "boom" in local musicians during the tourist season, but when the tourists went home, the opportunities dried up and contracts were not renewed. Worse yet, said Neita, rumor had it that some clubs and hotels would be hiring American musicians to attract patrons.

The threat of foreign talent taking away work for local musicians was real. It was just the push that some Jamaican musicians needed to get involved and throw their support behind unionizing. The *Daily Gleaner* reported that though Kingston clubs weren't hiring foreign talent, the North Coast clubs were, "including such big name big bands as Guy Lombardo."[28] Ivy Graydon's committee, while meeting at her home, unanimously agreed in November of 1952 to form the Jamaican Musicians Union. It was a separate body within the National Labour Congress (NLC) that was formed to "protect the general interests of local musicians, such as standard rates of contracts and the equitable award of contracts."[29] One of their first orders of business was to ask the Hotels' Association to ban importing foreign musicians. The president of the NLC pointed to the fact that Cuba had recently passed similar legislation. The union was not successful in this pursuit, as countless international artists performed in Jamaica over the years. In June 1955, the name of the union appears in the *Daily Gleaner* as the Jamaica Federation of Musicians, and in subsequent years they grew in membership and impact.

The last announcement for a performance of Ivy Graydon and Her Orchestra appears in the *Daily Gleaner* in November of 1963. After that, it was radio silence—literally. Shillingford explains, "We are told that the band broke up because of the lateness of one band member who was warned on a previous occasion. While waiting to play one night at her weekly scheduled half-hour musical interlude on RJR [Radio Jamaica Rediffusion], we understand that one musician was late and she promptly walked off the set and that was the end of that. The announcement soon followed on air, 'There will be no musical interlude tonight due to technical difficulties.' Lesson learnt—you had better be there when Miss Ivy struck that first chord. No form of indiscipline, she couldn't deal with it. So if you are late or you forgot something, she had no patience. It was because of that lack of patience, I can see her just walking out. That was the end of that. They tried to get her to continue and she just said no."[30]

Phillipps says it was the drummer who was the final straw:

> When she was going on a job, she made sure the boys knew that they were to be there, especially the drummer since the drummer takes a lot of time to set up his instrument, so she would warn him that wherever she is going that the drum should be there before her, so that when she walked on the stage and touched the key, everybody is ready. Nobody could be late. If they were late, they were out. She was very strict with that. You can not come in late for an engagement. In these years they used to have a program that would come on the radio which come on about 7:30. She kept warning this particular one who is arriving when she is arriving and that did not sit well with her. He should be there before her, so this particular night now, they are making preparations to go on the air and the guy wasn't there. He didn't turn up. So she turned to the station manager and said, "Now look, I'm very sorry, but I have to cancel this engagement for now, and for good." She ended just like that. Just like that. Oh yes and the boys cried because they wanted to continue with her, but that guy came late and he knew that was not allowed, so she just stopped it before any further complications with anybody and just told the station manager now you can just release me from my contract. Shortly after that, she migrated.

In 1966, Ivy Graydon moved from Jamaica to New York. She gave up her orchestra, gave up her job as a clerk with the Jamaica Defence Force that she had had for 22 years, left music behind and migrated. She studied nursing and lived and worked there for a number of years. The *Daily Gleaner* reported in 1973 that Graydon returned to Jamaica for the winter holidays, noting that she was employed as the "Assistant Secretary to the Medical Adviser of the Blue Cross in New York."[31] She also worked as a nurse, according to Phillipps. "She went and worked in nursing until she retired again." She returned to Jamaica permanently in the late 1970s. She married Jackie Scott, her constant companion, who died four years before Ivy. Ivy passed away on May 6, 2010, at the age of 97. "She was really a good mother," Phillipps says, adding that she is proud of her.

Myrna Hague Bradshaw, who knew Ivy Graydon well over the years, commented about the pioneering orchestra leader, "She must have been an excellent musician or else she would not have had the admiration of the men under her command at that time nor would she have been able to maintain the band for so long."[32] Phillipps says her mother gained the respect of the men in her band because of her talent, but also because of who she was as a bandleader. She took care of her band. "She was very strong. I can tell you that, very strong. She was one person that respected everybody and that's why they give it back to her. The men in the band loved her because she looked out for them. Nobody could do anything before asking her permission and the men loved that. But she kept quiet. She was not a person who was shouting. She was very quiet and that's the way that she conducted the orchestra too. She doesn't want any loud talking or unnecessary noise, and they loved her. They loved her," she says. Graydon's dedication to music and love for the stage paved the way not only for many women who were encouraged by her talent and tenacity, but also for the men to whom she provided opportunity and the ability to organize for proper industry treatment.

Janet Enright

The improvising horns of ska, the theme-and-variation call-and-response, the syncopated rhythms and hits of the hi-hat, are firmly based in jazz. Countless ska musicians of the 60s cut their chops in jazz: Tommy McCook, Don Drummond, Roland Alphonso, Lloyd Brevett, Lloyd Knibb, Jackie Mittoo, Johnny "Dizzy" Moore, Carlos Malcolm, Vivian Hall, Eddie "Tan Tan" Thornton, Rico Rodriguez, and the list goes on and on. There were also those such as Bertie King, Joe Harriott, Dizzy Reece, Harold McNair, and Wilton Gaynair, who were trained in jazz and stayed in jazz, although they left for Europe to try to eek out a better living. There were a few who continued to perform jazz on Jamaican soil even though the music in the studios and on the stages had switched to ska. One of those musicians, Janet Enright, was the only female musician to perform with many of these greats.

Janet Enright established her career in jazz and remained in jazz, and even though she is careful to point out that she did not perform ska, the two genres are intertwined. "The only connection I feel is the fact that I have worked in jazz with Tommy McCook, Roland Alphonso, and Don Drummond. If you listen to and observe ska, regardless of the feel or the rhythm, the improvisation on top is jazz," Enright says.[33] She influenced musicians with her impressive skill and fellowship, and she earned her nickname, "Little Giant," from a British promoter who noticed her big talent and small stature when she first appeared in London for concerts.

Janet was the fifth of six children born to Sydney and Estrella Enright. "I'm from a very musical family," she says. She grew up in a well-to-do area of Kingston called Drumblair, near Constant Springs, which was also a neighborhood that Norman and Edna Manley called home. It was a close community, a connected community. "My mother was a dress maker and she used to make things for people like the Manleys and Louise Bennett, so I was very community oriented and talented in the arts. I could sew and embroider and they asked me to join a little community group in the backyard of Norman Manley's home and so we used to go there and teach a lot of people and children how to sew and do all sorts of things, arts and crafts. I became known and people began to talk to me," she says.

That interest in the arts soon spread to music when one day Janet heard someone walk past her home playing a ukulele. Janet's father called the player over to the gate to talk to him about his beautiful playing, and it was then that Janet first met Ernest Ranglin. In fact, it was Janet's father who encouraged Ranglin to put down the ukulele and take up the guitar, since her father was an avid guitar player himself. Janet says she began to take an interest in jazz improvisation by listening keenly to recordings of the great Charlie Parker, Ella Fitzgerald, and numerous other African American performers. Janet was smitten with the sound of the guitar, having heard her father and Ranglin play. She began to teach herself the instrument, taught herself to read music, and soon her community of friends and family recognized her natural talent and fostered her growth—although not her mother, who preferred to nurture her more socially-acceptable talents such as sewing and craftwork. "My mother thought, at the time, that playing the guitar was not very feminine. Oh my gosh she would punish me if she saw me playing the guitar, and when I say punishing, I don't mean abusing, but she wanted me to go make a dress for my dolly or something. We had roles and the roles were established in those days," she says.

But the calling came. Those in the music business, and those who hosted events, even the most important people in the country, came to visit and call on Janet. She says,

> People began to talk to me. They had a business and they would say, "well come play," and I didn't even know what I was doing. Louise [Bennett] one day came to my mother for some dress or something like that and she said, "I didn't know Janet played the guitar too," so they physically dragged me, I'm not joking, she had me by one hand, Norman Manley had me by the other hand. Remember, I'm about 12 years old. And in Jamaica they had what was called lunch hour concerts and Louise Bennett was singing there and so she wanted me to back her. So I did that thing and when I finished I run off and hide. I was really terrified. And Louise would say do this and do that when she was having some sort of dinner party and I'd play with her, mento, and I used to love mento so I just strum the guitar and play mento with her. The next thing I know, when I was older, 14, it was Eric Deans.

Eric Deans was a renowned clarinetist who fronted his own orchestra at the Colony Club on Halfway Tree Road. He began directing his band in 1944 and attracted society people or tourists with his jazz standards. He had grown to acquire this residency through performing at clubs around Jamaica, including the Bournemouth Club and the Pepperpot, with a band he called The Liberators. He also performed at the Bournemouth Club with his "Latin-American Band." Deans was billed as the "Merengue King."[34] He performed at the Springfield Club and led the Springfield Club Orchestra. He performed at the Galleon Club in Ocho Rios and led the Galleon Club Orchestra. He played swing, he played Latin tunes, he played jazz, and Jamaicans labeled him for the rest of his days as an "impresario." His band at the Colony Club was a source of employment for the young boys at the Alpha Boys' School, and Deans would frequently scout at the school, offering boys a job before they even finished out their term, with the blessing of Sister Mary Ignatius Davies.

So when Eric Deans asked Janet to join his group of musicians, despite her inhibition and reticence, she went. She remembers, "Somebody came to the house and said they heard about the Enrights and that there was an all-girl orchestra that Eric Deans has formed and they would like to have me play the guitar." According to music journalist Hartley Neita, there were seven girls in the band, "Cherrie on drums, Monica on bass, Mary on piano, Olive on trombone, Ruth on alto sax, and Kay Russell-Munro on tenor sax," along with Janet Enright on guitar.[35] Janet continues:

> The thing is, the person says they have been practicing for one year but it was November and they were supposed to open New Year's Eve night. So my father says, "Well my daughter does not have any professional teacher, she's just a natural." I was shy and I was terrified, really terrified. But they got me into it. Then I went and what Eric Deans did was make the trumpeter teach the female trumpeter, the trombonist, which was Don Drummond, was teaching the female trombonist, but there was not a guitarist in the band. Ernest Ranglin left at that time and was in Haiti or something but there was nobody to instruct me, however, being naturally talented, I caught up. Wilton Gaynair was teaching the saxophonist but those two, Wilton and Don, just took a musical liking to me.

Perhaps it was Janet's skill and tenacity underneath that shell of shyness that the two professionals liked. Perhaps they saw the promise in this 14-year-old girl who possessed natural ability beyond her years. But Enright wasn't so sure of herself, and she certainly wasn't sure about the all-girls orchestra. She recalls,

> The night we opened, which was New Year's Eve night, the girls were happy and the audience was ecstatic. The girls were overjoyed with all the accolades and compliments paid them by the audience and musicians, but I was embarrassed to know that they were celebrating their frequent mistakes during the performance! And when we finished playing, I literally ran off the stage and hid myself at the back of the club and cried, only to be found afterwards by Wilton Gaynair and Don Drummond who, after listening to my woes, they along with Mr. Dudley McMillan [owner of the Colony Club] invited me to return inside. Wilton said, "What happen to ya, little one?" That's what they used to call me. And I said, "I'm so embarrassed." They said, "Why?" I said, "Because everyone's so happy and they made so many mistakes, we look stupid!" I was not at all amused at the girls' lack of professionalism. Now remember, I just practice with them one month and a half. It was the Eric Deans All-Girl Orchestra. The thing is, because I said that, they bought into it much more than I was emoting. Mr. McMillan said to me, "Will you mind coming and playing then, since you think they are not up to your standards," which was sarcastic but funny. He was trying to encourage me. "Since the girls are not up to your standards, would you like to come back inside and play even one tune with the male band, because I know you think they are a great band." It was true. I thought they were a great orchestra. And I said, "But I only know a few chords," and I'm going on with my usual insecurities. And Wilton said, "Look, the band has disappointed you, right? We have never disappointed you, right? Just come and play two tunes, stand up for what you like." Wilton chose two tunes and I played. I played two tunes, one I know was a straight jazz song and the next was a Latin-jazz thing, I don't remember the names of the tunes now. But I know I was having fun as much as I could and it really went over wonderfully.... It was the beginning of my profession as the first female jazz guitarist in Jamaica.

When it came to Enright, women weren't the inspiration for her musical leadership. It was strong men. Gaynair and Drummond served as mentors, as companions to Enright, who was young and timid. They were like big brothers to her, although that caused a bit of difficulty when it came to Janet's father, who saw the two as "wayward boys" from Alpha, not from the upscale society the family was accustomed to. "Here's the catch," Enright says of her success that first night on stage with the male band:

> At the end of the second tune near the end, I hear nothing coming from the guitar, so I happily thought I had touched the volume knob, so I'm turning it up and seeing that nothing is happening. I just heard a voice behind me which was Cluett Johnson, a fantastic bass player, he has this commanding sort of take-over attitude, and he said, "Stand up and take a bow, stand up and take a bow," and I said, "But I'm not finished." He said "Stand up and take a bow," so of course I just listened to him because I respected that man so much and I just took a bow and I ended the tune. When I went over and was packing up the guitar and I look around, to the back of the band stood my father. He had unplugged the guitar because he sent his nice little middle class daughter to play with some nice middle class little girls and naturally he would come to pick me up and take me wherever and he came and he saw his daughter in the middle of two prisoners. Uptown people at the time were snobbish. And he was so mad. Because there were all nice middle-class girls and then I am *sandwiched*, was his word, between two *prisoners*, which he was referring to Alpha. He said, "You're in punishment. You're not going to play the guitar for two years," or something like that. Wilton knew about it because they befriended me and I don't remember how we would keep in touch, but we kept in touch, Wilton and Don, and they got Mr. McMillan and they all talked to my father. McMillan was the owner of the Colony Club and he had one of the top, leading advertising companies in Jamaica. They let me continue but I did not go back to the Eric Deans Band.

It was at this time that Wilton Gaynair and Don Drummond had also left the Eric Deans Orchestra. With Janet Enright, they formed a combo of their own. "Wilton Gaynair left the band and formed Wilton Gaynair and The All-Stars. It had Drummond now on the trombone, myself on the guitar, and Foggy Mullings on piano, Cluett Johnson on bass, Donald Jarrett on drums—a hot little group with a bunch more, about seven and every now and then you'd have a guest singer, a jazz singer like Sheila Rickards. She was a great little jazz singer and she was young like myself at the time," Enright says.

To have a career in music in the 1950s and 1960s was to move from job to job, band to band, and that is certainly what women like Rickards did, as did Enright. She says,

> I have worked with just about every band in Jamaica. I have worked with Mapletoft [Poule] because after Wilton's group I went to the north coast. Wilton migrated to England and so he contacted my parents that I should take his job at the Tower Isle Hotel in Ocho Rios and he said I should take his job but I was still going to school so he said to just come down and play on the weekends. And I started on the north coast and then after that I had a little group of my own. I had the distinction of being called the first teenager that had her own group. It was called the Janet Enright Combo. And so my pianist was my best friend at the time, because we all grew up in Constant Spring. It was Leslie Butler.

Enright ended up marrying and then divorcing Leslie Butler, and they experienced a fruitful career while performing together. "Even though we are divorced now there is a friendship. There was Leslie on piano and we had Larry McDonald on percussion and then after that I decided to go solo and just do concerts, like Mapletoft Poule would play and I would be one of the guests, and Baba Motta, Sonny Bradshaw—I can't remember a band I have not worked with!" she says. She also performed with Don Drummond and His All-Stars at the Bournemouth Club with fellow musicians Cluett Johnson on bass, Foggy Mullings on piano, Papa San on drums, Bobby Gaynair on tenor saxophone, Jack Jones on alto saxophone, and vocalist Hugh Miller.

Her performances were met with rave reviews. *Daily Gleaner* articles proclaimed that she "did an excellent job," that "very lively were the crowds," and that she was "one of the nation's fine musicians."[36] So esteemed was Enright that she was sought to perform with national and international artists when they came to entertain crowds in Jamaica such as Sarah Vaughan, Carmen McRae, and Dave Brubeck. Enright remembers,

> Wilton and myself were chosen to play with Carmen McRae when she came to Jamaica. I have traveled and opened on stages for Ella Fitzgerald. I started traveling when I was about 16. When Dave Brubeck came to Jamaica, the man who brought him to Jamaica, Upton Hill I think was his name, he chose only two Jamaicans to play as guest stars with Brubeck which was Don Drummond and myself. I could not believe it. Of course other ill-mannered musicians crowded the band and they came on and tried to jam, but Don and I were chosen of all Jamaicans to perform with Dave Brubeck. He turned around at the piano and looked at me and what he said afterward was he could not believe my ability to improvise. That was my gift. Yes, that really was my gift to really improvise, so that was a high point.

Dave Brubeck arrived in Kingston's Palisadoes Airport on March 16, 1959, and he and his band were temporarily quarantined for not having had their yellow fever vaccinations. The next day Brubeck and his band visited the Alpha Boys' School. The *Daily Gleaner* stated,

> Strains of music in the true Birdland style filled one of the classrooms at the Alpha Boys' School for a few minutes when Dave Brubeck paid a short visit there on Monday afternoon. Mr. Brubeck and his son Christopher played an improvisation on "St. Louis Blues" and another short piece with local musician Lennie Hibbert. Mr. Brubeck later listened to the Alpha Band play "Old Comrades," "Slide Mongoose," and a vibes solo, "On the Track," by Ezekiel Nelson. Mr. Brubeck was presented with the music for "Slide Mongoose" by Glen DaCosta. He was met by the Social Welfare Officer of the school,

Mr. Garfield Clarke and Mr. Lennie Hibbert, who conducted the band. He was shown around the school by Sister Marie Therese who is in charge, and Sister Mary Ignatius, her assistant.[37]

The *Daily Gleaner* detailed the performance Brubeck gave the night before: "In a one-hour session at Sabina Park last night, Dave Brubeck again thrilled the hearts of thousands of Jamaicans with his 'downbeat' music ... Enwright [*sic*] of the Courtleigh Manor Band was also a crowd pleaser. For the next hour the crowd was treated to an almost continuous session of jazz as musician after musician came to the microphone and blew his solo."[38] Why was Don Drummond left out of the article? Perhaps because he was seen as a "prisoner," a "downtown musician"; but Enright confirms his invitational performance.

Janet Enright didn't do much recording, and in fact much of her career predates the major recording era in the 1960s forward. Plus, jazz is by nature a live music and so any recordings of Enright are rare. One is with Cecil Lloyd and His Orchestra, an album entitled *Carnival at the Tower Isle*. Selections on this recording include "Take Her to Jamaica," "Colon Man," "Lullaby of Birdland," "Cumanchero," "Ardela Told Me," "Banana," "Cuban Mambo," "Blue Skies," "Just a Moment More," "Two Different Worlds," "Calypso Medley," and "Tower Island Magic." The album was meant as a souvenir for tourists to take home and to let them "relive the moments of your own carnival at the Tower Isle." Musicians on the album include Sam Watson, Fred Parkins, Bobby Gaynair, Peter Johnson, Roy Shurland, and Janet Enright. The tunes were mostly mento versions of American ballads.

In March 1963, the *Daily Gleaner* confirmed that Janet Enright was pregnant by her husband, Leslie Butler. "If ever a musical offspring was destined for a musical future, this one will surely be it," exclaimed the writer in the "Merry-Go-Round" column.[39] That daughter, named Nova, "is beautiful inside and out," says Janet. She remembers trying to balance her pregnancy and life with a newborn with her career. "I stopped working at almost about five months since I was starting to show because I am so skinny and I didn't go back after six months. By this time now Leslie had taken over as the Leslie Butler Group and that didn't work out too well because he wasn't very liked by the musicians. The musicians didn't get along with him so he got fired from here, he got fired from there. I never put together a group again after that. I was just working for one person, one person, one person, doing shows and that was it until years down the road," she says.

Enright enjoyed working with the variety of musicians in the jazz world, who were almost exclusively men. That didn't bother Janet one bit. She was treated royally by her fellow musicians and by the clubs they played in, and if she wasn't, her comrades made sure she got her due. "I got the best treatment," she says, "the best of care." She continued,

> I played at the best of places and I didn't have to change my clothes in bathrooms, I was really very well treated. After the all-girls thing I never work in a group that had another woman. Not that it was my decision, it just happened that way. So I was surrounded by what I call these brothers. They took care of me. I remember Wilton went up to someone once and said, "How much are you paying Jan?" Everybody called me Jan. "So how much are you paying Jan for a performance?" And the promoter said so-in-so and Wilton said, "So why are you paying me five pounds and you're paying Jan two pounds? We are all doing this show. She is playing from the first note down to the last. I demand that she has to get five." That type of protection. Sometimes they would say "don't play at that place." Wilton was such a dear friend to me until the day he died, and he was living in Germany then. Everybody in his family knew not to come between Wilton and his sister, it was a beautiful relationship, and I was just blessed that I could have real friends that didn't cross the line. I'm not saying

that stuff never happened with one or two. But I had very good friends in the music world. There are women who complain that they were taken advantage of, as a woman in a man's world. I got the opposite.

Enright remembers Don Drummond fondly as well and says his foundation in jazz during those early years served as inspiration for his ska compositions with the Skatalites:

> Don Drummond was a great jazz musician before he went over into ska. Tommy plays what they would call soloing, his solo work in jazz and so did Don and so did Roland. There is a dynamic trumpeter and he also played with a jazz form, Dizzy Moore, and I remember being friendly with them. Don would say to me that the reason he switched over into the ska was that he was tired of playing the foreign stock arrangements because in early jazz that's what we used to do, stock arrangements. We played stock jazz for dancing, dancing jazz. After independence he got a brain wave, a disturbance, but he wanted to write something more on the Jamaican side of music. He used to love mento and he used to like revival music, Pukkumina, he would love that and so his whole inspiration for this Jamaicanization was through those sources. Though he wrote and composed a lot of music, he had the rhythm going in ska. If you listen to his improvisation, a lot of it was simple, beautiful, and sad but on the other hand it had a dynamic jazz solo. My favorite Don Drummond tune is "Don Cosmic." Beautiful. It's a sort of what we would call a cha-cha, a Cuban beat, but his work over the music, over the rhythm, regardless of the ska rhythm or Latin rhythm, he improvised with jazz.

Driven by her passion for jazz and Jamaican revival and mento rhythms, Janet formed another group called Truth with Orville Hammond on piano, Larry Silvera on bass, "Finey" on drums, and a dynamic percussion team consisting of Larry McDonald, Karley Messado, and Pat Lewis. After numerous successful performances locally, Enright was forced to retire. She no longer performs, having suffered three major injuries to her arms and hands, one involving a knife stabbing from a jealous musician on a cruise ship assignment, another involving a taxi-cab door, and another involving a sticky hotel window. Plus, her guitar was stolen by police after she lent it to a Rastafarian musician whose camp in the hills was raided. They claimed the Rasta had hidden his ganja inside the guitar cavity, but the sound of the package rustling around was nothing but Janet's extra pack of guitar strings, for that is where she stored her replacements. It was never returned. "Where is the guitar? No court, no charges, no nothing." But she produced Papa Michigan and General Smiley in 1980 for their tune "One Love Jam Down," and she co-arranged and performed the song "One Light Four Wheel" under the name "Jahnet Enwright" with Maxine Walters.

Despite her success, her years of working with the greats, of leading her own bands, Janet Enright still questions how she is received by others: "I thought they liked me for the novelty because every time you read about 'jazz female,' or 'the first woman to play jazz guitar,' or 'the first female to go in another country,' or 'the first female in the Caribbean,' and I wondered, can't you find other words besides female or woman? Are all of these people liking me because of the novelty, or do they like *me*?" She is quiet, modest, not one to brag about her pioneering skill, and even though she doesn't perform anymore, she still finds plenty of ways to manifest her boundless creativity. "I am multitalented and I can do all sorts of things. I write film scripts and I also used to have a boutique and I used to design clothing," she says.

As for advice to women, she says, "I have none. I don't know anything about women, how they think, why they do what they do. I grew up in the music world with men and I grew up with four brothers. I have never had an alcoholic drink in my life, I have never smoked a cigarette in my life, and I am surrounded by smoke. I was never even tempted and I think that is why the guys kind of adopted me like a sister, to take care of me, because I wasn't like the average female that has to do things to go where they want to go. My advice to women is women should stop trying to emasculate men, for like it or not, it is a man's world."

Adina Edwards

Adina Edwards was a blind performer who sang and accompanied herself. She was a self-taught accordion and keyboard player and always performed spiritual and gospel music, but in 1972 she recorded for Byron Lee. Her career started in 1934 when she sang a song called "Welcome" for her school recital at the Salvation Army School for the Blind.[40] She also performed there in 1939 for a holiday program where she received such applause for her performance of "You Can Smile" that she came out to do an encore.[41] In July of 1946 she performed for a recital which was covered by the *Daily Gleaner*. The headline read, "Blind Soprano to Give Song Recital." The article stated,

> On Wednesday evening July 31 a song recital unique in Jamaica's musical history will be given when Miss Adina Edwards twenty-year-old blind soprano will give a recital of songs at Bartley's Silver City Club. Possessed of a warm, colourful voice, Adina Edwards is certain to satisfy her audience with the songs she has chosen for this programme from Negro Spirituals to the light classical. The singer is being presented by Mr. Granville Campbell who will act as her accompanist for the evening while Mr. E. Roosevelt Hinchcliffe will contribute violin solos as fitting interludes to the programme.[42]

In 1949, Adina was presented with a cash donation of five pounds, 18 shillings, and three pence, which was collected from the audience at Eric Coverley's New Year Morning Show at the Ward Theatre in Kingston. Adina sang the song "Because" and was accompanied by Granville Campbell, following it with an encore of "Ah, Sweet Mystery of Life." She received "tumultuous applause from the audience," according to the *Daily Gleaner* article, which prompted Coverley to comment, "This girl is not here because she is blind but because she can sing. I am asking you to help her." Audience members placed money into hats while Adina performed "Red Hot Boogie Woogie" on the piano.[43]

In 1959, Adina performed on a famous launch pad of talent, the *Vere Johns Opportunity Hour*, although she did not win. Joe Higgs and Roy Wilson sang "Manny Oh" to take first place, the Blues Busters took second place, and Adina placed third with her vocal rendition of "The Lord Got the Whole World in His Hands."[44]

Jamaica Gleaner columnist Roy Black wrote, "Little is known about Adina Edwards, except that she made a big impact with her gospel-tinged, 1972 Tommy Cowan–produced recording 'Don't Forget to Remember Me.' She started her career as an inauspicious blind musical entertainer, who accepted collections for her performances on the streets until Byron Lee recorded that hit for her."[45] In early 1972, Adina's accordion broke. She obtained a new one through the effort of local admirers.

In 1973, Dynamic Sounds recorded her album *Soul of Adina*. Boris Gardiner performed on bass, Peter Ashbourne on keyboard and violin, and Marjorie Whylie and Dawn Forrester sang back up. Then in March 1974, Dynamic Sounds terminated a five-year contract with Adina after only 15 months. She was broke. She vowed she would not return to playing for pennies on the streets and so a local promoter, Constantine Morris, planned a benefit concert with proceeds to benefit Adina. A *Daily Gleaner* article stated,

Adina Edwards' accordion, on display at the Jamaica Music Museum in Kingston (photograph by Heather Augustyn).

> Dynamic Sounds' decision to terminate the contract sometime last week follows reports of disputes developing between the artiste and the company. She insists that she had not been treated as she expected by the company. Efforts to contact the company on two successive days for comment on the issue failed. Mrs. Shelia Lee, senior executive of the company who is in charge of the artistes, is off work. Not available either is chief executive, Mr. Byron Lee. Another executive of the company, Mr. Neville Lee contacted on Wednesday, had no comment, and was in fact unaware that the contract had been terminated.... News of the termination of the contract reached the singer by way of a letter signed by Mrs. Lee, which gave no reason for the termination. The letter pointed out that ... when the royalties earned was placed against monies advanced to the singer by the company on a weekly basis, it was found that she was in debt to the company to the tune of $747.04. The letter also informed the singer that as long as her past recordings were being sold by the company, quarterly royalty statements will be sent to her, credited against the outstanding debit balance.[46]

In December 1982, Adina performed in the Salute to Our Musical Heritage show at the National Arena with Ken Boothe, The Heptones, King Stitt, Bunny and Scully, U-Roy, Derrick Harriott, the Gaylads, Lascelles Perkins, Dennis Brown, Delroy Wilson, Theophilus Beckford, Marcia Griffiths, Jackie Edwards, Lord Comic, Val Bennett, Stranger Cole, Toots and the Maytals, Tommy McCook, Derrick Morgan, and Pam Pam and Gloria Kid. In 1983 she performed in an all-island gospel festival and was still performing for audiences in June 2000. A *Jamaica Gleaner* article interviewed her before the gospel show:

> Adina Edwards, an enduring gospel artiste, said most gospel songs earned the message of love and that men and women were not loving each other. Gospel singing is becoming like olden days when

music was composed and most male performers nowadays cannot bother to reach perfection in their craft. "Women are into experimentation until they get it right. I am doing a song called 'Real Real' and I am applying all kinds of techniques to let it appeal to people," she said. Adina has now taken her singing ministry to a higher level where she is no longer singing for adults on the sidewalk, but participating in school devotions.[47]

The following year she gave another gospel performance for a Mother's Day celebration at which the Alpha Boys Band also performed. "I am very excited about the concert," she stated in the *Jamaica Gleaner* article. "Already I am getting a lot of support. I will be performing all of my favourites, songs like 'Keep the Love Light Burning,' 'When Waking Up This Morning,' and 'Just a Closer Walk with God.' People always like to hear 'Don't Forget to Remember,' which was produced by Tommy Cowan and promoted by Byron Lee. I will never sit back and allow my disability to defeat me," she said.[48]

In 2001, an article on female musicians who had adopted children, including Lady Saw, told the story of Adina Edwards, who had also adopted a child. Adina Edwards has had her daughter, Amoie, since she was two days old. "At that time she was very sick and God help me to make her better. I do not call her an adoption and she does not call me anything but mother because she never knew any other. She is my sixth child. The most special thing about Amoie is that she a pretty girl and to think she loves this blind, ugly, old woman. It's very touching. I love her. Whenever I needed any of my children they were always there. And when I called them to flog them, they would come and I wouldn't bother," she said.[49] The article also stated that Adina had run a large nursery in the 1970s in Kencot, Kingston, where she was responsible for over 48 children. Adina Edwards died in 2008. Her accordion is on display in downtown Kingston at the Jamaican Music Museum.

The Carnations

Decades before all-female ska bands such as the Bodysnatchers and the Deltones made rude girls a thing to be proud of, a little-known ska band composed of all girls brought crowds all over Kingston during the 1960s to their feet to skank. The Carnations were a group of schoolgirls, friends, and acquaintances, who performed at parties and clubs but never recorded in the studio, so their energetic horns and rhythms are only memories.

Christine Levy, trumpeter and vocalist for The Carnations, remembers that the band was formed after her best friend at Excelsior High School, Donna Paul, heard the school was putting together a band and they both decided to give it a go:

> I think I was around 13 at the time and we decided to go try out. She got an instrument and I was the last person and when it came to me there were no instruments, so I used to go to rehearsals with Donna because she's my best friend, and the person who was teaching the band, his name was Reverend Eyr, he saw me. I guess I must have looked interested so he said, "Would you like to try the trumpet?" And of course at 13 you think everything is dead easy, don't you? And he gave it to me and of course I couldn't blow a note and then he showed me how and it started from there. He actually gave me his trumpet to go home and practice. I was a part of the band after that.[50]

The school band was a typical school band, not unlike a marching band, and they performed at school functions, at the Manning Cup, an inter-school soccer tournament at Sabina Park, and during independence celebrations throughout Kingston. It was through

Members of The Carnations perform on television for the show *Jamaica Bandstand*. Front row (*left to right*), Ingrid Chin (bass guitar), Jean Levy (steel guitar), Margaret Wong (congo drums), Althea Morais (keyboard), Christine Levy (trumpet and vocals). Back row (*left to right*), Marie Crompton-Nichols (guitar), Pam Mosely (guitar), and Richard Chin (drums) (photograph courtesy Richard Chin).

this school band and through her knowledge of her instrument that Christine learned of an opportunity to perform for another new band that was forming—but this one was different than the Excelsior High School Band. In fact, this one was different from any other band that existed. It was an all-girl ska band.

Christine says, "I heard through the grapevine—of course everything is through the grapevine in Jamaica! I heard they were looking to form a girl's band. My friend Marie, she plays a guitar and she was my age at the time and we decided, hey, let's go check this out and of course we did and they said, 'okay, you guys can be part of the band.' But we weren't any big thing. I was still learning on the trumpet. It's not like I was formally taught, but because we were novel and new they said we were the best thing. I mean, we were just having the time of our lives and we weren't paid a penny."

The members of the new all-girl band, The Carnations, included Christine Levy on trumpet and vocals, Ingrid Chin on bass guitar, Jeanne Levy on steel guitar, Margaret Wong on lead vocals and congo drums, Althea Morais on keyboard, Marie Crompton-Nichols on guitar, Pam Mosely on guitar, and Richard Chin on drums. Richard was a male in the all-female band and was the brother to Ingrid Chin, the two who put together the entire band. Richard explains, "It was an all-girl band. It was my sister who formed the band and I was the only boy, the drummer, the only boy that was in it."[51] Christine, who later married Richard, says, "He kept a very low profile because he was supposed to be a girl. He wasn't supposed to be a boy. Hardly anybody noticed him because we were the front line."

But Richard was critical to the formation of the group, as was his family who influenced his interest in music and helped to manage the direction of the band. "My uncle had a band and I used to just look at the drummer every time he was playing. I used to spend hours just looking at him play and one day I just said, 'I know I can play,' and I did. His band was Kes Chin and the Souvenirs," says Chin. Kes Chin was a popular club act, ska with a Latin flavor, featuring Chin, Dennis Sindrey on guitar, Lowell Morris on drums, Peter Stoddart on keyboard, and Audley Williams on bass and steel guitar. Stoddart and Sindrey were also members of the Caribs, and Lester Sterling of the Skatalites also performed at one time with Kes Chin and the Souvenirs. Richard's father and Kes's brother, Keyoung Chin, managed The Carnations. "He managed us all right," says Christine Levy. "In those days we didn't know what that meant. If we were paid a pound a gig we were lucky. We bunked on beaches if we had an overnight. At Dunn's River Falls we used to fall asleep and the waves would wake us in the morning. And we used to sleep on barstools, but it was fun, so I don't want to taint it. It was just pure fun. We enjoyed sleeping on the stools, we enjoyed sleeping on the beach. It was not like today and we never thought for one moment, 'oh, we're famous.' We didn't know the word, so it was really a time of fun, girls having fun, that's all it was."

Lead vocalist and congo drum player Margaret Wong says that she came into the band because she grew up in the music business.

> My two brothers also sing with the number one band at the time, which was called The Mighty Vikings. So Victor and Sonny were my brothers. I was about 16 and being in the music field I knew about Kes Chin who was Ingrid's uncle and Kes's brother was Keyoung, so he decided he wanted to form an all-girl band. I got reeled into this all-girls band so I was the vocalist, and if they needed, a drummer, for television work or something. When we had to play out all night long, then Richard would play the drums and I would just sing. So for the all-girls look, whenever we had something smaller, I could play the drums. I would not play all night long for that and I was mainly a singer. So that's how I got involved, coming from a musical family. My sister also played with the number one band in Jamaica, Byron Lee and the Dragonaires. Florence Wong. She started around 1957 or 1958 playing keyboard. She started with him in the early years of forming his band and played with him for over three years. She played all the softer-type tunes, for New Year's Eve, birthday parties, etc. She did not do any recordings with him and she didn't go to the World's Fair with him because she was there when he first started. They would practice at St. George's.[52]

Their performances were professional, and Margaret Wong made sure of that, she says: "I had pink and the rest of the girls had this yellow pants outfit with a jacket, really nice. I always dressed differently than they did, being the singer. We got some clothes made and it was the nicest times for us. Everywhere we went everyone enjoyed us. We were really liked in that era. We were unique. Nowadays you have all-girls groups, but 40 years ago you never heard of an all-girl group. People asked for us because we were so unique. People wanted that uniqueness and we were professional, always on time, dressed neat."

Perhaps because of the connection with other ska bands of the day, and perhaps because the youth in Jamaica during the 1960s listened to popular music, The Carnations performed ska. They never wrote any of their own songs, but instead they performed standards, as jazz musicians would, for the patrons of the clubs. "We used to play dance music, everything, we play jazz, we play ska, we play everything. In those days you play all sort of different music. We play other people's music. We used to play some Skatalites songs. We play a lot of songs. We play in Cayman. We play in Miami, and we play a lot of nightclubs in Kingston, at the hotels and things like that," says Richard Chin.

Christine Levy also says their repertoire was ska because that's what the crowds demanded in the mid–1960s in the clubs. "I was young enough to know that everybody did ska. It was *the* music. Therefore it had to encompass the whole society. It just was ska. I still love the music, very much so. People just came to dance and sing along with what they knew. It was songs by Don Drummond and 'Ska, Ska, Ska,' by Byron Lee, and we did that too. We didn't write any songs at all," she says. Richard says, "We never did any recording, we did it because it was just fun." Marie Crompton-Nichols concurs, "We weren't playing our own music. We did ska and we did rocksteady or jump up. We were playing songs like 'Letter to Mommy and Daddy' [Barbara Lynn] and 'Forty Miles of Bad Road' [Duane Eddy] was one I used to do the lead in."[53]

The crowds were civilized, not like today, Levy says, although her mother made sure the girls were protected. Levy says,

> Crowds were normal. They would come there and dance. Nobody got drunk. Nobody got rude. Nobody got fed up. Nobody stole. It was just normal people enjoying themselves and enjoying us. My mom was a little perturbed at first, but she decided if she chaperones she would be okay with it. Everybody tells me that I'm rebellious, and I must have been rebellious in those days, but I would have gone anyway, she couldn't have held me back. When you think about it, I'm going to play music, and I found my love [Richard Chin], I would have been as rebellious as you can think. She must have seen that and decided to chaperone. She went around with us until I was maybe 18. By that time I was engaged. But in school I was failing everything because I was having the time of my life so I was sleeping in school! We were out late at the clubs. When you look back now, as an adult, those clubs became seedy. They weren't but they appeared that way when I became an adult. We used to play at Sombrero. We used to play at Ding-Ho on the way to Palisadoes.

The clubs treated the girls well, especially since they were young and upper class. "When we go to all these places," says Richard, "they would set up separate tables so that everybody could sit, eat, and have a drink. In a boy band you just have to go to the bar and get your own something. But they have special tables set up for the ladies and we would just sit and eat and have a drink and then we were ready to go on and play again it was really special."

Marie Crompton-Nichols says that the clubs at which they performed were frequented by tourists and the upper classes, so they were treated well as musicians. "We played at Club Maracas and Brown Jug, those were in Ocho Rios. We had a lot of different types of crowds, a lot of sailors when the ship was docking in Ocho Rios. We played in Kingston at the Flamingo Hotel and we used to play downtown at the Myrtle Bank Hotel for Carlton Alexander. He would have office parties down there and we played a couple of times. It was nice, it was really nice. He himself used to come and take me and introduce me to some people that he know. They were upper class at the Myrtle Bank," she says. They performed for a number of society functions, such as business functions at the Jaycees Headquarters, fundraisers for the Polio Foundation, the Rotary Ball at the National Arena, the Hillview Gardens Association's Grand Gala Parade, and business openings and other functions.

Margaret Wong says they also performed for gatherings around the country. "We played for the Commonwealth Games. We were chosen to play for that and we played for all the American artists who came down, like Ruby and the Romantics, Little Royal, The Platters. We work with those artists that come from the states and we would either be the first band or we would back them up. Then when Toots and the Maytals did 'Bam Bam,' [winner of the first Festival Song Competition] in 1966. We did that with Toots and the Maytals and were on the parade float doing that song with them," she says.

They also performed for other headlining acts such as Tommy McCook and the Supersonics, Hortense Ellis, Alton Ellis, and Byron Lee and the Dragonaires. The Carnations were also involved in the "dazzling floor show," although not every member was part of the performance. Christine says,

> I remember Richard used to have to play for Margarita and Madame Wasp. I remember because my mom led us all out of the club when it was time for the rhumba dancers. She led all us girls out of the club, outside. I thought it was something bad. And even though she led us out we were looking through the cracks to see why we were not allowed, and man, that girl, Margarita! It was just like you would see belly dancing today, that sort of hip wiggle, you know? It was an art, it wasn't a downgrading thing, but in those days she was showing her belly, wasn't she? And the boobs were going—they were covered, so in our days, that wouldn't be right for young kids to see.

Marie Crompton-Nichols says it was quite an education. "I got exposed to a lot of things I never knew before and a lot of things I never see before, because I was 14 you know. We used to play for rhumba dancers, belly dancers. It was the first I was being exposed to that sort of dancing," she says. For Richard, though, those memories of playing for the rhumba girls are fond ones. "I didn't mind it!" he says with a chuckle. "You know Margarita and Madame Wasp, when we used to go to the clubs like Club Havana and Club Maracas in Ocho Rios, whenever we go to those places I had to look at them and play the drums. I had to look at them because when they do a certain move I had to play the cymbals, so as a young boy I felt very privileged. I play for Margarita, I play for a lot of rhumba dancers."

When the girls grew up and graduated from high school, many of them met their mates and got married or went their own ways. Still, the music went on. Christine says,

> They disbanded the girl's band because they were all getting married or had interest in wanting different things. They started a mixed band now and I was put out of it because there was no room for a trumpeter. They came upon a song and they said "who is going to sing it," because Margaret wasn't there either and the boys in the band couldn't sing it and one person said, "Where's Chris who used to sing back up? Try Chris," and it look as if I sang the hell out of the song because they took me back. By then it was a family thing. It was me, Marie, Richard, Ingrid, and then we started to have other people in.

Marie Crompton-Nichols married Richard's brother, Patrick Chin. The new band was no longer called The Carnations; it was now called The Avengers. Instead of advertisements calling them "The Caribbean's No. 1 All Girls' Band," or "Jamaica's No. 1 All Girl Orchestra," Ingrid Chin and the Avengers, sometimes also called Ingrid Chin and the Mighty Avengers, was now billed as "The only Girl and Boy band in the Caribbean."[54]

It is important to note that The Carnations and their subsequent group, The Avengers, comprised a number of Chinese-Jamaican musicians. Chinese-Jamaicans were instrumental in the music industry, and so the fact that the members of both of these bands were related not only to each other but to members of other bands is not unusual, as interest in this field was prevalent. Chinese-Jamaicans were known for establishing a number of businesses throughout the country, which has been documented in books such as *The Shopkeepers* by Ray Chen, as well as films such as Jeanette Kong's *The Chiney Shop* and Generoso Fierro and Christina Xu's *Always Together: Chinese-Jamaicans in Reggae*. Music was another form of business. There were a number of Chinese producers in Jamaica during the calypso era, such as Ivan Chin and his band Chin's Calypso Sextet (which he was not a member of, only producer); and in the ska era including Justin Yap, Leslie Kong, and Vincent Chin. Others had their own record shops such as Neville Cha

Fong of KG's Records or their own sound systems and shop, such as pioneer Tom "The Great Sebastian" Wong.

There were Chinese artists such as Ernest Ranglin, who was half Chinese, half Jamaican. And there were bands with a number of Chinese musicians and vocalists like The Vagabonds, composed of Lloyd Chang on vocals, Herman Sang on keyboards, Stanley Yap on drums, leader Colston Chen, and bassist Phil Chen, who would go on to play with such artists as Jeff Beck, Ron Wood, Keith Richards, Pete Townsend, Eric Clapton, Rod Stewart and Bob Marley. The Vagabonds were managed by Chinese-Jamaican Cecil Moo Young. Kes Chin and the Souvenirs were led by a Chinese-Jamaican, and The Mighty Vikings were Sonny and Victor Wong, Margaret's brothers. Byron Lee and the Dragonaires featured Keith Lyn and were led by Lee, a Chinese-Jamaican who later went on to establish Dynamic Sounds, the enormously successful recording studio.

Clubs were many times owned by Chinese-Jamaicans such as Club Havana, which was owned by Conrad Chin. This club changed names to the Ding-Ho Club in 1968 and was known for serving "the Tastiest Chinese Food This Side of Kingston."[55] The Golden Dragon, where The Carnations performed a number of times, was located opposite Halfway Tree Park on Constant Spring Road and was owned by Winston Lee, who renovated the club to include a restaurant that served Chinese food. A dragon sculpture featured a large tail that separated the patio from the parking lot, a head with flashing eyes, and smoke coming from its nostrils. The Lee family had owned and operated a restaurant by the same name in Port Antonio. The Golden Dragon hosted Chinese New Year celebrations. They were known not only for top-notch music, especially from Byron Lee and the Dragonaires and Ingrid Chin and the Carnations, but also for their sweet and sour sauce, which could be purchased by the bottle to take home.

Just as more and more Chinese-Jamaicans entered the music industry and reggae took center stage, so too did more women, although women faced challenges when they grew older. For many of the women, being in a band was just an activity they did when they were younger and when family life began to conflict, they chose to leave the band. But for others, like the women who continued on with The Avengers, it was all about finding balance. Christine Levy, who married Richard and became Christine Chin, gave up the trumpet and had children, although she continued to sing while balancing the role of mother. She relates:

> I gave up the trumpet because I was vain. I grew up, you see, and I got vain. I didn't want a tough lip. I was too young or naïve to realize the benefits of keeping that going. The same way I got it is the way I left it. I got it easy so I left it easy. And it was a stepping stone to my singing career which is what has taken off all through the rest of my life. I'm not famous, by the way. I'm glad because I couldn't deal with that. I remember freezing the first time The Carnations went on stage. I couldn't blow a note. I froze. I don't like being center stage, so singing now was with the band and other singers. Whatever solo work I did was at places where you go to eat a meal and I would be in the background with this guy on a synthesizer and I would sing. My children were my priority. Even before I got married I remember telling my mom I wanted to be a wife and mother, that would be my career, and I fulfilled that. That's my claim to fame. There's nothing else that's more important than that in my eyes. The music came if and when. I used to take the little ones in a sleeping basket if we went to play and they'd be right there. They'd sleep while I played. If I had to go and spend the night at a hotel, they're there. They'd play in the pool and enjoy the hotel. And all the way through it, it was still fun. Nothing to do with money or fame or anything. When I came to England with the two little girls, Tami and Tessi, the other three had grown up by then, I met a guy here who played synthesizer and that's what happened too. Here I went to jazz festivals and took part so I got a chance to experience that as well.

Marie Crompton-Nichols married Ingrid's brother, Patrick Chin, and together they have two children. She too says it was tough to balance a career in music with family life, but she was able to manage to enjoy both her children and her artistic passion, although it took extra discipline:

> I got married very very young. I was like 16. I've been married now 46 years but I got married very young and it was kind of hard. But I could still manage. Because I didn't work otherwise and the playing is usually at night, I was home all day. But I used to practice a lot because when you're up there playing and you know you can play you sort of have this high…. What I used to make sure of is that I don't make mistakes because I tell myself, look, if you are a woman and you are up there playing and there's mistakes made … you understand? I made sure I wasn't the one who make a mistake and make some sort of a blunder and mess up everything.

Christine Levy continued a career in music, singing not only for keyboardists at clubs and restaurants over the years, but also for broadcast. "When I moved to England I did what seems like thousands of jingles. I was a jingle maker. I used to be the jingle queen, the voice that does different jingles for radio and television, voiceovers. I used to be very good at that," she says. Christine and Richard passed their love of music on to their children, especially Tami and Tessanne, their two youngest daughters. Richard and Christine built a music studio called "The Underground" in their family home, and they taught the girls to follow their passion in life. As a result, they both have successful musical careers. Tessanne toured with Jimmy Cliff as a backup singer for three years before going solo and opening for Gladys Knight, Patti Labelle, and Peabo Bryson. She has collaborated with Shaggy and won the 2013 season of NBC's *The Voice*. She is now a popular national hero, mentioned in the same breath as Usain Bolt for bringing pride to Jamaica. Tami, who spells her last name Chynn, has toured with Shaggy as a backup singer and collaborated with Sean Paul, Beenie Man, and Lady Saw. She opened for the New Kids on the Block on their 2008 tour, has performed on a Pepsi commercial, and wrote a song that Jennifer Lopez has recorded, "Hypnotico." She is married to dancehall artist Wayne Marshall and she also designs clothing.

Marie Crompton-Nichols has also continued to perform over the years and has never quit. "I was with The Avengers and when the girls petered out I was still there. I was still there when it was all male and I was one female. I've been playing all these years. The last band I was with was called 50/50 and I left them in about 2006 but I've always played," she says. Marie grew up playing guitar. She got her first one at age 10 from her father, and now she is passing along that tradition to the next generation. She says, "I am teaching my grandson. We jam together. My fingers are not so wonderful because of arthritis, but I still love playing."

To say that Margaret Wong continued in the entertainment industry would be an understatement. She is now married and uses her middle name and married name, so she is known as Suzy Chan. Margaret says,

> I moved to the U.S. in October 1968 and was still a member of The Avengers until I left Jamaica. I was working at an insurance company when I was singing with the band and when I left I went to New York to live with my sister. My Uncle Lenny, who is not my real uncle but we call him Uncle Lenny, lived next door to the Ed Sullivan Theater…. He used to know everyone in show business. So he introduced me to Carmine Caruso who was the teacher for Herb Alpert; Blood, Sweat, and Tears; Chicago. He was a musical mentor for these people. He was a horn player. So I told him I want to get back into show business and he said, "Well, take your time. It's difficult up here," but one of his friends was an agent and I got a call from them and he said, "There's a band that's looking for an Oriental singer" and so that leader called me up and said, "Look, you have nothing to lose, all you

have to do is I'll fly you to Buffalo, then you sing for me. If I don't like you I'll fly you back, no expense for you. If I like you, you'll start being on the road." Well that was my career in America, just like that.

Within six months of living in America, Margaret was working for Warner Brothers in New York and traveling on the road for the Dave Yuen Show Group. "We did hotels. He was Canadian so we did the Canadian Pacific hotels too—Winnipeg, Regina, Saskatchewan, that area. We did a lot of Pennsylvania, up-state New York. After I was with him for maybe five years I decided to form my own band and branch out and it ended up being in the New York Sheraton. My band was called The Wong and Wite Way," she says with a laugh. Through this new band, Margaret met others in the business who hired her band to perform in Chinese nightclubs on the east coast, including one in Boston where she met her husband, Grandmaster Pui Chan, a kung fu master.

Margaret, whose parents were shopkeepers with an interest in music, continued to combine her love for music and business when she moved her family from New York to Orlando. "My two brothers live here and we formed The Version Band about 30 years ago and we only disbanded in 2009. I was singing up to that time. We are still in show business in a way because we do the Lion Dance and the Dragon Dance for events. We do Disney and Epcot and all those and I do all the emceeing for the shows in Orlando. I am still behind the microphone and do singing at the church," says Margaret, whose daughter Mimi has made a documentary about her father the kung fu master, as well as practicing kung fu herself. Margaret says, "She teaches kung fu and she was the martial arts consultant behind the Disney movie Mulan and they would draw her techniques. She went to Los Angeles and did stunt work for Mortal Kombat." Margaret Wong (now Suzy Chan) and her husband Grandmaster Pui Chan own and operate the Wah Lum Kung Fu Temple in Orlando. Suzy Chan teaches Tai Chi and has written a book on using the practice to battle cancer based on her own experience.

Although The Carnations may have not recorded nor written any of their own music, they were critical to showing that there were places for musicians in all facets of the industry, as well as showing that there were places for women. For those who had no aspirations to be a star, for those who simply wanted to perform, to share their love for the music, like The Carnations and The Avengers, their demonstration and interpretation of ska was no less important than anyone else's. They inspired other women, they inspired other musicians, and they inspired their children and grandchildren to continue to carry the torch of Jamaican music.

CHAPTER THREE

Mento and Calypso

When the Jolly Boys released their version of Amy Winehouse's "Rehab" in 2011, many first-time listeners were enamored of the unusual sound. What was this strange style that presented a pop classic in such an interesting way? Who were these senior citizens, clad so dapperly, crooning on a small stage in some tropical setting? And what was that instrument, that box that one man sat upon, plinking pieces of metal with his fingers? It may have been the first introduction to mento for many uninitiated, but one quick Google search would show that this music had long been part of the Jolly Boys' repertoire, and it had long been part of Jamaican culture. Few women, however, had had the opportunity to showcase their talents. Fortunately for the genres of mento and its cousin calypso, there were a number of women who were able to shine through.

Lady Earle

Little is known of Lady Earle, a mento singer who performed in the mid–1950s—so little that experts are even unsure of her real name. *The Star* in 1956 shows a photo of Lady Earle, smiling on stage during a performance, maracas in hand behind the microphone. The caption reads, "Most popular contestant was Lady Earle from Savanna-la-Mar. She was the only woman calypso band leader in the contest and with her group played and sang a spirited trio of Jamaica mentoes to win the Five Guinea mento prize."[1] The judges of this competition were Mrs. Louise Bennett Coverley (Miss Lou), Sidney James, Ivan Harris, Vere Johns (of the Vere Johns Opportunity Hour competition and other entertainment), Stanley Motta (Jamaica's first recording studio owner), Max Henry, and Mapletoft Poulle (orchestra leader and composer of Jamaica's national anthem).

According to writer Richard Noblett, the contest was organized by Miss Lou's husband as a way to show the more wholesome side of mento after a local Catholic bishop attempted to have "lewd calypsos" censored in the wake of the popularity of "Night Food," written by Everard Williams: "Eric Coverly, husband of famed Jamaican entertainer, Louise Bennett, promoted a Calypso Band Contest as an 'effort to show the world that these songs, expressive of the West Indian soul, had their appeal and need not go over the borderline of decency, to be popular.' Organised into elimination heats in Montego Bay, Savanna-la-Mer [*sic*], St. Ann's Bay and Kingston, with the final taking place in the island's capital in June."[2]

Lord Tanamo was a competitor at this contest, but Lady Earle was victorious over him. Noblett continues:

> The entrants were, in the end, a roll call of Mento/Calypso artists and bands. In the Kingston heat, Count Lasher, Lord Tanamo (reported as Lord Tallahwah!), Sir Horace and Chin's Radio Quintet appeared, with Lasher winning with his "Calypso Cha Cha" and Tanamo placing second with a rendition of "Mango Tree," which may be the same song recorded in London by Lord Kitchener. The final, on June 11th, was won by Monty Reynolds' Silver Seas Calypso Band, second was Count Berry's Band with vocalist Lord Lebby, and third came Count Lasher. Tanamo received an honourable mention, this time as "Lord Tanama," again for "Mango Tree."[3]

Noblett makes no mention at all of Lady Earle, once again erasing women from history.

Disregarding women's role in Jamaican music had a direct impact on the lives of the women themselves, as seen in the events that followed this single contest. One woman, Miss Lou, recognized another woman, Lady Earle, who was featured in a photo and a paragraph in the local newspaper. One cannot know the circumstances of Lady Earle's life to determine how or why she did not continue to have a career in music, as she then disappears from the scene. But for many of the men at this event, many who received lesser awards, their success did evolve: "As winners of the Kingston heat, both Lasher and Tanamo were in a position to capitalise on this exposure. Both acquired recording deals and headlined shows."[4]

Louise and Blossom Lamb

Many classify Louise and Blossom Lamb as mento singers, since they recorded songs written by mento lyricist Everard Williams for Stanley Motta in the 1950s. Mento ethnomusicologist Daniel T. Neely says they are more "all-around entertainers."[5] Listen to a tune like "Cutting Wood" or "Give Me Perfect Love," and it's hard to tell the difference. Certainly, the mento elements are all there, but the women's voices have much more variety and tonal quality than their male counterparts. Neely contends, rightly so, that just recording or performing a mento song does not necessarily make them mento singers. The fact that these women were allowed into the musical space in the 1950s, with Louise Lamb being the only female to record in the 1950s besides Miss Lou,[6] is worthy of note, even if the genre is fluid.

Blossom Lamb was born in Greenwich Town in Kingston. She was a pretty girl and won many beauty competitions. Her mother died when Blossom was just 13 years old, so she grew up with her grandmother. At age 21, Blossom had her first child, and shortly thereafter she had another, although she wasn't married at the time, which was controversial for her family. She did marry Clive Evans and had three more children. In total, she had three daughters and two sons. Blossom and Clive (known to his friends and family as Jimmy) were married for 40 years before he died of a heart attack in 2000.[7] Journalist Hartley Neita declared Blossom a "singer with a style of her own."[8] He wrote that she was a "slim-figured, husky-voiced girl" and that she had gone to Nassau, Bahamas, in 1955 to perform for a year in a residency at the Paul Meeres Club. He said that her style was charming and that she received criticism constructively to improve her singing skill. She left that residency in 1956 to return to Jamaica to perform at the Imperial Hotel and the Buena Vista. She was also offered the opportunity to travel to Miami to perform on television shows with Bahamian calypsonian George Synonette, though it is not known whether or not this came to fruition.

Born in Kingston, Louise Lamb was Blossom's cousin. She married Carlton Morales and together they had three children, two sons and a daughter. One of those sons went on to play guitar for Julian Lennon (John Lennon's son) in the 1980s, and the other son performed bass guitar, touring with his band in the U.S. and Norway. Louise and Blossom began performing either solo or together at locations around Kingston in the early 1940s. In 1944, Louise performed at the Ward Theatre with Miss Lou and others in the lineup. It was a show called *Hot Chocolate*, an all-star musical that she had performed in since 1940. In 1949 Louise performed at the Wickie Wackie and was billed as "Louise Lamb, the Heptie-Hutie Song-bird." The advertisement continued: "Hear her dramatize the dynamic and popular hit 'Dont You Worry 'Bout Dat Mule.'"[9] It is unknown was a "Heptie-Hutie" is. Louise also performed with the Roy Coburn Orchestra, the Eric Deans Orchestra, and the Redver Cooke Orchestra. In 1953, Blossom Lamb, who was described by the *Jamaica Star* as "a beautiful Indian girl with a sure manner at the microphone,"[10] won the weekly amateur night contest at the Glass Bucket Club. That same year, Louise was described by the *Jamaica Star* as one of Jamaica's leading female jazz singers.[11] In 1956, the cousins performed together at the YWCA auditorium on North Street in Kingston, promoted by the Ivory Club, at a show called *Evening with the Lambs*.[12] It was presented by the Jazz Committee and featured the Lambs along with Foggy Mullings on vocals and May Foster on piano. Blossom performed in 1957 for the *Harold Forbes Show*, backed up by Frankie Bonitto and the Rainbow Orchestra,[13] and Louise recorded a number of mento songs for Stanley Motta in the late 1950s.

After meeting Martin Luther King, Jr., on his visit to Jamaica in the 1960s when he stopped by Blossom's craft stall at the souvenir market in Kingston, she struck up a conversation with him and invited him to their family home in Harbour View for fried fish and bammy. King asked her if she ever thought about hosting her own Mother of the Year award after he commented that she was a wonderful mother and should be a role model to other mothers. Encouraged, she began the contest in the early 1980s.[14] She also owned her own store, Blossom's Dollar Shop and Calypso Records stores.

Calypso Rose

Though Calypso Rose was Tobagonian and not Jamaican, Jamaica's music, especially mento, is inextricably linked to calypso, so it is only fitting that the Caribbean's greatest female calypsonian be discussed in the context of the music of Jamaica. McArtha Linda Sandy-Lewis, better known as Calypso Rose, had enormous influence on women performers in Jamaica, as she demonstrated that a powerful lady could take center stage in a male-dominated industry. It is for this reason that many female musicians and vocalists idolized Calypso Rose and covered her songs in the ska and rocksteady genres.

"I was born in Tobago, April 27, 1940," says Calypso Rose. "I was the fifth child of 13."[15] It was a pleasant childhood—her father was a fisherman, a Spiritual Baptist preacher, and a busy man, having sired seven of his 13 children out of wedlock. Her mother was a homemaker and a seamstress, and she sold McArtha's father's fish in the market. They named her after the World War II General Douglas MacArthur. In an interview with Marco Werman for the *World*, McArtha says her mother admired the general: "They used to be dropping leaflets in Tobago about what was going on in the war. And at night the planes would come and drop the leaflets and drop food and rice and all different things so she loved that. So she says, 'This baby I'm carrying, if it's a boy I'm going to call him Macarthur. And if it's a girl I'm going to call her McArtha.' And there I came, so that's how I got the name McArtha [laughs]."[16]

McArtha didn't grow up on calypso but she certainly heard music, and she loved it. "My father had a radio and with the radio you have to use a big battery, a big car battery with a bamboo pole with wire, so we used to hear more country western. So I grew up on more country coming from the U.S.," she says. But it wasn't until McArtha moved to nearby Trinidad that she began writing her own calypsos. She remembers, "My uncle's girlfriend, she didn't have any kids and she was with my uncle, my father's brother. And she wanted a child. So my uncle told her to go to Tobago and my brother have a lot of kids and she could take one. And she came on a Saturday and my mother had us line up in a line and she choose me. She came to me and she ask me if I want to go to live with her in Trinidad and I shook my head and said yes. She took me to Trinidad at age eight, and I grew up with her."

Her aunt, Edith Robinson, gave McArtha a good life. "I was so glad," she once told a reporter, "no more fighting for roast sweet potato for breakfast and bush tea."[17] But McArtha visited her siblings and parents frequently, so it wasn't a sorrowful exchange. "My aunt normally send me back, one Easter this year, next year she would send me for Christmas—she would split up the vacation time," she says. Her aunt loved her, provided for her, and she also introduced her to calypso, an art form that would change her life. "She had a lot of records from The Mighty Spoiler [Theophilus Philip], Attila the Hun [Raymond Quevedo], King Radio [Norman Span], Roaring Lion [Hubert Raphael Charles] and all these calypsonians. And in those days they had the Victrola where you crank up the handle to play those big records and I used to listen to all these guys singing this and that," she says.

It is important to take a quick look at the history of calypso to understand how McArtha's use of this art form was an integral part of the culture. Calypsos were first performed during Carnival in Trinidad as far back as 1784 by a professional singer known as Jean between stick-fighting bouts as an entertainment interlude. Calypsos were sung in an African tongue, patois, or French creole, and it wasn't until the late 1800s when Richard the Lion Heart, Norman LeBlanc, introduced the first English calypsos. To prepare for Carnival, calypso artists assembled in a tent days before the event to write and practice, but the form was also extemporaneous, the artists improvising on the spot to compete against one another with fresh material. Soon audiences were not only attending Carnival to participate in the festivities including hearing the calypsos, but also to attend the tent practices, which then became an event all their own.

To complement the boastful challenges that constituted the content of the calypsos, singers, called chantrels, took stage names that reflected their prowess, a convention that many ska artists and ska producers practiced in the years that followed. Calypso monikers like King Pharaoh, Mighty Duke, Lord Superior, Black Prince, Lord Executor, Mighty Sparrow, and Lord Inventor are part of this trend. The songs were witty and funny, could be narrative or expository of the singers' abilities and skill, ridiculed and besmirched the rival (frequently the slave master and his exploitation), and were displays of verbal bravado. Musically, calypso incorporated the same instruments of Carnival—drums, graters, shakers, stick percussion, and stringed instruments. The voices that provided backup to the chantrel were normally women's. Bands dressed in colorful, fancy costumes of velvet, fine silk, or other fabrics trimmed with ribbons, braids, plumes, and gilt decorations to set themselves apart from other bands and make an impression on the judges of the competition. Music and performance were one and the same. Everyone participated, both the musicians and the audience, in a shared experience of musical communion.

McArtha composed her first calypso at age 15, based on an event she witnessed in the streets as a child. The tune was so good that it gave McArtha her first big break. It also gave her a way to express herself in a manner she had not been able to before:

> I like singing, so at school one time I wrote a calypso and I sung it in the school when they had a function and the teachers were happy to hear me. At that time when I was small I could hardly speak because I had a stammering tongue. But singing, yes, I love to sing. So my aunt send me one time to the market, Sunday morning to shop and I saw an incident in the market. A guy run up and snatch a pair of glasses out of a lady eye and start running, and in Tobago you never see or hear about those things, so it amaze me to know what could happen in Trinidad. So I wrote a calypso advising Tobagonians to "stay in your house, stay in your land and raise your fowls, because Jane went into the market to buy piece of ice, and a fellow snatched her glasses from out she eyes." So 1955 I went home. Eric Williams had become the first prime minister. He was the first prime minister of Trinidad and Tobago and he went to Tobago to speak to the Tobagonians. I was home on vacation and there was something they called the Council in Tobago and I told a lady I want to sing. They say, "You can sing?" I say, "Yea." Okay, and I went and I sang, the same song I wrote advising Tobagonians to stay in the land and Dr. Williams came to me and he said, "What's your name?" I told him, "My name McArtha Sandy" and he said, "Oh you very good, you should be in the calypso tent in Trinidad." So when I went back to Trinidad I told my aunt what took place and what Dr. Williams said. And my aunt said, "Well if Dr. Williams says you're good, I will take you down to the calypso, the original young brigade, and talk to the managers down there." So she took me down there and she spoke to two managers, nicknames, we call them Spike and Mr. Piggy. And I sang "Glass Thief" and I sang a song they call "Can Can," and they said, "Oh, you're good, you're good."

She had impressed government officials and the calypso tent managers with her talent, and now it was her turn to stun the crowds with her charisma. But first, she had to choose a name. "They asked me, 'What is your calypso name?' So being as I come from Tobago, I said Crusoe Kid. They said, 'No, no, no, no, no, we are going to change your name. We are going to call you Calypso Rose because rose is the mother of all flowers.' And that's where it all started. They told me the tent is opening up very soon so you gotta come to rehearse and that's how I started in the calypso tent," she says.

Calypso Rose wasn't the very first female calypsonian, as at least one other had come before her. "There was a lady before me called Lady Iere. Lord and Lady Iere, but she was very old. Lord was her husband. But I was the only female in the calypso tent," Calypso Rose says. Anne S. Gottreich writes, "Lady Iere (Edna Thomas nee Pierre) began singing with her husband, Randolph Thomas, Lord Iere."[18] She notes that Iere is an Arawak word for hummingbird and the indigenous name for Trinidad, "Land of the Hummingbird." Gottreich continues, "Theirs was the first husband and wife calypso duet in Trinidad. It has been suggested that Lady Iere came on the calypso scene only after her husband, Lord Iere, was unsuccessful; as a last resort to save his own reputation, he included his wife, who then became popular on her own." Lord Iere made his calypso debut in the mid-thirties, and his wife joined him in 1942. Lady Iere never wrote her own material, but she won the first Calypso Queen competition in 1956 against a sole challenger, Pearl White; there is no information on this challenger.

Even before Lady Iere, there was a calypso singer named Lady Trinidad, whose real name was Thelma Lane. Gottreich writes that Lady Trinidad "had a career in the mid–1930s and is acknowledged as the first woman to sing on stage in 1937. She began with 'Yankee bands' singing American pop music. She did not write her own material, and she never recorded any calypsos. 'Old Man's Darling' and 'Advice to Every Young Woman' were her popular calypsos at the time."[19] Some place Lady Trinidad's stage debut in 1935 in the Crystal Palace Tent on Nelson Street in Port-of-Spain. She was followed by Lady Baldwin (Mavis Baldwin) in 1936 and Lady MacDonald (Doris MacDonald) in 1937. But it was Lady Trinidad who is credited with being the first female calypsonian to make a record.

Lady Iere and Lady Trinidad weren't writing their own material like Calypso Rose, who came right at the tail end of Lady Iere's time. "I was the only female in the calypso tent but they took good care of me because I was accepted to the tent. It wasn't the only tent in Port-Au-Spain in Trinidad. There were three tents and the Original Young Brigade had the only female because at that time Lady Iere had just ended her days," Calypso Rose says. She remembers the days when she performed for the crowds:

> In the calypso tent there is the stage. In front of you there are the seats where people are sittin' down listenin' to the show and behind you will be the band, they will be playin' for you. And if you're good you go off stage, they will clap to give you encore to bring you back. Every night I be getting encore. Encore every night and during the week, from Sunday, Monday, Tuesday, we will perform on the outskirts of Port-Au-Spain, we will go in the country and villages to perform because there are people in the country that couldn't come into the city to the tent, so they will take us out to all these deep places. The people used to open their homes for us to sleep overnight and then we travel the next morning to the next town and perform and we back in Port-Au-Spain Wednesday for the calypso tent, Wednesday right through. I loved it. I loved it. I loved to see the people happy with whatever song I sing, happy, they be cheering and I was so skinny I used to be jumpin' up a lot. I have seen clips of when I was younger, I say, "Oh my god, that's me?!" I'm flyin' in space [laughs]. Yes, yes, yes.

The subject matter of Calypso Rose's songs was in many ways typical for a calypso—events of the day, relationships, life—but in other ways it was unique to the experience of being a woman. But as Kim Johnson, musicologist, points out, Calypso Rose was exceptional in this regard. "The male attitude was bragging and the female attitude was nagging. Calypso Rose didn't fall for that. It was almost like creating a new form. She defined women's role in a very female-centered way, but not demeaning to men," Johnson says in the film *Calypso Rose: The Lioness of the Jungle*.[20] Some of the topics came to Calypso Rose through experiences with her ancestors. She remembers,

> My mother's grandmother, my great grandmother, she came to Tobago as a slave. She did not come to Tobago on her own, she was kidnapped, bought, and sold by the French and end up in Tobago. She came from Guinea, Africa. She was a Guinean and she was very frail and old. Every evening she used to stoop down with her long dress with long sleeves and the frills around her neck and she used to stoop down and smoke the pipe and watch Mount Irvine Bay, the beach. That is the area she arrive in, that she landed, and one evening when she smokin' the pipe I hear she cry out, "Ah, mi pickney, no man know de burial ground." And I didn't know what my great granny had meant, but after I grew up, what she mean was my child, nobody know where they will be buried when they die. That is it. And I tell myself I had to write something for my granny. [Sings] "Sittin' on another man land, you only sufferin'. Toilin' on another man land, you gettin' nothin'. My country create and raise me up, wherever I was placed, I'm going to find it. I want to go, but the land is too far. Oh yes, I want to go, I am begging Jah. Over yonder, where there's many many moons yonder, I want to go, back to Africa." I wrote that in honor of my granny.

Other songs dealt with international and national issues, such as labor disputes:

> "Sweet Brown Sugar" I wrote as a way to address an event in Trinidad and Tobago. Dr. Eric Williams went into cabinet and form a law. Domestic servants had been working for $20 a month. All night, going to bed at 12 a.m., getting up at 5 a.m. to prepare the master's meal and take care of the kids, prepare them for school and wash and iron—for $20 a month, and I wrote about that. And there was a journalist from Italy, came to Trinidad, that was in 1979 and when she heard the calypso she went back to Italy and she wrote a story. And then Dr. Williams read the story and went into cabinet and they passed a law, that no domestic servant could work for nothing less than $1,200 a month. I'm glad that I lived for that.

Calypso Rose also tackled other worldly issues, such as climate change and natural disasters. "Hurricane Flora came and hit Tobago [September 30, 1963] and there were eight lives lost, and I wrote a calypso called 'Hurricane Flora.' I wrote about the world is changing vast and rapidly that even the blind could plainly see, the cold country becomin' hot and the hot country becomin' cold, tornadoes sweepin' Japan and earthquake in the Caribbean. And I did not know that these things would come to pass—look at Haiti and Japan and look at what is happening today," she says.

The calypsonian notes that the chorus of her song "Hurricane Flora" was written from a hymn. She also wrote two gospel songs in 1968, "I Am What I Am," and "Ezekiel Comin'," which was done by design, to address a group of her critics. Calypso Rose explains,

> There were a lot of females from all different church groups calling me to meetings. "Why are you singin' calypso? You shouldn't be singin' calypso—calypso is a man's world!" And they be puttin' the pressure on me, puttin' the pressure on me, until I got so mad, the last time I attend a meeting I say, "Let me tell you something. The Lord has given me the ability to create and write. He has given me the voice to sing. I couldn't speak but he gave me the voice to sing. And this is what I am doing and I will not be like the foolish virgin who bury her talent in the soil." And I got up, and I walk out. It was a heavy load and a long long road to walk night and day, that's why I pray and pray and pray. I ask for wisdom like in Solomon, I am what I am. And I am the first entertainer, calypsonian to ever write gospel and put it in a calypso, but they never put it on the radio because they say I was blasphemin'. You cannot bring calypso in the word of God because anything come out of Africa, because calypso and the beat come out of Africa, and anything come out of Africa is the devil. And now look, so many calypsonian, the Mighty Sparrow wrote a gospel album and so many Jamaican artists have written gospel in calypso and reggae beat. I am the one who open the door.

To have faced such opposition from her own kind, her own sisters, was close to the heart. But Calypso Rose had done battle for her fellow women, for the right to sing and speak out as a female, for years. Even as a child she fought, quite literally, against the men who attacked her. "I was raped. I had been raped when I was 18 years of age and had my right hand broke and two of my ribs fractured in Trinidad," Calypso Rose says. "I got raped by three men coming from a junior political meeting. And after they finish using my body, they put a knife to my stomach to take my life. Once you're raped you never forget that. It goes through your life until you die," she said during an interview for her film.[21]

It was for this reason that Calypso Rose says she was never intimate with a man. She did get married, but the marriage was more of a business arrangement. She says,

> My husband, Aubrey Lewis, was from St. Croix, from the U.S. Virgin Islands and I was four years older than him. He died in 1976, a long time ago. I married in Puerto Rico because we were working in a club in Puerto Rico and he was the keyboard person and I was the singer and I did not know the laws in Puerto Rico and I was working there without a working visa. Immigration came and

took my passport and stop me from workin', stop me from performing and the tourism attendance come and asking for me and the band leader's asking for me, so one morning my door knock and there was Aubrey and he say, "I hear what happen to you. You want to get married?" I say, "Who?" He say, "We can get married. We don't have to be involved. I can marry you and they cannot put you out." So we get married. I went and I bought the ring and two of the workers who used to dance the limbo were our givers and so we got married, but we never consummate the marriage because he had respected my life because I was raped.[22]

Aubrey respected Calypso Rose as a person and so too did the other men she performed with, largely because Calypso Rose respected herself. She was a strong woman. "Respect yourself always," she says. "Respect is great. If I did not respect myself, all the men in the calypso tent, the musicians, the tent manager, would have been talking about me like a dog, but not one of them could point their finger in my face. I have been approached, yes, but I stood my ground and I backed them off. So respect yourself and whatever you want to do in life, you have the faith and you go with it. The Lord is going to bless you and bring the blessings." But that was tough for Calypso Rose because the response she received by standing tough was not always positive. In her documentary she says, "Because they couldn't go to bed with me they gave me all kinds of names. She's a lesbian, she don't like man, and all kind of things, and I didn't mind what they say about me. I am still smiling and I am still standing!"

The industry was tough for Calypso Rose as one of the only women in the business. The music industry in Trinidad was dominated by men. "All men, all men, all men, all men. They pay me less. The contracted singers used to get their money as contracted, and whatever they leave in the kitty, they would share it among the helpers, a dollar, a dollar, a dollar, a dollar, until it ends," she says.[23] That was the money that was doled out to Calypso Rose. A dollar among the helpers. That didn't stop Calypso Rose, who went on to write some 800 calypso songs, recording many of them for Charlie's Calypso Records in the recording studio in Port-Au-Spain. She also recorded her most famous song, "Fire in Mi Wire," for Mighty Sparrow's recording studio, National Recording. This song was covered by numerous artists over the years, most notably Millicent "Patsy" Todd in Jamaica on Sonia Pottinger's Gay Feet label in 1963.

When Calypso Rose did find success in the tent, it was taken away from her. The calypso tent is all about competition, and organizers felt that it wasn't a level playing field with a woman in the ring. In 1968, Calypso Rose won the Carnival Road March, a prestigious calypso competition in Trinidad, but the title was taken away from her and given instead to Lord Kitchener. The committee said that Calypso Rose's song was too short, although it was three verses long instead of the standard two. In fact, Calypso Rose was the first calypsonian to write a three-verse calypso, and soon everyone followed suit and began writing a three-verse format. "Then they said they couldn't give woman a world match in front of a man," she said.[24] It wasn't until 1977 that Calypso Rose was finally allowed to take the title she had earned. She won the Carnival Road March with her song "Tempo," and the following year won with "Soca Jam."

It was in regard to another title that Calypso Rose really changed the landscape of calypso competition, literally changing the name of the title. The Calypso King competition, also held during Carnival in Trinidad, had been held since 1939. It was won year after year after year by a male calypsonian until 1978, when Calypso Rose won with her songs "I Thank Thee" and "Her Majesty." How could the committee crown Calypso Rose, a female, with a title of Calypso King? They were forced to change the name of the competition, not just for the winner that year, but for all years, to a gender-neutral name. "They change the name from Calypso King to Calypso Monarch. I win the Monarch. I took all the prizes and I took all my music internationally," she says.[25]

In the Calypso Rose documentary, Dr. Patricia Mohammed of the University of the West Indies says, "The role of women in Caribbean society is a very paradoxical one. On one hand we are given a lot of importance. Generally we are supposed to be mothers and daughters and sisters and the carriers of culture, but on the other hand we are supposed to be silent, quiet, not be public, not defy those rules that are allotted to us, so if you are a performer, you come out on stage, the automatic assumption is that you must somehow be loose, have low morals, and so on."[26] Calypso Rose fought those stereotypes. She fought harder than the men for recognition, a testament to her talent. "I am a powerful woman," she says in her documentary, "very powerful. Nothing could stop me then, in the 50s, in the 60s, in the 70s, and now. I started in 1955 and I am still here today. I pass through three heart attacks and I am still here today. And I pass through two cancer, I am a cancer survivor and I am still here today, so nothing can stop me. I am like a river overflowing. You try to stop me, I am going to find room to pass."[27]

Calypso Rose still records and performs all over the world. In 2019 she performed at the WOMAD and Coachella festivals, just to name two. It was the first time a calypsonian had performed an entire set at Coachella, and at 78 years old, she is the oldest to perform at the festival, introducing thousands, even millions, of young people to her artform. That same year she released "Amazing Grace," a cover of the iconic gospel song, in collaboration with Tim Armstrong of Rancid and the Interrupters.

Chapter Four

Jazz

In 1962, the full-length album *Jazz Jamaica from the Workshop* was produced. It is still today considered a classic, with jazz from Don Drummond, Tommy McCook, and Roland Alphonso, among others. Sonny Bradshaw observed in the liner notes that jazz musicians in Jamaica served an important role, especially in the wake of Jamaican independence, which the album celebrated. Absent from this commentary and the offerings on the album, and most recordings for that matter, were women in jazz and the role they played in shaping Jamaican identity, before independence, during, and after. The following are just two of the vocalists who have contributed greatly to jazz in Jamaica, though many others started in jazz and segued into other genres, in addition to the female jazz instrumentalists, discussed in other chapters.

Totlyn Jackson

Her debut on the North Shore in Ocho Rios at the Silver Seas Hotel received such a tremendous review that she couldn't help but be destined for stardom. "Breaking into fame last night ... was Totlyn Jackson, 23-year-old Jamaican girl who draws 'bravoes' from the crowded hotel audience with her sweet, hot renditions of the old favorites 'L'Amour, L'Amour' and 'Blue Moon,' 'Sweet Sue,' 'Body and Soul,' and so forth," stated the *Daily Gleaner*, June 28, 1953:

> Totlyn, backed up by the Silver Liners, a quintet built around a bass fiddle, two guitars and the unusual maracas, sits with the boy quietly until her turn at the "mike" comes. Then she takes over so that even the too noisy background music cannot mute the tremendous range of her voice. Unlike husky-throated blues singers, Totlyn is not only unafraid of the high notes on her numbers, but rides to them easily via breaks of her own creation, so that the listener is carried right up there with her. Her unformalised voice is allowed its full play in all her numbers, save when she is being drowned out by either of the bands, this will be rectified as she gains confidence and holds on to instead of giving up the mike for all comers. Stuart Sharpe [hotel manager] knows he has a gold mine in Totlyn.

Totlyn Jackson was born in 1930 in a small village in Port Maria, St. Mary. Her father worked for the government, so the family had a bit of status in their town, and their mother was a skilled dressmaker who took care of the home and raised Totlyn and her three siblings—sisters Claire and Peggy and brother Peploe. The family was extremely involved in the Hampstead Presbyterian Church and other social and civic organizations in the community, so Totlyn had the opportunity to sing in the church choir and participate in Christmas and other holiday performances. Plus, there was an organ in the family home, so Totlyn taught herself to play and sing, and she also began taking piano lessons from a neighbor. She was born with a club foot, which was aggravated by an operation in her childhood. As a result, she always had a significant physical deformity, but she never let that stop her from a career in the spotlight.

When Totlyn was 19 years old she moved to Kingston after winning a scholarship to Lincoln College. It was an enormous change for Totlyn, moving from a small village where her family enjoyed social status to a city where she was an unknown. She joined the choir at North Street Cathedral as a soprano and then, like many other talented vocalists and musicians, Totlyn decided to try her hand at the *Vere Johns Opportunity Hour*. Accompanied by Frankie Bonitto, Totlyn won by singing "With a Song in My Heart." She then entered a contest at the upscale Colony Club, where Eric Deans led the orchestra.

Totlyn was young and innocent when she was taken under Eric Deans' wing. She recalls,

> Coming out of a church situation, I was wearing boots and socks and an inappropriate dress, but Eric [Deans] knew what he was doing with me. Eric had inherited a big band folio—we didn't call it jazz—I didn't know anything about jazz. I was treated as a curiosity but I didn't know it then! ... I began to work with Eric and was making a name for myself at the Bournemouth Club every Friday where I came into my own.... I was the only full-time professional singer; the others were part-time with daytime jobs. Friday nights at the Bournemouth and Sonny's [Bradshaw] got in touch with me for the first big band concert at the Ward; by this time everyone thought of me as a jazz singer because of this concert, and I could sight-read, so I was easy to work with.[1]

In 1954 she caught the attention of *Star* newspaper music writer Hartley Neita, which no doubt increased her visibility. He wrote that he saw her perform and was astounded by her talent. "Heaven forbid that Totlyn Jackson's talent should remain hidden under the proverbial bushel, taken out only now and then for a brief dusting," said Neita. He argued that the small number of club appearances she was given was too little for her skill: "A singer with a voice like hers should be heard on her own weekly radio programme. No stage show should be regarded as complete without her presence. So how about some of you people who can do something about it, pitching in with a helping hand?" Neita appealed to his audience.[2]

Totlyn Jackson also performed at the Bournemouth Beach Club with Lester Hall's Orchestra, featuring Don Drummond, and she frequently sang with Baba Motta's Band, the Zodiacs, Sonny Bradshaw's Orchestra, and Herman Lewis and the Glass Bucket Band. She performed in a show at the Carib Theatre on February 5, 1966, with the son of Frank Sinatra, the 18-piece Tommy Dorsey Orchestra, and the Caribs. She even performed for Prime Minister Norman Manley's birthday on July 3, 1956, singing a song composed for him by Frank Clarice of Little London in Westmoreland that moved Manley to tears. Her only recording on the island was for WIRL—"Island in the Sun," with the B side "Yellow Bird," in 1963 with the Audley Williams Combo.

While Totlyn's life was beginning to thrive in Kingston, her family's life back in Port Maria was crumbling. Her mother and father split up and her mother came to stay with Totlyn. But Totlyn had been living in the home of one of her professors at Lincoln College as part of the scholarship arrangement, and her mother couldn't live there. So Totlyn moved her fractured family into the home of Joe Issa, owner of Issa's department store:

"One day my two sisters and brother arrived, because Dada said that if I was big enough to look after Mama, I could look after them too." According to vocalist and jazz expert Myrna Hague, "Her father was probably resentful of her [Totlyn's] show of independence, and because of whatever had gone on between her mother and him, he no longer wanted them or perhaps responsibility of them."[3]

Soon, Totlyn had yet another family member to care for while balancing her career. She met an advertising executive from New York on his travels to the island when he came to Glass Bucket Club for one of her performances. "I eventually became pregnant. I didn't want to get married. I had seen how unhappy these wives were, including my mother. I wondered, 'Should I have this child?' There was no one to ask this kind of intimate question."[4] But she did have the child, a son named Franz. His father, Jack Conroy, the ad executive, died in a car accident shortly before Franz was born. Totlyn never married—not then, not ever. But she did have her share of boyfriends: "That's where [the Glass Bucket] I met my contacts and my boyfriends. I wanted a first-class life and so what I needed was people who could take me onto that plateau, to take me up."[5]

One of those boyfriends who took her career up was a man named Michael Rouse. She left Jamaica to go to London with him in 1960. She also left her son to be raised by her mother. "I went to London to join him [Michael Rouse] when he offered to handle my career, and then he became a fully-fledged impresario who was handling people like Juliet Greco, Los Paraguayos, Gilbert Becaud, Miriam Makeba, and others of that ilk. We eventually broke up because he couldn't sell me and I resented that. When I complained he said that he loved me too much. I thought that was crap but friends said that it was possible because he was afraid of losing me…. He couldn't or wouldn't arrange a tour for me. He was not a very good businessman," she said.[6]

After five years in London, Totlyn arranged to have her mother and son brought to London. She relied on her connections to find lodging, since she had severed the relationship with Rouse, and found people to support her. She was able to find success in London and did tour many countries over the years. The *Daily Gleaner*'s "Merry-Go-Round" column on November 27, 1964, states, "I have news from London that songstress Totlyn Jackson, last year's 'Star Award' winner, is the success of the autumn season. To quote from *Theatre World*, Britain's leading theatrical magazine, 'some new acts have emerged over the past month, the best of whom was Totlyn Jackson, a polished and sophisticated Jamaican singer who starred at Quaglino's and the Allegro.'"

In a *New Amsterdam News* article by socialite Poppy Cannon White on November 2, 1963, those in New York are told to "watch out" for Totlyn, and her talent is lauded. "It is impossible for anyone within the sound or sight of the strange voice and beauty to tear attention away from her. She holds a roomful of people taut and tight as if in a vice. Tiny, regal looking, and sounding a little like Eartha Kitt, with a swan throat and a small proud head, lil Nefertiti, queen of Egypt. Five feet tall and a size seven at the most! Her trademark is a shimmering mermaid gown that she designed herself five years ago, although it has plunges and clings like the latest from Paris. Flowing close as possible to her knees, the gown bursts into a fin of blue foam to the floor. This clever dress, like her exotic calm face, hides tragedy. She was born with a club foot," writes Cannon White.

Totlyn hid her club foot well, under this mermaid dress. Neita described her condition in his appeal for more opportunity for the artist. "Because of a slight disability of one leg, as a child she was unable to play hopscotch and ring games with her friends. As she was not athletic she sewed and as she sewed she sang herself, and the neighbours, hearing the sweet, wistful lilt of her voice, got her into the union choir of the Kirk Presbyterian Church in her home town, Port Maria."[7] A dozen years later, she would be standing on stages all over the world.

In 1968, Totlyn Jackson traveled to the Soviet Union. She recalled, "It all seemed very strange behind the Iron Curtain. I'd like to go there again, mind you. It was interesting and I met some very nice people, but it certainly is different.... They believed that because it [Jamaica] was near Cuba that it was also Communist. I got a very warm reception in the beginning, because it was believed I was a Communist and came from Communist Jamaica. When it was realized that neither Jamaica nor myself were Communist the reception though cordial, cooled considerably.... There are irritations about being a traveler in Russia, not the least of them is that if you run out of cosmetics you either can't get any replacements, or they are of very poor quality and, of course, deodorants are unheard of."[8]

Over the decades, Totlyn Jackson continued to perform. She traveled to sing in Czechoslovakia, Romania, Germany, Holland, Scandinavia, England, and Canada, and she even lived in Dallas, Texas and Florida during the 1980s and 1990s. She resided in London until her death on June 15, 2015. More significant than her tours or talents, what Totlyn Jackson did for women was to show that they can take center stage alone, although there are sacrifices to be made. Totlyn was never able to have a traditional family—she never married, and she didn't raise her only child, who resented her for it and was estranged from her. But she did pursue her dream and paved the way for other women to follow, perhaps finding the road a bit easier. Women like Totlyn had to make choices. Some chose to leave their profession to have children, others brought their children with them and tried to balance a career, while those like Totlyn chose the career over the children and family. Before we judge any of the women for the hard choices they had to make, remember that men didn't have to face such dilemmas. For this reason alone, we should give these women, like Totlyn Jackson, credit.

Sheila Rickards

Sheila was born a preemie, weighing only three pounds at birth, which was just seven months into her mother's pregnancy in 1942. Perhaps this is why she was described in articles later in life as "tiny," standing five feet, one inch tall. She was talked about as "pert" with a "light excited voice." She says she got her start after being discovered by pianist Baba Motta. "I started at age 6. I've always been singing as long as I can remember, and Baba Motta was a friend of my family and he heard me singing and that's how I started. I started with *Lannaman's Children's Hour* on the radio and I started from there. I won three years in a row and the fourth year they told me not to come back," says Rickards.[9]

Sheila then had the chance to compete at the *Vere Johns Opportunity Hour* in 1956, where her talent for singing jazz was recognized. She says, "Whenever he was going to do a show he would call me and ask me to come. It was very natural to me because that's what I had been doing my whole life. There were a few of us—Jimmy Tucker, Hugh Francis—and a few of us that used to go around, he'd always call us and ask us to go wherever he was going to do a show, Montego Bay, Ocho Rios, wherever. Vere Johns was always very nice to us. He never paid anything, but he was a nice man and my father trusted him to take care of us. My father wouldn't let me go anywhere unless I was going to be taken care of."

Sheila Rickards' father, Ferdinand Arthur Rickards, was a contractor for the Sugar Manufacturers Association. "My father had a fleet of trucks. He was what he called a haulage contractor. At one time he had 17 trucks. My father was also a singer," she says. He helped foster his daughter's love for music by purchasing records for the family phonograph. There were over 200 records in their Greenwich Town home, which was quite a substantial amount in the 1960s for a family to own. Her father said, "Sheila was born to be a singer, she's been singing since she was four years old, started music when she was seven, very musical like her mother and sisters."[10] Sheila says, "We are all musical, my whole entire family was musical. There was always music in the house. Whoever was up first would put the hi-fi on. We'd start with something classical or very low so it would slowly wake up other people. There was dancing and all of the kids from the neighborhood was always at my house. My father made sure we had every board game, every card game, ping pong, and my mother would cook supper for these kids and they were the parents for the entire neighborhood." Sheila's mother, Melvina, was a chef, cooking for weddings and events including some at the Jamaica White House, she says.

Sheila was hired to perform with Baba Motta at the Myrtle Bank Hotel, though she was just eight or nine years old. She says, "My dad would take me, I would do my numbers, and I would come home and have to go to school in the morning. I did the very first in-house television show, I remember Alexander Bustamante, who was prime minister at that time, was at the show and it was a show done at RJR, Radio Jamaica Rediffusion, and he came to my dressing room that I shared with three other girls, but I was the only singer, and he came to me and he said, 'Do you know who I am?' I said, 'Yes, Sir Alexander Bustamante,' and he said, 'No, I'm Buster, don't forget that ever. I'm Buster to you.' I'll never forget that. He was a very nice man."

Sheila Rickards also performed regularly at the Glass Bucket for long runs, as well as on the North Coast and for Sonny Bradshaw and overseas. As she tells it, "I went to the Bahamas, I went to Australia, I went to England, I went to Europe, I was all over. I sang when the Queen [Elizabeth] came to Jamaica [November 1953]. I was a little girl, I must have been about 7 or 8 and she came to the cricket field [Sabina Park]. I got to sing Greensleeves for her and gave her bouquet of orchids."

When Sheila was just a teenager, she moved to the United States and stayed with a trusted confidante as she tried to build her career, but she soon returned to Jamaica:

> I had gone when I was 14 years old to see if I could make a break in the business. Everywhere I went it was not what I expected it to be. People were not honest, and everybody wanted something in return, if you know what I'm saying. And I was a little Catholic girl and I couldn't deal with it at all. Happy Goday [music producer], who was called the Maker of Stars, became a friend of mine, because I was sent to him, that he was a star maker. Richmond Organization, that was the name of his company. All he had me do was come to Columbus Circle everyday and had me put music sheets together because I read music and he never gave me an opportunity at all, never, and I got fed up. Charles Aznavour from Paris, who I had met in Paris years before, he came over and he saw me and he sat down at the piano and he wrote a song for me. The song was called "Once Upon a Summertime" [*sic*; "There Is a Time"]. And I can remember, Happy gave the song to Liza Minnelli. Judy Garland's daughter, she did not need a break, right? So he gave the song to her, and that was the last straw. I felt like it was beneath my dignity and I did not need to put up with it and that probably is why I never made it in America. It was the American business. The American business. Everybody wanted something and I'm a little Catholic girl and I'll be damned if I'm going to be on the casting

couch for anybody, I don't care who you are. They say you have to give a little if you want to get some, and that isn't what God meant for me.

But Rickards did continue her career in Jamaica. She also performed with the Caribs, and guitarist Dennis Sindrey remembers her as a person of great integrity and talent. "She was a favorite of mine not only as a great singer, but also as a great person. I know that you are probably aware how difficult it can be for female artists to maintain their morality when faced with the pressure of some of the unscrupulous male producers and entertainers. Sheila was always able to maintain an impeccable reputation and earned the respect of the musicians she worked with. When I was producing radio and TV commercials, she was an asset for me in that she could adapt her style as required by the content of the commercial. She was also a participant in some of the floorshows that we, the Caribs, staged at the Sheraton Kingston Hotel," Sindrey says.[11] She also performed with Carlos Malcolm, Lord Jellicoe, Lennie Hibbert, Roland Alphonso, Byron Lee, Jimmy Cliff, Derrick Morgan, Totlyn Jackson, Tony Gregory, Keith Stewart, Hortense Ellis, and dozens of others. She performed for advertisements on Jamaican radio and television, and she was a stage performer as well. "Not only was I a singer, but I was an actress." She was billed as the "I'm gonna live girl" after one of her performances at the Ward Theatre Pantomime, where she sang a song with these words.[12] She performed on stage with Louise Bennett-Coverley and Ranny Williams in shows such as *Finian's Rainbow*.

Sheila also opened for Sammy Davis Jr. when he came to Jamaica, and she became well acquainted with him and his wife. In fact, she even babysat their eight-year-old child for a couple of days[13]:

Sheila Rickards performs at the Big Beat show at the Carib Theatre on August 3, 1959 (copyright The Gleaner Company [Media] Limited).

> We had Sammy Davis Jr. and his entourage come to my house, we had Sam Cooke. Sam Cooke just gave me his daughter in the middle of the street and my father couldn't believe it. He sent me a telegram and said, "Meet me at the airport." Well we were late getting there and when we were going, they were coming to Kingston and we stopped in the middle of the street, he gave me his daughter and her suitcase and said, "Take care of her for a week or so because Barbara and I are going to have a second honeymoon." Okay! So she stayed at my house about nine days and Louis Satchmo came to my

house a couple of times. I had Count Basie, not he himself, but boys from the band I knew. My mother cooked a whole big thing for them. Dave Brubeck and Paul Desmond, when I was working in Montego Bay and I had a big house called White Horses and they came and stayed at the house and we had a jam session that lasted for three days—I'll never forget it.

Sheila was married with a son while living for a period of time in England. She explains, "My father is from England so I've been coming and going, coming and going. I went to school over there. My son was six months when I lost my first husband. He died because he wanted to come home. It was a one-car accident ... he was working away from home and he wanted to come home that night. I told him to take a rest and he just didn't listen. He said, 'I miss you and I miss my baby and I want to come home,' and he never made it home. He was a certified public accountant, a mathematician, and he audited hospital books."

Sheila returned to the United States again in the mid–1970s, though not to attempt another career in show business. She says it was just to have a better life. She says that after her father died, she came back to New York and worked at Hearst Magazines in the accounts department, where she oversaw 12 magazines and was in charge of 137 women and 10 men. "There was no sitting on my hands. I am well educated because my parents made sure I was properly educated," she says. However, she chose not to raise her son in New York and moved to California. "I just wanted a new life and that's what I found—a new life."

It is because she wanted a new life and wanted to leave show business behind for good that she says she somewhat disappeared. Record collector and filmmaker Chris Flanagan went on the hunt to find Sheila for a decade and was able to finally locate her. He started his search after he discovered one of Rickards' recordings for Bunny Lee, a tune called "Jamaican Fruit." This song is haunting, with lyrics that talk of the slave trade, and is a fairly obvious reference to Billie Holiday's "Strange Fruit." Flanagan negotiated rights to re-release the song and searched for Rickards for over a decade. That search, which found Flanagan traveling to numerous cities to interview musicians and producers, concluded with a documentary on the quest, as well as finally locating the long-lost Sheila Rickards. Flanagan says, "When I found Sheila's music in a musty Canadian thrift store, I had no idea of the journey it was going to take me on or how completely this obsession would take over my life. At first, I didn't even know who I was looking for as the song was credited only to 'Shella Record' and was unlike any reggae song I'd ever heard. I set off on a 10-year search to try to find Sheila from Toronto to Kingston, Jamaica, all across the states and even Australia. I consulted private detectives, reggae legends, and even a psychic until finally I found her."[14]

"I didn't want to be found," says Rickards. "I did not wish to be found. No. I was done with the business. I was totally soured on the business. It left a bitter taste in my mouth. I don't want to be a singer anymore. I want to sing for my own joy, which is what I did. I just left. I'd go to small clubs where I knew the musicians and we'd jam and have a good time, but I shied away from the business really badly."

Still, when she talks about her career and her life, she talks about it all with just as much excitement about her experiences as disdain for the unscrupulous actors she encountered. It is because of her strong sense of integrity and confident identity that Sheila Rickards is the pride of Jamaica. She says, "I've done a lot of things in Jamaica. I've done a lot of things for my country. As a matter of fact, I was sent two medals and a proclamation, an Officer [*sic*, "Order"] of Distinction. It was proclaimed in August, but it came to my door on my birthday in November. That's the best birthday present I ever had!" she says. That Order of Distinction was awarded to Sheila in 2018 for her "contribution to the cultural arts, in particular the fields of music and dance."[15] Sheila and her husband Bart have been married for over four decades and they reside in the United States. Her son is an EMT in Alaska.

Dr. Myrna Hague

She is class personified—grace, elegance, and sassy style. Dr. Myrna Hague, born in Jamaica, began her singing career in the UK but brought it back home for her people. Every year she continues to perform as well as to educate the public on the importance of their musical heritage. She carries the torch not only for women in Jamaican music but also for all Jamaican music to make sure the history is remembered correctly.

Born in Buff Bay, Portland, north of the Blue Mountains on the coast of the Caribbean Sea, Myrna Joyce Hague was the second of four children. Her father, Clarence Hague, played the organ. Her mother, Ivy May Abrahams, sang in the church choir, and one of her sisters played the piano. Myrna says,

> There were lots of family—aunties, lots of aunties, a very extended family life, and I'd go from one auntie's house to the next. I didn't stay in Buff Bay for a very long time. We moved to Kingston, and then I went back to Buff Bay for a short while to stay with an aunt who then died very quickly, and so I was back to Kingston again. My parents parted quite early. My father was a schoolteacher known as Teacher Hague, and his father was a schoolteacher too, and so he followed in the tradition of both of his parents—both of my grandparents were schoolteachers. When he died he was the head of the agricultural department at a secondary school. He was a teacher all his life. My mom started off as a housewife but when they parted, by that time she had learned to sew. She was a dressmaker, and when she went to the UK to live, she continued. She went to one of the factories there in the East End and by the time she came back to Jamaica she started her own business, a boutique in Ocho Rios making uniforms for most of the hotels, because she was that good. She had contracts for all of the major hotels in Ocho Rios, so my mother was basically a dressmaker. I have two sisters and one brother. I have a big sister, a brother who follows me, and then my last sister.[16]

In 1956, Myrna migrated to England with her mother. Hague says, "My parents parted, and my dad stayed in Jamaica. He remarried, and my mom took off for the UK. At that point she had only my big sister and me, we are both Hagues. My brother and my last sister are Abrahams from my mother's second marriage. I was 10 when we went to the UK." When she was 16 years old, Myrna left school and went to work as a secretary. After one year she decided to attend college. She studied dance and theater at North London College, and she was working as a model when she was discovered by the only agent for black talent in England during this time, Pearl Connor. Myrna began performing as a singer, and she says that she had always known from early in her life that she wanted to be an entertainer, and a certain level of entertainer:

> My girlfriends and I in the UK, we used to go to dances, the blue beat dances, as teenager and had a good time and we loved it. But my headspace was somewhere else because I had already developed a love for jazz. I had already decided that I wanted to be a jazz singer, I had already decided what kind of career I wanted, and this music did not suggest itself to me as something that would have any sort of longevity. And I was already thinking career, not just a job or some way to have fun, but career. So blue beat did not present itself to me as something that I wanted, and I already envisioned myself in the image of a Lena Horne. I knew from the time that I was about 12 what I wanted to be and how I wanted to look. I already had my self-image all carved out. My mother is a very elegant woman,

and also because she is a dressmaker she always made beautiful clothes for herself and for me, so I already had this image of wanting to dress up and to have a certain kind of look. Lena Horne was the lady for me. Lena Horne was my fashion idol and my artistic idol, the way she sang and presented herself onstage. So I knew very early where I was heading. I was listening to Sarah Vaughan, Dinah Washington, Ella Fitzgerald, and my favorite male singer was Sammy Davis Jr. So these were my show business idols that I was looking to for inspiration for how to sing and what to sing and how to craft. When I was a teenager, I used to get my pocket money and buy theater tickets and show tickets and sit up in the cheapest seats and go to see these people, performers, whenever they came to the UK. Sometimes my mom and I would go together, and we saw Nat King Cole together and all of the people together, but I hardly ever went with my girlfriends because they didn't want to go to those things. They just wanted to go to blue beat dances. But my head was already in a totally different place.

Hague says that in addition to her showbiz role models, her mother was also one; she modeled a certain level of living and tenacity for success:

Dr. Myrna Hague Bradshaw, jazz vocalist, speaks about her dissertation on jazz at the National Institute of Jamaica in 2013 (photograph by Heather Augustyn).

My mother was terribly ambitious, both for herself and for her children. She moved to Stilton, which was a Jewish community that became a West Indian community over time, but at the time when we lived there it was a Jewish community. When it began to change, my mom moved and she went to Stamford Hill, which was another community, and then as Stamford Hill and Topham became West Indian communities, she moved. And the last placed she lived was in Essex in suburbia, the only black family in Gants Hill. I didn't have any white friends really, but there was a quality of life my mom wanted. All of her friends were West Indians, all of her women friends. We always had big dinner parties at our house on the weekend and her women friends were just as ambitious for themselves and their kids as she was. They were always moving, this set of middle class aspiring Caribbean women and men who had dreams of a certain quality of life for themselves and their kids.

Hague began to tour in England and Europe, especially in Italy, where she would stay for extended periods of time to perform for an entire season. It was on a contract that Myrna went to perform in Italy, but she ended up staying for six years at the Moulin Rouge nightclub in Florence. She also toured Austria, Switzerland, and Beirut; she says that she "didn't particularly like being on the road, but I don't know any other way of life." She added, "Over the years, I have become the fastest and most expert suitcase packer in the West."[17]

In 1975, Hague decided to return to Jamaica, but it wasn't initially to further her career, it was to rest and connect with family. She says,

> I came to Jamaica on holiday, really. I had been working in the UK, I had been living and working in Italy, and then I began to get a little emotionally drained and stressed out, and I wasn't getting over it because I was on my own, I had no family and friendships were few and far between because I was going from city to city, from job to job. At one point my doctor said, "Where's your family?" and he said, "You need to go home because what's wrong is not physical." So I came to Jamaica and I started to come every winter for a few years and just spend six weeks and then go back. I also came on the invitation of an actor named Charles Hyatt, who was part of the Caribbean entertainment community. He had been invited to Jamaica to do some shows and he said to me, "Why don't you come and be a guest because it's a good chance for Jamaicans to know you." He said, "You were going to go on holiday anyway, so why don't you come?" It was in the middle of summer, June or July, and I came and it went very well. It was the first time I ever worked with the Sonny Bradshaw 7, they were the band, they were his friends and it was at the Courtleigh Hotel on Oxford Road.

It was after this performance that word got out that there was an incredible talent on the stage, and so the next move for enterprising producers was to get this powerful voice into the studio. Myrna says,

> I went back to Ocho Rios, where my parents live, and Coxsone made contact and said, "Why don't you come to Kingston and let's see if we can record you." This was about 1972. So I came into Kingston, stayed with the family and went to the studio. I took some of my arrangements with me, and Coxsone went through what I had and picked some things he thought that I would want to do and proposed some other things, and we made the album *Melody Life*. After I made the album I didn't really think anything more of it. It was my first encounter with reggae and my first encounter with Jamaican musicians. It was a totally new ballgame for me. It was a whole different world.

Myrna Hague's career began to evolve in the Caribbean and so she slowly moved back home. She says,

> I went back to the UK and back to Italy but I decided that I would come back [to Jamaica] in the winter, and it was a good time to come because I got called to do quite a bit of work, starting off with the Playboy Club. I did the Hilton Hotel and that was fun too and interesting. I got to work with some really good musicians, working in the hotels. So I began to transition because at that point I was beginning to get bored with going around in Europe. I wasn't being offered any record deals there, and the industry was changing, from the supper club scene to more of a pop music scene. Discotheques were coming in and the whole scene was changing, and a different kind of music was happening. So I started to think in terms of transition. I decided I was just going to go back and take up residence in London, but everything was changing in London and I was not quite sure what I was going to do. So I started to come to Jamaica every winter and stay longer and longer. More and more work was being offered, and so I was staying longer and longer.

In 1976, Hague performed with Jimmy Cliff in the Second Caribbean Festival of Arts. Critics lauded her style and described her as "somewhere between soul and Shirley Bassey."[18] It helped to give Myrna incredible exposure. "Carifesta, a Caribbean Festival of Arts, was going around the Caribbean," Myrna remembers, "and in 1976 it came to Jamaica and Buddy Pouyatt was a major artistic mover in Kingston." She continues,

> He got in touch with me and said, "We would like you to appear at Carifesta. The Jamaica Big Band is going to play, and we think you should sing with the Jamaica Big Band; however, you have to sing Caribbean songs, original Caribbean songs." I had been singing jazz and popular music, popular standards. I wasn't singing any R&B or reggae or anything like that. I was singing show music, standards, and some jazz. So I spoke with Ralph Holding, who was a hugely talented musician and he was a band leader at the Hilton, and I said to Ralph, "I need some music." He promptly wrote two original compositions for me. Then I went to the JBC library and decided to research some original

Caribbean folk songs, and I found the Haitian song "Choucounne," which was very popular in Jamaican, known as "Yellow Bird," but it's originally a Haitian song. And I liked it, so I learned it. I learned the dictation in French, and that and the two original songs that Ralph Holding wrote for me, and I translated "Feelings," which was originally a Spanish song that had been done in English and was quite popular at the time, and that was my repertoire for the show. And Ralph Holding wrote all the big band arrangements, brought them in and we rehearsed them with the Big Band under the direction of Sonny Bradshaw, and this was the show at the Carib. It was televised live. So it gave me an immediate visibility and it gave me an entree, as it were.

With Hague's career now established in Jamaica, offers continued to roll in. "Soon after that [Carifesta] I was called by JBC and was offered my own television series, 'An Evening with Myrna Hague,' for six weeks. Actually, a folk singer, Stewart, who had his own show on television, called me and asked me if I would be a guest on his show. That was the first thing. And after I was on his show, I was offered my own television series. And that pretty much gave me a strong visibility and it went on from that, really," she says.

In 1977 Myrna Hague became secretary of the Jamaican Federation of Musicians, a position she held for six years. Here, and at her performances, Hague grew to know Sonny Bradshaw even more. He had performed trumpet for her sets, hired musicians for her songs, and arranged music for her. But Myrna says he also gave her tremendous professional advice that helped to establish her career in Jamaica in those early days:

> I remember the first time I was asked to perform at the Hilton, and the money was so ridiculous that I called him because he was president of the musicians union at the time, and I said, "I've been called to work on a regular basis for the whole of the season. I'm going to be here six or eight weeks, but they're offering me X, what do I do? It's a lot less," and he said, "Yes, it's less than you're accustomed to, but if I were you, I would take it and make your name. Then you can ask what you want." It was excellent advice. So I did, because I really didn't need the money. I was living at home with my parents, I didn't have rent to pay or food to buy or anything, and so it was okay. And it gave me the opportunity to begin to ground myself in the Jamaican musical environment, to get to know musicians and to begin to understand the culture. I felt that it was important for me to reground myself.

Hague also became a voice tutor at the Jamaica School of Music, and in 1992 she earned her bachelor of arts in music from the University of West Indies at Mona, all while still maintaining her career. Myrna was winner of the Caribbean Broadcasting Union Song Festival 1990, she won the Jamaica Music Industry Award for jazz a number of times, and she was both the Jamaica Federation of Musicians Award winner and Special Merit Award in 1993.

Myrna Hague is an independent woman, a successful woman, a professional woman, but she also is one half of the team that established the Ocho Rios International Jazz Festival on the island. Myrna Hague became Myrna Hague-Bradshaw when she married Sonny Bradshaw in 1995. Sonny's children, not by Myrna, are daughter Karen Hall-Bradshaw and son Carey Bradshaw; daughter Bridgette Bradshaw was murdered by a boyfriend who killed himself; and his very first child, Christian, died of natural causes early in life.

The Ocho Rios International Jazz Festival was established in 1991. Prior to this, Sonny Bradshaw established Reggae Sunsplash. But, as he explained, he had a different vision inspired by Myrna:

> My present wife [Myrna Hague] was one influence. She wanted it [Ocho Rios International Jazz Festival] done. Because, out of Jamaica came reggae, reggae, reggae, and the showplace for reggae was Reggae Sunsplash. I was working with the Ministry at that time, The Ministry of Welfare and ... they

were promoting the ska, because it's a wonderful music. It ahhm, let me see how to put it ... let me see now ... well because Reggae Sunsplash was representing the popular music of the day in Montego Bay, Kingston had all the other entertainment facilities, sports, football, cricket, and all that. Ocho Rios had nothing. And so we decided that we would make Ocho Rios the jazz centre. So we started the festival in Ocho Rios because the other areas of the music and entertainment industry were elsewhere.... That's why I don't want to use the Ocho Rios Jazz Festival to be a pop music festival. Because the pop music is already established. And now it's Reggae Sunfest, which has taken over from Reggae Sunsplash. They're covering that quite well. And in Kingston they're covering all the other all the other entertainment. See theatre, we have more theatres now than any other time, and plays, everything. But Ocho Rios, it don't really have nothing you know, but a lot of hotels and the sand and the sea, and every other country has that. So Ocho Rios should be so glad to have the jazz festival here. And so we have persevered with that. That's why our festival is a jazz festival.[19]

The Ocho Rios International Jazz Festival has featured the greatest names in Jamaican jazz as well as the best international artists, a youth program, daily free concerts, a large-scale photo exhibition, and events. It has established a Jazz Hall of Fame, which recognizes Jamaican and Caribbean musicians "who have distinguished themselves internationally while contributing to the development of the art form."[20] While Sonny Bradshaw was alive, Myrna served as assistant director to him. And after Sonny died in 2009, Myrna took over to continue his legacy.

Dr. Myrna Hague has always loved jazz, as a singer and as an aficionado. She has gone back to school and recently completed work on her PhD at the University of the West Indies, with a dissertation on jazz in the Caribbean, and she has gone back to the studio. In 2003, Hague teamed up with Earl "Chinna" Smith on guitar, Oral Brown on percussion, Denver Smith on drums, and Ozou'ne on keyboard and bass to record the Sarah Vaughan tune "Broken-Hearted Melody." She also covered Bob Andy's song "Honey." In 2014 she re-recorded her album *Melody Life* and revisited the songs she once recorded at Studio One. The new version of the album features Rupert Bent on guitar, Christopher McDonald on keyboard, Desi Jones on drums, Howard Foulds on saxophone, and Adrian Henry on bass. Myrna launched the album with a performance at Hope Gardens on April 27, 2014. She says that she decided to re-record the album due to requests from her fans:

Everytime I am on the stage, I'm being called out to sings songs from *Melody Life*. At first I just thought it was just a guy from a radio station or something, but then I started to hear it more, and so I started to learn a couple of the songs and have them ready just in case. Then the whole thing became like a thundering knock at my door. People started to ask me, "When are you going to re-record *Melody Life*?" It couldn't be released as it was because the technology has changed so much. The two tracks that Coxsone used would be totally unacceptable today, and so my thinking then was, let's just do it over. I've taken out "Time After Time" and "On a Clear Day" and I replaced it with "Waiting in Vain," which is a Sonny Bradshaw original arrangement; original composition is Bob Marley, but original big band arrangement that Sonny had done for me and I reused; and I'm also doing the Bob Andy song, "Honey," which I got to sing for his fundraising concert. They are basically the same but fresh, based on the quality of the musicians, which is much better, and the technology is much better, which is nice. I think it is going to be a success in Europe and that is really what I'm looking for at this moment. We all had a really good time and the musicians themselves had fun.[21]

Hague recognizes that women have difficulty in the music industry, especially in Jamaica, but she has been fortunate not to face those challenges. She says,

I personally have not faced some of the challenges that I could have faced as a woman because by the time that I came into the recording industry I was already an established performer. I wasn't looking for anybody to break me into show business. I wasn't looking for a break. I came already with stuff, so I was making a record to underscore what I had already done. If you listen to *Melody Life*, half of the songs come right out of my repertoir of material that I had already been singing. If you listen to the voice, it's already well formed. The style of singing is already pretty much well formed, so I'm not looking for a break here. The next album that I made, *Send in the Clowns*, I produced it myself. I was my own executive producer. I wanted to do what I wanted to do, and at that point, all of the recording companies and studios were into reggae but there was not a lot of quality musical content for me. It didn't satisfy me. I like reggae, but I like quality music. It doesn't have to be genius, but it has to be acceptable levels.

Dr. Myrna Hague was awarded the Musgrave Silver Medal by the Institute of Jamaica in 2016 for "outstanding merit in the field of music,"[22] and she continues to bring a stellar quality of music to stages all over the world. She is a true Jamaican diva in the best sense of the word.

Chapter Five

Ska

It would be interesting to catalog all songs in the Jamaican ska genre from 1959 through 1965 or so to determine what percentage of them were instrumentals and what percentage of them contained prominent vocals, meaning more than mere toasting. One would venture to guess that a larger percentage, perhaps a decent larger percentage, would be instrumentals. This is due to the fact that the ska genre emerged from jazz and featured jazz-trained and classically trained musicians. Ska also emerged from mento and American rhythm and blues, however, so there was a tendency to add in some vocals from time to time.

The vocalists who got their start in ska or stayed in ska were used repeatedly in recordings—Derrick Morgan, Stranger Cole, Owen Grey, Roy Panton, and, of course, a number of crucial women. While these women mostly sang duets with the men, owing to the American rhythm-and-blues style of the time as well as to social and cultural reasons, a few women did have the chance to spread their wings a bit more and perhaps solo now and then—either within a song or on a stand-alone recording. These are a few of the women who are the songbirds of ska.

Millicent Todd

Millicent "Patsy" Todd was just a teenage girl when ska first became popular in the early 1960s. She was born on September 23, 1944, grew up in Fletcher's Land in West Kingston, and was Prince Buster's next-door neighbor. She attended All Saints School and left at age 14. Although she wasn't raised in a particularly musical home, and the Catholic Church she attended didn't have much to offer in the way of music since the program was still presented in Latin in those days, she did listen to the music coming from America. "I'm somebody who liked to listen to the radio, and I really got interested in this group, Frankie Lymon and the Teenagers. I used to hear them singing and I used to sing after them," she says.[1]

Her mother, whom she refers to as "Miss Kitty," realizing Todd's talent, helped to get her daughter's start. Miss Kitty approached Derrick Morgan on Orange Street, a street in downtown Kingston known for its record shops and studios, and told him of her daughter's talent—although today Todd says she has only heard the story from Morgan and didn't know the details:

Derrick told me the story because I didn't know anything about it. He said he saw this woman and she told him she had a daughter that could sing. And I saw this guy came to my gate, knock on my gate. I'm looking at him and he's saying he's Derrick Morgan, and I say to myself, "So?" And he said, "I heard you can sing," and I'm looking at him wondering what he's talking about. And he said, "Could you sing something for me?" and I said, "Why?" And he said, "I just want to hear something." And I did. But as far as I'm concerned, I didn't know who this guy was, what he wanted. Somebody just come appear to you, telling you he hear you can sing and if you would do a song with him. And at first I was kind of, something ain't right here. But then he told me a story about another artist that the song was about, and this guy, I hated him, still do. And when he said that, I was ready to sing that song. And I did. And we have this producer, Duke Reid, God rest his soul, a nice man, and he start shooting up the place. My God! I was so scared! I ran! And they said, "No! That's a good thing! When he hears something that he likes that's going to make a hit, this is what he does!" So that experience was great for me and after that it was history. The song was "Love Not to Brag."

Millicent "Patsy" Todd, backstage at a performance with Stranger Cole in Minneapolis, 2016 (photograph by Heather Augustyn).

The man who inspired the song was Eric "Monty" Morris, who grew up with Morgan and was known to be boastful. He and Morgan were vocal competitors.

Todd was young, and the music industry could be an unkind environment, especially with so much skilled talent, so many professional musicians in the studio and producers wanting to record a hit song to play at the sound system later that night. "It was hard. Very hard," says Todd:

> I was 15, 16 years old. And it was hard because you didn't have a say. I didn't get the chance to go to rehearsal and things like that. I would go to the studio and my partner would tell me, "This is so-and-so and so-and-so," and I would write it down, and I would sing from the paper, that was it. I don't remember what it was, what I did or how much record I did. I didn't have a say, to say to the musicians, "Would you play this," or "Would you play that." They would kill me. You just take what they give you and that's it. The musicians that we had were great musicians. I think they could play with anyone in this entire world. They knew music, they knew what they were doing. They were absolutely fantastic. But they were very egotistical. You know, it was either just them or nothing. The problem when you have a band that every musician in that band could be the leader, it's very hard. That's how great they were.

She was young, innocent, naïve, but her talent transcended. Graeme Goodall, engineer at Federal Records, recalled her work in the studio. "I loved her dearly. She was a very nice person, very pleasant to work with, very polite. She was not so much a leader, but she was very very good and she, like most of the vocalists of the day, understood that this was her big break," Goodall says.[2]

Derrick and Patsy continued to record hit after hit as a duo, including "Feel So Fine," "Are You Going to Marry Me," "Crying in the Chapel," and countless others. Perhaps the most well-known song the duo recorded was "Housewife's Choice" in 1962 for producer Leslie Kong. This song was originally named "You Don't Know How Much I Love You," but Marie Garth, legendary radio host, had so many housewives call in to the station to request the tune that she renamed it, and future pressings reflected this name change. The song also became popular in the United Kingdom as West Indian immigrants played the tune, which was released on the Island Records label. Derrick and Patsy were a hit. They were the perfect boy-girl duo singing sweet songs of love and romance. They were so big that when popular American artists came to perform in Kingston, so too did Derrick and Patsy as part of the Jamaican spectacular. They performed at shows with Ray Charles, Ben E. King, and Sammy Davis Jr. Derrick would record with a number of female vocalists in duets, including Gloria Franklin (who also performed as Gloria and the Dreamlets), Naomi Phillips (who also recorded with Doreen Shaffer), Hortense Ellis, Paulette Morgan (Derrick's sister), Yvonne Harrison (also called Yvonne Adams), and Jennifer and the Mohawks (Jennifer Jones).

When Derrick Morgan left to go to England to try his hand at success overseas, Patsy Todd was approached by another singer with the offer to perform duets. She recalls, "Stranger [Cole] came to talk to me. He said that Duke Reid sent him and he said he wanted to do some record and the only way that Duke Reid would record him [was] if I sang with him. And it kind of hit me off guard because Derrick was in England, and I said to him, 'I don't know about that, I have to think about it,' and then I saw this guy really needed to do this. He believed he could make himself better and do something that he love and getting paid for it, you know, a charge was in him. And I said okay, I tell him yes. And that's how Stranger Cole and I came about." One of their biggest hits was the song, "When I Call Your Name," which they recorded for Duke Reid. Other classics include "Down the Train Line," "Yeah Yeah Baby," "Give Me the Right," and "Love Divine"; there were plenty more. The tunes were also classic boy-girl duets, inviting and harmonious. Most were recorded in 1964 for Sonia Pottinger and Duke Reid. Stranger remembers his days with Patsy. "Mr. Reid was the one who asked me to sing with her. He told me to go to her and asked me to sing with her. So 'When I Call Your Name' we recorded, and we do many many more songs together. She was not shy, she was much braver than I. She make hit record before I do, with Derrick Morgan, so she was a more limelighted artist than I was. I think that was a blessing for me to have a lady with more hit songs before me. I am very lucky to sing with her, and I think she is very lucky to sing with me," says Stranger.[3]

Patsy Todd wasn't just a duet artist. She was also an artist in her own right—Queen Patsy. At a time when women weren't doing much solo work at all, Patsy paved the way for strong female vocalists. One of her tunes, "A Man Is a Two Face," is not a ska or rocksteady song, but is true to the American R&B tradition with soulful vocals, music by Lynn Taitt and the Jets. The lyrics offer advice from a mother to a daughter that she shares with other women about how a man will smile and sweet talk but leave you singing the blues in the night. It was not the submissive songs of innocent love she sang with Stranger and Derrick. It was a song of empowerment and knowledge and sisterhood. It was Patsy Todd's take on "These Boots Are Made for Walkin'," both in sound and in spirit. She was physically without a man by her side, as in her duets, and she, as a solo artist, was all woman. Her voice transforms in this song from the way it was in her duos. She is no longer the little teenager—she is informed, guiding, warning. The flip side of this recording on Sonia Pottinger's Gay Feet label is "It's So Hard Without You," where Patsy sings that there is nothing she can do without her man. What do we make of this paradox? Certainly, these songs reflect the emotions women feel in relationships—the phases and complexities.

Two of the other solo songs that Patsy Todd recorded for Producer Sonia Pottinger were "Fire in Mi Wire" and "Pata Pata Rock Steady," which were unique in their content. "Fire in Mi Wire" is a calypso tune originally written by Calypso Rose, whose lyrics are the typical sexual innuendo of calypso and soca, but certainly not typical of those sung by a female up to this point. "Pata Pata Rock Steady" was also a song written by a female artist in 1957—by Dorothy Masuka for singer Miriam Makeba, both South African artists. "Fire in Mi Wire" and "Pata Pata Rock Steady" were songs that showed Patsy's take-charge side and celebrated the creativity of other women. Of "Fire in Mi Wire," Todd says, "I wanted to prove a point that I could do other styles. I would take chances to see what I could do. I never had a say in any of the songs I sang with the duets, so this was an opportunity to try different things." "Pata Pata" was not the only Miriam Makeba song Patsy Todd covered. She also recorded "The Retreat Song," also titled "Jikele Maweni," which had a distinct African feel, especially since it was sung in the Xhosa language, whose lyrics tell of a vicious stick fight—not the typical teenage love song.

Patsy Todd traveled overseas to share her talent, to the U.S. with Byron Lee and the Dragonaires, and to Belize. She sang on over 100 recordings. But she left it all behind in 1968, as the music left ska and rocksteady behind. She simply grew tired of the industry and moved to New York to start a new life. Todd says,

> I went to Belize with Byron Lee and they had some recording shop [studio] and when I went there, I wanted to get some orders for Miss Pottinger [Sonia Pottinger]. And when I went there, I had three records on the chart, number one, number two, and number three. And it just blowed my mind. I am standing here with record number one, number two, and number three in their country and I don't have any money. And that day I decided when I go back to Jamaica, that was it. And I decided that if I stayed there, that's all I really knew how to do. And I called a friend of mine and I said I just want some time to think and she said, "Why don't you come up?" and I came to America and I didn't go back. I didn't go back. That was it. That was in 1968. There's been a lot of ups and downs because I came. I was by myself. When I was in Jamaica it's not like I even lived by myself. I lived with my parents, so coming here, living with my girlfriend and her mother, it was kind of strange, but it's a choice I made. I figured to myself that if I went back, it would be showing that what I did, I had to turn back and I said come hell or high water I'm not going to do it. So I know I made a choice and the choice I made at the time, it was very hard because coming to America and you have no skill but what you left home with. The music here is totally different. Their music, their way of thinking, their this, their that, there's no way to know where to even start to get your foot in. So I was just saying to myself, "Well this is it, this is your choice, you've got to stick with it." As they say, you've made your bed, you have to lie in it. But fortunately, I was lucky that I got a job. I was working in a hospital in a cardio-care unit, the secretary there for the floor, and the people that we worked with, we were like family. In fact, they didn't even know the life I had before I came. Because that was my life. That was my personal business and I tell no one, so no one knew what I did.

Patsy took the stage for the first time in 33 years at the Legends of Ska Concert, organized by Brad Klein in Toronto in 2002. Since then, Patsy has occasionally returned to the stage to perform, alongside her duo partners, Stranger and Derrick Morgan, as well as on her own.

Doreen Shaffer

Despite the fact that she takes center stage in the spotlight night after night, year after year, using the microphone to reach the hearts of crowds all over the world, Doreen Shaffer can be fiercely private. She will never reveal her age. She won't even tell you the year of her birth, because she knows you can do the math. And even though she exudes warm spirit and love like a member of your own family, don't for a second think that she is a caretaker or a mother figure. She is no one's mama but her own kin, and she is tough and talented. She had to be, to last this long.

Doreen Shaffer was born Monica Shaffer in the center of Kingston, Jamaica, and she was raised by her mother, Lurlene. Doreen's father, Herbert Shaffer, was German and held a job that was very demanding, requiring much time away from the home. "I only grew up with my mom. I didn't grow up with my father. My father was a liaison officer for U.S. farm work … there was an office on East Street and the men would go there for their health examination. He was the one who was in charge of all that. My mother raised the kids and worked for a company called Royal Mill and she used to be a messenger for them. I had two brothers and I was the only girl. I was the last child. My mother was married to Cardoza, was his name. I didn't grow up with him. By the time she had me, she was divorced. I didn't know much of him. He was Jewish. My eldest brother was Shaffer. We both are Shaffers," she says.[4]

Doreen Shaffer performing at the 2018 Supernova Ska Festival in Virginia (photograph by Heather Augustyn).

With so much responsibility to manage on her own, Lurlene Shaffer ran a tight ship. Doreen says, "I was brought up where I couldn't take friends home from school. She was a strict mother. I didn't go anywhere. From school, I go home. She would start the meal and go to work and I would have to come home and finish up, so I was always in a hurry to get home. If you are late, you are in trouble."

Doreen says she remembers her mother singing around the home, which was an inspiration, but the real opportunity came in church and school:

> My mama, I would hear her singing when we go to church and she was always singing around the house. But there was no music around of such, no music of such, say like somebody was in that field. So I started singing at school a lot. I did a lot of school plays and like that. In Kingston, Jamaica, I went to elementary school. I attended Calabar Elementary on East Queen Street in Central Kingston. The school was at the back of the church. It's Baptist, but I used to attend church at Wesley Methodist, but I went to Calabar. When I leave school there, I went on to night school at Durham College. I don't know if it's in existence anymore. So that's where it really started for me, singing around classmates, and they would say, "You should sing." I grew up with that in the back of my mind. That's a project I'm going to get involved in.

Shaffer's husband, Joseph Johnson, had a connection to Coxsone Dodd, and he encouraged her to pursue a musical career. "I used to sing in school, for concerts or on Fridays and I knew a song from it, from singing. I spoke with his uncle and he told me where Coxsone was and I went there, to Studio One on Brentford Road. Because I had the intention to try out the music, I wanted to see what I could do. To sing cover songs is nice but I wanted to do my own thing. At the time there was this Dinah Washington song on the air that played a lot, so I took it and write some lyrics to see if it would go with it and sing on my own. I got involved in the music at 18," she says.

That audition at Studio One launched Doreen's career as a vocalist for the seminal ska band The Skatalites, who, at that time, were a group of studio musicians who performed not only at Studio One for recordings but for all producers during the early 1960s, as well as in clubs throughout the country. Doreen remembers,

> When I got there, there were some other people there and what I was hearing, they were saying to other people was, you come back in a month, you come back in another two weeks, or so, and I couldn't understand when he said to some people, you come back in one year [laughs]. However, he said to me, when I got there, there were some other musicians that make up The Skatalites—[Lloyd] Brevett was there, [Lloyd] Knibb was there, I think Jackie Mittoo was there, but the first person I met was Lloyd Knibb. [Coxsone] introduce me to Lloyd Knibb, the very good drummer, and after I sung a song to him, he said I must come back the following day. So I was happy about that. I went back and after I did my recording, he said he had Jackie Opel and he wanted to do a duet. He said Jackie was coming the next day or following two days. The next day that I was there, Jackie Opel came and he [Coxsone] introduced me to Jackie Opel and he said he liked my voice and we'd be a good blend for a duet. And so that's how it started, with Jackie and Doreen.

Jackie and Doreen recorded a number of singles for Studio One in 1964 and 1965, including "Adorable You," "Every Beat of My Heart," "The Vow," "Welcome You Back Home," and "You and I." It wasn't the easiest partnership, but Doreen remains respectful of the situation. "There was a lot of unpleasantness and I don't want to go back to that. It will hurt me. But he's a very good singer. He was having his own problems. We didn't get to rehearse much most of the time. I would go by their house and his girlfriend is there and want to make a scene, and we were both by Bournemouth Beach and we did some rehearsals there. It wasn't regular, but whenever it was possible. But they were always arguing at home, and the first time I went and I saw that and he said he don't mind if I come and I said, 'No I'm not coming back,'" she says. But rehearsing wasn't always part of the plan in those days, so Doreen continued despite the challenges.

Doreen was asked to join The Skatalites as one of their four vocalists, and she accepted. "Lloyd Knibb said, 'We'd love to have you in the band.' I said yes. At that time, when the band was formed, we had four vocalists at that time, I being the only female. You have Jackie Opel, Lord Tanamo, you have Tony DaCosta, and myself. Then we started in shows and traveling all over the country," says Shaffer. As the only female in the band of virtuosos, many with egos to boot, it wasn't easy going. "It's not all roses for female singers at that time. It wasn't the best. It was rough. It wasn't all that easy, but the good outweighs the bad. Later in the years, everybody was obsessed with us, but at that time, you were in a man's world. I was very determined that I was going to do it. I wasn't going to let anyone hold me back. That was my disposition. I was quite clear, I wanted to do it and I'm going to do it and stick with it and thank God it's been good," she says.

After The Skatalites broke up in 1965, Shaffer continued singing, establishing herself further as an artist, but not without a snafu that could have killed her career. Shaffer relates,

> I started with The Skatalites in 1964 when the band formed and then we were off for a year and we got a job at the Bournemouth Beach Club in Jamaica, so I was there and I performed and someone was very interested in my performance and I was offered a job in the Bahamas. Unfortunately, that didn't come about. It should have been, because you have these cruise ships that used to come there, and they would dock. So I got a letter from them stating that they wanted me. I was supposed to attend an audition, which unfortunately, where I was living, I didn't really get nothing in the ghetto, the tenement, you know. Somebody took the letter and destroyed it. But I found out. They sent me another letter that they were waiting for me in Miami. So when I got the letter, all of this had gone. The date passed and I couldn't make it. They said they were waiting for me almost a week, but like I said before, the letter was destroyed. They had got someone from Florida. Someone there got the opportunity I should have gotten.

But fortunately, Shaffer's talent was still in demand. "I went to the Bahamas finally. The people still were interested. They still make preparations for me. And I was there for like 18 months. I work at a club called The Island House and it was lovely. It was great. I wasn't too open, and I didn't know what was going on around me, but I had a chaperone. I had someone there. Someone would always take me around and she get everything done, so I was half comfortable. That was good. I was in my late 20s, about 28," says Shaffer.

While in the Bahamas, Shaffer became a mother. "My first child was in Nassau. Kellier was the first girl, and she lives there. She got married there and decided to stay there. Her father in the early days, people were migrating to England, and he went off to England. And I have two children with my husband, Joseph Johnson, a boy and a girl. We used to be neighbors in Jamaica," she says. Shaffer also had another daughter in 1969 with Tommy McCook, although she is private about that relationship and the resulting tragedy, understandably. Doreen explains, "I lost my daughter in 1988. That was the child I had with Tommy McCook. It was tragic. She drowned at a relative's pool. She was 19 and just graduated. She was very bright. She won a music pageant. Some of these things I try to block out. Her name was Denise McCook."

After Shaffer finished her work in the Bahamas, she returned to her native Jamaica and continued her career. "I came back to Jamaica and then I started recording. It was at the end of '79, I think, that I did 'Sugar Sugar.' That was moving for me," she says. "Sugar Sugar" is a song that Shaffer regularly sings with the modern incarnation of The

Skatalites; it was written for Shaffer by Laurel Aitken. Her other classics with The Skatalites include "You're Wondering Now" and "Can't You See." "Most of the time, after the band broke up, I would do concerts around the island with a lot of other artists, some of them passed on. The New Caledonians, Delroy Wilson, The Itals, a few of them that I really worked with," she says.

Doreen's name has been spelled a number of different of ways over the years, including "Schaffer," "Schafer," "Schaeffer," "Chauffer," and "Shafer." She performed solo and did duets with Slim Smith, Clive Bonnie, Leon Hyatt, and Tony Gregory. She worked with producer Bunny Lee and also spent some time working with Naomi Phillips, who had previously recorded duets with Derrick Morgan and Clive Bonnie. "She wasn't in the music all that much but had a very good voice," says Shaffer. "I happened to be at Byron Lee's one day and somebody introduced her to me, and she told me where I could get in touch with her, and I went and I listen to her and she had a very good voice, but her determination was not there and she start judging if I'm getting money and you're not getting—I don't want to be caught up in that, so that was one of the problems we had because you keep judging me and I wasn't happy about that. I got to do something with her and I know we could have gone further."

In 1983, when the Sunsplash Festival took place, Shaffer was part of the Skatalites reunion. "I was still living in Jamaica and I think it was the Sunsplash organizers, they were the ones who got in touch with them [the members of The Skatalites] in some way, and I was informed that they were going to come down for Sunsplash and they wanted me to be a part of it. But everybody was away. I hadn't seen them for a good while. So that was quite exciting, meeting everybody again. But I didn't get back with them until I got to the U.S., that's what I'm saying. Sunsplash was in '83, but they went on to London and I wasn't a part of that," says Shaffer.

Shaffer had a busy personal life, and in the 1970s, before the reunion, she took time off from singing professionally to raise her family. "In my 20s, I was having kids. I have four kids." Even though she had children and took a break, she still came back to her music career. "Because I'm going to do what, if I stop? Most of my time was just with music. I don't do anything else. So I always put away something and I feel if I have the energy, I go out there and do it." Shaffer moved to the U.S. in 1992 after living in Jamaica her entire life. When Shaeffer arrived in the U.S., word of her presence quickly spread to the members of The Skatalites, and Coxsone's wife, Norma Dodd, facilitated the reunion. "Ms. Dodd took me down to Central Park. They were having some concert. They were part of this festival and she took me directly because she knew where to find them and she was the one who took me there. So I was happy, meetin' and greetin'. So we decided, they said, 'Well, you are here now, you've got to work with us,'" Shaffer says.

She has toured with The Skatalites ever since then, to countries including Brazil, France, England, the Netherlands, Luxembourg, Spain, Mexico, Argentina, Germany, Denmark, Sweden, Finland, Russia, the U.S., Canada, the Czech Republic, Poland, and Japan. She has also performed with the Moon Invaders and other bands. "It's exciting. We have a lot of dates and a lot of audiences. It's very interesting. It's advanced, you know. Wherever we go, we have a full house, I would say. It's quite commending to know that after all these years, it pays off, all the time," Shaffer says.

Touring year after year with the members of The Skatalites, as well as fronting other orchestras like The Western Standard Time Ska Orchestra at the Supernova Ska Festival in 2018, has been a labor of love for Shaffer, even though being on the road and performing late at night in clubs is a difficult lifestyle for a grandmother in her 70s. "It's quite exhausting. We're doing shows and our nights are very hectic, so it's quite an experience, but I'm doing that, and I thank God. I enjoy being on the road, but at the same time, you need your rest and you need to be with your family," she says. "But music is fun. If you enjoy it, it is worth it. A sacrifice. A lot of sacrifice. It's a lot of devotion because it takes up a lot of your time," says Shaffer. And what do her grandkids think of Grandma Shaffer? "Very awesome," she says with a sweet laugh.

Shaffer says she plans to keep bringing her music to fans all over the world even though she is the only original member still alive with the band. "I hope for The Skatalites everything good. Even better than last year, that everyone will be around and we put out more good music," she says, acknowledging that although the music appeals to generations young and old, the youth keep it alive. "The young ones, they go crazy. The kids, they are very excited and very into it, so I'm happy for that. The energy from the audience, that's what keeps me," Shaffer says.

The popularity of The Skatalites after all these years is due to those who founded the sound and founded The Skatalites, the true pioneers. The music they established led to modern versions of ska and other incarnations of the jazz and mento blend. "You have a lot of dub music and hip hop going on, which is a part of the musical scene. Some people really want to hear instruments, to hear the band, the orchestra, and the music. These are great musicians, I have to give them credit, you know, because from Roland, Tommy, coming right down, Don Drummond, they were really good," she says.

But she is careful to point out that she is no one's mother except her own children's, despite touring with musicians who have become like family. "I am nobody's mother, no. I don't take that responsibility. We are all there working, and I don't get into business that's not mine. I'm not your mother so I shouldn't tell you what to do. That's why I'm there so long! I don't judge. But I do try to help everyone. You don't have to be my grandchild or my child. If people have a problem, whatever I can do for that person, I do. I like to listen to people and I don't see myself as, 'It's all about me.' I'm not that person. I make time for people because I'm not living in a world by myself. So wherever I go in the world, I have friends," she says.

Yvonne Harrison

With Derrick Morgan as a cousin and Glen Adams as a brother, Yvonne Harrison could say that music is in her blood. She was billed as "The Nightingale," as "Jamaica's Patti Page." Yvonne Harrison was born in Kingston in the Vineyard Town neighborhood. She says her household was a musical one, although she was encouraged to focus on school. "My mother was a singer in her days. I grew up with my father. I went to my father when I was very young, so I grew up with him. My father was a very strict person and he was all about school. It wasn't until I left at a later age that I started the singing. In those days we didn't know about dating and partying and stuff like that. When you go to a party, like Excelsior have a Christmas party, you go at three o'clock and you come home [laughs]. My mother supported me after I go to live with her, and my brother start working, so it was the two of us—I start first and then he after. He start doing keyboard and I traveled out of the island to work with different groups," Yvonne says.[5]

She says that her brother, Glen Adams, was a half-brother (same mother, different fathers), and so sometimes people confused her surname with his and called her Yvonne Adams; because of this some of her recordings are misnamed. Her brother Glen, born on November 27, 1945, became a performer after appearing as part of a vocal group on the *Vere Johns Opportunity Hour* talent show. Coxsone Dodd spotted Adams when he was rehearsing a song one day, a song that was written by Yvonne called "Wonderthirst," or as the song is more widely known, "Look Before You Leap." Adams went on to form a duo with Ken Boothe, Ken and Glen, and together they took second place with the tune "I Remember" in the famous Festival Song Competition in 1966. The Festival Song Competition was a creation of Edward Seaga to promote Jamaican music island-wide and internationally. Adams and Boothe also sang backup for Stranger Cole on the classic song "Uno Dos Tres." Adams went on to form The Heptones with Barry Llewelyn, Joseph Forester, Jackson Jones, and Earl Morgan. He sang solo and backup for Bunny Lee, played keyboards on

Yvonne Harrison performing at the Manhattan Center in New York City with Roland Alphonso and the Outer Limits in the early 1980s (courtesy Yvonne Harrison).

"Bangarang," and played in sessions for The Hippy Boys and The Upsetters. He worked for Herman Chin Loy and toured the UK with Lee "Scratch" Perry and the Upsetters, as well as performing for The Wailers during their time with Perry. Adams established Capo Records in the U.S. and moved to Brooklyn in 1975. He continued to perform, record, and produce until his death in 2010. "He was with Lee Perry and he branched out on his own. He performed all over, mainly in Europe and he had a studio in Brooklyn," says Harrison.

When Yvonne Harrison started singing in school, the experience soon led to a career. "When it was Christmas time at school, they would have the lighting of the Christmas tree and we'd go and sing carols, and they would have a concert at school and I would participate. From there I joined a group called Robin and the Nightingales, and we did a lot of rehearsals and also we tried to do some recording, but it never pan out. The recording never came to anything. It was one guy and two girls, including myself," she says. Little else is known of The Nightingales, especially since they didn't record; however, when Yvonne Harrison then continued her career as part of a duo or as a solo vocalist, she was billed at times as "the Nightingale," so one can assume that The Nightingales had some recognition on the entertainment circuit.

Because her cousin Derrick Morgan was a successful vocalist in the early 1960s, he and Yvonne did some recording as a duo—Derrick and Yvonne. She says, "I started singing with Derrick Morgan, who is also my cousin, and I started with Derrick and did a couple of performances and recordings." Those songs, "Meekly Wait," "Oh Zella," "Lorraine," and "Day In and Day Out," were recorded for Prince Buster in 1962. "I was about 18 or 19," says Harrison. "You weren't thinking about money. It was an accomplishment to hear your name on the radio and see your name, that you're going to perform. So I guess we were young, money was of no value to us, so to speak. If you get it, you get it, if you don't, you don't."

Yvonne then moved to a number of different duo partners, as was common during the studio days. "There were a couple of other artists that I worked with, a guy named Lloyd Clark, we sang the song 'Love You,' and I did a couple of songs with other guys, because in those days somebody would come to you and say, 'Can you do a tune with me?' and you did it and you hear nothing more about it," she says. In 1962, Yvonne Harrison also recorded with Lascelles Perkins on a song called "Tango Lips (Lips Red as Wine)" for Coxsone Dodd; with Theophilus Beckford on a song called "Burnette" for Prince Buster; with Theophilus Beckford on a song called "Run Away (Gone Away and Leave Me)" for King Edwards; and with Basil Gabbidon (founding member of Steel Pulse) on a song called "Boy Meets Girl (Baby Bay)" for Vincent Chin. "You always feel safer with a partner because you feel protected. In those times you feel protected having a partner because he does the negotiating," she says.

It wasn't until 1964 that Yvonne recorded with Roy Panton. "Don't ask me how Roy and I got together. I don't remember. I think it was Derrick who told him about me. Roy and I did a lot of stage show and were all-island tours with Byron Lee, we were the local artists when the foreign artists came to Jamaica—to name a few, Jackie Wilson, Solomon Burke, the Drifters, and quite a few others," says Yvonne. Most of the songs they recorded in 1964 and 1965 were for Lindon O. Pottinger, Sonia Pottinger's husband before they parted ways and she took over the company, as well as Prince Buster. She says, "After Roy and I separated musically, I did a song with Clancy Eccles, 'Roll River Jordan.' I did backup with Prince Buster on some songs, then I went into Pantomime, which is a yearly play that opens up at Christmas time and goes until maybe February or March. The show was always at the Ward Theatre, and I was in that play. After that I did some solo songs," says Harrison, "'The Chase,' 'Near to You,' and 'Take My Hand,' for Ken Lack." Ken Lack, whose real name was Blondel Calneck, was one of The Skatalites' managers over the years, along with P.J. Patterson, who helped manage their pay with the Jamaican Federation of Musicians; Shay Vishawadia for a short time in the mid–1990s; and of course Ken Stewart, long-time and essential manager. She recorded for Ken Lack in 1967 and 1968, and she also recorded for Pottinger again in 1966 with the song "We Had a Date." When she performed at nightclubs, she sometimes went by the name Toni Marie.

It was after her solo work in Jamaica that Yvonne left the island to try her hand at success in the U.S.:

> I left. I migrated to the United States and I have five children and I got married, which is how I end up going to New York because my husband went and we came after. My four children were born in Jamaica, one in New York. Unfortunately, one passed away in 2006, my daughter, but they all live in the States. I was working for a time in nightclubs, and I teamed up with Roland Alphonso and we did several shows together—one in particular was at the Manhattan Center with Mighty Sparrow. I work with another band—the band leader ... the owner of the band, was Owen Barclay—and you had artists

like Keith Rowe from Keith and Tex, and we had a couple of artists from Jamaica that were working with the band. I was the female singer of the band. This was in the late 70s. I was living in Brooklyn, and I worked in Manhattan for Blue Cross and Blue Shield. I was a dental correspondent and then I got promoted to medical rep. My co-workers didn't know about my musical career. My department was moving upstate, and I have a sister who lives in Canada and I came to visit her and fell in love with Canada, because after living in New York, it's a fast pace, and I decided to come up here and set up because I'm a licensed cosmetologist.

Yvonne's life is parallel to Patsy Todd's in many ways. They both had successful singing careers in Jamaica and then moved to the United States to find work in a completely unrelated field where co-workers were unaware of their previous lives. And both returned to performing in later years. For Yvonne, that involved more than just music, though—it meant finding her singing partner Roy Panton. The two fell in love. As Yvonne tells it,

> I lived in Kitchener for a while. I came over in '91, lived in Kitchener, all this time not knowing that Roy Panton, my partner all those years, was living in Canada. I thought he was in England and he thought I was still in New York. It wasn't until I decided to move down to Jamaica in '97 and I was there for a while, when Michael Barnett who puts on a show, *Heineken Startime*, he wanted me to do a show with Derrick Morgan on the show. Michael Barnett is also a good friend of my nephew. So in talking to him he asked me, "Where is Roy?" So I said he is in England, and just then it was Merritone (producer Winston Blake) who was in Canada, in a show, and he happened to see Roy. Merritone was at the show and said he knows where Roy is, he has connections. And so they wanted to put on the 60th birthday party for Byron Lee in Jamaica, and so the plan was to bring Roy down and we do the show. So, not seeing Roy in over 40 years, I decided to come back up to Canada, meet with him to do some rehearsals and see if our voices were still in working condition. Unfortunately, the show didn't come off because of funds, but I think it was a way of Roy and I connecting. I met him in August of 2005 and we were together in October and got married on June 23, 2011.

It was the rekindling of a musical career too, for Yvonne as well as the duo of Roy and Yvonne. But Yvonne points out that the two never had a romantic relationship in the early years. "When we sang before, it was business because I was involved with somebody else and he was married, and I keep out of that thing because back home it was a known fact that when a female and male work together there's something hanky panky going on. But I stayed out of that because I didn't want to get involved in that kind of thing. He used to tell me he was afraid to hold my hand because when he hold my hand I pull it away when we are on stage," says Yvonne.

Roy and Yvonne have returned to performing. They tour the world and have recorded new songs, in addition to bringing their classics to the stage. Yvonne says,

> I was talking to Patsy Todd, and she just came back from performing a show and she hadn't performed for a long time, and I'm saying to her, "Doesn't it feel good to be back out there?" It feels good. I love it and I just pray to the good Lord to give me a long life so I can continue. I was just talking about how our own color, our own people, do not give us the support. We did a show in Mexico, and you and would be surprised to know the young kids, they appreciate us so much that the night before the show we have autograph signing and picture taking and I even sign somebody's stomach! [laughs] I end up dancing with them. Listen, these people pay big money to come see you. Most of them, they don't have it, but they come and they support you. So you can't be too big to interact with them. "Hey, I appreciate you just the same way you appreciate me and thank you for being there." Because had it not been for them, there would be no show, so even now they call us their Mexican friends! It's a very nice feeling. We did an album in Washington for Tony Liquidator and we have a 7 inch, too. I write some new music, about four new songs.

Yvonne Harrison today has a thriving musical career again and a family. "I have one daughter, she is into the business, but she is not a singer. She is a choreographer. She was on 'The Voice.' Her name is Hi-Hat and she did a lot of movies, 'Bring It On,' 'Nutty Professor,' 'How She Moves,' and 'Step Up 3D.'" It appears that music and performing truly are in the family blood.

Kendris Fagan

Louis Armstrong was always hugely popular in Jamaica. The radio stations from New Orleans, Armstrong's hometown, could be picked up by Kingston transistors on a clear night, so there was plenty of popularity on the airwaves. And anytime Armstrong toured or performed in the states, the *Daily Gleaner* covered his every move. He had also performed in Jamaica a number of times to crowds that craved the sounds of jazz. So it is no surprise that there would be those who tried to perform like Armstrong. What may be a surprise was that emulator was a young female, not on trumpet, but rather a vocalist.

Kendris Fagan, sometimes spelled Kentris or Kentrist, went by her stage name Girl Satchmo. She got her start, like so many other entertainers, on the *Vere Johns Opportunity Hour* talent show after working as a fish vendor in Kingston. She also competed in other competitions, such as one called *Artiste Parade*. The newspaper article read, "TONIGHT the series of Friday night shows called 'Artiste Parade' will wind up with the presentation of the grand finalists first at the Regal Theatre at 8 o'clock; then at Johnson's Drive Inn Club at midnight. The finalists as lined up are Owen Grey, Kentris Fagan, Audley Lyon, vocalists; cycle acrobat George Nelson; dancers Pluggy and Beryl, and Edgar and Rosie; Cobra man N. Forbes; saxophonist Lester Stirling [sic] and limboists Dorothy Plunkett and Milton Dawes. Music will be supplied as usual by Baron Lewis' Orchestra. Coply Johnson will compare the shows."[6] Girl Satchmo had performed previously at Johnson's Drive Inn and Club with popular artists of the day, such as Laurel Aitken and Owen Grey.

Girl Satchmo performed with the circuit of performers who were popular during this era, no matter if they were vocalists or musicians, or if they were dancers or comedians. This kind of show was common on stages throughout Kingston during the late 1950s and 1960s. They were stage shows meant to appeal to a wide audience and frequently took place on the outdoor stages at movie theaters during the day, or in the evening when movies weren't screened so the venue could continue the flow of revenue. Another example of Girl Satchmo's participation in one of these shows took place in 1960 at the Palace Theatre when she performed on the same bill with jazz vocalist Totlyn Jackson and Margarita, rhumba dancer and girlfriend to Don Drummond, before she died at his hands. Laurel Aitken and The Jiving Juniors also performed in this show.

Girl Satchmo sang with the froggy deep growl of Louis Armstrong. *Daily Gleaner* columnist K.R. Abrahams recalled various meetings with celebrities; one of those remembered was Louis Armstrong (whose nickname was "Satchmo") during one of his visits to Kingston. Abrahams states, "It was a part of his welcome that he should hear a local female artist with the stage name Girl Satchmo do an imitation of his style of singing. On his arriving at the then famed Myrtle Bank Hotel in Kingston sure enough I was among the crowd there to see him. Satchmo was laughing and in fine form, the quintessence of bonhomie. I got near enough to him to ask what he thought of Girl Satchmo's imitation of his singing. Satchmo with an expansive grin on his face replied, 'That gal sure sing more like me than me.'"[7]

Girl Satchmo began recording as her alter ego in 1961. Her first song, "Darling," was a huge hit and was recorded on the Starline label for Ken Khouri. The B side was a tune called "Satchmo's Mash Potato," credited to Girl Satchmo and Swinging Mashers. It was released the same year in the UK on the Blue Beat label for Emil Shalit. In 1962 she released the song "My New Honey," a duet with Karl Rowe, and "Twist Around Town," credited to Girl Satchmo and the Blue Beats in the UK and to just Girl Satchmo in Jamaica. From 1963 to 1966, her releases were only on the Blue Beat label in the UK; they included "Brother Joe," "Don't Be Sad," "Blue Beat Chariot," "Rhythm of the New Beat," and "Nature of Love." She is credited as Girl Satchmo, Girl Satchmo and the Blue Beats, and Girl Satchmo and Les Dawson Combo.

In the late 1960s, Girl Satchmo then turned to a different label for her recordings, and she partnered with Tommy McCook and the Supersonics for producer Duke Reid on Treasure Isle in Jamaica, and Fab and Trojan in the UK. The songs, "I'm Coming Home" and "Take You for a Ride," still featured her gravely growl that punctuated her natural singing style. But Girl Satchmo was more than a novelty act—she had real talent and real business acumen. In 1971 she founded her own record label, Kangaroo, and released her own single, "Crazy but Good," as Girl Satchmo and Reggae Kings. She produced the song as well. The same year she put out the song "I Found Out Pt. 1" with B side "I Found Out Pt. 2" as Girl Satchmo; she also produced.

Girl Satchmo toured Germany and had immigrated to England by the end of the 1960s. She had been traveling there since the mid–1960s, when Vere Johns paid her way to England since she was very close with Johns and his wife. She once wrote them a letter saying, "Thanks to you and Mrs. Johns for all I am today. You brought me up and made me an artiste." Girl Satchmo traveled back and forth between England and Jamaica to perform. She performed in London at the St. Pancras Town Hall and numerous nightclubs, and she returned to Jamaica in the early 1970s, as noted in a newspaper article with the headline "Girl Satchmo for Independence jump up." The article stated, "Girl Satchmo, popular Jamaican singer, returned from England after residing there for a number of years to take part in the big Independence Jump Up stage show at the Regal Theatre tomorrow morning, starting at 10.30. Girl Satchmo sings in the style of the late and great Louis (Satchmo) Armstrong. Other Jamaican artistes taking part will be the Festival '71 winners."[8] She apparently returned to Jamaica from time to time to scout new entertainment for her label, according to an article from 1974 titled "Jamaican Singers in London Doing Well Says Girl Satchmo." It states,

> Jamaica's female singer/producer and talent scout Girl Satchmo is currently in the island negotiating with top artistes for a series of performances in London during the Independence holiday. Girl Satchmo, who produces on the Kangaroo label works in association with Count Shelly, a Jamaican who operates Shelly's Recording Company in London. Together both have been engaged in a series of promotions at places such as Angel Edmonton and the Regal Ballroom with the two most popular shows being the Easter and Labour Day concerts. Girl Satchmo herself is also holding her own, concentrating on gospel recordings. She has formed a group called the Gospelaires and so far two tunes have been released. They're "Just a closer walk with thee" and "In Loving Kindness." Their LP will be released shortly.[9]

Girl Satchmo had converted to singing gospel music after she heard the music performed at a church in Jamaica. She changed genres, leaving ska and reggae behind, and she also left something else behind—her stage name. An article from 1975 states,

> Four members of the Gospel Singing Group known as The Gospelaires including Hugh Spence, guitarist and vocalist, and three females—Pauline Stephenson, Iverlin Narcisse and Norma Mason,

all singers left the Island on Monday August 11, for England on vacation. During their stay they will be guests of Kentris Grant Ex-Girl Satchmo—well known Radio and T.V. Artist who has given up "Pop" for Gospel Singing. The Gospelaires actually comprised eight members including Sister Kentris Grant. This group was formed over two years ago by Rev. Wilfred Narcisse—Overseer of the Church of God Faith Assemblies, with Headquarters at 10 Lincoln Road, Kingston 16, Jamaica. Primarily it was formed for involvement in Gospel Campaigns, Conventions and other Religious Programmes where a larger Choral Group would be less adaptable. It was during one of their live sessions that Ex-Girl Satchmo heard them and not only was impressed but gave her heart to the Lord. She finally joined the Group and there and then the Group entered the recording business. One LP "Just a Closer Walk" and a 45 "He will Set You Free" have been released and others are in the making.[10]

Francisca Francis

Francisca Francis, whose real name was Isolyn, was born in Kingston on May 11, 1918. She attended the Convent of Mercy School and St. John's College and immediately entered the entertainment field upon graduation. She was a vocalist during the 1940s and 1950s, performing the blues. In 1947, Francisca married Kingsley Sterling, but she continued to perform for such greats as band leader Sonny Bradshaw. "We used to work together back in the early days. She was very close to me because we used to live in the same area. She was like family. She sang with Roy White's band which was based on Beeston Street. She was their guest singer and I used to play with that band. Later, when I formed my band she appeared with me as a guest singer specializing in the blues. She was the only one of her kind at the time, boasting that Diana [*sic*] Washington sound which made her popular," said Bradshaw.[11] Francisca sang with a number of other bands including those led by Steve Dick, George Moxey, Redver Cooke, Doc Bramwell, the Don Drummond Four, and Milton McPherson. She also performed in the all-star musical *Hot Chocolate* with Louise Lamb and Miss Lou, and she performed cabaret with Robert Lightbourne. She was billed as "The Dynamic Queen of the Blues." Her friends described her as having a kind and warm spirit.

Francisca frequently sang without a microphone or any amplification for her large hotel audiences. She had a love for the blues, although she would also sing jazz. "I sing the blues. I live it. I see the whole story. I also enjoy singing spirituals and songs such as 'Nobody Knows the Trouble I've Seen,' 'Carry Me Back to Old Virginny,' and 'Old Black Joe.' I never studied. I just sing. I like jazz as well as blues—but blues I like best," she said.[12] Francisca eventually moved to Europe to pursue contracts with clubs and continued to perform for soldiers and children all over the world. She had one son, Oswald Decambre, and died on October 30, 1998.

Beverly Kelso and Cherry Green (Smith)

When we think of the Wailers, we naturally think of Bob Marley, Peter Tosh, Junior Braithwaite, and Bunny Livingston. But take a look at those early photos of the group and you will see a sweet girl who first met Bob Marley when she was just 16 years old. She knew this boy not as Robert or Bobby or Nesta, but as the name he was called in Trench Town—Lester. And from 1964 to 1966, Kelso was a member of the Wailing Wailers—an original member, a founding member.

Beverly Kelso was born on April 14, 1948. Her father, Herbert Kelso, was a plumber in Kingston and her mother, Ruby Kelso née Gayle, ran the household. She was one of seven children—three girls and four boys. She attended Denham Town primary school. She first lived in Denham Town and then moved to Trench Town on Fifth Street. Beverly was a tomboy and played sports with all of the boys in the neighborhood. She grew up singing, too, and would even visit the Ellis household. Kelso recalls, "It was nice living on Fifth Street. You have Alton Ellis—all the members in Alton Ellis' family could sing. Sister Hortense, his brother Irvin and another brother, it's like they all used to sing. So, what we used to do, like everybody would sometime go by Alton's house when they have rehearsal. And sometime we'd all just sit there on the side of the road and somebody would start to sing something. But I was a quiet one. I never bother. I just shut up and listen. But I loved singing. But I was so shy."[13]

Beverly continued that her knowledge of music came not only from the neighborhood but also from the radio and the sound systems. Kelso says, "We would all go to these dance halls like Friday night, Saturday night and you'd hear King Stitt, all the dance hall sound that is there. I would stay on the street because we as kids they wouldn't let us in. Friday night we would be outside with everybody until if you wanna go to sleep, you go to sleep. But we would stay out all night. And you don't get tired."[14]

Beverly sang for her school choir when she was just 10 years old, and with this choir she sang a solo for the Queen of England when she visited Scotts Kirk, a historic Presbyterian church in Kingston. At the urging of two of her childhood friends, Beverly went to Chocomo Lawn to perform, and she sang the popular Patti LaBelle song "Down the Aisle." It was after this performance that Beverly's life changed, since one of the people listening in the crowd that day was none other than Bob Marley. "I'll never forget how I started with Bob Marley and the other Wailers! I was about 16 at the time and performin' in one of what we used to call 'fun clubs.' This one club was a place on Wellington Road that teenage people could go to in the early evenin' to dance and show their talent. It was about 3 p.m. and I was singin' down the aisle of the club when Bob walked in and saw me. After my song he came right over and asked if I wanted to sing with his group. I started laughin' and he said, 'Nuh, I'm serious!' So I told him, 'Anytime you're ready.' This was in 1963. The next Wednesday he come over to my house on Columbus Road and told me to be at the studio Thursday, the next day, to record!" Kelso said.[15]

Beverly had not known Bob Marley from the neighborhood in Trench Town even though they grew up just streets apart from each other. "My first impression of him was ordinary. Ordinary. I didn't think of him as nobody special, you know?" she said. "But he was very polite. Never sad. Even that evening he was just smiling. He was just looking at me, like, oh, pretty girl. That's what I have in my mind. So I went up and when I went there Peter, Bunny, and Junior was sitting under a tree on K's workbench. Bob wasn't there. So I asked for Bob and they said Bob went to get the guitar or something. And Bob came and introduced me to Peter, Bunny, and Junior. But I didn't call him Bob and nobody in Trench Town called him Bob. He introduced himself to me as Lester. And then they started to play. So we rehearsed 'Simmer Down' the same evening."[16] The song was written and performed by guitarist Ernest Ranglin as well as the members of The Skatalites.

The recording took place at 13 Brentford Road, Studio One, the famous studio of Coxsone Dodd. "When I got there we had 10 minutes' rehearsal, and Bob just had me doin' this chorus of 'Simmer down, simmer down,' over and over behind him. It was done so fast, but the next thing I know our recordin' is a success, and we must do stage shows everywhere at theaters like the Palace, and travelin' between Kingston and Montego Bay. My sister made this gold dress for me, to match these gold outfits that Mr. Dodd had given the Wailers the money for. And Mr. Dodd had a picture taken of us for publicity. I couldn't believe it was all happenin'!" said Kelso.[17]

Although we know now that Studio One was a place of business and making money, it is important to consider that Kelso and the Wailing Wailers were all teenagers in these days. It is hard to take Bob Marley and the Wailers out of the context we know them in today, with their serious messages of revolution and spirituality. But back then they were silly kids. They were having fun. They were friends having a good time. Of the walk to Studio One from Trench Town each day, Kelso said,

> They would walk and sing, they would walk and carry on with a lot of clowning. Bob would be pushing Bunny, Bunny would be pushing Bob, Peter, and they laugh and they clown and they tease each other. They would laugh at people. The little things that they talk, you just sit down and just crack up. At that time they didn't used to smoke, nobody never smoked, you know? And me and Junior was two little short one, so we would stay in the back, hold each other's hand and walking and start talking our little talk and Bunny and Peter would be there and Bob carrying on with them antics and going on. I'm telling you, you'd be around them you don't wanna move. I used to look up on them and they look up on me. With respect. They treat me like a sister and they treat me good.[18]

Studio One was a bustling place of music and musicians. The amount of recording was limited only by studio time, and everyone had a place. "Studio One was like our house. We lived at Studio One," said Kelso.

> The Skatalites was there, everybody. It was like every day or every other day we would be in the studio. If we're not recording for ourselves, we were backin up other people because we have other people coming and singing, like for instance, Tony Gregory or anybody else in the studio singing and want backup we would just come in and harmonize. Everybody would just backup, either you back sing, clap, whatever you wanna do over there to backup everybody. So we was in the studio most of the time. We were like a family. And there were times when we didn't go home. We would be in the studio like two, three days. When Junior was leaving to come to America they were doing an album and for like two, three days we would be in the studio. We didn't have a place to sleep. We didn't have a place to sleep. We didn't even have no time to sleep. It was just fun in the studio. We would eat and would sit down and get a little nap, you know. Sometimes I would run home and come right back. We have the privilege to go into that studio that most people they couldn't come in. Jackie Opel was there. He was my guy. I used to sit with Jackie Opel most of the time in a little room right there. And if I'm not with Jackie Opel I would be right at the control board with Sidney Bucknor. I did like Sidney. I would talk to Sidney more than anybody else, and Jackie Opel. Jackie Opel was very nice, quiet. He always have his girlfriend with him. He talked different from Jamaicans and Bob would tease him.[19]

When Beverly would travel to Studio One from Trench Town, she says, she and the Wailing Wailers would take a short cut through the Calvary Cemetery and pass by Rita Anderson's home. Rita had a baby, and so Kelso began stopping to chat with her and visit with the baby, although the rest of the Wailing Wailers didn't stop and would become angry with Beverly for the delay. When Anderson told Kelso about a song she had written called "Opportunity," Kelso encouraged her to bring it to the studio, and Coxsone Dodd welcomed her. Anderson brought her two fellow vocalists, Constantine Walker and Marlene Gifford, and the Soulettes recorded their first song the very next day. Not only did Beverly help to launch their career; her connection also brought Rita Anderson and Bob Marley together. They were married on February 10, 1966.

In addition to "Simmer Down," Beverly sang the following songs with the Wailing Wailers: "It Hurts to Be Alone," "Lonesome Feeling," "Amen," "Climb the Ladder," "Destiny," "Do It Right," "Donna," "Don't Ever Leave Me," "Do You Remember," "Go Jimmy Go," "Habits," "I Am Going Home," "I Don't Need Your Love," "I Made a Mistake," "Let the Lord Be Seen in You," "Nobody Knows," "Straight and Narrow Way," "There She Goes," "Tell Them Lord," "True Confessions," "White Christmas," "Where Will I Find," and "Your Love." But her time with the group lasted only until 1966, and she decided to leave. She said, "I stopped singin' because of Bob's attitude about the music. We would be practicing a song like 'Lonesome Feelings' or 'It Hurts to Be Alone'—so many songs I can't remember them all—and if you make a mistake he would jump down on you and be very tough, because that's the way he was taught. But I was too quiet and shy, and I'd start crying and say, 'Oh, I'm gonna leave.' Sometimes I would cry, and he would apologize and say, 'Oh, Beverly, you know how I am.' But the attitude was hard to take, and I left by 1966."[20]

Bunny Livingston has claimed that Kelso just couldn't "keep up" and that the musicians—like The Skatalites, who performed the music for the Wailing Wailers—were seminal musicians who demanded perfection. But Kelso says there was also another reason, which she told to author Timothy White. "I didn't like them smoking when we'd go into the studio! It's airtight there in the studio and with all that smoke you'd take a deep breath and choke and start coughing. And they'd get mad and say, 'Oh, it just because you don't smoke! This is the thing to do!' So I couldn't support it—and I couldn't quarrel about it," Kelso said.[21]

Kelso adds that she didn't receive any money for her work at Studio One. She told author Roger Steffens, "I know I didn't get any. I know Peter didn't get any because Peter would get upset and say Bunny and Bob is brothers, so, they're keeping it in the family. I didn't see really nobody getting any money." She told Steffens that a few years later when she went to visit Bob Marley at 56 Hope Road during the time he was with Cindy Breakspeare, Bob didn't even recognize her despite their formative years together as teenagers in Trench Town and in the studio. "He was just looking at me and gazing. He was just like in another world, looking at me and gazing and, 'What your name? Who are you?' Yeah. And I said, 'What?' My girlfriend was just laughing and I start to cry. And I said, 'What happened to you Bob?' You know, I start to cry. I was living at Forest Hill and I feel down and I actually walked home to Forest Hill that day."[22]

In 1979, Beverly moved to New York City in the Jamaica neighborhood of Queens, where a number of West Indians immigrated. She lives in the Bronx today. She performed from time to time in Brooklyn with a group of friends who performed in reggae clubs, but she preferred to stay out of the limelight. She was recognized in 2012 at Tribute to the Greats, an award and performance festival in Jamaica organized by King Omar, also known as Kingsley Goodison. Beverly's brother, Rudolph "Garth" Dennis, was a founding member of Black Uhuru and a member of the Wailing Souls. "I am proud that I was part of the group," Kelso said of her days with the Wailing Wailers. "And I could tell anybody that I enjoyed myself when I was with the group. I liked them all like family. I was happy to be with them. I was proud to be with them. Proud of myself being with the Wailers, one of the Wailers."[23]

Junior Braithwaite was only 13 years old at the time "Simmer Down" was recorded. He was with the Wailing Wailers for eight months before he left in 1964 to join the rest of his family, who had already moved, in America. It was after Braithwaite's departure that Cherry Green became more a part of the Wailing Wailers, although she had previously helped to sing harmonies a number of times for the band.

Cherry Green (sometimes called Cherry Smith) was born Ermine Ortense Bramwell on August 22, 1943, and, like the other members of the Wailing Wailers, she grew up in Trench Town. Because she had a light-colored, reddish complexion, she acquired the name Cherry. The last name Green was the surname of her half-brother, Carlton Green. Before she moved to Trench Town she lived in Jones Town; her father was a dentist. After he died they had to take a room in a house in Trench Town. Cherry's mother, Alma, worked for a family member who owned a mattress store. She was a skilled seamstress and made the children's clothing. Like Beverly, Cherry says she was a tomboy and played sports with the boys in the neighborhood. But she loved music and was an avid listener of Duke Reid's *Treasure Isle Time* radio show, which was broadcast on Saturday evenings on the yard radio.

Cherry Green says her mother liked to sing, and so she too grew up singing in her neighborhood, harmonizing. She sang for her church, school, and performed in school theater productions. With neighbors like Hortense and Alton Ellis, Lascelles Perkins, Jimmy Tucker, Roy Wilson, and Joe Higgs, it's no wonder that Cherry Green began singing with the musicians of the day. Cherry Green says of her days in Trench Town, "We used to rehearse back in the back yard. We didn't even have electric light, you know, only kerosene oil, torch, or the fire that my brother make. But we had a good old time. And now it's history," she said.[24]

Why didn't she appear on numerous recordings as Beverly Kelso did? Cherry Green had a daughter for whom to care. She not only had to care for her child; she also had to earn a living to raise her child, as she was the only parent in the child's life. Money from recording wasn't enough to put food on the table. She had to get a regular day job. She began working for Caribbean Preserving, handling grapefruit. Her position in the Wailing Wailers was filled by Beverly Kelso. Still, Cherry Green was able to get a few recordings in before she moved to Miami in 1969 and became a nurse. When Braithwaite left there was a space that needed to be filled, and because the grapefruit job was seasonal, she says, she stepped in for the following recordings: "Amen," "I Am Going Home," "Let the Lord Be Seen in You," "Lonesome Feelings," "Maga Dog," and "There She Goes." "You feel good to hear your voice on the radio. I can remember my daughter, she probably was three, and every time she hear 'Lonesome Feeling' she say, 'Hear my mother. Hear my mother,'" she said.[25] She left the band in 1966.

Cherry Green spent her life as a nurse. She was married twice and had only the one daughter, Audrey Hinton, and a granddaughter, Stephanie. Cherry Green, whose name by this time was Ermine Ortense Dempsey-Barker, died of a heart attack on September 24, 2008, in West Palm Beach, Florida. In her obituary in the *Guardian*, music historian David Katz wrote, "Although her tenure was brief, she made an important contribution to the popularity of the ska form, and to the development of Marley's career."[26]

CHAPTER SIX

Blue Beat

When Jamaican ska came to the United Kingdom, it was classified as "Blue Beat." This is because the British businessman who "licensed" the music—and this is in quotation marks because those monetary deals were suspect and certainly not advantageous, or many times even known, to the artists themselves—coined the term himself. Sigmund "Siggy" Jackson identified the American rhythm and blues influence in ska, calling it "bluesy,"[1] so the label that released Jamaican ska in the UK, one owned by Emil E. Shalit, was called Blue Beat. Hence, ska and blue beat are, for all intents and purposes, synonymous, but the latter signifies the genre's popularity in the UK and, in the case of some artists, internationally. Though she did not record for and was not released on the Blue Beat label, one female artist above all others has been associated with the blue beat movement because of her UK connection—Millie Small, the "Blue Beat Girl."

*Millie Small, OD**

If someone is unfamiliar with ska, chances are when they hear a few bars of "My Boy Lollipop," sung in one's best falsetto, they will respond, "Oh yeah, I know that song! That's ska?" Millie Small's song is so iconic that even today, some five decades after it was recorded, it still brings recognition to an entire genre of music, just as it was originally intended to do.

Millie Small was born Millicent Dolly May Small on October 6, 1947, in upper Clarendon, Jamaica. Her mother was named Elvie Smith, her father was named Christopher Small. "We were a very humble family really," she says:

> We were poor but not in poverty. I am the youngest of seven children. We were just a little family that just live. I was born in a little place called upper Clarendon, Jamaica. I was born there and then I left from upper Clarendon to the lower part of Clarendon. The lower part of Clarendon is where I went to school. It was called Milk River. My mother looked after me, but she used to work in the cane field in the farm, yes dear, and my father used to do the same thing as well. The cane fields, cane plantation, they dig a little hole in the ground and things, that's my background. But it was humble, it was beautiful, it was loving because my mama is loving, and I love my mama and I love my family. I was not from a big rich family, just a humble, sweet, poor family. Not poverty, but poor.[2]

*Order of Distinction, a Jamaican national award given for "outstanding and important services to Jamaica" (https://jis.gov.jm/information/awards/order-of-distinction/).

Small's family worked hard to provide for the children—four boys and three girls. Millie was the youngest. Her sisters were Estrie and Lou (Lou was a half-sister with a different father), and her brothers were Leeburt, Earl, Franklin, and John Brown (a half-brother with a different father). With so many children to feed, clothe, and care for, there was no time for music. There were no instruments in the home or record players or radios, but still, Small loved performing, loved singing, and told her family when she was only nine years old that she was going to be a film star or a singer.

"While I was going to school at Milk River School in Clarendon, I used to read the newspapers and there used to be songs in the newspapers that I used to copy. After doing that, I left school and I went to do a talent show," Small says. Many vocalists and musicians received the opportunity for a career in that way. Bob Marley, Jimmy Cliff, Alton Ellis, Hortense Ellis, John Holt, The Blues Busters, Derrick Harriott, Derrick Morgan, Lascelles Perkins, Higgs and Wilson, Bunny and Scully, Laurel Aitken, Wilfred "Jackie" Edwards, Girl Satchmo, Lloyd "Sparrow" Clarke, Jimmy Tucker, Margarita (Anita Mahfood), Charley Organaire, Roy Richards, and Rico Rodriguez all received their start on the *Vere Johns Opportunity Hour*. Millie Small also got her start on a talent show. "I did a talent show and I won second prize. I was 10 or 11 years old then," she says. The particular stage where Millie performed was in Montego Bay at the Palladium Theatre.

Shortly after that, Millie relocated to Kingston "to live with some friends," she says. During this time she visited Studio One, where Coxsone immediately recognized her talent and gave her the opportunity to record with vocalist Owen Grey. Roy Panton, who would later become her duet partner, recalls those early days: "Her first official song was with Owen Grey. That was 'Sugar Plum.' She recorded 'Sugar Plum' with Owen before she recorded with me, and during that session, when she record 'Sugar Plum' with Owen, I was in the studio at the time. As a matter of fact, Owen Grey did two songs with her, 'Sugar Plum' and 'Do You Know.' After Owen Grey recorded with her, obviously Owen Grey was always a solo singer, he wasn't going to team with anyone. Seeing that I had teamed previously with Monty Morris, Coxsone suggested we could team together. We became Roy and Millie."[3]

Millie says that Roy became a friend of hers, and it was the start of her career. "Roy was a friend of mine and we made a song called 'We'll Meet.'" This song was critical to the start of Millie's career and it led to much bigger things, things that even Millie couldn't have imagined at the time. Panton recalls, "We did 'We'll Meet,' which was a huge hit, number one on RJR/JBC for quite a few weeks. That sound basically put us on the map.... That was my first time working with Byron Lee, and we were on that show, the Ray Charles Show at the National Stadium. There were a lot of us—Roy and Millie, Jimmy Cliff, a whole set of artists, but that song was all over the place and got her working on stage. I think I was about 20 years old and she was about 14 or 15, something like that. We became a permanent partner, Roy and Millie, like Shirley and Lee in Jamaica at the time—she with the high-pitched voice, like Shirley. We never heard a voice like that before. Not even Shirley's voice was that high."

The duo of Owen and Millie recorded the songs "Sugar Plum," "Do You Know" with the B side of "Sit and Cry" in 1962, and "I Don't Want You (You Don't Want Me)" and "There'll Come a Day" in 1963, all for Coxsone. The duo of Roy and Millie recorded "Anybody Seen My Girl," "Starlight," "We'll Meet," "Dearest Love," and "Honeysuckle Rose" in 1962; "I'll Go," "Over and Over," "Cherry I Love You," "Marie," "Never Say Goodbye," "Oh Merna," "Oh Shirley," "This World," "You'll Always Be Mine," "You're the One," "I'll

Go," and "Cherita" in 1963; and "Seek and You Will Find" and "You Belong to Me" in 1964. She also recorded duets with Jackie Edwards as "Wilfred and Millicent," including the songs "The Vow," "I'll Never Believe in You," and "Do You Want Me Again." In 1966, after her hit with "My Boy Lollipop" she recorded the duo "Hey Boy, Hey Girl" with Jimmy Cliff. She recorded for Coxsone Dodd, Prince Buster, Lindon O. Pottinger, Vincent Chin, Roy Robinson, and Leslie Kong.

Panton continued, "And then she got the opportunity to go to England with Chris Blackwell. We talked about it and I told her, it's an opportunity, why not?" Chris Blackwell, before he was inducted into the Rock and Roll Hall of Fame in 2001, before he placed Jimmy Cliff as Ivanhoe Martin in "The Harder They Come," and before he signed Bob Marley, Jethro Tull, Robert Palmer, Cat Stevens, Steve Winwood, U2, Tom Waits, Toots and the Maytals, Third World, Black Uhuru, Burning Spear, and Sly and Robbie, among many others, was a rich kid looking for his way in life. "Chris's family was very very wealthy, but his family was very strict that you generated your own money," says Graeme Goodall, recording engineer for Federal Records and one of the three initial founders of Island Records with Blackwell and Leslie Kong.[4] The three had founded Island Records together in 1959 as a way to sell records not only for the Jamaican market but also for the English market. Previously, Blackwell had tried his hand at the motor scooter and scuba equipment rental business, and he had more successfully owned six Wurlitzer jukeboxes, which gave him entry into the music business, but it wasn't until Millie Small that he was able to really make a break.

Blackwell moved back to London in 1962 and tried to establish his career in music. Before success with Millie Small, Blackwell had released over 200 Jamaican records. "He used to pile them into his Mini Minor and flog them himself from record shop to record shop. Nobody ever played any of his stuff on the BBC or gave him much encouragement," writes Maureen Cleave, a *Daily Gleaner* reporter.[5] But when Blackwell heard Roy and Millie's "We'll Meet" and he recognized the star quality in that female voice, everything changed. Getting her to England to establish her career, however, wasn't an easy task. Goodall says,

> I used to send the stuff over to Chris when Chris Blackwell, Leslie Kong, and myself were partners in Island Records in England. And when Chris went over to England, he heard Millie and he called me and said, "I want her over in England right now. She's going to be big, I know it, I just feel it, she's got an unusual voice, get her to England." And Leslie and I were on the phone together on a conference call, and we said, "Okay Chris," and we hung up and I looked at Leslie, and Leslie looked at me, and we said, "Oh yeah?" She was 16! We had to go through a whole procedure—how do you move a 16-year-old Jamaican who—her father had gotten lost somewhere along the line and she wasn't in communication with her father, so then we had to get her mother and convince her that this was the thing to do. We had to get a passport for her and because she was 16 and we had to get all the approvals for that. We had an attorney at the time who was helping us. There wasn't any legal action involved, he was just guiding us through the steps. And remember, I was working at Federal Records, Chris was producing Beverley's Records, and this was going on, and then you're making sure she got on an airline, and my wife helped quite a bit there because she worked for BOAC [British Overseas Airways Corporation], so it was a combination effort and we got her to the UK. Then Chris took over as such.

Millie remembers her relationship with Blackwell fondly. "He was the one who heard 'We'll Meet,' and when he came to Jamaica, he went to meet me. So we met up with Chris Blackwell, and it was like old friends. He liked our song very much and he said that I should come over to England and start a little career and things, so he brought me to England in June 1963," she says. Blackwell acted as Millie's manager, but before they recorded the song that would propel both of their careers into international recognition, Small had to first be groomed into a young starlet. Small was enrolled in school to learn to speak without a thick Jamaican accent, and Blackwell also sent her to a number of classes to refine her skills. "Chris managed to get her a dance instructor and she was a natural dancer, but he got someone to teach her the moves that were familiar or would attract the interest of the huge population in England and get them interested in it. He got her a hairdresser. He got her a dentist. He got her somewhere to live. Chris had a secretary [Elsa Hoken, who was also leader of the Millie Fan Club], and she'd take her to South Kensington to the stores and put her in all these trendy mod clothes. And of course at 16 she couldn't even drive, so he had to get a car with a driver for her; Nicky Johnson was her driver at first," says Goodall.

"My Boy Lollipop" wasn't the first Millie song that Blackwell recorded and released. Three pop songs were recorded by Blackwell at Olympic Studios in central London—"Don't You Know," "Until You're Mine," and "Oh Davy." The single "Don't You Know" with "Until You're Mine" on the B side was released by a production company Blackwell had with two other partners called BPR (Blackwell, Peers, Robinson), which also produced Blackwell's single by the Caravelles, "You Don't Have to Be a Baby to Cry." But Millie's first venture didn't produce on the charts, and "Oh Davy" was never released. Still, Blackwell saw true star quality in his vocalist and so in February 1963, Blackwell recorded and released "My Boy Lollipop" on Fontana in the UK and in the U.S. on Smash Records. When Blackwell recorded "My Boy Lollipop," he had already heard the song years before when 16-year-old Barbie Gaye recorded it (spelled "My Boy Lollypop") in 1956 for the Darl label in the U.S. with the B side "Say You Understand." The song was originally written as "My Girl Lollypop" by Robert Spencer. However, there are two others listed as writers of the song—Morris Levy, real name Moishe Levy, who was the owner of Birdland (the jazz club named after Charlie Parker), founder of Roulette Records, and owner of over 80 record stores in addition to other music industry entities before his conviction for extortion and involvement in organized crime; and Johnny Roberts, an alleged gangster. According writer Rob Finnis, "Robert Spencer of the Cadillacs, a popular doo wop group of the day, actually wrote the song while Johnny Roberts, a New York wiseguy who managed pop and R&B acts on behalf of the mob, helped himself to a piece of the pie by naming himself co-writer. By the time Millie cut the song, the name of Morris Levy, the infamous head of Roulette Records, had replaced that of Roberts as the co-writer, which suggests the song was a negotiable asset in certain circles. (By the new millennium, the song registration compromised by listing all three as writers.)"[6] Finnis notes that the song by Barbie Gaye was played in heavy rotation on WINS-FM by Alan Freed, the famous New York DJ, and Gaye performed the song for Freed's Christmas show in December 1956 when she opened for Little Richard. Alan Freed is the DJ who coined the term "rock 'n' roll"; his career was shattered by his participation in the payola scandal.

To record his version, Chris Blackwell solicited the help of guitarist Ernest Ranglin. Ranglin says that he was the only Jamaican who performed on the record, and he had to teach the rest of the musicians how to play the ska version. Blackwell wanted an authentic ska sound that could be accepted by mainstream pop audiences, so the blend of British and Jamaican artists was the perfect recipe. The harmonica was performed not by a young Rod Stewart, as rumor has it, but by Pete Hogman of The Pete Hogman Blues Band and Hoggie and the Sharpetones. Pete Peterson performed on trumpet, and the rest of the musicians were members of a band called The Five Dimensions, a band from Birmingham. It was because Rod Stewart once performed for The Five Dimensions that the rumor of his involvement on "My Boy Lollipop" persists, but it simply isn't accurate.[7] Millie says the song, when it was recorded, wasn't a memorable experience, although she did thoroughly enjoy the performances afterwards. "When Chris Blackwell gave me the tune to learn at first," says Millie, "I did not like it, but I grow to like it the more I sang it over and over again. I did not feel any way in particular about it when I actually recorded it, I just went with the flow and did the best I could."

The reverb on the song came from "a sort of cupboard in the back of the studio that we used as a live chamber," said Blackwell. This creation had been Goodall's doing a few years earlier at Federal Records, and Blackwell replicated it at his London studio.[8] Goodall recalls,

> I remember when I said to Ken Khouri [owner of Federal Records], "We got a problem here. We've got to get some echo in here somehow." He said, "What does that require?" I said, "Well I could design an echo chamber. I could modify the equipment," which I did. I rebuilt a lot of it to make it a lot more professional and I said I'd design an echo chamber and tag it on the back there. He said, "That sounds good." All the walls were a different angle from one another. The Jamaicans that we got to build it refused totally to build it. And I remember one of them talking to Ken and they didn't figure that I could understand. They said, "It's not right, Mr. Khouri, it's not right. We cyaan build it because all the walls dem different," [laughs]. I figured it all out, these guys were used to putting up walls vertical, floors and ceilings horizontal and everything at 90-degree angles from one another. And Ken said, "I don't know what he's doing but trust me, you've got to do it his way." So we built it that way, and I think that was one of the primary things, because when we started adding reverb it brought it into a completely different era. And that was the start of Federal Records.

Blackwell used this reverb effect to give a fuller sound to Millie's voice since it was a mono record.

When "My Boy Lollipop" was recorded, Chris Blackwell specifically selected this tune since he had the vision to see it could have great crossover appeal—with Jamaican and West Indian audiences in the islands and in the UK, as well as mainstream pop audiences in the UK and America. Goodall says, "Millie was a lynchpin. She was a link. See, Chris understood the American market in those days. Whether you liked it or not, the English market only succeeded because of the American market." But Blackwell, almost perplexingly, released the song that he knew would be a smash hit on a different label—not Island, but Fontana, a subsidiary of Philips Records. In an interview with *Interview Magazine*, Blackwell explains why: "I licensed it to Philips because of something I'd learned from understanding the American independent record business, which was that if an independent label had a hit, then it was pretty much guaranteed that they'd be out of business, because most of the time, these small labels couldn't collect that money from the stores fast enough to pay the pressing plant to make more records in order to meet the demand. When I heard 'My Boy Lollipop,' I knew it was a hit. I also knew it was way beyond what Island could handle, plus it was much more slick than something that we would put out, so I licensed it to Philips."

The song was a huge hit. Millie Small's voice on this song, and on all her others, is the hook. It has been described as "chirping," "chuckling," "bubbling," and "effervescent."[9] It was small but big. It was lively and exciting. It brought ska into the mainstream. Released in March 1964, the song went down in record books as the third biggest hit of the year in the UK, just behind The Beatles and The Rolling Stones. *The Daily Express* heralded her success, saying, "There hasn't been a voice like it since Shirley Temple,"[10] which, to be clear, was quite a compliment. It reached number two on UK charts. She appeared on television shows in the UK and performed with The Beatles, whom she described as "very nice boys!" The song also charted in the United States, Nigeria, Australia, and New Zealand. It reached number two in Australia and number one in Scandinavia. It charted in no less than 12 countries. It was released in the United States on Smash Records, a subsidiary of Mercury Records, which distributed Fontana recordings. Such artists as James Brown, Jerry Lee Lewis, and Frankie Valli were signed to the Smash label, so it is no wonder that Millie found success with this market. Within just five weeks of its release, "My Boy Lollipop" sold over a half-million copies and went to number two on the U.S. Billboard Hot 100 chart. To date it has sold over seven million copies worldwide.

Immediately, Chris Blackwell launched a worldwide tour for Millie Small, which was essential to the success of her career and continuing the success of the song. Critical to the tour was getting Small airplay on radio and television. "When she got the hit record," recalls Goodall, "Chris was managing performances—TV performances, live performances, the release of the product overseas, so Chris was the, how do I put this, the controlling big brother of all of that—everything, everything, everything—telling her what to say. I did a couple of open-ended interviews with her because I was broadcasting-based and just asked her questions and she gave responses so—this is what America wanted was her responses—so they could insert their own disc jockeys into it. It was the norm in those days, so Chris and I would prepare these lists of questions, I'd ask her the questions, then we'd record it on tape and edit out the questions. And this was the sort of thing that Chris did."

Millie Small hit the road as soon as her song began to chart. "My first big tour was in Norway. And even now it is one of my favorite countries, and it was very successful there. And I've been to New Zealand, another of my favorite countries, and Singapore," says Small. In September 1964, Millie came to the United States on tour for a series of shows. She flew into New York City and was met by press, including Murray "The K" Kaufman, the Radio Hall of Fame DJ from WINS-FM, the top DJ in New York, who was responsible for bringing fame to the likes of Dionne Warwick and Bobby Darin. "Chris said, 'We're taking her across to the Brooklyn Fox!'" says Goodall. The Brooklyn Fox was an opulent theater built in 1921 that was the site of popular concerts hosted by Murray "The K." "It was my introduction to American pop artist concerts. What a difference there! Millie made her introduction into the Brooklyn Fox, which was produced by Murray 'The K.' And it was phenomenal! It included the New Beats with their song 'Bread and Butter,' and Dusty Springfield, and The Supremes were on that show," Goodall says. Also on that bill were Marvin Gaye headlining, The Miracles, Martha and the Vandellas, The Contours, The Temptations, The Searchers, Jay and the Americans, The Dovells, Little Anthony and the Imperials, and The Shangri-Las, in addition to Millie Small. The stage featured two flags on the backdrop: the American flag and the Union Jack, to represent the American and British artists that performed, with a large K in the middle to signify the popular DJ's affiliation. According to the *Los Angeles Sentinel* (November 5, 1964), the show set box office records: "For each of the six shows that they perform daily, there is a line extending from the box office completely around the block, four abreast. This is the first time that such a show comprised of Motown artists and top European artist has ever appeared at the Brooklyn Fox together."

Millie Small went all over the world to promote her song with Chris Blackwell at her side. She performed in numerous countries on television and radio, as well as live. "When she did do these tours, overseas to Asia and places like that, Chris went with her. She was very easy to manage, and she wasn't a prima donna at all. She was a very pleasant soul and very easy to get along with. Of course, there was a lot of male interest in Millie, and Chris had to be very much on guard for that, if for no other reason [than] the bad press that you could get. But not Millie, she was a pleasant person, and when she went to a party she just bubbled. And there was a lot of the party scene going on with music, and when she'd walk into a party she just glistened. She just sparkled. She never embarrassed anyone, least of all she never embarrassed Chris and the record company as so many of the artists did in those days," Goodall says.

There were performances in many countries, including Singapore and others throughout Asia, and Goodall recalls how that came to be:

> At one time, Chris said to me, "I want you to go out," and I was planning to go to Australia anyway to see my mother, and he said, "Can you drop by Singapore? There's a guy out there that wants to put on a tour of Millie Small throughout Asia." I said, "Yeah, why not?" So I went to Australia and on the way back I stopped off at Singapore, stayed at the Raffles Hotel, and it was a good time. So this man called me and said he wanted to put on these tours, and I said fine. He said, "I'm sending this car for you." So this Rolls Royce came up with a beautiful English lady who said, "Mr. So-in-So said I must take care of your wife." So Fay goes immediately off in this Rolls Royce, and she later told me she was very embarrassed because she took her to all these high-class shops and poor Fay had about five dollars in her pocket. So I went to see this preview of one of his movies, one of these awful Chinese movies where a guy sees his love in the distance and he runs to her and it takes about 20 minutes for them to meet, and it was about 2½ hours and I sat through the whole thing. And I said, "So you own quite a few cinemas?" and he said, "Yeah," and I said, "How many?" and he said 1,200. So I went back to Chris and I said, "I think this guy is on the level!" [laughs]. And that's the sort of thing that went on with Millie, and Chris, I have to say, did a great job of it.

At the end of July 1964, Millie Small came to the U.S. to do performances for stage and television and hosted a press conference at the famed Rainbow Room at Rockefeller Center. *The New York Amsterdam News* reported on her visit in late July, "Millie Small is the only girl who has ever been able to challenge the popularity of the Beatles," under the headline "Millie Small the Lollipop Queen Impresses Here."[11] The reporter, James L. Hicks Jr., seemed enamored with Small, writing, "Millie is the most pleasant girl I have ever met. She has a wonderful personality and she smiles all the time and is not shy at all." He quoted her as saying, "I'm 16 and I have a flat of my own in London and I make more money in a week than I earned in my entire life before coming to London." The reporter also comments that Millie began dating boys when she moved to London and says "she was such a big hit in London she performed before a Duke and a Princess" and "learned to curtsy in high heeled shoes." The article goes on to report that Millie is "five feet eight, weighs 100 pounds and her favorite vocalists are Lesley Gore, Dusty Springfield, Elvis Presley, and Fats Domino"; adding that both Quincy Jones and Lesley Gore were present at Millie's "party," along with the consul general of Jamaica and his two daughters. The reporter ran a photo of Millie Small signing an autograph for him. Small also performed for events surrounding the second anniversary of Jamaican independence, which was celebrated in New York after Governor Nelson Rockefeller proclaimed August 2 through August 8 as Jamaica Independence Week for the state of New York. She also received a gold disc during this visit, an award that commemorated selling one million copies of her record.

It was a whirlwind. Just before her appearance in New York for Independence celebrations, she visited Jamaica for a few days to perform in their independence celebrations. She appeared at the Denbigh Agricultural and Industrial Show for an hour-long meet-and-greet as well as a number of "independence 'Lollipop' shows"[12] at the Palladium Theater in Montego Bay, and two shows at the Carib Theatre with Otis Redding, Inex Foxx, and Patti LaBelle. The concerts were sponsored by Canada Dry. Her return to Jamaica was covered on the front page of the *Daily Gleaner*. She was a star. It was a hero's welcome, or a heroine's welcome. "Chris had me organize her return to Jamaica for the Independence celebration," says Goodall. "There was a motorcade from the airport, which was quite phenomenal, the reception in Jamaica. I think the only person who had more response than her was Haile Selassie." Millie arrived from Montego Bay at Palisadoes Airport wearing a "chic navy blue coat and pleated skirt, white knee-high socks and black pumps with brown hair blowing in the wind as she ran into the arms of her mother," read the newspaper story on her return.[13] Canada Dry presented her with a giant lollipop decorated with carnations and Roy Panton, her one-time singing partner, was there to greet her as well.

"Millie was the star of the show," says Panton of her performances on that return visit. As the motorcade proceeded from the airport down the street, fishermen dropped their nets, bathers jumped out of the ocean to wave to Millie as she drove past. Buses stopped in the street, children yelled and cheered, and crowds lined the streets all the way to the Stony Hill Hotel, where she lodged. Her father and brothers were with her, too, as Millie met with dignitaries and government officials. She visited the offices of the *Daily Gleaner*, and she dined with the director of tourism. Millie even drew a large crowd outside the government offices as she came to visit Prime Minister Alexander Bustamante, who was out of town on business—although that message never made it to Millie, and she showed up. The minister of development and welfare, Edward Seaga, entertained her instead. The attorney general, Victor Grant, presented her with a gold medallion on behalf of the prime minister as a gesture of appreciation. A film crew documented her visit for television broadcast back in England on Global TV, affiliated with Associated Rediffusion, for an estimated 40 million viewers. The producer, Elkan Allan, was originator of the British music show *Ready, Steady, Go!* He flew in a film crew of eight people including producer Rollo Gamble for the one-hour special *Millie in Jamaica*, which aired in the UK on January 6, 1965.

Millie also had a role in promoting Jamaica at the 1964 World's Fair in New York City. When Edward Seaga, then minister of culture, selected the band he formerly managed—Byron Lee and the Dragonaires—and other musicians, singers, and dancers to represent Jamaica at the 1964 World's Fair in New York City, he used the popular downtown music, the ska, to sell his country to tourists. Hiring Ronnie Nasralla to package the music and dance was essential to promotional success. "Let me tell you how it started," says Nasralla:

> One day, Eddie Seaga, who was my close friend, called me and told me he heard a music that was breaking out in Western Kingston called ska, and he asked if I could promote it for him, so I said, "Well, I'd like to learn about it." And we organized and I said, "Well Byron Lee is the best person to promote it." So we get together with Byron Lee down in Western Kingston, and I learned the ska music. Eddie organized a dance at the Chocomo Lawn in Western Kingston—it's like an outdoor nightclub. And Byron played there, and all the ska artists performed with Byron, and it was a sensation. Eddie said to me, "Move around the crowd and see what they are doing on the dance floor and see if you can come up with a brochure about how to dance the ska." So I did that, saw the people dancing around and came up with a brochure about a week after, how to dance the ska, give them

different steps in the ska, and something that they could use to promote ska worldwide. That brochure was used by the government. They put it in all the record albums, and it was sent all over the world. I was asked to go to the states and promote the ska with somebody, and I got Jannette Phillips to dance with me. Jannette was a dancer, a belly dancer, a friend of my sister. We took pictures doing the different steps and the brochure was produced. I went to the states and performed ska for all different television shows and taught different people how to do the ska, went to dance schools and taught them how to teach the ska. At that same time, Byron Lee was in New York and he performed at the Singer Bowl, and Jannette and I danced and a few other people I organized and taught danced on the stage, and Millie Small performed and it was a sensation.[14]

Unfortunately, Jannette Marie Phillips, now Jannette Miles, wife of Raymond Miles, a wealthy souvenir and clothing merchandiser in Jamaica, did not want to speak of her days as a ska dancer and said she doesn't want to "relive that part of her past. It was a long long time ago."[15] Her wedding announcement in the November 2, 1965, *Daily Gleaner* said of Jannette, "The former Miss Phillips has been to the United States and around the Caribbean on several occasions, demonstrating the Ska." Wedding music was provided by Byron Lee and the Dragonaires.

Millie was at the World's Fair to represent her country and spread her popularity and fame to her homeland. The headline in the *Daily Gleaner* that heralded her visit to the U.S. read, "Millie leaves saying 'I love you all.'"[16] The soiree was held at the Singer Bowl, a stadium that was built in Queens specifically for the 1964 World's Fair and went on to host concerts by The Who, The Doors, Led Zeppelin, and Jimi Hendrix as well as sporting events before it closed its doors in 1977. The party was held on August 12, 1964, from 6 p.m. until 10 p.m. The entire day was designated "Millie Small Day" by New York World's Fair officials. The party at the Singer Bowl introduced fairgoers to the ska as "a sensational new dance craze by the Jamaicans who started it," stated the *New York Amsterdam News*.[17] "Starred on the show was Millie Small whose Ska-beat recording of 'My Boy Lollipop' has been a best-selling record for the past 14 weeks. Included on the program were Byron Lee and his 12-piece Jamaica Ska Band; Jimmy Cliff, a popular vocalist; the Blues Busters, and several talented dancers who were flown to the Fair from Kingston, Jamaica especially for the concert." A total of 17 acts appeared at the Singer Bowl from Jamaica that night, and it was attended by dignitaries including Arthur Murray and his wife, and Miss Jamaica (Miss World 1963, Carole Joan Crawford). During the days surrounding the ska party at the Singer Bowl, other performances were held for fairgoers by the likes of Benny Goodman, Louis Armstrong, Duke Ellington, Count Basie, and Dave Brubeck. Ska came full circle, in a way, at the World's Fair—the jazz orchestras and musicians that had once influenced the creation of ska now performed on the same stage as the bands that evolved into the Jamaican form.

When asked about the World's Fair, Small replies, "Yes, I remember that, I remember that," and she adds that she remembers one other significant detail of the event. "Martin Luther King was there that day. And I was introduced to him and he was a very very cool, serious man, and that was it. I was there with my manager Chris Blackwell. He was my manager then. So when it was the Millie Small event at the Fair, that's when I met Mr. King and I also met his son, his first son, I met him as well. So two Kings I met," she says with a little laugh.

While Millie was in the U.S. for the World's Fair, Fontana released her first full LP album, titled *More Millie*. Ernest Ranglin performed on a number of the tunes, which included "What Am I Living For" and a cover of the classic Jiving Juniors song "Sugar Dandy." Millie continued touring after the Independence celebrations and the New York

World's Fair, immediately traveling to Ireland for seven days and then going to Germany for four days, New Jersey for two days, then England for radio and television appearances; she also starred in Pantomime shows. It is no wonder that in the middle of her touring, Millie collapsed and was ordered to have complete rest for a few days. Speaking to reporters from the Battersea General Hospital in London, Millie sent best wishes to Panton and Panton's wife and mother, as well as a message to her mother in May Pen, Clarendon: "Don't fret. I am alive and can still sing Lollipop."

But the significance of this song comes not from the amount of touring or appearances or places on charts; instead it comes from the impact it had on the music that followed. For Chris Blackwell, Millie's success set the foundation of Island Records. Goodall says, "Chris, up until that point, was concentrating on Jamaican records and Jamaican records solely. He tried to put this song by the Caravelles, 'You Don't Have to Be a Baby to Cry,' in the charts, but then when we got Millie Small and it broke the charts, it changed Chris's whole concept of music. Then it became Island Records and then Island Records had the capital and the organization to go into bigger better things. When you think about it deeply, this gave Chris the ability to work Bob Marley, right?"

Chris Blackwell had bet on a sure thing, a star who would pay off in dividends so he could go on to find further talent. Goodall relates,

> Once when we were walking down lower Regent Street, Chris went into a betting shop and he went in there and put some money on his horse and he came back out and we did some mastering work, some disc mastering, and he came out and said, "Just a minute Graeme, I'm going to go in and collect my winnings," and he went in there, went straight to the winning desk and collected his money. "Are you kidding me?" I said. He said, "Yeah, I always win," and that was the attitude he always took. He said, "When I gamble, I always gamble enough that if I lose it hurts me." This is Chris's great life that he went on with. So having a hit record with Fontana—then the money started coming in, and people started taking notice of him. If Chris Blackwell called you, you answered the phone, okay? Chris had the access to BBC, to pirate radio, to booking agents, so Millie actually opened that door for him. I don't think he made a fortune from her, but Bob Marley was a lot of Chris's success and later fame. Millie was an essential link.

What "My Boy Lollipop" did for ska was to make it a recognizable genre for the masses, in England, in America, in Australia and Europe and Scandinavia, around the world. As author Colin Grant writes, "'My Boy Lollipop' marked a pivotal moment in the evolution of Jamaican culture. Not only was it a huge international hit, filling the coffers of Chris Blackwell's London-based Island Records; but back home in Jamaica, among the record-buying middle classes, it uncoupled the freight of negative associations they had attached to ska. The lyrics of 'My Boy Lollipop' may not have stood much analysis, but its unambiguous financial success prompted speculators and other businessmen to take a punt on ska artists."[18] Those artists, such as Toots and the Maytals, Byron Lee and the Dragonaires, and The Skatalites, were finally getting some uptown play. Radio stations and newspapers that were once afraid to play or report on ska suddenly couldn't get enough. Ska came out of the yards and into the airwaves. Sure, Byron Lee, Edward Seaga, Ronnie Nasralla and the crew at the World's Fair had a hand in bridging ska's class divide, but so too did Millie Small on a much larger scale. Internationally, ska was a recognizable word. Before 1964, the word "ska" had never appeared in a newspaper, not even in newspapers in Kingston itself, although it did appear as "sca" as early as October 1963. But after "My Boy Lollipop," the word "ska" was visible in print everywhere. Millie Small had a part in that. And certainly Chris Blackwell had a part in that. In fact, the first time that the word "ska" appears in the *Daily Gleaner* is on March 17, 1964, in an article titled "The 'Ska' hits London—but they call it Blue Beat," where the journalist, Maureen Cleave, admits she "got the story from a rather handsome young man of 26 with reddish hair called Chris Blackwell." The article also references Millie and "My Boy Lollipop," so the song was obviously released by then and was already having impact.

Millie's song, albeit at the hands of Chris Blackwell, paved the way for other artists to showcase their talents overseas. Howard Campbell, journalist for the *Jamaica Gleaner*, states, "She set the pace for other Jamaican hitmakers in Britain (Desmond Dekker, Dave Barker and Ansell [sic] Collins, Ken Boothe and Junior Murvin).... Within four years of its release ['My Boy Lollipop'], Jamaican pop music exploded in Britain. Dekker hit it big with Israelites, followed by Barker and Collins' funky 'Double Barrell' in 1969. In the mid and late 1970s Boothe ('Everything I Own'), Murvin ('Police and Thieves') and Althea and Donna ('Uptown Top Ranking') all invaded the British national chart."[19] Others such as Laurel Aitken and Prince Buster also came to England to enjoy Jamaican music's wave of success, introducing their sounds to the working class youth who would then shape it years later into something of their own.

"My Boy Lollipop" brought ska to the world. Ska had existed for years before, as early as 1959 with Theophilus Beckford's "Easy Snappin'" (released in 1959 but recorded in 1956) and with more authenticity from the likes of The Skatalites, but it took this form of ska, a pop version that was perhaps more palatable to the populace, to break through. "Small will always be remembered as the first Jamaican artiste to expose Jamaican music on a wide scale to an international audience," writes *Jamaica Gleaner* journalist and music historian Roy Black.[20]

"I was young, so I did not think about the impact at the time of 'My Boy Lollipop's' success," says Millie. "One thing for sure, it open the door for all Jamaican artists, male or female, that follows thereafter up to this point. Also it was the first ska disc to make it globally and the influence it carries still exists and is evident today. This disc is the only ska recording that sold over seven million copies to date, of which no other female Jamaican artist has surpassed yet."

Millie Small went on to record more songs, some of which had moderate success on the charts, such as "Sweet William" and "Oh Henry," which were released on June 15, 1964. Although the "Sweet William" had 100,000 orders before it was even released, none of Millie's other songs reached the same level of popularity as her smash hit. She also sang backup for the Spencer Davis Group on the song "I'm Blue," an Ike Turner song, which Chris Blackwell again hoped would have strong crossover appeal. In 1966 she recorded a number of songs with Jamaican vocalist Jackie Edwards, who had relocated to London, and over seven months the two toured New Zealand, Australia, Singapore, Kenya, Uganda, Tanzania, Nigeria, Ghana, Liberia, Norway, Sweden, Denmark, and Finland before spending time in Jamaica. By the time Millie's contract with Island and Fontana had elapsed in the summer of 1968, she had produced 70 recordings and four LP albums for them.

In 1969, Millie signed a one-year contract with Decca and recorded the songs "Readin', Writin', Arithmetic" and "I Want You Never to Stop." She performed on stage in Manchester at Houldsworth Hall on March 31, 1970, almost exactly six years after the release of her hit. The *Daily Gleaner* reporter Clayton Goodwin remarked of the performance, "It was the first time that I had seen Miss Small in a one night stand since the halcyon days of 1964 and nothing had changed—except that Millie had grown even more attractive with maturity, and her better-controlled voice was able to overcome the poor acoustics of the hall."[21] That same year she also performed at Wembley Stadium for the Caribbean Music Festival with Toots and the Maytals, Desmond Dekker, Bob and Marcia, and The Pioneers, among others. Besides singing, Millie performed in a number of plays in England, plus Pantomime, but she says she prefers vocal performances.

As the decade transitioned from the '60s to the '70s, so too did Millie begin to transition from an impish little girl into a sexy young woman. She posed nude on the cover of her *Time Will Tell* album, which was released by Trojan in the 1970s, and although her back is facing the camera, she is, strangely, riding a giant banana. She posed topless in 1971 for *Mayfair*, a men's magazine akin to *Playboy*, and she lived for a period of time in Singapore. "I lived in Singapore for about a year and a half. I went there on invitation of a friend of mine, and while I was there he thought he could get me some job, which he did, and I went down very well in Singapore.... Singapore was the first country I traveled to in the Far East, and I've been there many times, but the last time I've been there was in 1970. Oh my dear, when I was there it was very very nice there, and I loved it so much and I did very well there," Millie says. She also returned to Kingston to perform at the National Stadium in 1971 for an Easter extravaganza.

Millie Small dabbled in the fashion business for a while, opening a shop in London called Millie's Bazaar, which housed 18 smaller individual shops. Millie had many suitors, including actor Gary Bond, who co-owned her shop, and Peter Asher, a record executive and part of the duo Peter and Gordon. She was also engaged for a time to an English art historian and painter named Eddie Wolfram, although the two never married. Wolfram went on to produce Millie as she tried to work with The Pyramids and to work with Graeme Goodall's label Doctor Bird, which soon folded, before turning to Trojan for the release of one single, "Enoch Power," a song that was widely banned despite its theme of racial unity. Millie has never been married, and she says she doesn't wish to be, either. She does have a daughter, Jaelee Small, born in December 1984, who is a full-time professional session singer in the UK. Millie says, "As a mom, I'm a nice little girl. I have a daughter called Jaelee who is my pride and joy and I am her pride and joy. She is my baby and I am her little mommy."

Newspaper articles in Jamaica expressed wishes that Millie would return to receive her Order of Distinction in 2011, but she had Edward Seaga accept the award for her. "In Jamaica, I heard about it," says Millie of the prestigious honor, "but I haven't accepted it yet. Seaga accepted it on my behalf." Although Millie hasn't recorded or performed and has been reclusive in the past many years, she does still have aspirations to return to the musical stage. "I will be recording later on, some time, some time. I am a spiritual person. I meditate and at the moment I'm creating my dream. I do a lot of mediation in my work here at home, and through meditation I am creating my dream, and in that dream will be something wonderful for every one of us. But I can't tell you much about it now, you see? I am so in love with the good people in this world and the beautiful animals and plants, I cannot wait to go back out and start showing myself and looking at all of you," she says.

Millie Small died on May 5, 2020, in London at the age of 73.

Others

There are a small number of women who recorded on the Blue Beat label about whom little or nothing is known. To further complicate tracing the history of these women, when they married they frequently changed their maiden names, or they recorded under false names or names given to them by the producer.

Beverly Mills, sometime spelled Beverley Mills, was a singer with Ezz Reco and The Launchers. They featured Jamaican saxophonist Johnny Hope, drummer Ezz Reco (real name Ezzard Reid) and both Boysie Grant and Beverly Mills as vocalists. Grant had been a member of Ivy Graydon's orchestra in the 1950s, and he regularly performed in night clubs. In 1964, Mills recorded with Boysie Grant, backed by Ezz Reco and The Launchers, in a cover of the Jimmy Cliff tune called "King of Kings." She also recorded "The Bluest Beat," "Please Come Back," and "Little Girl." She moved to England with the group in 1964 in an attempt to capitalize on the ska trend. A photograph owned by Getty Images dated February 14, 1964, shot by Edward Miller, features the caption "Singer-dancers Beverly Mills and Boysie Grant do the 'Blue Beat,' a dance brought to Britain by West Indian immigrants, which looks set to sweep all other popular dances off the dance floors. Present at this reception held in London was the high commissioner of Jamaica Mr. HL Lindo."[22]

Other women who recorded on the Blue Beat label include a vocalist called "Brigitte Bond." The song "Oh Yeah Baby," with the flip side "Blue Beat Baby," was recorded in 1964 by Brigitte Bond and the Blue Beats. There were also Joyce Bond, Cindy Star and the Rude Boys, "Jeannie" (who recorded with Kent Brown), Annette Clarke, and additional women featured in other chapters.[23]

Chapter Seven

Rocksteady

It is perhaps appropriate at this stage to discuss the fact that genres are not distinct in sound nor in time period. Genres are fluid. Artists are fluid. Genres are classifications that are helpful in many ways, but when it comes to defining a particular artist's catalogue, especially if that artist performed and recorded for many years, even decades, these classifications can be problematic. Such is the case here. As an example, the work from artist Patsy Todd spans multiple genres—ska, rocksteady, soul, reggae. So placing Todd in a chapter on ska is really a matter of personal preference. She easily could go in this chapter on rocksteady since a large amount of her work, and certainly much of her solo work, falls in the rocksteady category. The point here is that the stories of these artists are more important than placing them in musical taxonomies. So let us suspend that strain and move forward with exploring the lives of these pioneering ladies.

Hortense Ellis

In the song "Woman of the Ghetto," written by Marlena Shaw, singer Hortense Ellis asks the legislator how to raise children in the ghetto. She is strong, proud, free, and black, and her children are just like those of the politician, who are no different, crying when they have pain, closing their eyes when they sleep, but not seeing the same ugly sites as those in the ghetto. It is no coincidence that Ellis chose this tune to record. She, too, was a woman of the ghetto with many mouths to feed. She felt the struggle she painfully wailed of in her music, and despite great admiration from virtually all who hear the depths and heights of her vocal range and abilities, Hortense Ellis, like so many others in Jamaican music history, never received recognition even close to matching her immense talent. In fact, Hortense Ellis has been largely ignored.

"I'm the very first female singer in Jamaica. I've been through the R&B, rocksteady, and ska eras. When I began my singing career, there was no Marcia, no Rita, no Judith, there were only singers like Totlyn Jackson and Sheila Rickards, and they were jazz and cabaret singers. I was the first, whose voice was heard on the radio all over the island," said Hortense Ellis.[1] She was born on April 18, 1941, in Trench Town. Owen "Blakka" Ellis, Jamaican comedian and Hortense's nephew, remembers, "I lived on First Street with my mother's family but I'd visit my dad who lived on Third Street."[2] His dad was Leslie Ellis, Hortense's brother. There was also Alton Ellis, the successful vocalist; Irving; Mertlyn;

Lilieth, who went by the nickname Cherry; Veronica; and Hortense, who went by the nickname Tiny. Their father Percival was a railroad worker, and mother Beatrice ran a fruit stall. "It was a musical family, but more of a musical community than household," says Blakka. "Trench Town was designed with very small houses, so everything spilled out into the yard and onto the streets. And Hortense was not so much a singer in those times but was more a comedian. She would be doing wonderful spectacles imitating people, doing a belly dance, more a humorist than a singer in the early days," he says. Christel Reid, Hortense's oldest child, says she remembers her mother as a comedian too. "Comedians run in the family," she says, noting that Blakka and Ity Ellis, Hortense's two nephews, are showbiz personalities with successful careers in comedy, but Hortense too was a jokester. "Sometimes just by talking, she would get us laughing, all of us. We are just a family of happy people," says Reid.³

Hortense Ellis at Studio One in the 1990s (photograph by Ron Vester).

But when Hortense turned 18, she decided to try her hand at showbiz, not as a comedian—although there would have been room for that in Jamaica's Pantomime and variety show venues—but as the singer we know and love. She got her start through the same means as so many other great musicians and artists, the *Vere Johns Opportunity Hour*. Blakka says, "She won Vere Johns. It was like a monthly competition. She won one month and Alton won another month, then she won the grand finals over him." The song that Hortense Ellis wowed the crowds with in 1959, the same crowd that cheered her on the loudest to win her the championship, was "I'm Not Saying No at All," by Frankie Lymon. According to writer David Katz, it was Alton Ellis who chose the song for her to sing.⁴ She continued to compete at the *Vere Johns Opportunity Hour* and racked up six semifinals and four finals. "I used to perform at the Majestic, Palace, Ambassador, and Odeon Theatres in the '50s at the *Vere Johns Opportunity Hour*, but I began singing professionally in 1961," she said.⁵

Before she recorded a single tune, Hortense had her first child, Christel, in 1960, but she was already singing on the stages of Kingston. "She had me in 1960. She told me she sang Saturday night and she had me the next morning at five o'clock. She was 19 when she had me," Reid says. Then in 1961, Hortense Ellis recorded her first three songs for Coxsone Dodd on his World Disc label: "Eddie My Love" and "Loving Girl," billed as Hortense Ellis and the Blues Blasters, and "All by Ourselves (All by Myself)," billed as Lascelles Perkins and Hortense Ellis. It was her ability that made her desirable. "She had a massive, massive range, a very very high pitch and she could come down to a deep baritone," Blakka says. Reid adds, "She was a beautiful singer. Anybody I tell Hortense Ellis was my mother, they say, 'That girl could sing!' I remember one time she got an award, the First Lady of Song." That award, given by the *Star*, came in 1964, but she had been using the moniker on her advertisements a year earlier while performing at the State Theatre with the Mercuries.

By 1962, Hortense Ellis was on the road, touring with Byron Lee and the Dragonaires to the Bahamas and Trinidad as well as performing with Lee's band for holiday shows in Kingston, such as the *Easter Spectacular, New Year's Show*, and *Christmas Mornings*. These holiday stage shows were very popular in Jamaican culture and featured a full lineup of performers. At one of those shows called *Heptime* in December 1966 at the National Arena, Hortense performed with the Mighty Sparrow, Marcia Griffiths, The Gaylads, The Clarendonians, The Techniques, and Roy Richards. Hortense performed songs by Dionne Warwick and had previously been covering Patti LaBelle's songs, says an article which reviewed the show. In August 1967 as part of independence anniversary celebrations, Hortense Ellis performed in one of the country's street concerts with The Jamaicans, The Paragons, Derrick Harriott, Winston Samuels, Count Ossie, The Techniques, Desmond Dekker and the Aces, The Clarendonians, Stranger and Patsy, and her brother, Alton and the Flames.

While Hortense did record and perform with her brother from time to time, their personal relationship over the years was difficult. "It has been said that he never ever forgave her for winning over him in the grand finals [of *Vere Johns Opportunity Hour*]," says Blakka. "They were close, understand, but there was always some tension between them that never got resolved, and I'm told the tension originate from the fact that she won the grand finals and he came in second or third. There definitely was some competition. There was always a question about who was the best singer in the family. My dad (Leslie) sang with Alton as a backup singer, and Irving was a steel pan player and claims that he is the best singer, but my dad argued that he could sing as good as Alton, so there was always that friendly rivalry among them," he says. Reid says that the relationship with Alton was good early on, but as their careers developed they didn't always see eye to eye. "Something went wrong in the latter part, something went wrong. I don't know what it is, but they weren't on any speaking terms at one point and in a lot of parts," she says.

Hortense continued to record and perform as a solo artist and as part of a duo with artists such as Derrick Morgan, Delroy Wilson, Jackie Edwards, Jackie Opel, Johnny Clarke, Lloyd Charmers, Stranger Cole, Peter Austin, Dillinger, and Clint Eastwood. In addition to recording for Coxsone Dodd, Hortense Ellis also recorded for producers Ken Lack, Duke Reid, Lord Koos, Clive Chin, Bunny Lee, Prince Buster, and Lee "Scratch" Perry. She also recorded under the names Queen Tiney, Dawn Love, and Mahalia Saunders. Mahalia was Hortense Ellis's middle name, and Saunders was her married name after she married Mikey "Junior" Saunders in 1971. The couple divorced a few years later.

Hortense Ellis was known for not only her voice but also her tough personality. "Coming to You Softly" may have been one of Hortense Ellis's hit songs, but it definitely wasn't her way of doing things. Blakka says, "She was very slim, wiry, very very slim, never gained weight, small build, looked very quiet and looked very unassuming, and then she raised her voice and got noticed. She was very strong, very determined. She carved her own path. She would not be told what was appropriate or right or acceptable— it was what her heart said. She never lived by societal rules, she simply did what she felt was right. She was always in a fight with somebody, a verbal fight, because she wasn't a physical fighter and she would raise her voice loudly. She was always ranting about somebody who didn't pay her."

Blakka remembers one of those times when a promoter tried to take advantage of her as well as him, since they both performed at the same show together. "I remember later on when I became an adult and I became an emcee and a comedian. I did a show with her in St. Elizabeth. Everybody who did the show, at the end of the show, was having a problem getting paid. And all the performers were waiting around, mumblin', grumblin', getting antsy, and she raised her voice. She was the one who spoke out loudly, angrily, with a profanity-laced demand for her money. She never backed down from that, never backed down," he says. Christel Reid says that being taken advantage of by men in the industry was always one of her constant battles. "Her challenge as a woman in the singing industry is that the producers weren't being fair. They'd have you doing a show and very little finance coming back from it. Very little pay, very little pay," she says.

Perhaps Hortense Ellis was so concerned with her pay because she had mouths to feed. Over the course of her 59 years, Hortense had nine children, 26 grandchildren, and two great-grandchildren. "My mother had nine of us, eight girls and one boy," says Christel:

> I'm the first one. There were challenges for her while she was away on her shows but my grandmother, her mother, played a big role. She lived with her and my grandfather. I left her at six years old to come and live with my father. I remember my father coming and taking me away at six years old. I have a different father from her husband. She had four of us from different fathers and then she got married and then she had five from him, five girls. My dad tried to take me from her, and he wanted me to go with him, so he took me from her. I don't know what led to the taking away, but I remember him coming and taking me away on his bike, his motorbike, a motorcycle. I hadn't gone back to live with her until her death. She's always around and she bring everything for us, clothes and everything, groceries, and she keep us together, all our brothers and sisters, we are never apart, up to this day.

The fact that Hortense Ellis was a mother of so many children made having a successful career even more difficult for her than for other women. "Life for women in ska, and it's women in show business really, whether they were in ska or in jazz or in classical music, have to make hard choices," says Dr. Myrna Hague, vocalist, musicologist, and widow of musician and orchestra leader Sonny Bradshaw.[6] "Whatever choices they made, the choices are hurtful and the reward is based on the choice you make. You have to decide, really, what is it worth to you? What is it that you really want and what are you prepared to give up for what you're going to get? And sometimes you don't get what you think you're going to get." Hortense Ellis loved her family. She was a mother first and a singer second. That affected her career. Writer Lorna Goodison says, "Hortense was so powerful. She had enormous talent but she had a lot of children. So she got this reputation for being always pregnant, and it was hard."[7]

Performing and recording throughout the 1960s, 1970s, and even a few times in the early 1980s, Hortense Ellis moved to Miami for a period of time and spent most of her time on her family and home life. Reid says:

> She was everybody's mother. She love plants, beautiful flowers, she loved to garden. She loved pretty things—crystal vases, crystal figurines—she bought a lot of those and she love shopping. When she started getting grandchildren, a whole lotta stuff, buy, buy, buy for them. I gave her her first grandchild in 1978 and he was spoiled! She was nice to us, her children. And she loved having parties.

> When party announced we are always around her. She's never far from us. My mom always say that she was happy she had so many girls, she was happy she got to always go to the hospital for new grandchildren, not to the police station, not to the lockup! And everybody knows when she's going to get another grandchild, everyone knows about it. Whenever someone was at the hospital, she was right there to receive her, to take home her grandchild.

Blakka says that when it came to choosing between family and career there was no contest—family came first: "She did defer a number of offers and turn down a number of gigs because while she was always certainly singing, she was more focused on her role as mother than she was on her career. If it was interfering with her motherly duty she'd say, 'Sorry, I can't do it. My kids need me.' Her son lived in the country, and when he came to Kingston and left in the morning to drive back, she would make him a bowl of porridge so he could have some porridge back home. She's that kind of mother."

Hortense Ellis died on October 1, 2000, at only 59 years of age. "She died very young," Reid says. "The lungs, the air pockets in the lungs, they were damaged because she used to smoke. She stopped for quite a while, but the damage was already set in." Her funeral was held on November 9, 2000, at the Andrew's Seventh Day Adventist Church on Hope Road in Kingston. Bunny and Scully, Ken Boothe, Stranger Cole and Alton Ellis gave musical tributes at the service, and Desmond Young, president of the Jamaican Federation of Musicians, Marcia Griffiths, and Derrick Morgan were in attendance, along with dozens of others. These family and friends, as well as millions of fans throughout the world, recognize the depth of Hortense Ellis's spirit and talent, even if the industry didn't. "Artistes from that era are not given the recognition they deserve, but other artistes who recently came on the scene have been given awards and so on," said Hortense Ellis just a few years before her death. "But we, the artistes, who sang because we loved it, not even a kind thought."[8]

The Webber Sisters

Many who have heard the song "Stop That Train" are familiar with the Keith and Tex version. The tune, produced by Derrick Harriott in 1967, the slow rocksteady groove with perfect harmonies and Lynn Taitt's loping train whistle of a guitar, was not the first recording of the classic. The first version, recorded in 1965, was a ska song credited to The Spanishtonians, a band whose identity has long plagued collectors and historians. This song has such a different feel from its successor that they could be two completely different songs; this is exemplary of the change that Jamaican music experienced during these years—the change in rhythm, slowing from ska to rocksteady; the reduction in the number of horns or elimination altogether; and the tone of the vocals, from lively and punctuated to smooth and slippery. But the mystery has long been, who are The Spanishtonians? Who is this female voice? And who wrote the song? According to Winston Jones, the answer to all of these questions is Winston Jones and The Tonettes, also known as The Webber Sisters.[9]

Cynthia Webber was born in 1941 and Merlene Webber in 1947. They also had a brother David. They grew up on Spanish Town Road in Kingston. Getting their start singing in church, the three siblings formed a group and would sometimes perform together, or sometimes as a duet, depending on schedules or desires. The *Vere Johns Opportunity Hour* gave them their big break, like most other artists of this era. Merlene recalls, "From an early age of about ten going on, I used to dance jitterbug, me and my brother, for *Vere Johns Opportunity Hour* at Majestic Theatre and all over the country, all over, and my sister sing at all of the shows and festivals in the early days. Then me and she start to sing together as a group. But we were doing well with Vere Johns and all those people." Cynthia adds, "The call us King Webber and Queen Webber. When my sister dances with my brother, they would be King and Queen Webber and with me when I am singing it is the same, King and Queen Webber. They did most of the Vere Johns stuff and any concert in the city or travel out to the town and do the jitterbug, and I used to sing on occasion at the popular clubs in town. A lot of dancing."[10]

Before long, David Webber went on to form The Gladiators with Albert Griffiths and Errol Grandison, his two childhood friends. So Cynthia and Merlene began singing at clubs around Kingston. "The Glass Bucket was a classy club," says Cynthia of one of the places they performed. Merlene adds, "They sit down and have a drink and they have time when they get up and dance. They listen to the music and we sing and they dance." They also started recording for Studio One. The Tonettes, sometimes spelled the Tonnettes, recorded "Love That Is Real," "Pretty Baby," and "Tell Me You're Mine."

The following year they teamed up with Winston Jones to form Winston and the Tonettes. Jones lived near the Webber family. "We lived in the same neighborhood and form a group together," says Jones. "We grew up together and everybody go up to Studio One on Sunday. That's when he picks the ones to do the recording. Twenty different groups waiting to go into the studio." Together they recorded "You Make Me Cry," "I Love You," and the now classic "Stop That Train," which was incorrectly credited to the Spanishtonians. Jones explains,

> I wrote that song. I did that song in 1964 for Prince Buster. I recorded it and I wasn't with The Spanishtonians, but we go to the same studio. They put The Spanishtonians on the label just to throw me off. It was Winston and the Tonettes, but they put The Spanishtonians. It was me, Winston Jones and Cynthia and Merlene Webber. Prince Buster put the Spanishtonians name on it, to throw us off, because in those days there are different people's names on them songs, so you don't know what's what. You're not going to take a plane and go to England or go to America, so they would do that. In Jamaica, it's very trickyful and weird in Jamaica. When these producers record the artist name, they don't put the name right on the record when they sell it abroad. It is you singing the record, but they don't put your name on the record. So when these guys start to travel around now, go to America, go to Florida, go to London and different place, then they realize, that is their record and they're not making the money. The question is, who wrote the song. I wrote the song. I wrote the song. I don't see my name on it. I see a mixed-up name on it. If I tell you how much money I make for "Stop That Train" you'd cry tears. Nothing.

Both Cynthia and Merlene concur that it was Winston Jones who wrote it and the three of them that recorded it. "'Stop That Train' we did, both of us sing with Winston Jones. No, it's not The Spanishtonians, that is a mistake. That sounds like Prince Buster all right. He was demanding. He always want things done his way or no way at all. He was drastic, he was very drastic. Your name is there and everything, but they do the collecting. We get nothing. Even the material—you write the song, you compose the song and yet they take all the credit for it," says Merlene. They all say that the other songs credited to The Spanishtonians, including "Rudie Gets Plenty," were not Winston and the Tonettes nor the Webber Sisters. Kenroy Fyffe, a confirmed member of the actual Spanishtonians, says that it was a woman named Beverly who sang vocals on "Rudie Gets Plenty" and confirms they did not record "Stop That Train." Could this be the same Beverly, Beverly Mills, who sang with Ezz Reco and Boysie Grant and The Launchers? This is the group that is credited with launching blue beat in the UK before Millie Small. Their first song was a remake of Jimmy Cliff's "King of Kings" in 1964. Or could it be Hazel Wright? The voice is very similar and evocative of the baby voice that many Jamaican vocalists employed, imitative of their idol, Shirley of Shirley and Lee.

It wasn't the first or last time Cynthia and Merlene would have difficulty due to unscrupulous producers—in fact, it would only get worse. Merlene says, "It was tough for women. To be honest, the femininity of a woman is completely different from the male. Sometimes they treat you very tender, sometimes they just rob you, yeah. That's how they are. When it come to the financial part of it, they are all rotten, they don't do justice. Not one of them." Coxsone Dodd was another of the producers they sought for work, moving back and forth between Dodd and Prince Buster, but Merlene says one wasn't better than another. "He was the main boss that we have. In Jamaica you pick up anything you can get. Suffercation. Prince Buster ask us to do a song and Coxsone was mad. He suffer us for a while." Cynthia says, "When things weren't going well for us with Coxsone we were drawn to Prince Buster because the bigger money and the treatment had you coming and going." "When you were hungry," adds Merlene with a laugh.

Some of the music that Winston and The Tonettes recorded for Coxsone in those years was never released, claims Jones. "We record a lot of things for Studio One, but it never come out. Even before Coxsone died I ask him about some of the songs and what he did with them, and he say he still have them, so I'll bring them back one by one. I didn't get paid for them, so I'll record them again for myself," he says.

Cynthia and Merlene both recorded as The Tonettes in their early years and as The Webber Sisters later, plus they both sang backup for a number of artists. "We used to do harmony work with Bob Marley when I-Threes [his regular backup; see ch. 8] weren't around; we would do something with him also. We didn't mind it, we glad when they call us to do backup, anything, you know. We need the money, so we always go and do it. Sometimes you make people your starship from that because people hear ya and want to know who it is, and they employ you because the more backup you get the more employ you get, so we never mind that," says Merlene. "We did quite a lot for those guys in those days—Ken Parker, Tony Gregory, Jimmy Cliff—all the leading reggae artists," Cynthia says. And they also released a number of their own songs, singing together as well as separately, throughout the late 1960s, and an LP in 1982 called *I & I Love You Honey*.

Still, it was tough—tough for women. Cynthia says, "We have promoters who want to be more than friends, more than producers, and that sexuality push us apart. We can say we didn't stay on top long time because of sexual advances, being able to live up to their standards of sexual advance. They make advances and with one or two in those days you would get involved with and they make you promises that don't really work, then you have to just sort of break off and try for yourself again. It's a bumpy road." Merlene adds, "And some of them just take it," referring to producer Bunny Lee. Merlene and Bunny Lee are the parents of Errol Lee, born on August 27, 1968. He was musically trained by his mother and Cynthia and today is a talented singer and performer. "It was hard," says Merlene. "I eat from the rent, that's how I live. And so when I get a show I would go, and that's how it was." Merlene immigrated to Canada when Errol was 10 years old and her other child was 3 years old. She sent for them three years later. Cynthia is also a mother, to three children, and she lives a few miles away from her sister in Canada.

Both Merlene and Cynthia still sing today, and they give thanks for the opportunities they have had. "When life gets a little better you have to thank God for the best and move on, that's what I did," says Cynthia. "I say, whatever you believe in, lead with that belief and compose songs because that is the greatest now, to be able to compose and build a dream from that and follow that dream, for your work, to touch hearts. It's a life but it cannot be lived unless you live it for others," she says. As far as Merlene, her advice to other women is simple. She says, "Look before you leap."

Phyllis Dillon, OD

Those outside of the island might only know of Linstead, Jamaica, by the folk song that made the town in the parish of St. Catherine popular. "Linstead Market" is perhaps the most popular Jamaican folk song of all time: "Me carry me akee a Linstead market / Not a quatty worth sell. / Oh what a losses! / Not a quatty worth sell. / Me carry me akee a Linstead market. / Not a quatty worth sell. / Oh not a light, not a bite! / Not a quatty worth sell."[11] These words tell of the struggle of a woman, a *higgler*, to provide for her children, who will now have to go hungry. In many ways, this ackee seller is not unlike Phyllis Dillon, who also struggled to make money with her work, to provide for her children, and who also came from the village known as Linstead.

Born on New Year's Day in 1948, Phyllis Dillon started her singing career as a young girl in Linstead singing for her church and little concerts and festivals around town. "Singing means so much to me as a person, that when anyone asked what I wanted to be when I grew up, I always said 'I want to make records!'" she said.[12] But her family wasn't supportive of her career at the beginning, since girls in the entertainment industry were not seen favorably in the public eye. In fact, she says her father threatened to disown her. But Phyllis was a strong girl, even early in life, and she stubbornly pursued her dream. She began performing with a young Roy Panton, who was also a resident of Linstead. The two were vocalists for the Linstead band, The Vulcans. "She was a good performer, also a very good singer. She was easy to work with and I had no problem working with her," says Roy Panton.[13] The Vulcans performed not only in Linstead but all over the island in Ocho Rios, Montego Bay, and Kingston, where they appeared at the Glass Bucket Club. Of the Glass Bucket, Byron Lee once said, "When you go to the Glass Bucket you had to have a reputation. Glass Bucket mash up the night. Glass Bucket was for the rich and famous and then for the people. Ska played that role."[14] The Glass Bucket Club opened on December 22, 1934, on Half Way Tree Road in Kingston. It was owned by Bob Webster and later Joe Abner. This area of Kingston was a border between uptown and downtown, and the club certainly catered to high-class clientele. Because the club welcomed the upper classes and tourists, the entertainment offered was in accord with established tastes and was frequently dictated by trends in the U.S., such as vaudeville. But when tastes changed from vaudeville to the sounds of big band orchestras, the Glass Bucket adapted. It was here, at the Glass Bucket in 1956, that great American jazz singer Sarah Vaughan came to perform in mid–July. Don Drummond played trombone as part of Vaughan's musical backup, and Vaughan was so impressed with his playing that she said he likely ranked in the top five trombonists in the world.

It was at the Glass Bucket that Phyllis Dillon met Lynn Taitt after The Vulcans performed. Taitt complimented her singing and suggested she begin recording. He took her a few days later to meet Duke Reid at Treasure Isle. She was just 19 years old when she recorded her first song for Reid, a tune called "Don't Stay Away" that she had written herself. She recorded the song late in 1965; it was released early in 1966 and quickly shot up the Jamaican charts to the number one spot. In 1967 she recorded perhaps her most well-known song, "Perfidia," a tune made popular in 1940 by the great Xavier Cugat, who had also once performed at the Glass Bucket Club. Other Jamaican artists would go on to record this song, including Laurel Aitken, Johnny Clarke, Pam Hall, and Watty Burnett. Dillon recorded songs with Oliver St. Patrick and the Diamonds, Tommy McCook and the Supersonics, and she performed duets with Alton Ellis and Hopeton Lewis. She also recorded as Phyllis Dillon and the Revolutionaries, and as Shirley Kay. On almost all of the songs recorded by Phyllis Dillon, Lynn Taitt was involved. Other musicians she worked with included Lloyd Knibb and Winston Grennan.

Influenced by the American singers popular in Jamaica during this era, including Dionne Warwick, Sarah Vaughan, Connie Francis, and Patti Page, Phyllis continued to record hit after hit for Duke Reid. She once said she stayed with him only because it was easier to stay with one crook than go around to many crooks. Like so many other musicians, and like so many other women, Dillon didn't receive any financial gains from her work, but she said she found Reid to be a nice person and they worked well together. Her song "It's Rockin' Time," also known as "Rock Steady," was written by Phyllis. She says that she had to revise her first version of the composition because Reid said it wasn't exciting enough. She also recorded for Sonia Pottinger, who, along with Duke Reid, produced the huge hit "Don't Touch My Tomato." It was a song once made popular by Josephine Baker and was a traditional calypso song recorded by Lord Lebby (Noel Williams) as well as George Symonette.

Like many calypso songs, "Don't Touch My Tomato" was filled with sexual innuendo. The lyrics, when performed by a confident and sensual Josephine Baker, as well as a strong and assured Phyllis Dillon, had a kind of sexual power, calling the shots, rejecting, teasing. In today's culture of slackness and twerking, it is difficult to fully comprehend the impact a song like this had. No longer was the female singing the sweet love song—now she was taking back control of her own sexuality.

Phyllis performed songs that she wrote herself, as well as an ample selection of cover songs from the likes of Perry Como, Frank Sinatra, The Wailers, and Stephen Stills over the years. She enjoyed performing but simply was not making any money at all, and so in 1967 she left Jamaica and immigrated to the United States, settling in New York. She returned to Jamaica to record from time to time and became involved with a group called The Buccaneers, a band of Jamaicans who had also settled in New York. She still wasn't able to make a living performing, and so she turned to temporary jobs to earn money. She married and had two children, and in 1971 at the age of 23, she left singing altogether, worked at a bank and raised her family.

After staying away from the entertainment industry for two decades, Phyllis made her return. She was encouraged by Michael Barnett, a director of MKB Productions, who produced the Get Ready Rock Steady tours. In 1991, Phyllis made her re-debut for a rock-steady show at the National Arena in Kingston, where she performed for over 5,000 attendees. She was reinvigorated and returned to the art she once loved, undeterred by the corruption in years past. Phyllis's performance received rave reviews. She and Hopeton Lewis sang their song "Get on the Right Track" for the first time together in 24 years.

She starred regularly for Barnett's *Heineken Startime* concerts with other performers such as Derrick Morgan, Leroy Sibbles, U-Roy, Alton Ellis, Pat Kelly, Lloyd Parks, Stranger

Cole, Derrick Harriott, and John Holt. She performed around the globe for those who longed to hear her soulful soprano in the flesh. She performed in New York, London, France, Germany, Belgium, Spain, and Japan, as well as in her native Jamaica. "Music is my life, it's what I know," Dillon said.[15] In 1998, Lynn Taitt coaxed Phyllis back into the recording studio, and the two made an album of songs written by Taitt and Phyllis, as well as Phyllis's brother. On April 15, 2004, Phyllis Dillon died of cancer in New York. She was just 56 years old. She had divorced and was survived by her two children, Nigel and Janice. In 2009, Phyllis Dillon was posthumously awarded the Order of Distinction (OD) for her contribution to the development of popular Jamaican music.

Chapter Eight

Reggae

Ask the average non–Jamaican to identify one female reggae artist, and chances are they will either identify the three women who back up Bob Marley in flowing skirts and head wraps (though not by name), or they'll come up completely empty. However, perhaps because of the lyrical melodies in reggae that allowed women to spotlight more of their vocal talents, and perhaps because society had advanced in terms of opportunities, more women in reggae than in any earlier Jamaican genres performed and recorded. Women in reggae were far more than accents for male singers; they were headliners, they were best-selling recording artists, they were legends.

Norma Fraser

Being introduced by Rita Marley to her son Ziggy as a "legend" is akin to knighthood, sainthood, a coronation. But it is completely comprehensible that such a singer should receive such an honor when it was she, Norma Fraser, who taught Rita Marley how to sing in the first place, counseled her to marry Bob, and went on to lead the life of not only a virtuoso vocalist but also a centered, spiritual, strong woman.

Norma Fraser was born in St. Andrew in Jamaica and attended Merle Grove High School. Although she loved music as a child, she never realized she had any talent, nor aspired to it. "My father could sight read. He could look at a musical piece and just sing the notes, but I had no musical talent at all. None. But I loved music. I grew up in St. Andrew in the suburbs of Kingston. We used to have a lot of American artists who would come do concerts, and my parents would give me money to go to matinees because kids would go to matinees at the Carib Theatre, Ward Theatre. I was there all the time, just to see them, because I love music. I would meet a lot of them too—Sam Cooke and his wife; Paul Anka. I loved all types of music and we just go to listen. I had no aspirations really of becoming a singer," she says.[1] In fact, like the rest of her family, Norma first became a schoolteacher. But she realized it wasn't her calling as she turned to her passion, music.

Norma remembers the days of the "sound system" dances, although she says they typically attracted a bit of a rougher crowd for a young girl, and so she favored attending the theater and club shows instead. Still, she says the sound systems influenced her:

> The sound systems were huge. Everywhere you went you heard what was coming out of these studios. My parents were sophisticated. In my family there were three girls and two boys and I'm the fourth one. My mom and dad are educators, which is why education in our family was so paramount. Oh yes, God yes, great educators. The Frasers are teachers. So I wasn't allowed to go to the sound systems, but my brother had a dance once at one of our homes and he had one of the best sound systems come to play. He knew nothing about the downtown language or the money or anything, and here I am—I wasn't even singing then—and I said, "Let me stand by the gate." He didn't want me to stand at the gate, and I had a feeling they would steal from him because here's this educated boy, but he knows nothing about that kind of life. So I stayed at the gate, but they still ripped him off and took all the money and he didn't do it again. But I learned a lot about the sound system because they played some good music at my brother's dance. The sound system brought all the records and the top records. And the sound system that had the best records, he's the one that had the best following.

But Norma's involvement in music went from spectator to participant when she realized that the music was not just up there on the stages of the theaters but within her as well. She says, "One day I was in the shower and I said, 'Well, let's see if I can sing,' and I just opened my mouth and something came out and I said, 'Wow man! I can sing! I can sing!' Just like that. It was weird!" So Norma formed a band, a small group of fellow artists, and they began to practice and perform to cut their chops. "We had this little group. There were three of us, Dwight Pinkney, who was a great guitar player, and another guy and they called him Weedy Head. That was like a nickname," she says with a laugh. Pinkney went on to become a successful guitar player with his bands The Sharks, Zap Pow, and Roots Radics. He performed backup for The Wailers on their song "Put It On" and for artists such as Culture, Gregory Isaacs, Yellowman, Bunny Wailer, and The Itals. Weedy Head's real identity is not known. "We were Catholics and we went to the CYO, the Catholic Youth Organization, and we formed our group. So we came up with this song, 'Money Can't Buy Love,' and so we were all singing, practicing. Dwight said, 'Let's go and audition with Roland Alphonso,' and Roland Alphonso took me and said, 'I want her, she has good ears. You guys need to go plant yam or something, enough for you,' and I think Dwight took it to heart and he practice, practice, practice so much he became an accomplished musician. I started to sing with Roland's group. It was a trio. That's the way it started," she says.

The first song that Norma Fraser recorded was a tune called "We'll Be Lovers," a duet with Lord Creator, in 1961. The song was an instant hit and stayed on the Jamaican charts for over a year. She also recorded a tune with Lord Creator called "Come On Baby," and both songs were recorded for Vincent Chin on the Randy's label. But all of Norma Fraser's subsequent songs were recorded at Studio One for Coxsone Dodd. It is extremely unusual during the early 1960s for an artist to record so exclusively for only one producer. Typically, musicians and vocalists would move from studio to studio to seek work—Coxsone Dodd, Duke Reid, King Edwards, Prince Buster, Leslie Kong, Justin Yap, Vincent Chin—making the rounds. There were no contracts, and if there were, they were never honored. But Norma Fraser recorded only for Coxsone Dodd, and she says he was good for her career:

> Coxsone Dodd was extremely powerful, but he was very unassuming. But I think that was a ploy so you would think he is in your corner, he is going to take care of you. "I'm here for you, you don't have to ask me for money now, you know I'll take care of you, just come and do a recording now and I'll take care of you." He didn't act very authoritative, not at all. He had a very easy way about him. He would use the word "Jackson." He call everybody "Jackson." If he say Jackson he would

disarm you. "Oh man, how you doing, Jackson?" He'd call you and say come on in to the studio and do some work, and after you finish he'd say, "Why don't you do two more?" and he's so pleasing that you just go in and do two more. He sees "ching-a-ling!" I was very selective and loyal, I'm that kind of person. The only person I recorded for outside of Coxsone was Randy's, with Lord Creator, and then I went to Coxsone. I didn't go all over the place like a lot of these artists. Very loyal. Super loyal. A lot of these guys, even girls, record for everybody, and they got nothing.

Studio One was the epicenter of the music industry during the 1960s. It was here that she first met Bob Marley and Rita Anderson, becoming close friends to them both. In an interview with a journalist, Fraser told her memories of teaching Rita to sing. "Rita was not a singer but would show up at the studio grounds often. She asked me to teach her how to sing and I did. She then latched on to Bob Marley and would do some backup ooohs behind them," she said.[2] Fraser also told a reporter about a time that Rita consulted her about marrying Bob. "Rita Marley asked me if she should marry Bob and I told her 'Yes, yes.' Rita and myself were friends before I met Bob. She would always hang out at Studio One hoping to get a break, but she could not sing at the time. I taught Rita how to sing. She now refers to me as 'The Legend.'" She and Rita and Bob continued a strong relationship over the decades.

At Studio One, Norma composed many of her own songs. The process of creation, not the music industry, was most important to Norma, but she quickly learned the naïve can suffer for their art, and she grew wise through experience. "I wrote when I was with Studio One. It was natural for me. I didn't really understand that music was a business. Ernest Ranglin arranged some songs for me; I wrote them and he took them to England, they made money. I didn't even know anything about that, I just wrote them. I didn't understand that side, that music was a business. You're not just a performer, you need to be cognizant that there's a business side to this, or economics," Fraser says.

She performed at the Carib Theatre, Ward Theatre, State Theatre, Majestic Theatre, the Copa, and the Ocean View Club in Montego Bay, and she worked with such artists as Ken Boothe, Derrick Harriott, Hortense Ellis, Hopeton Lewis, Desmond Dekker, Delroy Wilson, The Claredonians, The Soul Brothers, Roland Alphonso and another member of the future Skatalites, Jackie Mittoo, who was known for auditioning musicians. She says, "Jackie Mittoo was really the motivating factor, the driving force, and I would just come in and he'd say 'Sing,' and he would just arrange at the same time. Awesome. Just genius, just arranging. We didn't do no rehearsals, those guys were just pros."

She says that the musicians in the studio were more than just professional—they were polite to her and never made her feel uncomfortable. They treated her like a professional as well. "All the musicians were respectful to me because of the way I carried myself, and they know that I'm from uptown. I'm educated, I'm respected. With the other girls they wouldn't do that. But with me they didn't dare. Around me they didn't even curse. Class is embedded in that culture. I remember when I had shows and Roland would pick me up; when he took me home he'd say, 'We need to go because I told Mrs. Fraser I'd have you home at a certain time,' and he'd take me back home," Fraser says.

Spending time with downtown artists in the downtown studios may have ruffled a few feathers in Norma's family, but she stayed true to herself because she had a passion not only for the music but also for the culture and the people. "Jamaica, they're so classist. If you're from this family you have to behave a certain way and you better not deviate from that norm. If you live uptown you're educated, but I was the one who would bring people home from down in the streets because I've always loved the underdog, always," she says. These themes of life and hope made it into the songs Norma wrote: "Hope and love and the human condition. These are things out there that may pose a challenge to us, for us, but together we can solve it together, as a group, the people who are all together on this planet here. We are all one. We are all here to solve problems and if we don't, we die together. You against me, me against you? No, no, no."

Norma Fraser took these messages of love and hope and unity to the stages where she performed and the studios where she recorded. Sure, she recorded her takes on a number of other people's compositions, such as Aretha Franklin's "Respect" and Cat Stevens' "The First Cut Is the Deepest," but she also performed her own compositions around the island with performers of every ilk. "Johnson's Drive-Inn was big. I performed there a bit. I was with a bunch of bands. I was with The Cavaliers, The Sheiks. When I was with The Cavaliers it was a line-up of all of The Skatalites—Jackie Mittoo, Lloyd Spence, Lynn Taitt, Lloyd Knibb, Lester Sterling, Headley Bennett, Bobby Gaynair, the best, the best, and here I am in the front. And we performed in the best clubs, like Club Havana, Jamaica's Latin Quarter, and I perform with Desmond Dekker. I did a song with Lloyd Brynner called 'Malika,' a duet. He was a very very close friend from Trinidad. He would come to Jamaica and go to the studio and we would perform in Montego Bay. I was huge at one time. Big productions," she says.

When Fraser went to Montego Bay, she secured a residency at one of the most prestigious clubs in the tourist hot spot, Club 35. This club opened in Montego Bay on December 21, 1963, and was a membership club that also welcomed tourists. It was a supper club (a dining establishment with a social club) that also featured other types of entertainment including magicians. Lord Brynner frequently produced calypso shows at Club 35. Fraser says she enjoyed her time at Club 35 and was fortunate to get the work. "I got a fantastic gig there when I was very young. I was the featured vocalist. It was a very prestigious club. They were mostly tourist, suit and tie," she says.

Fraser was never satisfied with being relegated to the back of the band when singing, but center stage was a tough gig to find in those days. "There weren't too many women," she says. "But I didn't realize it at the time, didn't categorize it like that or label it that way. There were just a lot of men, really." Journalists of the time noted Fraser's success against the backdrop of the male-dominated industry:

> Female vocalists are now quite scarce on the local pop scene. Ever since it became fashionable for men to sing falsetto accompaniment to pop tunes, the girls have practically disappeared from the show scene. When you do find a girl as part of a group, she's usually just making one more of the many "ooh" and "baybee" sounds which seem necessary for most tunes. For this reason it has been interesting to find a new record out which features a Jamaican girl. She's Norma Fraser.... Norma sings everything—jazz, pop, ballads and even calypsos. But she finds the field for women vocalists in Jamaica is very limited. On the pop scene, it is group stuff which the fans are buying and the successful groups are mainly all-male. But, according to Norma, she's not disheartened. In her travels, she has established contacts which should bring return engagements in various places. For the home scene, she would like to link up with a good band. She thinks show business, with all its uncertainty, beats school teaching any day.[3]

When the ska and rocksteady era changed over to reggae, Norma sang for some of the artists who have now become legendary. But it isn't her performances that she remembers from this time as much as the friendships she made, which are still a critical part of her spirit. In 1966 she performed with The Wailers on "I Stand Predominant" and on Peter Tosh's "Rasta Shook Them Up." But the end of the '60s signaled an end to Norma's musical career in Jamaica, as she left the country, disenfranchised with the direction of the industry. Even though Bob Marley asked her to join his group, she declined. She moved to the United States in 1970 and virtually left the entertainment business altogether, except for performing for Bella Abzug, a congresswoman from New York, during her campaign for election. Abzug was instrumental in the support of gay rights, and while in Congress she introduced the very first national gay rights bill, the Equality Act of 1974. She co-authored the bill with fellow congressman Ed Koch, who went on to become mayor of New York. Abzug once said, "I've been described as a tough and noisy woman, a prizefighter, a man-hater, you name it. They call me Battling Bella."[4]

As much as Fraser may have been an instrument of social equality herself, standing tall among the men of her day, she is not a fighter, not one to battle in that sense of the word. Instead she is a collaborator, a comrade, a friend. She is still friends with Rita Marley today and remembers Bob Marley fondly. "Bob and I were alike, very giving and sharing. We'd give you the shirt off our back. If you want it, you can have it. He was a good person. There are two things I value, and that's honesty and integrity, no matter who you are. You have those two things and you're my friend for life," she says.

In America, Norma returned to her roots in more than one way. First, she got her master's degree in gerontology and psychotherapy. Education was always important to the Fraser family. Second, after two decades away, she came back to music. In the 1990s she supported Inner Circle and Yellowman on their tours, and she went on a solo tour to Colorado and Texas. She still regularly performs on the West Coast; she resides in Oregon. She has released a number of solo albums in recent years including *Get Up Stand Up*, *One More Chance*, *C'mon Baby*, and *Hot Again* on her own label, Gyftt Records. She says, "I'm getting back to my music now because over the past years, so many people have come up to me to tell me how the music has bettered their lives. They've encouraged me to come back. I'm more mature now and truly understand how music can bring joy to people's lives."

Marcia Griffiths, OD, with the Gaylettes, the Soulettes, and the I-Threes

When one thinks of Marcia Griffiths one might envision a fabric-swathed singer swaying peacefully with her two sistren behind a jumping Bob Marley in denim and locks. Or one might recall hearing her voice through a DJ's speaker on a tripod stand above a group of family members at a wedding as they stepped and turned in unison to the "Electric Slide." So what does Marcia Griffiths have to do with the early days of Jamaican music? Like many reggae and contemporary musicians from Jamaica, Griffiths began her career in ska and rocksteady. She has performed continually as a vocalist for over 50 years.

Marcia Llyneth Griffiths was born on November 23, 1949, in Kingston. She was part of a warm and loving family and describes her childhood as pleasant despite the fact that they had few resources to go around. "In my growing up years we had a whole lot of love in our family. When we didn't have bread to put on the table, the love that we had kept us together. We were just bonded in love—the whole family—my father, mother, grandmother, my three sisters, and my one brother, and whoever else was there as a family member, we never knew any other way other than love. Growing up we would go to church together and do things together as a family. As little kids we hear our parents talking with each other, adults, and we would sit and listen, talking about days gone by, and it was just so beautiful. If I had a choice to be young again and eliminate my memories from my childhood growing up until now, I would prefer to keep my memories and my experience," says Griffiths.[5]

Her mother Beatrice and her father Joseph made a happy home for the family. Her father was a furniture maker and her mother raised the children. Griffiths says, "I still have some beautiful furniture in my house that he made. My mom gave us all the love and support we needed as a family. She stayed at home and took care of us and made sure everything was right, and whatever little we had, she would stretch it to make sure everyone was fine. Most children would say their mommies are the best cooks, but all the children who knew my mother, they have no doubt, they never hesitate to say my mother was the best cook. My mother was Indian, and she made not only things with curry or roti, she made every other dish you could think of. My mother's father was from India and my father was Jamaican from St. Elizabeth. I grew up right in Kingston, I was in Hannah Town." Hannah Town is located just south of Trench Town and north of the former location of Back O Wall, a settlement that was bulldozed and burned by Edward Seaga—without warning to residents—to build Tivoli Gardens.

Marcia attended Kingston Senior School and began singing at an early age. She says, "I sang in church and school, all the concerts when we were getting holiday concerts in the school—I would be very active in singing and dancing and acting and doing everything. I was just enjoying all that, as a young child coming up. I never had any vision of singing as a professional. I was just having fun singing. My other sisters are fantastic singers too, so we were all active, in school and church, singing all the time. The only reason why they are not in show business today is they were very, very shy. I was the bravest one. I remember my dad singing Archie Lewis and all those other guys who sang way back when. My dad even wrote a song for me, but I never recorded it—but I always remember that song."

Marcia's father was not a soft person. With a family to support, he was the one who set the rules in the home: "He was a caretaker and he was very strict. I was not allowed to speak with any strange guys … or touch anyone. He was very, very strict. Ever since we were born, we knew our father like that. We were so afraid of him. My mother was like an angel. Never ever had to flog us at any time. Dad was the one who did all that. We were good kids, but I was very afraid of him, so I do the right thing. He had to go with me to concerts because me and my sisters were young (and I was the youngest of the three) and he was the one who insist to go everywhere."

Marcia's love for music extended beyond her school and church. Even though her father was strict, her older sister was able to take her around the city to hear musicians perform. One of Marcia's older sisters lived in Rockfort on the southeast side of the city. It was while visiting her one day that she heard a group that would go on to become popular on the island. It was also the start of a relationship that would become legendary. "The Paragons were rehearsing. They were a group of three guys, and Bob Andy was a part of that group. He formed that group. And when we stopped up at the rehearsal with those guys—I'm a little girl and I was with my eldest sister—and we stopped and we were listening to them, and before she left that room they were rehearsing in, she was pulling my arm through the door and I said, 'I can sing too, you know,' and Barry, one of the guys, said, 'Sing a song for me.' And Patti LaBelle was popular in Jamaica, she had a song called 'Down the Aisle,' and I started singing that song and they said, 'Wow, this little girl has a big voice.' So after I left that rehearsal I never saw those guys again. It was not until I was at Studio One—when I went there one day, I saw them walk in the studio and Barry said to the other two guys, 'Hey look! It's Patti LaBelle!' They were very surprised to see me there and that's how I met them back," she says.

How Marcia Griffiths came to find herself at Studio One is a story of being in the right place at the right time, although in Kingston during the 1960s, right places were plentiful, as musicians of all types were springing up all around—sound systems on corner after corner, trombones and trumpets in Coxsone Dodd's and Duke Reid's and Leslie Kong's studios, vocalists on the stages of the Ward and the Palace, and drums in the Wareika Hills. Singing in her yard one day, Marcia was discovered by a young Phillip James, member of the popular singing duo, the Blues Busters, with Lloyd Campbell. Griffiths remembers,

> That's the man who discovered me. He came because he was visiting his girlfriend right where I was living. I wasn't allowed to be outside after 8 o'clock at any time. He came there before eight, and he heard me singing right by the gate with another guy who used to live in the same place where we were. The guy was playing his guitar and I was singing and harmonizing the guy.... He heard me singing with this guy and harmonizing, and he stopped and he said, "This little girl can sing." And I looked at him and said, "I have another song that I can sing for you." And I sang a couple of songs for him and he said, "Man, I have to get you on the show Easter Monday morning." ... He went to Byron Lee and he told him he heard this little girl and he would love to have her on the show and Byron said, "No way. My show is already planned, nobody else is coming on the show." So they just refused me, and he insisted and he insisted and he insisted and he said, "You have to listen to this little girl, Byron." Byron said, "Okay, let her come to the rehearsal. One song," and I went to the rehearsal and the musicians, Byron Lee and the Dragonaires, the musicians weren't with it to back me at all. They also were refusing me. They didn't want to learn the song and anyway they finally learn the one song that I rehearsed, "No Time to Lose" by Carla Thomas. Phillip was very happy that at least I came to the rehearsal and he's going to expose me now because he just kept saying, "Boy, I've never heard a singer like you." And he said to me, "Little girl, don't get nervous," and I said, "No!"

Marcia Griffiths performing in 1969 (copyright The Gleaner Company [Media] Limited).

Byron Lee agreed to allow Marcia Griffiths perform with them at the Easter show, but the musicians in his band weren't so supportive. She says,

> I went to the Carib Theatre that morning with my dad. He came with me and when they call me on stage, I walked out there. I was more anxious to go on stage than

anything else because I wanted to show everybody what I could do. I don't know anything about being shy or nervous, I just know that I am going out there to sing. So I went on stage and I'm there, standing on stage, waiting for the guitar to start the song, cause the guitar starts that song, and there is nothing happening. It's like they are doing everything on purpose just to mess me up. Even at that tender age, I heard a voice say to me, "Little girl, start singing," because the audience got to start sounding a little uneasy. I am standing there, and the band is just playing rubbish, like they forgot everything. I know it was the voice of God, and I just started singing the song all by myself and they had to follow me. Yes, they followed me and let me tell you, I've never had an experience like that, because in those days when you are emulating a singer that inspires you like Aretha Franklin and all those big female singers.... You dot every *i* and you cross every *t*, so if you close your eyes, you would think that was Carla Thomas singing, but I do every slur and I'm harmonizing at the same time and every time I make a slur the audience just goes up in a roar. Every time I am doing something that they're not expecting—because I'm 99 pounds, one skinny little, and they're not expecting that from me at all—the audience just went wild. And when I finished, the audience just could not stop. The emcee was Tony Verity. He went on stage and they yelled, "Bring her back! Do the same song! Bring her back!" But I didn't go back, but that was my big moment on Easter Monday morning.

Despite the rocky start, the performance went so well that Griffiths' musical career was instantly ignited. "That very same day I went on television and I was taken straight to Studio One recording studio and I was not auditioned or anything. I went straight into the studio and started recording," she says.

Marcia Griffiths' first recording on Coxsone's Supreme label was "Wall of Love." She began as a vocalist on her own, and she performed regularly with Byron Lee and the Dragonaires. She recorded a number of hits for Studio One including "Truly," "Funny," "I Cry Alone," and others, but it was the song "Feel Like Jumping" that took over the charts. "It was not until '67 that I got that hit, 'Feel Like Jumping,'" says Griffiths. The rocksteady song was written by Bob Andy, and Jackie Mittoo, keyboardist for the Skatalites and essential musician at Studio One, was the song's musical arranger. And Marcia performed on stage for the American artists who toured the Jamaica. "I performed with every one that came because I became the one lone female that was reigning, winning all the awards. So everybody that came to our little island, all the American artists, I would be a part of it—Carla Thomas came there, Ben E. King, every single one, Patti LaBelle came a couple of times, Gladys Knight. A lot of American artists," she says.

Coxsone also paired Griffiths with other singers. "I started out as a solo singer and even though Coxsone was putting me with all these other guys, he was just seeking a hit song for me because he was so overwhelmed with my talent. I've never ever relinquished my solo career," she says. Those duo partners included Tony Gregory, Bob Marley, Owen Boyce, Jeff Dixon, Ernest Wilson, Jimmy Riley, Beres Hammond, and of course, Bob Andy. The duo of Bob and Marcia, a pairing of Griffiths with that Paragon she met previously at rehearsal in Rockfort, would prove to be an incredibly popular combination; the two even released their own album of hits. But Bob Andy was more than just a singing partner for Marcia—he was a mentor. Griffiths remembers, "Being a young girl in a male dominated business, you're vulnerable to all kinds of things. Mr. Dodd was the one who was so desperate for me to have a hit song, so what he did was have me doing collaborations with Bob Marley, Tony Gregory, Bob Andy, and so forth. Bob Andy had to start writing songs for me, which is how we start being friendly, and everything started there. Bob was writing everything for me at that point, he was writing all of my songs. Song after song after song. He was more experienced, a little older, and was definitely a big brother, definitely." Bob Andy wrote "Mark My Word," "Tell Me Now," "Feel Like Jumping," and "Melody Life" for Marcia Griffiths. They were all recorded for Studio One.

Bob and Marcia came together as a vocal duo at the suggestion of record producer Harry Johnson, who was known as Harry J. Johnson had produced the song "No More Heartaches" by The Beltones, a tune that is arguably the first reggae song. Johnson was able to take the attributes of both Griffiths and Andy to create a pop sensation in both Jamaica and England.

Bob Andy, who was born Keith Anderson, had been recording as a solo star with his first big hit, "I've Got to Go Back Home," in 1966, and as a member of The Paragons with Tyrone (Don) Evans and Howard Barrett, later joined by John Holt. Bob Andy was the song writer for The Paragons, as he was for Marcia Griffiths as Bob and Marcia. He had been inspired by Bob Dylan to become a songwriter. Andy left The Paragons in 1964. Evans and Barrett split to go to Duke Reid, and Andy went to Coxsone Dodd, first as a record salesman and then as a songwriter and artist. But Bob and Marcia left Coxsone to record with Johnson since they weren't getting enough money from Dodd.

Bob and Marcia were a big hit in Jamaica as well as overseas. Their biggest success came in 1970, when they recorded the classic "Young, Gifted and Black," a song originally by Nina Simone based on the autobiography of Lorraine Hansbury. The single sold 500,000 copies in the UK and Europe and the entire album by the same name sold well too. Bob and Marcia continued to record and had another hit with "Pied Piper" in 1971. This song was a cover song as well; it was by Crispian St. Peters, who had written and recorded it five years earlier in the UK. The Bob and Andy version was much less mod and instead was smooth and soulful, with just enough flute to recall St. Peters' tune.

To promote their success, Bob and Marcia appeared on the hit British show *Top of the Pops* and toured England, Europe, and Holland with such headlining stars as Elton John and Rod Stewart. They appeared on television shows in Holland, and they also sang backup for Johnny Nash. They recorded additional songs for Harry J. which were shelved for years until the contract with CBS ran out and Andy was able to release them on his Nectar Records label. Andy continued to work with Johnson over the years, but when Griffiths and Andy returned to Jamaica after touring, they both decided to pursue solo careers.

Griffiths decided to record for producer Sonia Pottinger on her High Note label. "She was the only female producer that we had. She was absolutely amazing. She was understanding. Whenever you are comfortable and relaxed you work better. Working with her, I found that better things come out of me. I can always come in and kid with her, and she understands and give me inspiration, to think about my songs," says Griffiths. She recorded the song "Toil (Talk)" in 1969 before returning to record a number of additional songs for Pottinger from 1975 to 1979.

In the mid–1970s, Marcia Griffiths career took a new direction as she formed a singing group with two other women—Rita Marley and Judy Mowatt. Together the women were known as The I-Three, sometimes called The I-Threes, and they were the backup singers for none other than Bob Marley. "I met Rita in Studio One when I went there in '64. Rita, Peter, Bunny—but Bunny and myself went to kindergarten school together, way back. So he was the one I knew there when I was there. So when I met Rita, Judy wasn't singing yet, but Judy would tell me that when I was on a stage and I used to perform, she used to look through the hole to watch me performing there. She would come and watch me. But she started out as The Gaylettes," says Griffiths.

In a 1981 interview, Judy Mowatt explained how she began her singing career, first with the all-female singing trio The Gaylettes.

> I was born in 1952 in a little village in St. Andrew and I started singing there as a little girl with my grandmother. I was raised by my grandmother and I used to go down to the gulley every day and sing to the trees and the breeze and she always tell me, "Girl one day, you are going to be a singer," but I always wanted to be a preacher. I wanted to be a gospel preacher. When I realize the work I am doing now, I am doing preaching but it's in a different fashion. It's in the music. I have started with the Gaylettes. First of all I was a creative dancer. I always liked singing but I was very shy at the time and I didn't want to go up there on my own, I was afraid of the limelight. So I teamed up with a group called the Estraleta Dancers. We went to places like Grand Cayman, we performed in these areas, Ocho Rios, Montego Bay. One evening we were in the bathroom after the rehearsal and two sisters from the Gaylettes, the group had mashed up, they split and one of the sisters left and they heard me singing, I was always singing in my little spare time and they said, "Boy you have a good voice and we're looking for a lead singer for the group," and I went into the group and we went down to a company called Federal Records in Jamaica, the Khouris owned it, and we went for an audition.... Well there was a brother there called Henry Buckley, he's a very good songwriter and a singer but he hasn't gotten much exposure as a singer, but as a songwriter, and he had a song that was giving him problem, he couldn't find the background vocal group to sing background singing for the song, so they told us to try. They gave us the lines and the phrases and they told us to try and do some work on it. And after we finish doing it they were so impressed that they asked Henry to write a couple of songs for us and the first song he wrote for us was called "Silent River Runs Deep" and that was number one on the Jamaican Hit Parade chart on both stations, RJR and JBC. And that's how we got started. That was about in 1965 with Beryl Lawson and Merle Clemonson. We stayed together about four years.[6]

Mowatt says The Gaylettes, whose songs were more soul or American rhythm and blues than ska, recorded songs such as "I Like Your World," and "Son of a Preacher Man." She said, "In Jamaica at that time nobody write their own material, as we hear a foreign song we always adapt it because the producer at that time never instill in you to do something of your own composition. He always wants to make money off the other person's composition so as he hears a song he says, 'Listen to this,' and he would write out the words and we cut it the next day, press it that same evening and then it's months after and you never even know how much it has sold because we were so enthusiastic about singing and getting our voices on record.... We were being exploited because you were never told how much your songs were sold and you were given a small money and you have to be behind these people every day, I mean you work for them and even lunch money in the day you have to go there begging them for lunch when they have your record is selling and they make it look as if you owe them, when it's these people owe you."

Mowatt had a daughter, Yashemabeth, with reggae artist Freddie McGregor. Yashemabeth began singing backup vocals for her mother Judy at age nine. "My mother has influenced me tremendously, but more so as an individual versus being an entertainer. My mother raised her five children on her own and was always a very independent woman who taught that through work we will see our rewards," said Yashemabeth McGregor.[7] Mowatt raised her children while touring and singing all over the world. Judy made hard choices and faced challenges along the way that were unique to the female position. Reporter Tanya Batson once wrote, "Judy Mowatt's success also stands as a testament to the need for confident assertion. Like many women in the business, Judy Mowatt was also involved with a man whom she says tried to control her music. She pointed out that he wanted total control of her, telling her what to wear and what to sing. She was still determined not to be controlled, however, and thus her response was 'No *iyah*!' Her position as one of the queens of reggae resulted from this stance."[8]

The Gaylettes broke up in 1970 when Lawson and Clemonson moved to America. Mowatt went on to record as a solo artist with producer Sonia Pottinger as Julianne or Julian, since she was under contract with Federal Records. She had known Pottinger since 1964, when the Gaylettes recorded a number of songs for Lindon Pottinger on the Gay Disc label, which Sonia took over after she split from Lindon.

The Soulettes, Rita Marley's vocal trio, comprised Marlene Gifford, a childhood friend of Marley's, and Constantine Walker, Marley's cousin. Marlene Gifford was sometimes replaced by Hortense Lewis, and vocalists Nora Dean and Cecile Campbell also sang from time to time. Nora Dean, born in 1952, was also a successful soloist, with such hits as the bawdy "Barbwire (in Your Underpants)," "Mojo Girl," "Heartaches," and "Wreck a Buddy," which she performed with The Soul Sisters. Rita Marley wasn't Rita Marley during the days of The Soulettes; she was Alpharita Anderson, born in Cuba before moving to Trench Town in Kingston at a young age.

In 1965 she recorded as Girl Wonder on Dodd's Port-O-Jam label, a single called "Cutting Wood" with the B side "Mommy Out De Light." "Cutting Wood" was a mento song by Louise Lamb cut on the Crystal label in 1956. (Louise and her cousin Blossom Lamb were popular jazz singers in Kingston during the mid–1950s; see ch. 3). Because of Rita Marley's marriage to Bob Marley, much has been written on her life, so a focus on The Soulettes is more germane to this discussion. The Soulettes, who were sometimes billed as The Sweet Soulettes, performed live at venues including the Sombrero Club, the Ferry Club, and the Carib Theatre. A review of one of their performances from 1971 features comments that would likely never appear for male performers. "Their harmony sends needle like action in your body; like a romance approaching a blissful climax," states the journalist "R.R."[9] The Soulettes began recording for Coxsone Dodd as early as 1965 and were later produced by Bob Marley and Lee "Scratch" Perry. In 1971, Allan "Skill" Cole, a famous Jamaican soccer player and close personal friend to Bob Marley, took over management for The Soulettes, along with The Wailers (who had previously been managed by Lee "Scratch" Perry) and The Pipers (who were previously called The Wailing Souls and before that, The Renegades).

Griffiths met Rita Marley in 1964. She remembers when she first met Judy Mowatt at Studio One:

> Rita was in the Soulettes, and Judy had the Gaylettes. I heard that Judy was a good singer, but I never actually get the chance to meet her, until one day Mr. Dodd had us coming in separately to do some harmonies for him at Studio One, and none of us knew that we were going to meet up there. So that was something that I think was ordained by God. We all three met there and did some work for Mr. Dodd and some harmonies on some different recordings that he had there. So that was a time I had a weekend at a popular club called House of Chen. It was a very popular place, and I was doing the entire weekend there—Friday, Saturday, and Sunday. I said, "Girls, would you like to come and do some harmonies for me?" And they were excited, and they said, "Sure, we want to come," and they came and did Friday, Saturday, and Sunday. On the last night we did a little jam thing on the stage. The Sweet Inspirations were the biggest group in Jamaica. Whitney Houston's mother was a part of that group—Cissy Houston—and every song they made was a hit song in Jamaica. We did some of those songs on stage for a little jam session, and the audience went wild. And people say, "Why don't you girls get together and form a group?" and everybody encourage us. I said, "Yeah, why don't we do that?" So we decided yes, we're going to do it. And I decide "Let's call ourselves I-Threes"; and Rita said, "I-Three?" I said, yes, as if we're saying We-Threes, we say I-Threes. So that's how everything started with the group right there and then. It was like another thing that was ordained again. That group was formed at the same time that Bob, Peter, and Bunny had a fall out. When he heard that we had a group formed, he just ask us to come in and do "Natty Dread." Yep. That was the beginning of history.

It was 1974 when The I-Three officially formed, says Marcia, and one year later she had a son. She had two more with Errol Thompson, a disc jockey for the Jamaica Broadcasting Corporation, who died in 1983 (not to be confused with Errol Thompson, the recording engineer who was prolific in the 1970s and died in 2004). She essentially raised her children on her own, which was a challenge considering she chose to continue her music career. And having her first child right at the start of her touring with Bob Marley as a member of The I-Three was like being thrown straight into the fire. "Oh, it was not easy at all!" she says. "Everything I earned went into having someone ... capable to take care of him, and calling on the phone every single day, three, four times to make sure everything is good. And when I get the opportunity to take him, I'm gone with him on the road. We had a good sister who was traveling with us, who give us food, so I would ask permission from Bob if I could take him, and I take him along a lot of times. I had two other children. Number one for me is family. That come before everything else," says Griffiths.

The success of The I-Three is well known and well documented. They performed for Bob Marley from 1974 until his death in 1981. All three women then pursued solo careers or projects of their own. Griffiths never took a break from performing. Notable is a song that Griffiths recorded in 1981—the song "Woman a Come," which was originally written and performed by Margarita Mahfood for Duke Reid in 1964 with Baba Brooks. Mahfood was Don Drummond's lover before she died at his hands on January 2, 1965. Griffiths knew Mahfood and lived in the same neighborhood, Rockfort. "I knew that girl personally. Bunny Wailer was the one that suggested that song, and he was the only who did the cover of that song for me. I recorded it, but it was his suggestion that I do that song. It's a simple song but it has strong meaning. When she says 'Woman a Come, Jah dawta from Ethiopian [sic, Venturian] border,' you know? It's just simple but it's very effective. When I heard that song first I said that song is hardly saying anything much, but it is simple and powerful. And I like the idea when Bunny suggested I do that song, and the arrangements that he put to that song made it so fantastic. Margarita was a beautiful girl, and she was also so very talented. I was very moved when I found out she was the writer. She is not just a beautiful girl. She is deeper than I thought, who thought about the things she wrote," Griffiths says.

Marcia Griffiths had also worked with Bunny Wailer, her childhood friend, to record "Electric Boogie," that staple of all wedding receptions. The song was recorded in 1982 but it wasn't until 1989 that the song really took off after a DJ in Washington, DC, began playing it frequently. The dance that now accompanies this song, the "Electric Slide," was originally created by choreographer Ric Silver of Connecticut in 1976, before the song was recorded. The dance is described by the copyright certificate held by Silver as a "Four Wall Dance Fugue."

From a very young age, singing was in Griffiths' blood, and she has never stopped making music a part of her life. "As a little girl, every day I listen to the radio and I hear all these ladies sing beautiful songs—Dionne Warwick, Carla Thomas, Nancy Wilson. The first song I can remember I started singing was Ruby and the Romantics' [sings] 'Our Day Will Come,' and my father used to say, 'Don't worry my love, your day will come one day.' I used to love that song. But when I hear all these female singers on the radio doing some beautiful songs, I used to just sing on top of it, and if I could find any harmonies I would harmonize the songs they are doing. I knew these songs like the back of my hand. No matter how many harmonies in the song, I would find another harmony to sing. If a fly passed me by, I would harmonize that fly. I just loved singing harmony," she says.

Many have called Marcia Griffiths a role model, especially women. She came from meager beginnings and through skill, strength, determination, and an unwillingness to be shaken by obstacles thrown in her path, she persevered and became a star. She is arguably the most successful woman in Jamaican music, yesterday and today. Griffiths says, "As someone who is celebrating 50 years in the business, I am not one of the artists that just count the years and say, well because I start in '64 till now it's 50 years—I'm talking about consecutive work, always working, always traveling. I'm just always in the mix. It's always hard work. So I pat myself on my shoulder for that. Love and blessings."

Dawn Penn

Many Jamaicans received their musical tutelage in church. Regardless of financial ability and access, the church was a place where children could learn to sing with harmony, be surrounded by the sounds of the organ, feel rhythm and tempo, and participate or perform in front of an audience. Dawn Penn's grandparents were Quakers (Quakers originated in the United Kingdom and traveled to Pennsylvania and Delaware to establish sects of their group before settling in the Caribbean), so she certainly had a childhood in the church, and it was here that she too cut her musical chops.

Born in 1952 to William MacFarlane Penn and Emelyn Penn, Dawn Penn was one of three girls. Her sisters, Claudette and Audrey, were always by her side. She grew up first at 133 Luke Lane, where her family occupied two rooms in a ten-room tenement yard. Penn remembers the activity on nearby Orange Street and North Street, even from a young age. In her book, *Story of My Life*, Penn writes,

> Prince Buster's Record Shop could be found up Orange Street before you get to Charles Street. He became a Muslim and started a mosque on the premises. Coxson's Record Shop—"Musik City" was in the same block—on the opposite side of Prince Buster's Record shop on Orange Street and Producer Leslie Kong operated Beverley's Records at the corner of North and Orange Streets. Later on Beverley's Records installed a lounge area and put a piano in the room. Jimmy Cliff, Millie Small, Owen Grey, and Jackie Edwards had all been there long before my time.... Many years afterwards, the Clarendonians, Desmond Dekker and the Aces, and I used to meet up either at Beverley's or at the Boxing Ring/Race Course [now called Heroes Circle] to practice on the piano on the premises. Later on in 1996 I was touring with Desmond Dacres, also known as Desmond Dekker in Europe doing 30 shows after taking the boat from Ram's Gate, crossing the channel to Holland, ending up in Marseille, or Calais in France.[10]

So how did Dawn go from tenement yard to the stage with Desmond Dekker? Penn's father worked for the United Fruit Company and would go to the wharf for three days at a time to load ships, but he was also an active member of the Salvation Army located at Bramwell Booth Memorial Hall, 19 North Parade (near Randy's Records). Dawn would attend church with her family, then Sunday school. "My dad was very strict and used to wear a belt that exposed his bullets and gun in a holster. It wasn't a good thing to get him upset," writes Penn. One of the members of this congregation was Miss Campbell, who taught piano lessons; Dawn began at age eight. Dawn was also mentored by two women who were members of the North Street Congregational Church Choir, and Dawn admired their beautiful voices. Dawn attended both churches, and she also attended a week-long camp each year hosted by the Salvation Army's Singing Company. "My sisters and I were members of the young people's choir for the church. We learned to play the tambourine (decorated with colorful ribbons)," she writes.[11]

When Dawn was ten years old, her parents moved to a home at 148 Church Street. She began taking piano lessons from a more formal, classical teacher, Mrs. Lena Robinson, who taught scales, theory, and "the rudiments of music and sight-reading sheet music." She not only had a strict father who helped to shape her discipline and nature for achievement, but also had a schoolteacher who demanded much from her students and was even abusive. Despite this, Dawn says, the teacher was an influence on her life. Her name was Linda Robinson, known as Miss Rob, and she was headmistress of North Street Congregational Primary School, where Dawn took private education lessons on Saturdays to prepare for her high school entrance exams. "Miss Rob was a schoolteacher. She used to hold the cane, go up on her toes, and come down on your hand on the back. If you did something wrong, like you didn't do your homework, or if you were rude in the class, or any fighting or anything, she's going to beat you. The boys used to get beatings on their butts so they would put a book in their clothes and when she found that out, she would beat you more. Sometimes we would get five lashes, ten lashes. But that discipline that we got made us into who we are today," she said.[12]

Dawn was also surrounded by music in the home. "My dad played the organ in the house that you had to put your foot on it and pump it to get the sound, and he played the box guitar which was in the house, and he played the accordion as well. And he took us to learn the piano because he knew the teacher on the next road. Pat, Audrey, and I, we used to go around and sing in church, and I used to play for them. I wasn't singing at that time. We used to call ourselves the Penn Sisters. We used to go to different churches, and they used to sing gospel songs and I used to back them up on the piano," she says. "My mom was a nurse and she worked in the hospital, Kingston Public Hospital. She came up in the ranks. From 18 she was in nursing. She was American." Her mother was also involved in the Salvation Army choir.

When Dawn was just entering high school, her family moved to 6 Marlborough Road, and she attended St. Hugh's High School. After performing in concerts for the Salvation Army and churches, Dawn entered another contest, encouraged by her piano teacher. Dawn and another student named Hazel Stewart performed in the classical duet category for a performance at the Ward Theatre commemorating Jamaica's Independence celebrations. They came in first place. But Dawn also decided to enter another category on her own—in this one, singing instead of playing the piano. It was in the pop music category. Instead of Dawn Penn, she chose a pen name, Connie McGann, because, she says, "Some of my friends said my real name wasn't sounding good." She performed her own accompaniment on organ and sang a song she herself had composed called "Make Up Your Mind." The performance took place at the Tropical Theatre, and she received second place. A vocalist named Beverley Simmonds came in first. Simmonds went on to record on the Pama, Stag, and Island record labels in the late 1960s.

Dawn says that as a result of the contest, she was awarded a scholarship for additional musical education. She continued her work in piano and also studied violin with a woman named Miss Scott. At the same time, Dawn started copying some of the popular styles of the day—rhythm and blues, ska, and rocksteady. "I thought I knew everything about music, and anytime I heard music playing on the radio, I would try to play the song on the piano by ear," she says. She was hearing the popular music not only on the radio but also on the stages around Kingston. She writes,

> One Sunday afternoon my sisters and I left Sunday school and went to a dance by Tommy McCook and the Skatalites at the Orange Bowl on Orange Street. It was getting late that afternoon and my dad was looking for my sisters and me. He asked a lady who lived on the way if she saw us and she told him we had passed up the street. While on the premises I heard that my dad was at the gate paying to get in the venue. Luckily for us we were able to take off by scaling the fence and rushed home to reach before he returned.... I was a frequent follower of Tommy McCook and the Skatalites with singer Doreen Schaeffer [sic], Lord Creator and Jackie Mittoo who fascinated me as he played jazz and sounded like Jimmy Smith on the organ. My sisters and I used to follow Merritone's sessions almost everywhere they went even when they went out of town. My sister Pat, and another girl and I backed the Jamaicans, doing a dance routine while they were performing their hit song "Baba Boom Time" for the Independence Festival Competition. I used to be at Sombrero Club—Molynes Road on Wednesdays—that was the beginning of the weekend for me. Johnsons' Drive-Inn to listen to Granville Williams and his band, Byron Lee and the Dragonaires at the Ruin Club in Ocho Rios on Sunday nights and Carlos Malcolm and his band at Club Havana off Windward Road. I later played organ for an all-girls band called The Carnations. We rehearsed at their family home in Havendale.[13]

She adds that she frequented the *Vere Johns Opportunity Hour* at the Palace Theatre to watch the performances, as well as the Pantomime at the Ward Theatre.

Dawn got her first taste of broadcast performance while working at the Jamaica Broadcasting Company: "I studied filing, bookkeeping, typing, and Pitman's shorthand at Kingston Senior School in the evenings," she writes.

> I pursued and received a diploma in journalism for radio and TV script writing with the Canadian Institute of Science and Technology long before technology became a household name. Later on I got a job as a reporter in the news room at JBC Radio Station.... We used to get the news from overseas sources like from Reuters or CNN and we would cut, splice, edit, and time the news for the afternoon broadcast. One afternoon while I was in the canteen the TV director, Mr. Desmond Elliott, asked me if I could come and sing one of my songs he named "Don't Sleep on the Subway," or "I'll Let You Go," as the artist had left the building and they had to be on the air in 10 minutes.... Almost every weekend onwards I was on this programme.

Dawn Penn later released the song "Don't Sleep in the Subway Darling" under the name Suzette.

Dawn explains how she began her career in recording, although to her, it wasn't a career, it was just something she did for fun. "I wouldn't even call it work. I record a few tracks for Coxsone. Sometimes they want you to just record the song and they don't pay you anything, you just come and record as a project, so I find out that he record like that. But the first song that was recorded of me was a song called, 'When I'm Gonna Be Free.' I didn't know it was recorded. I was actually playing the piano at Beverley's and this guy recorded me and I didn't know anything about that song that I record until about eight years ago. At the time I thought my first recording was at Coxsone's," she says.

The first song that Dawn Penn recorded for Coxsone was called "You Don't Love Me." She remembers the musical process in her memoir:

> I had some friends who visited Studio One regularly including my friend Cherry who got married to Tyrone Evans of the Paragons and one Sunday in 1967. I followed them there and did an audition. I sang, "You Don't Love Me," and Mr. Dodd said I had a jazzy voice. He gave me some tips on how I should sing the song and said that I should return the following day to record. Musically, Jackie Mittoo and I arranged the music for the song using major 9th, augmented and diminished chords. I was sitting beside him on the seat as he put them in to make the chords sound fat and big. Johnny Moore arranged his solo part that he played on coronet. Nonetheless I was set to do this track backed by Tommy McCook and the Skatalites including Lloyd Brevett who stood and played his string bass while Roland Alphonso played his saxophone. Also in the recording, the band made a mistake—they

should have changed the progression chords and they didn't. It didn't sound too noticeable and they kept it instead of starting all over.[14]

She elaborated on this during a conversation, saying, "If you know music, and you know the song, you will figure it out. The band was playing the theme because in those days, when we record, everyone has to be on the same page. Everyone had to listen to each other. If there was any mistake you have to start from scratch.... They play the song but they construct part of the song with bridges, where they are supposed to change the chord, and the song they didn't change the chord there. We just ride it out. Johnny Moore, who played the solo, ... he had a problem with his girlfriend and that's why he played like that."

It was a time of musical communion when musicians and vocalists were in abundance at the studios. "I used to work with Bob Marley when Johnny Nash worked with him, that's even before he formed the I-Threes. It was just Bob, Peter, and Bunny was there, and we used to be upstairs at Randy's every afternoon from three until after morning, recording and creating songs," Dawn says. She adds that later in life, when she worked in the banking industry, she helped to secure a loan for Bob Marley so that he could fund equipment for his Tuff Gong studio.

But money never came from the music for Dawn. The issue of not being paid for songs was part of the landscape in Jamaican music during this era, and although it may not have affected Dawn so much during her youth since she held other jobs in the business sector, it certainly affected her over the course of her life, since her songs were incredibly successful and earned big money for the producers. She recorded not only for Coxone but also for others:

> I moved to Prince Buster's place and did one of my original material, "Blue Yes Blue," written by me alone. The saxophonist was Mr. Val Bennett and Gladdie [Gladstone Anderson] on keyboard, a pick-up studio band with Lynn Taitt—they later called themselves The Jets. On another note, I played the violin on one of my original track called "Here's the Key," recorded for Prince Buster as well. I went to Duke Reid's studio at Bond Street. He had a liquor store managed by his wife, and he was doing an album project with Phyllis Dillon from Linstead. At the time I had a song, "I Just Can't Forget About You"; this she sang, and I sang "Why Did You Lie," my originals. Boris Gardiner was playing in the session, and Boris and I, along with the band, created an instrumental track called "Moody Ska." Mr. Reid was an ex-policeman and he wore twelve rings on his ten fingers. If you were not recording or singing as you should, he would just fire some gunshots and the scare alone would make you neither miss the key note nor the words. Also if you sang a hit, he would follow the same procedure, plus he had his police friends visiting him from time to time.... Loads of singers were there, including Alton Ellis and the Flames, The Jamaicans, The Melodians, and many more. I always went to record for Prince Buster. Prince Buster hasn't paid me either. And his lawyer is saying to prove that I am the writer of the songs. Prince Buster put his name like he wrote the songs I sung for him. He never did write no songs for me though. And you know what Coxsone told me? Coxsone told me he wrote "No No No," and he put his name and then I put my name on it.

"No No No (You Don't Love Me)" was Penn's most successful song, recorded in 1967 for Studio One. "Because I was a woman, I haven't got any royalties from all these years I did ska and rocksteady and all this different music. We didn't treat our music as a business, so we never had a manager, knew about publishing and all these things, so it was a problem. We never knew until 20 or 30 years later that it went worldwide. We were never getting royalties or anything like that."

Fortunately, Dawn Penn had not made music her occupation, and she was able to fall back on other careers to sustain her. "It was hard, but I had another job, so I wasn't depending on the music for money. I was earning money outside of the music," she says. Penn worked for the Jamaica Telephone Company, where she met Cynthia Schloss, who also worked there. "She sings so well, and I say to her, 'Why you don't do singing?' She actually took up singing, did some music and she got married to Merritone. But she passed on, it's so sad. She's a beautiful woman. I encouraged her to sing and record as well," Penn says.

Penn worked in other jobs as well and left Jamaica to pursue her family history. "My dad was from Tortola, and he lived in Cuba for 32 years. He start in Tortola and he moved to Santo Domingo to find his brothers because of bad treatment from his aunt," she says. So, in the middle of what seemed to be a successful singing career, she picked up and moved to Tortola. She also lived in St. Thomas:

> I stopped doing music. I left Jamaica in 1970. I was in Tortola for 17 years. I had worked with an airline that goes in the eastern Caribbean. So I was learning how to write up tickets for travel and things like that. Then I worked for six years as a bank official, posting accounts; and my last job in the bank was to give loans to people who needed a personal loan.... I also worked for the government during the time I was there. I worked for the chief medical officer, which is what they call the prime minister. Then I worked for a man called Chuck, Charles Tobias. He used to come to the UK to do this thing where they hunt foxes. He was a shooter and, he used to make Potter's Rum, which was a combination of three different rums from Guyana, Jamaica, and Barbados.

During these years, Dawn had eight children. "I went back to Jamaica in 1987. And then I left from Jamaica and went to the U.S., and I lived in the Bronx in Little Italy, and then I went to Brooklyn as well. I had six boys and two girls. They were born in the Virgin Islands. It's a lot. I used to get them off to school and drop off the little ones at the daycare center and then pick them up in the afternoon. I had a helper who would cook the food and wash. That's how I grew up—we had a helper as well who would come in the house. I never leave my kids anywhere. They were always with me wherever I go," she says.

Even though she had other careers to fall back on, from broadcaster to telephone operator to bank loan manager, and she was able to raise her children successfully, Penn still feels slighted by the music industry, as do countless others who were never given their due. She says,

> I'm not getting any royalties from 1960—whatever. They cannot pay royalties from back in that time, they only go from 1968. That's how they keep the criminality alive, because they collect the money and not pay it out and buy a house or a new car. Meanwhile, the people have nowhere to live or have to pay rent. That's what happened. Some people take it to heart. Some people start to drink. I know one guy who was drinking rum and chasing it with another alcohol drink, and he got cirrhosis of the liver. And you had another one who went on crack. But some decided to become something. One became a tailor, things other than music, because they are not getting anything, but you always hear the song on the radio. So it's a bit upsetting. I know quite a few who died of a broken heart.

Susan Cadogan

Susan Cadogan says that over the years, the newspaper articles that depicted her as a quiet little librarian bug her. She says she felt they painted her out to be a "homely girl." Admittedly she was naïve, unskilled in the ways of record label executives who telephoned her and immediately whisked her off to foreign lands, young and alone, who choreographed television presentations and sent fancy cars that drove through throngs of teenagers screaming her name; of commercializing producers who dressed her in revealing costumes, circling her, eyeing her, making comments as if she were not even there; and of reporters from the biggest newspapers, clamoring to tell her story, from a quiet library assistant to an international superstar. Susan Cadogan was no homely girl. She was strong inside, smart inside, and yes, beautiful on the outside and inside as well, but it would take years for her to realize her strengths, since she was shy and unaware of the powers of her voice.

Susan grew up in Belize, although she was born in Kingston on November 2, 1951. She explains, "My father is a Belizean. Belize was called British Honduras in those days. When they got married, they went to Belize to live. Every time mom was going to have a baby she'd go to Jamaica to have the baby because Belize was not up to par with their medical facilities. So she went to Jamaica, had me, and brought me back to Belize as a little baby. It was underdeveloped and up to now there are dirt roads in the capital."[15]

Susan's father was a minister and her mother took care of the family. She says,

> Daddy is a Methodist minister. He was Reverend Claude Cadogan. Everybody knows him in Belize, and there are places that are named after him. In Jamaica he got his honorary degree from the University of the West Indies, and he also got an Order of Distinction from the Jamaican government. He's really very eloquent and very oratory-like because he preaches and he still types (at 99 years old), and people call him because he is very knowledgeable about Methodism and certain things. And poor little mum now has been a loving devoted wife and mother. That's a job though. She was engaged at 16, married at 18, and they're still married today. A couple of times in our lives she said she always wanted to be a teacher, but daddy came, wanted a wife. She really worked hard, and you couldn't find a more giving, wonderful person. She was a supreme mother.

Susan, who was born Allison Anne Cadogan, had two brothers and one sister. "I was Allison, the heroine of a book daddy was reading, Anne after Princess Ann who was born the same year or a little before me, but with an 'e,' like the French spell it. Jean was the eldest, and they always called us by our middle name. Lola Jean was named after my mother, Mark was Claude Ainsley Mark after Daddy. Daddy is Claude, Mommy is Lola, and I am Allison Anne, and we are all called Jean, Mark, Anne, all middle names," she explains.

Because of her father's occupation as a minister, the family moved frequently as his assignments dictated. "When we went to Jamaica first, I used to stay with my grandparents, the three of us, and when Daddy came he was stationed in Montego Bay, so I went to school at the Montego Bay Primary School, and eleven years after me, up came Paul, my little brother. He was what we call a 'wash belly' in Jamaica. I don't know why they call it that. But along comes this little person and for me, I was no longer the baby of the family," she says.

It was a musical household, especially since Susan's father was involved in the church. Her mother was a singer, and they had access to recorded music at home. It was here that Susan began to develop her own love of singing. She says,

> Mommy sang with one of these trained soprano voices, classical. Up in Montego Bay she used to sing in the choir there. I never sang anywhere but at home. I used to love the records, and my sister did too. We had a record changer that was locked up with a padlock from Paul, because from when he was a little baby he was fascinated with it. When I used to sing he'd sit on the floor and just watch me. And I learned to play the piano. I used to play the piano by ear then. We had a piano and we used to play and sing. When we moved to Kingston and I passed my exams to go to high school, my grandmother sent me to piano lessons and I did go up to grade three, distinction in one, and distinction in two, but I just couldn't stand the discipline of the thing. I just wanted to play. You have to go through theory as well as the practical, and I just wanted to play. I fell out of it after a while, and

after that when I played and made a mistake, I would have to stop and start from the beginning, as I played from memory. After that, I really didn't think about music at all.

Lola Cadogan, Susan's mother, recorded songs on shellac, but not for commercial consumption, only for her own satisfaction: "My mother's records were never released for sale. She just made a few for her personal use because the songs were so good. She did 'O Holy Night' on a 78, and we had it for a long time. She used to go to practice every week for her choral group. Every year they would have a performance with the Jamaica Philharmonic Orchestra, and they would have musicians from Canada, and it was wonderful. And she would enter festivals, and we have her trophies from the 1960s. Now that she's in her state of mind, she doesn't remember, but she is something and she'll burst out into song, 'Jerusalem, Jerusalem' [sings]. As old as she is, she still sings now. And she sings, 'Hurt So Good!'"

But before Susan made her hit single, "Hurt So Good," and her many others, she pursued a different direction in life:

Right when I left school is when I had my love life, and I had my two sons before I went to the library, one at 19, the second one at 21. We were brought up so strict and you don't talk about certain things, and when I look back, I just think I wanted love for myself, growing up with my grandparents and moving moving moving everywhere with Daddy always away. I remember feeling so unattractive as a young girl, homely and shy. I was chubby. When I went to Excelsior High School I think I was more aware and started to exercise. I remember I took this pill (Apisate) and I used to have two grapefruits for my breakfast, grapefruit at lunch, a little dinner and I would put on music and exercise and sweat and I would sing the whole side of a Supremes record, and I just got thinner and thinner.... I knew all the lyrics of songs from the Everly Brothers and Ben E. King. I used sing aloud when they had Rediffusion [RJR, the island radio station]; I would never ever think that I was going to be a singer. Some people just want to be a singer, from when they are 16 they are performing and they pursue a career—I never ever did, ever. When I was up at the university living with my aunt—Daddy might have been in Antigua, and my mom was with him and my brother—because at that time I was too old to go with them—so I was living with my aunt up at the university campus and I needed to work, and I applied to a bank because I was just looking for a job, but when I went to the interview they asked, "Why do you want this job? Why do you want a career in banking?" and I said, "Well, I really like money, you know!" [laughs]. And I never got the job, and I was getting downhearted, when I applied for a job at the library. As soon as I applied for it, they gave me the job. That was in 1973, and I was able to walk to work, and I discovered this ability to organize.... I loved my work and organized away, everything, and I became a very capable assistant.

It was while Susan worked at the library that her best friend from school days launched Susan's singing career. Through connections in the most unlikely places, Susan was destined for stardom:

My good friend Theresa used to work at the JBC in the library department. She would tell me how Bob Marley and other singers used to come arguing for airplay. In those days the lists of songs were made up in the library and given to the deejay so he couldn't play what he want, because of Payola and all those kind of things. So what the DJ played, the record library staff compiled, made it up each program. So her boyfriend was a DJ, Jerry Lewis, and he wrote a song and wanted to record it. He asked Theresa to sing it, but she told him, "My friend loves to sing, let her sing it." They came and took me down to the studio to record it. I didn't know where I was, but I was at the Black Ark and this little man, he came out with his rings and little beard and I recorded the song, "Love of My Life." I was kind of shy, but Theresa was really shy, and both of us were supposed to sing it as a duet. But when we went into the studio with these huge headphones on and the music started, Theresa didn't sing anything and I sang the whole thing by myself. And that was my first song. When I finished and went back into the control room with Scratch, he says to Jerry, "I love your singer, you know." He said to me, "Do you know this song, 'Hurt So Good?'" And I knew it and he said, "You want to sing it for me?" So I said okay and went back to the mic. Scratch said, "Okay, run it through," and after I had he said, "Yea mon, sing it again … just like that." And I sang it again, and he took the two tracks and bashed them together to double track my voice. Then there was the trio The Diamonds (The Mighty Diamonds they are called today), who did the background voices. Scratch said, "You have a sexy voice, you know?" He had been trying to find somebody to sing it and had tried some other people. And he said, "What's your name?" and I said, "Anne," and he said, "No, you mean Suz-Anne, now that sound sexy!" and that's how I got the name Susan. But all the rigmarole we have been through, and in those days, I didn't even know he had released it. He said he loved my voice and he gave me a little practice and gave me a cassette of songs and said, "Learn these songs—do you want to sing them for me?" I was so excited I couldn't believe it. He said to come back and the next time I went there I met Glen Adams and Bunny Rugs, the lead singer from Third World, Family Man, and the drummer Ben Bow. He played barefoot. He used to send Glen to pick me up and bring me to the studio to record all the songs that are on that album, *Susan Cadogan*. To date it is still my best-selling album, even though I have nine, but that Perry album—people say there is something about it that no other producer has ever been able to make. I don't know what it is, I just sing [laughs]. I didn't know all these guys liked me, because I was so shy, and Glen is the one who warmed his way to my affection. Perry and himself had one fight over me. He ran Glen out of his house! But Perry always showed me respect and I was respectful of him—I never had any problems with Scratch.

But issues over payment and rights and production soon reared its ugly head, as they frequently did for musicians during these years, especially women. Susan says,

> My uncle, who was a lawyer, said, "How are you singing all these songs, what are the legal facts, do you know?" So I went and told Scratch and his wife, Pauline said, "Don't worry about it," and they had some sheet of typewriting things they gave me, and they gave me $100. But it didn't matter to me. I only wanted to sing. I didn't realize the bigger aspect of it, even though I was 22 or 23, so next thing you know, I didn't know he had released "Hurt So Good" as a 45. In Jamaica, "Hurt So Good" never really got exposure and airplay, but "Love My Life," which was my first single, was playing. I remember one morning I woke up and I heard the xylophone and Alan Magnus saying, "I don't know who you are, but you sing like a bird!" [laughs]. "Love My Life" came out as "Anne" in the beginning, and however it filtered to London, they changed it to "Susan." Up until now I don't know anything, never gotten anything. Last year, Jerry Lewis said that Universal had claimed the song and he is going to get the money, but I don't know. It happened to a lot of Jamaicans who had hits on BBC. From Boris Gardiner through to Althea and Donna and Ken Boothe. The Jamaican producers didn't do things right. Trojan says anything Perry did belonged to them, but he sent "Hurt So Good" to somebody else, and that's when Pete Waterman heard it and took it to Magnet and said, "Listen to this. I think this is a hit song." I don't know who exchanged money, but I didn't get any.

What Susan did get, however, was the opportunity to launch her career in England. She recalls, "I got this call one day after work that 'Hurt So Good' is on the charts and I have to come, and I said, 'Well, what happened to Mr. Perry?' I'm not to worry, he's coming too, but they need me now to do a TV show, out of the blue. It didn't occur to me the magnitude of the thing, you know? The ticket came and my aunt said the day after I left, 'This little man came asking for you and I told him you went to England. He left, he drove off in a temper,' and that was Scratch, that was Perry. I don't think he even had a phone, but Glen Adams said I should have told him, but it happened so fast. I was to go on TV, and I got there the day before. So they zoomed me in, and these men measured me up and took me down to the record company." That record company was Magnet Records, a London-based pop record label founded by Michael Levy, where Peter Waterman worked. The label also signed Bob Andy and Bad Manners over the years, and they aimed to become a "kind of Motown" and "sift out the crossover material," said Waterman in an interview with Vivien Goldman in 1976.[16]

Cadogan helped Magnet Records to gain success with "Hurt So Good," which sold over a half-million copies in only one year. Trying to turn Cadogan into a superstar who could continue to churn out hits and bring in cash was the aim of Waterman and Magnet, as Susan explains:

> I've worn glasses since I was about 10 or 11, and they have thick lenses, and I had just cut my hair afro style, so when I went they took off my glasses and they walk around me, inspecting me up and down. Michael Levy, I remember him saying "She's not a bad looking girl, but the glasses have to go." I was fitted for contacts, but in those days we had to wait. Somebody else said singers have to have big hair, and they took me and got this huge afro wig. Next thing you know, they pick me up early to go to BBC to re-record "Hurt So Good" for *Top of the Pops*, so you record in the morning and you mime the evening of the show. In the evening you go in your dressing room and the dressmakers came in with a red jumpsuit with a big hole cut out, showing my navel, showing up the sides of my breasts. I dissolved into tears. I said, "I can't wear this!" And a little lady had to come and sew in a piece of cloth and they took a brooch to hold the thing together. I still have that brooch! I went into makeup, and when they went to put on the false eyelashes the lady said, "Oh I don't think so, her lashes are very long." I felt good! But I was so naïve and not into the star thing. I don't know anything about performing or anything. I still hadn't got the contacts, but they took off my glasses and I couldn't see well, and they put me on this little round thing and tried to get this lady to choreograph me. I told her I prefer to just sing. I am from Jamaica, I am dancing reggae, and she is going to teach me how to move to the song? So I remember them saying, "She'll be okay so don't bother with her." So when it was my turn, I was biting my lip because I'm so blooming shy. This was *Top of the Pops* at BBC Studios! I remember when I was driving in, they had this big time—I don't know if it was a Rolls Royce or what—and there were screaming children knocking on the windows saying, "Who is that? Who is that?" And they said, "Oh! It's Susan Cadogan! Ah!"—climbing all over the car, and I thought, "What the hell is this?" [laughs] because to me it was something new. I was never a rockstar or anything. So I sang the thing, and I couldn't see the solid sea of faces bobbing. I just pretended I was in my drawing room at home, doing what I used to do. And the record shot up 25 places after *Top of the Pops*, and I was on the next week again, went shopping down on Knights Bridge with Pete Waterman and a PR man named Barry. I stayed in a hotel room one morning and the *Daily Mirror*, *Telegraph*, one after each other they come and interview me, and all my headlines were like "Jamaican Cinderella," or "Susan Cadogan Stays in the Library," "Reluctant Susan stays in the Library"—those kind of things, all sort of negative sounding like I was just a homely girl.

Susan says that she had to be extremely guarded, especially since she was admittedly naïve in the ways of the music industry:

> They harass you as a woman, all the producers and things. JBC was going to do a show on me. The man who was in charge of the show, I spoke to him about the show, he said he's going to have this special show about me, and they'll interview me and I'll sing. When I got home he phoned me and asked when can he pick me up. I said, "What? You're going to do the show already?" He said, "Come come now, Susan, you know how this goes." I told him I'm not going out with him and I never heard another thing. When I went to JBC I was told they're not having the show again, and I lost my whole scrapbook of clippings from London. And that's happened to me a couple of time, because they always feel because you're a woman you'll go with them and they push you. He was a show producer at JBC and I think he was known for that sort of thing, but it was new to me and I was not involving myself in anything like that; I knew it was wrong. But the female producers and promoters, did they hit on the guys? [laughs]. But I must say, in London, Magnet Records treated me so well. I stayed in Holiday Inn for three months, food, clothes, transport, everything. And then they came to me and said, "Susan, you have to sign this contract so we can go ahead with a follow up and stuff." By that time, Perry hadn't come yet. I hadn't seen Perry. So I was there by myself, they're looking after me and I think that was my mistake, but what was I to do? I had to sign the contract. And they gave me £3,000. And they had been paying for everything. In the end, I paid for it because they took it out of the "Hurt So Good" money. I remember one evening Pete Waterman came into my dressing room and said it sold 34,000 in one day, so they made a lot of money. Pete Waterman got a Jaguar, but they said I don't need a car cause I can't drive. It was also said, what is the sense in getting the gold disc

because where am I going to hang it?—'cause we have mud walls in Jamaica. These are the things they used to say. Whether they were being funny or not, I didn't find them funny. When I did my interviews they told me he will talk, I mustn't talk too much because people won't understand me. I speak better English than some of the record people, even Pete! I don't speak patois unless I want to! So sometimes I wasn't too happy with them.

Despite her struggles with proper payment over the years, Susan's true joy comes from singing and her fans. She says she has never been married, and her two boys are very important to her. "My boys were in Jamaica with my aunt while I was in London. Sean was with mommy and daddy in Antigua. I went there and did many shows and had quite a few number one hits on their ZDK station; and P.J. [Patrick James] was there at my aunt's in Jamaica. When I came back, P.J. was shy of me. He was a baby and had not seen me for months! But my family embraced us all. They've always been there for me," says Susan, who today looks after her two grandchildren from time to time.

It was fortunate that she always had a stable career to fall back upon, since her singing career didn't prove as financially fruitful as it should have, thanks to the producers and promoters. However, she says her children and family don't really understand her passion for singing:

> Sometimes it bothers me that they [Sean and P.J.] don't seem to believe in my music. Not that they don't love music, but because I've never been financially successful or have anything to show for it, they think it's a joke and they think I keep on doing this for nothing—what's the sense? So during the years I used to go back to the library—probably four times I went back.... I had to earn, so I went back to the library, and every time I went back, they promote me. At the top of my post, I was acting librarian even though I was never professionally trained as a librarian. I remember I lobbied and made a big noise to personnel to tell them they were paying me like a non-librarian and as an acting librarian it was not fair, and I won that thing and got a whole heap of back money, not only for myself, but for the other girls.

The legacy that Susan Cadogan is leaving to Jamaican music is her domination in the genre known as lovers' rock, a genre so popular in England in the 1970s that The Clash even recorded a slow and sultry homage to the style with the obvious title, "Lover's Rock." Lovers' rock is a genre that Steve Barrow and Peter Dalton in their *Rough Guide to Reggae* argue is associated with "London 'blues parties' and discs by girl singers who sounded as if they were still worrying about their school reports."[17] They credit Louisa Marks with starting the style in her hit "Caught You in a Lie," but it has been said that Sharon Forreste first did "Silly Wasn't I" before Marks's tune, followed by "Love Don't Live Here Anymore." Other women such as Louisa Marks, Janet Kay, J.C. Lodge, Pam Hall, Carroll Thompson, and Deborahe Glascow, to name a few, then followed. So too did some men and groups perform lovers' rock, including Barry Boom, Junior Delgado, and Brown Sugar. Some were Jamaican performers; some were British. Jamaican Dennis Brown with his melodious voice definitely shines as a singer of some of the finest lovers' rock. Producer Neil Fraser, better known as the Mad Professor, is credited with establishing the careers of a number of lovers' rock artists by recording them on his Ariwa label, which he began out the living room of his home in south London.

Susan Cadogan reigned supreme in the genre of lovers' rock, especially after her reggae hit, "Hurt So Good," had stormed the BBC charts in April 1975. The sultry duet with Ruddy Thomas, "You Know How to Make Me Feel So Good," topped the black charts for eight weeks and entered the BBC charts. These were followed through the years by "Love of My Life," "Love Me Please," "Cause You Love Me Baby," and more recently, "Falling in Love with You," and "You're Mine," to name a few.

"I am really known for the lovey dovey songs that groove between rocksteady and reggae called lovers' rock, and it has been said by many that I have the 'sexiest voice in reggae!' I love sexy songs and most of my songs are about love, and you rock to them," says Susan with a laugh. Susan has written several songs under the umbrella of her Acado-music Publishing, and she has worked with producers Lee "Scratch" Perry, Owen "OB" Brown, Roy "Hawkeye" Forbes Allen, the Mad Professor, and Bruce White, to name a few. She recently celebrated 40 years in the industry and continues to record and perform today.

Althea Forrest and Donna Reid

When Althea and Donna sing "Check how we jamming and ting, love is all I bring inna mi khaki suit and ting," they really are—jamming, grooving, styling to the music in a military khaki shirt and skirt, cut across with a little purse, their heads wrapped in scarves. "We were little horrors! We were something else," says Althea Forrest, as she and Donna Reid dissolve into giggles over the memories.[18]

Althea and Donna met when they were just teenagers. Each of them had grown up with music in the family. "We grew up close to each other by Hope Road, by Devon House. My father was from St. Elizabeth, my mother was from St. Andrew. I have one brother and one sister. There was music playing all the time in our home," says Althea. Donna adds, "My parents were both born in Kinston, Jamaica, and I'm the first of three children. My grandfather owned many clubs. As a matter of fact, he was the first to book Tommy Cowan. He owned the Adastra Club. My grandfather was Clifford Reid. He also owned Sugar Hill and a couple of stalwart Jamaican spots."

Clifford Reid was a prominent business owner in Kingston. Reid owned the famous Sugar Hill Club, a restaurant and entertainment venue that brought in local shows and Cuban and American artists. Reid entertained foreign dignitaries at his club, which prospered throughout the 1940s and 1950s before it was sold and Peyton Place opened in its location, the club made popular by the Blake Brothers. The comedy team of Bim and Bam also frequently performed at the Sugar Hill Club, as did Ranny Williams, one of the founding members of Jamaica's Pantomime, along with Louise Bennett, known as Miss Lou (see ch. 1). Reid entertained crowds at his club after horse races at Caymanas Park, and calypsonian Lord Kitchener from Trinidad performed during the height of the club. The Sugar Hill Orchestra was the resident band, led by Don Hitchman. Members of the band included Arthur Harris on alto sax, Tommy McCook on tenor sax, Raymond Harper on trumpet, Ken Williams on drums, Bertie Williams on piano, and Gilly Gillespie on bass. Their performances were emceed by Ben "Hi-De-Ho" Bowers who also, from time to time, sang. One article from the late 1940s stated, "Manager Clifford Reid is quite proud of his band, too, for it is a brand new one with lots of possibilities."[19]

Clifford Reid was also owner of Club Adastra, which had also been called Adastra Gardens, in Rockfort. It suffered a major fire in December 1958. Loss was valued at £15,000, but Reid rebuilt and continued on. He also owned the Baby Grand. But Althea and Donna didn't meet at Clifford Reid's clubs, and they didn't meet in their neighborhood. Instead they met at a hotel on the north shore. Donna says, "We met as teenagers and that was it. We were friends and we never stopped. It was summertime, school was out. We went in Ocho Rios, the Mallards Beach Hotel." Althea says, "Our favorite place to stay was that hotel."

When the girls returned home, they not only continued their friendship but also began a musical career together. Althea Forrest already had some success with singing, and so she and Donna continued socializing in these same circles. "I started singing with Derrick Harriott when I was 13. That's when I made my first record," Althea says. She recorded "Hey Mister" and "Friends" in 1976 on Harriott's Crystal label, and in 1977 she sang a duet with Derrick Harriott called "Train of Desire." She continues, "I also did Festival songs. Winston McAnuff and I teamed up for a Festival song." That song was recorded in 1977, also for Derrick Harriott on his Crystal label, and was titled "Having a Party."

Althea and Donna began friendships with the musicians in the bands that performed at the studios around Kingston, especially since Donna's grandfather owned the clubs they performed in. Donna dated Gayman Alberga, who co-founded the Talent Corporation with Tommy Cowan and Warwick Lyn in 1975, a group that promoted musicians such as Dennis Brown, The Abyssinians, and Jacob "Killer" Miller, who dated Althea for a number of years. It was through their relationships with fellow musicians that Althea and Donna wrote their massively successful song "Uptown Top Ranking," which would land them in the spotlight. "We actually started being friends with Third World, and they would always mess with us, because in the daytime we dressed like dreads, and in the night, that's when we put our high heels and miniskirts on. They called us cosmo freaks and we would answer them in song, and that's how that really went," says Althea. Donna adds, "Yeah, that's how that came to fruition."

The song was recorded in 1977 for producers Joe Gibbs and Errol Thompson on the Joe Gibbs Record Globe label in Jamaica; on the Lightning label in the UK, a subsidiary of Warner Brothers; and on Sire in the U.S. Althea says, "At the time, I was dating Jacob 'Killer' Miller. We were young and having fun. We were close to Inner Circle, I mean Roger [Lewis] is my daughter's godfather, so we're still close." Donna says, "We did our first recording of 'Uptown Top Ranking' with them. And then Jacob took us to Joe Gibbs' studio, so that's a bone of contention that they have not let us live down, including just two weeks ago! Yes, we did it at Joe Gibbs' recording studio." Althea affirms that Gibbs used a rhythm track from the Alton Ellis song "I'm Still in Love" (which was covered by Marcia Aitken in her song "I'm Still in Love with You Boy") and a deejay track called "Three Piece Suit" by Trinity.

Almost immediately after recording that song, Donna relocated to Florida because, she says, it was "just the thing to do then." She was in search of opportunity and career. She had no idea that "Uptown Top Ranking" was ranking tops indeed. Donna says, "I moved to the U.S. shortly after recording the song. As a matter of fact, Althea had to call me and tell me the song was a hit! We didn't think it was going to do anything! It became number one, what can I tell you?" Althea says, "Yeah, we did it as a joke. We were just enjoying ourselves. We were just having fun—we did a recording, life goes on!"

But life certainly changed for the duo. Before they knew it, they were being whisked away to the United Kingdom, where they were celebrities. "We were managed by my dad because we needed chaperones. We were only 17 and 19 years old," says Donna. The song was released in the UK in December 1977, and it came on the British charts at number 32. One week later it was at number 18, and the following week it was at number two, and it soon toppled the number one record, Paul McCartney and Wings' "Mull of Kintyre." The news headline read, "'Top Ranking' duo strike gold." The article states, "On arrival they were immediately presented with a silver record signifying sales of over 250,000 copies. Within a couple of days, they received a gold disc which represents sale of over half million—the next step will be platinum which signifies a million seller."[20] The song was in the *Daily Gleaner's* top ten for 15 weeks and held the number one spot for six of those weeks.

They performed on *Top of the Pops* and other television and radio shows. They were in the UK promoting their song for six weeks. When asked about her memories of the tour, Althea says, laughing, "The most important thing for me is I wanted some food, some good food, and it was hard!" Donna adds, "And we wanted some sleep!" They both say that they were stunned at their popularity, and there were crowds everywhere they went. "They had to close Selfridges [a UK department store], where we were shopping. There was almost a riot! So whoever was in the store had to stay in the store until we were done," Althea says. "Because we shop! And we still do! We are shoppers to this day," Donna says. "We went home with like 13 suitcases, right Donna?" asks Althea. Donna replies, "About that, yeah!" and again they giggle like the teenagers they still are at heart.

Back home they were celebrities as well, but they say that they didn't feel like celebrities and it was all about having a great time as girls. "We were the same people we always were," says Donna. "Our parents were supportive of us. Maybe they wanted lawyers or doctors, but they knew that this was it, and they were supportive of whatever we decided to do," she says. Althea states, "All of our friends were in the industry too, so it was just a lot of fun. We had a really good time."

Althea and Donna released an entire album of songs with the same backing musicians as on their hit song—Sly and Robbie on drums and bass, Earl "Chinna" Smith on guitar, Bernard "Touter" Harvey on keyboards, Herman Marquis on alto sax, Tommy McCook on tenor sax, Vin Gordon "Don Drummond Jr." on trombone, and Noel Simms "Scully" on percussion. The album was titled *Uptown Top Ranking* and featured the songs "No More Fighting," "Jah Rastafari," "Make a Truce," "Oh Dread," "The West," "Jah Music," "If You Don't Love Jah," "Sorry," "They Wanna Just," and of course, their hit, "Uptown Top Ranking." They had intended to establish their own label, A&D, and they did for a while, as they explain. "We did, then we didn't follow up, but now we're back on track," Althea says. "We did it and had to take a hiatus for personal and other issues, but now we're back at it. We're going to test the water again and see what happens. Maybe we'll have a second and a third hit song!" says Donna.

Anyone who claims that Althea and Donna were a "one-hit wonder" is revealing their ignorance. Althea and Donna were pioneers and innovators more than they ever knew at the time that they recorded their now-classic song and the others that followed. "We were the first female deejays, that's number one," said Althea. "We were the first female deejays in the world. There was no Queen Latifah. Queen Latifah came after us. Salt-n-Pepa came after us, so we are really the first female deejays, the genre of music is considered deejay so that's what we did." Even in 1978, Althea and Donna were called, "Jamaica's first female duo," and since then they have been called a "popular female DJ duo" and "first female DJs" by the *Daily Gleaner*.[21]

Althea says that before Jacob "Killer" Miller died tragically in a car accident, they had split up but remained close friends; Jacob had even visited her the week prior. Shortly after Donna moved to the United States, Althea moved as well, and they both reside in Florida today. "I had kids, lost a child, and I've been married for twelve years. Three of my children are alive," says Althea, who is a housewife and a party planner. Donna has two children and didn't get married. She works for the State of Florida.

Even though they were surrounded by friends, Althea and Donna say that it wasn't all fun times in the studios during those days. "At that time, the industry was very male oriented. It was very chauvinistic. As young women in the industry, that's one of the reasons we stepped away from it, because the men expected that in order for us to get anywhere we would need to—you know—and we weren't going to do it. That's why we had Donna's father manage us, because that was not our style. That was not gonna happen," Althea says.

When asked if the *Daily Gleaner* headline was true, did they really "strike gold," Althea and Donna once again laugh, but this time not a giggle. This time the laugh contains a sardonic cast. "We didn't strike gold. Producers got the money. To this day we're still fighting to make the money. We have no records on our wall." Donna says, "They took our records for our wall. Give us something!" But it's more than just a record, an award, acknowledgment. It's about the financial legacy that their families have been deprived of. "So my kids, my grandkids have lost. And this still happens today—not to that extent, but it happens today," Althea says. Perhaps the legacy can't be measured in dollars and instead comes from something that cannot be measured at all, such as the pleasure brought to fans of their music, and the inspiration they give to little girls, teenage girls, and even women who see that it can be done, against the odds. "People love it. You can never recoup that original fever. It took the world by storm," Althea says.

Cynthia Richards

Cynthia Richards was born in 1944 in Duhaney Park in the northwest area of Kingston. She was a student at Denham Town Primary School. After singing in school and astounding teachers at an end-of-the-year performance, Richards appeared on the *Vere Johns Opportunity Hour*, the talent show that catapulted many Jamaican performers to stardom. Richards was no exception. She recorded "Chain of Love," "I Am Lonely," and "How Could I" for Coxsone Dodd in 1966. In 1968 she recorded duets with Clancy Eccles, who also served as producer. Her big break came in 1969 with the single "Foolish Fool," also produced by Clancy Eccles. It was an immediate hit in Jamaica and in England. The song was a cover of the song that Dee Dee Warwick had made popular (Dee Dee was Dionne's younger sister).

Cynthia was a member of the Jamaican band Skin, Flesh, and Bones, which over the years featured Lloyd Parks on bass, Jackie Jackson on bass, Sly Dunbar on drums, Ansel Collins on keyboards, Tarzan on keyboards, Ranchie MacLean on guitar, Hux Brown on guitar, and Rad Bryan on guitar. The group became The Revolutionaries when they performed with Studio One, but prior to that they went with Cynthia to New York to perform at the famed Apollo Theater.

Cynthia performed with a band called The VIPs in England in the early 1970s, and she received approval from crowds everywhere they performed. She said, "London has been really good to me in terms of acceptance. I have worked in clubs in Hammersmith and these have been immensely thrilling and rewarding." She was on tour in England for seven months. She left Jamaica for England in April 1970 after her two singles "If You're Ready Come Go with Me" and "For Your Love I Will Do Anything" were successful in the British market. "Due to special demands for these tunes, I was forced to hurry off on this tour and what a successful tour this was for me! I formed my own backing band, the VIPs and we toured all over England and even did a session with the 'Chosen Few' at the Empire Ballroom. I was honoured with an invitation to the Lyceum Ballroom on that memorable night when Bob Marley and the Wailers performed. They were just fantastic and how proud I felt to know that it was my Jamaican brothers getting such tremendous raves," said Richards.[22]

In 1972, Cynthia was chosen as one of 50 Jamaican artists to perform for shows in the U.S. after promoter Earl Harris scouted her. A *Daily Gleaner* article that detailed her success in the U.S., performing at Madison Square Garden, in San Francisco, and in England at the Count Suckle Cue Club and other locations, spoke of Cynthia with a definite bias against the other music coming out of Kingston. "Cynthia sings with conviction although her songs do not emphasize the colonialism and slavery that has been a part of Jamaica's heritage, neither does she fashion the usual lyrics about the drawls of the working class or ghetto life in the island. Instead what comes out in her songs is a theme which is profound and thrilling, a message significantly deep and personal. What she sings, if one will admit, conveys no trace of hostility. Without reservation, she is a professional," the journalist stated.[23]

Nora Dean

Nora Dean was born in 1952 in Spanishtown. She began her singing career as a backup singer for a number of musicians including Jimmy Cliff, and she was a member of The Ebony Sisters, The Soul Sisters, and The Soulettes, Rita Marley's group. She joined Cecile Campbell when The Soulettes lost one of their originals, and they recorded "Let It Be," a cover of the Beatles song. When it came time to tour, however, Nora was ill and replaced by Hortense Lewis. She underwent three operations for a stomach condition. Nora was just 16 years old.

Nora recorded her most popular song, "Barbwire (in Your Underpants)," in 1969 for producer Byron Smith. The song, some contend, began the dancehall characteristic of "slackness" or lewd and vulgar lyrics. She was paid £30 for the song over the course of nine months, which is a large amount of money compared to what most artists were paid. Perhaps that's because Nora had to beg for her pay. "'I had to go to Smitty's record shop each morning and stay until about 7 p.m. and he would give me a ten pound, or a five pound or a one pound, and the whole day I wouldn't eat a thing. I remember one day I stayed at the shop and counted 5,000 copies of the record sold."[24] She asked her publisher, Ted Powder, once to check on the sales of the record internationally, and he claimed that it had sold more than 13 million copies worldwide. However, he disappeared from Jamaica shortly afterwards, and she never saw him again.[25]

Nora Dean recorded singles for Duke Reid, Bunny Lee, Coxsone Dodd, Lee "Scratch" Perry, Ranny Williams, Vincent Chin, Jimmy Cliff, Sonia Pottinger, and many producers from 1968 through the 1970s. But then, Nora suddenly disappeared from the recording scene. She had earned no money from her successful recordings. So, bitter at the Jamaican producers, Nora went to live with her sister in New York. She left music altogether and began work as a nurse's aide. In 1981 she began singing again for her church choir. She left reggae and slackness behind. She changed her musical repertoire to gospel, recording such songs as "My Soul Loves Jesus" and "Battlefield." She claims that producers pressured her to record her overtly sexual songs and that they were out of character for her. In 1994 she married Albert McLean, a Jamaican who also moved to New York, and the two self-funded her album *My Soul Loves Jesus* in 1996. She recorded a number of gospel albums, the latest in 2006. She has an adopted daughter, Sharon.

Cynthia Schloss

Cynthia Leonie Schloss was born April 12, 1948, in Trench Town. She was the second child born, among three girls and three boys. She graduated from Trench Town Primary and Ardenne High School and sang in school choirs. Just after graduation, Cynthia took a job at the Jamaica Telephone Company as a telephone operator and worked there from 1966 to 1983. She worked with Dawn Penn, who encouraged her to sing.

Her opportunity for developing her musical career, and an opportunity for love, came when Cynthia was 24 years old and she met Winston "Merritone" Blake. She auditioned for his weekly amateur talent contest at the VIP Lounge, performing the song "I Only Live to Love You" by Cilia Black. Winston Blake became her manager, and her husband.

Cynthia had a string of successful lovers' rock songs, including "Surround Me with Love," "You Look Like Love," "Love Forever," and "As If I Didn't Know." She performed for years in the north coast hotels, and she toured with Byron Lee and the Dragonaires to Mexico, Belize, North America, the Cayman Islands, and Canada. Cynthia sang and danced with the Eddie Thomas Group, was a vocalist with the Jamaican Folk Singers and toured South Africa with them in 1997, and sang with the Jamaica Philharmonic Group. She performed at concerts throughout Jamaica and at times was accompanied by Marjorie Whylie. In 1985 she became sales director of United Bedding, which was owned by her husband Winston Blake and his brother Monte Blake.

Cynthia's big hit was "Love Forever," which was touted in the local papers:

> Her latest release "Love Forever" certainly ranks as one of the most beautiful recordings done this year. The impressive arrangements are done by Harold Butler, a talented keyboard specialist, who plays both piano and organ, the strings and mellotrons, heard on this particular song. In a recent chat with Cynthia she related the origin of "Love Forever" which is winning her many fans. "Harold, one of my favourite musicians, phoned me about this tune, which he said was specially written to suit my voice. I wasn't interested at first, but eventually accepted the offer. He went straight to the studio and laid the tracks in my key. When I heard the tape I felt this was my kind of stuff so off we went to the Federal studio. In a few minutes the song was completed because I took only one cut."[26]

Another article, a decade later in 1985, discussed Cynthia's career as well as her devotion to her family: "Her main occupation when she isn't working is her family. She has two children, Andre, and Divine, who is 10 months old. She often takes them on drives out into the country where she restores her flagging energies. The world of the theatre, plays and concerts etc. is another method of relaxation and entertainment that Cynthia enjoys."[27] Cynthia died in February 1999 of undetermined causes. Her husband, Winston "Merritone" Blake, died in February 2016.

Carlene Davis

Carlene Davis was born Carlene Sinclair in Clarendon, Jamaica, to a family with a tradition in music. Her grandfather, Uriah Rhooms, also known by his nickname "Bad

Move," was a virtuoso who played violin, cello, clarinet, saxophone, and guitar. He taught her music and performance, and she was raised by him until she was 13 years old. She attended Mt. Carrnel Presbyterian School and Colonel Ridge. In 1967, Carlene and her sister moved to Berkshire, England, to join their parents. She finished her education in England at Wilson's Secondary School, where she was a member of the choir. She was the only Jamaican in choir, and so she introduced her choirmaster to Jamaican folk songs such as "Linstead Market." After she graduated high school, Carlene took a secretary class from Reading Technical School and was able to secure a position with Sun Life Insurance, which allowed her to continue to perform during the evenings at clubs, pubs, and the Broden Army Camp.

It was during this time, the mid–1970s, that Carlene changed her name to Carlene Davis. She left England and moved to Toronto, where she joined the American Federation of Musicians (which also encompassed Canada) and started her own band. They performed in cocktail lounges and bars and performed popular country, folk, and rock songs. At the same time she worked as a secretary to help make ends meet. She performed in Caribbean clubs in Toronto and supported Jamaican acts that came through on tour, like Toots and the Maytals and Peter Tosh. She also met Bob Marley on his last worldwide tour. "I had a show the same night so he came by after his show to see me and came backstage afterwards," Carlene said.[28] In 1980, encouraged by those in the music scene, she returned to Jamaica to pursue her career.

Back in her home country, Carlene recorded an album and appeared with Tony Gregory on a JBC-TV special. She performed at Sunsplash '80 and began to establish exposure in Jamaica. She was noted for her vocal range. Carlene's hits include the songs "Like Old Friends Do," "Stealing Love," "The First Word in Memory Is Me," "Dial My Number," "It Must Be Love," "Going Down to Paradise," "Winnie Mandela," and "Santa Claus, Do You Ever Come to the Ghetto." She is married to Tommy Cowan, who was once a member of The Jamaicans and promoter/manager to Bob Marley, Dennis Brown, Peter Tosh, Bunny Wailer, and Judy Mowatt. Carlene and Tommy both own the Judah Recording Studio. Cowan recounts meeting Carlene:

> I first saw Carlene in 1979 at Dynamic Sounds studios on Bell Road, where I worked as marketing manager. I enquired about her and was told that she was a singer from Canada, and she was at the studio to record a song. Sometime after that there was a concert at the now Hilton Hotel and she was singing backup vocals for Ernie Smith. Her voice was so good that I felt she shouldn't be doing backup vocals as she had the potential to be a star. I asked Babsy Grange, who had organised the event, to introduce us, and that's when we met formally. At that time I was interested in her creative talent as I was struck by it, and I told her this. Our relationship developed over the years through a growing respect that I had for her because of her principles. We began to date but in order to pursue a relationship with her it meant that I had to let go of the lifestyle I had at the time. We were together for a long time until we got married in August 1995.[29]

Carlene, along with Papa San and Junior Tucker, performed the song "Colour of Love," which was written by Cowan. They donated the proceeds to Kobe, Japan, earthquake relief in 1996. That same year she was diagnosed with breast cancer and underwent chemotherapy treatments. She continued to perform, and the cancer went into remission. It was at this time that Carlene's musical repertoire switched from secular to Christian gospel music; she and her husband Tommy are outward exponents of Christianity. She has won over 30 awards, including Best Female Vocalist at the Caribbean Music Awards in 1990, the 2000 and 2001 Jamaican Federation of Musicians Awards for her gospel albums

Vessel and *Redeemed*, and Best Gospel Artiste of the Year Award in 2004 for the album *Author and Finisher*; and the CARICOM Hall of Fame Award in 2003. She has two children, Nathan Thomas and Naomi Chrystalice.

Lorna Bennett

Lorna Bennett was born on June 7, 1952, in Newton, Saint Elizabeth, in Jamaica. From an early age she loved music and performing and has memories of sitting on her living room floor with her sister Kay, harmonizing to songs by Diana Ross, Astrud Gilberto, and Nancy Wilson. She attended St. Andrew High School in Kingston. While in sixth form at Excelsior High School, she was approached to become a female singer in a group called The Bare Essentials Band. Lorna and Kay joined, along with Errol Lee, and they performed at the Epiphany Night Club in New Kingston each Wednesday night. It was there that musician Geoffrey Chung asked her to record a song called "Morning Has Broken," which he produced along with "Harry J" Johnson. Encouraged by her brother, Kenneth "Toney" Bennett, Lorna next recorded the Dusty Springfield ballad "Breakfast in Bed" (again for Chung and Harry J.). Chung gave the song a reggae arrangement, and Lorna's version was a huge hit. It stayed at the number one position on the Jamaican charts for six weeks.

After Lorna graduated from Excelsior, she decided to pursue both her musical career as well as a career in law. As a student at the University of the West Indies Mona Campus she continued to record, including the songs "Letter from Miami," "Chapel of Love," "Run Johnny Run," "Stay with You Awhile," and her album *This Is Lorna*. After graduation, Lorna went to Barbados to complete law school. She returned to Jamaica in 1974 and recorded "Dancing to My Own Heartbeat," produced by her brother. She performed at the Top O' Sheraton and other locations around Kingston, but in 1978 she returned to Saint Elizabeth, set up her own legal practice in Santa Cruz, and left her musical career behind. She took the advice of her brother, who told her to pursue a profession that was more rewarding and less brutal for women than music. She also married Michael Ollivierre, a calypso singer, and together they had two children, Oje and Leann. She owned her own gym called Firm Bodies.

In 2001, Lorna returned to the music business and continued to work with her brother. She appeared in holiday programs across the island and recorded a number of singles in 2006. She performed for the *Heineken Startime* shows and toured England, and she has recorded with Sly and Robbie and Spragga Benz. She is divorced from Michael and she manages her son's career. Oje is the Grammy-nominated artist known as Protoje.

Sheila Hylton

Sheila Hylton was born in Manchester, England, and moved to Jamaica when she was five years old to be raised by her maternal grandparents in Vineyard Town, east Kingston. Her mother moved to Australia and her father moved to Finland. Sheila's grandfather worked for Pan American Airways and was a jazz aficionado, so she was raised around jazz music and was influenced by a variety of music, from Billie Holiday, to Chaka Khan, to The Police and Sting later in life. Because she wanted to see more of the world, she decided to become a flight attendant for Air Jamaica and modeled as well. She began her recording career during the height of the reggae era in the mid–1970s, but she didn't enter the business through traditional routes, such as talent shows or studio try-outs. Instead, she worked as a secretary for "Harry J" Johnson's studio, and after observing and learning, she decided to show off a bit of her own vocalizations. Johnson recorded two cover songs for Sheila, "Life in the Country," which was originally recorded by The Ebonys, and "Don't Ask My Neighbour," which was first recorded by The Emotions. She also recorded "Breakfast in Bed" in 1979; it went to number 57 on the British charts. "She influenced me the first time I saw her modelling at a show," said Harry J. "I realised she had the fan appeal. After talking to her, I realised she had a good voice tone."[30] A number of her songs were written for her by Wilfred Jackie Edwards.

In 1981, Sheila's biggest hit, "The Bed's Too Big Without You," was distributed by Island Records. The song was a cover of a tune she heard in London while traveling as a flight attendant. She visited a record shop and bought The Police's *Reggatta de Blanc* and was so impressed by the reggae rhythm of "The Bed's Too Big Without You" that she immediately recorded her own version. "I called in Sly and Robbie to give their interpolation of 'Bed's Too Big Without You' and it became an instant hit in Jamaica. Radio and club DJs played it around the clock. Chris Blackwell heard it being played on the radio and contacted us saying it was a sure hit for the UK, and released it on Island Records," said Hylton.[31] Hylton has also recorded with Elvis D and Lushy Ranks from New York, and she moved to New York City in the 1980s. She has performed with Ken Boothe and Third World and has traveled all over the world to perform. She has also hosted events like the International Reggae and World Music Awards. In 2017 she released a song originally written for her by the late Dennis Brown called "True Love."

Sonya Spence

Sonya Spence (sometimes spelled Sonja) was born in Rest Store, Manchester, near Alligator Pond in Jamaica. She once said, "It was a very romantic place and my childhood memories are indelible."[32] She studied at Church Teacher's College and Mico College, as well as briefly at the University of the West Indies Mona, prior to entering the music industry. She got her break while working as a student teacher at the New Green All-Age School. She said, "I was practicing a song in the barber shop. The owner was a musician. He heard me singing 'Jet Plane' and liked it."[33] After the barber introduced Sonya to Lloyd Webster, he produced her Peter, Paul, and Mary cover, the most popular song of Sonya's musical career, "Leaving on a Jet Plane." She recorded the song with the band The Thunderbirds in Mandville in 1972. She also made popular the songs "Fantasy," "No Charge," "I Love You So," and "Talk Love." She performed at shows with Freddie McKay, Bongo Herman, and Vin Gordon in the mid–1970s.

A short time later, in 1977, Sonya immigrated to Canada and went back to school. She also visited Nigeria, where she launched an album, because her records sold so well there. She then returned home to Mandeville and became a teacher for 11 years, teaching English at the New Broughton School, Cross Keys Secondary, and Victoria All-Age School until 1995.

Like a large percentage of other Jamaican artists, Sonya received little pay for her music. "I would really like to know what is happening with my songs because somebody should be paying me some money. In those days I was very unfamiliar with the business behind the music," she said in a *Daily Gleaner* article, which said that she had hired a local copyright agency to investigate the issue.[34]

A *Jamaica Gleaner* article on August 25, 2000, said that Sonya left the music industry for a number of years and "went high on cocaine. She's not ashamed to speak about the folly of her ways and wants to be an instrument of positive direction for today's youth. 'The first thing I would say is keep far from drugs. Don't even try it. Resist that temptation because here you have the benefit of advice from people who have been down that road and it is just not worth it.'" Sonya died on February 17, 2007, after suffering for some time with liver complications. In a poem Spence wrote about crack cocaine in 1995 she stated, "It's a killer/ It will take your life away / If it gets you there is no coming back / You are a loser." Sonia had four daughters. She was 54 years old.

Olive "Senya" Grant

Olive "Senya" Grant was born in Kingston. She began her musical career in the early 1970s with the help of Aston "Family Man" Barrett, legendary bassist for The Wailers. It was in 1974 that Family Man took her to Randy's studio to record for him along with producer Clive Chin (son of Vincent Chin), who was instrumental in continuing his father's work for the label. She recorded, backed by The Wailers, and released songs such as "Oh Jah Come" and "Children of the Ghetto." In 1979, Family Man took Senya to record at the newly constructed Tuff Gong studio. They re-recorded "Children of the Ghetto" as a way to test the new equipment, as well as a new tune, "Natural Woman." She also recorded for Jimmy Cliff's Oneness label, including the song "Show Some Love," and she sang backup vocals on "Jerusalem" by Alpha Blondy and The Wailers.

Senya toured all over the world throughout the 1990s with The Wailers as a backup singer and after that worked for Reggae Sunsplash in administration and as manager of a restaurant. In addition, Senya raised her family. Senya died of a brain aneurysm on April 19, 2001.

Beverley Simmonds

Born on November 18, 1950, Beverley Simmons (sometimes spelled Beverly Simmonds or Beverly Simmons) lived in Waltham Park in Kingston with her mother and father. She started singing at church and was a member of the Anglican church choir. At age 16 she gained employment at the Ministry of Pension and National Insurance but continued her singing career. She twice entered and won the annual Jamaican National Singing Contest. In 1966 and 1967, Beverly won the Kingston and St. Andrew Parish Pop and Mento Contest in the pop solo section. In 1967 she won with her original composition titled "You Are a Deceiver." Beverly was frequently billed as "Our sweetheart of soul."[35] She also auditioned for a recording contract with Pama Records and beat out 125 applicants. At age 17, she went to London to record, resulting in 12 tracks on *Beverley Simmons Pays Tribute to Otis Redding*. Jamaican journalist Clayton J. Goodwin wrote of Simmons in the late 1960s, "She has a powerful voice, stronger beyond the usual power of one so young, and her employed nasality jerks the numbers out of the rhythms which we have come to expect from Redding-imitators. You will either love or loathe the little darling. Either way you cannot fail to notice her. Miss Simmons is a product of the same company that developed Joyce Bond, and she shows not a little of the early Joyce in her treatment of the numbers. Like Joyce she has the voice that will be a knockout at 'live' performances. Beverley has the attributes to be a valuable acquisition to the London club and recording scene."[36]

Chapter Nine

Dancehall

"Women have come a long way in the world of dancehall music," wrote journalist Germaine Smith in 2005. "Though originally the subject of bare-faced discrimination in the business, females have held their own in many aspects. From artiste managers to publicists to promoters to deejays themselves, the women have made it clear that testosterone alone does not run the dancehall world."[1] A number of women were able to find space in the dancehall arena in the 1970s and 1980s, though it was not easy. Identified for their vocal talent, command of the audience, lyrical creativity, and charisma and persona, these women of dancehall were progressive trailblazers.

Sister Nancy

"I'm a lady, I'm not a man. MC is my ambition," sang Sister Nancy in her classic "Bam-Bam," a dancehall song that completely reworked the Toots and the Maytals tune that won the first Festival Song Competition in 1966. Though Sister Nancy's hit song came out in 1982, she had begun her career in music in 1976 and had to work for many years to earn her place in the dancehall space, which was especially hard as a woman.

Sister Nancy was born Ophlin Russell on January 2, 1962. Her father was a revivalist pastor and as a result, the family were deeply religious. It was Sister Nancy's mother, however, who was responsible for supporting the large family, since her father suffered from illnesses. Her mother immigrated to the United States in 1978, and the following year Sister Nancy graduated from high school. By then, she had already begun to establish herself as a deejay, following in the footsteps of her older brother, Robert Russell, who is better known as Brigadier Jerry, the popular Jamaican deejay. She got her start by deejaying on Chalice sound system, Blackstar sound system, and finally the Stereophonic sound system that others such as Nicodemus, Dillinger, and her brother, Brigadier Jerry, deejayed on all around Kingston. Sister Nancy was one of the only female deejays in Jamaica at the time, and by some accounts, she was the first.

During one of Sister Nancy's performances, she caught the eye of producer Winston Riley. Riley had success himself as a member of the seminal vocal group The Techniques. He had established his own studio, producing his group's music as well as music from Johnny Osbourne and the successful "Double Barrel" from Ansel Collins, Sly Dunbar, and Dave Barker. He had also worked with Horace Andy, Pat Kelly, and Alton Ellis, when he discovered Sister Nancy and invited her to his studio to record. "'We did one single, two single, three single—then he said he wanted to do an album with me,' she recalled. 'I said I'm ready, I'll do it.'"² That album was *One Two*, and it was the only album she ever recorded. Three years later she married and had children.

"It was rough in those times," says Nancy, reflecting on her career. "Women had more responsibility than men in those days. The woman had to think about what she was doing with her life. For the men, some of them just get up, brush them teeth and go on the road to hang out at the studio whole day. She may not have so much time; she haffi think 'bout her family and what she do with her time. I personally never capable of doing it those times, so I never thought I could take it on."³

Sister Nancy says that she never discovered the popularity of "Bam Bam" until she migrated to the United States in 1996. "In those times, I never heard 'Bam Bam' play one time in Jamaica…. It was when I migrated in 1996, that I knew how big 'Bam Bam' is. I didn't know, I never had a clue because the producer never wanted me to know. He knew because he was traveling, and I was not…. Because when I did 'Bam Bam' I didn't get any money. Back in the days, they don't pay you. You just want your voice to be heard, you just want to hear your record play on the radio, and you feel good. So him [Winston Riley] never want me to know, didn't want to give me anything. I still didn't, for 32 years. I didn't get anything for it. Terrible," she says.⁴

Today, however, Sister Nancy is realizing some success from her classic song, thanks to the fact that it has been sampled by so many other artists. "Bam Bam" features prominently in Kanye West's "Famous" with Rihanna and has been generously sampled by such artists as Yellowman, Lauryn Hill, Chris Brown, Wiz Khalifa, and Jay-Z. In fact, it has been sampled over 80 times.⁵ Jay-Z even went to Kingston to record a video for his song "Bam," which samples Sister Nancy's version. He brought Sister Nancy with him to appear in the video, which also featured Damian Marley. Even today, when many songs from the 1980s have not withstood the test of time, this tune enters into the category of classic. The cerebral *New Yorker* aptly describing it as "perfection, a soul-hugging mix of horn dollops, crackly bass, and open space."⁶

When Sister Nancy's song was sampled for a Reebok commercial in 2014, she decided to take legal action and won. Though she was only able to reap 10 of the past 32 years of rewards for the song's success, it was still something. Being compensated for her work has meant that Sister Nancy could quit her job as a bank accountant, a job that she held for 15 years, and return to her first love—performing live. "I'm going to continue performing live, as I have many places to go still," she says. "I have records to release. I have like five new tunes that I have done that haven't been released yet. I'm gonna do more work, I just have to do what I have to do. I love live performance more than anything in the world, 'cause I know I'm good at it."⁷

Sister Nancy's contributions to dancehall and to Jamaican music as a whole were larger than one album, larger than one song. Sister Nancy was influential to the creativity of future artists and their own output and creativity—especially women. "I'm the first female DJ to perform on Reggae Sunsplash. The first woman DJ to leave Jamaica. The first woman DJ to take it internationally."⁸

Junie Ranks

Junie Ranks was born June Evans in Kingston but grew up in Old Harbour in St. Catherine. Even as a child she realized that she had an ability for pushing boundaries, a trait that would come in handy as a female in the mostly male world of Jamaican dancehall. She says: "At a young age I enjoyed being a challenge. I was always pushing myself to the limit which back then for a female wasn't considered the most proper thing to do. Sneaking out to perform at the community center youth club called 'Afreak,' I was always getting the crowd going. When I became a regular local act, that's when some of the sounds approached me. I began dee-jaying on ET Sound System and on Technique Disco and that's how I was discovered. I was always a challenge on the mic and would challenge anyone. Not only was I challenging men, but I was also challenging some of the biggest names in the industry."[9] She was influenced by Sister Nancy and General Echo and found she had a talent for singing but chose deejaying instead because of her competitive nature. "Singing was my first love, however like I said before, I like challenging things. Listening to artists such as Super Cat, Shabba Ranks, Admiral Bailey, etc. I started to mimic the style and just enjoyed the way the words would flow so rapidly with the riddim."[10]

Early on in her career she adopted her stage name, as she explains. "I was always rude when I was younger. At that time 'Ranks' was the name that was in style. So they began calling me Junie 'Ranks' and the name stuck."[11] She auditioned for Winston Riley, the same producer of Sister Nancy's *One Two* album and "Bam Bam," and in 1987 she recorded her song and was an instant star. Junie states, "I became famous when I did 'Gi Mi Di Buddy' as an answer to Admiral Bailey's 'Gimme Punanny' and 'Cry Fe Me Boops' which was the answer to Super Cat's 'See Boops Deh.' At the time I came out I was famous."[12] She also recorded for producers King Jammys and Donovan Germain and with other artists like Wayne Wonder and John Mouse. She was one of essentially two women in dancehall at the time, though soon a number of women took up the dancehall microphone, including Sister Charmaine, Lady G, Lady Ann, Macka Diamond, and Shelly Thunder, to name a few.

"The lack of female presence may be due to the industry wanting a certain type of style. That limitation makes it hard for females to be creative and have the ability to stay fresh in the music," Junie says.[13] Seeing that it was so tough to make a living as a female dancehall artist, Junie Ranks tried a different aspect of the music industry as well—promotion. "I used to keep shows and promote them, but as it comes on to producing, that was a no-no. I used to think about producing, but we were saying that it was so hard to get into. I used to think that it was a headache to do and to get the artistes to cooperate and get studio to book was too much headache for me," she said.[14] Junie Ranks left the music industry behind in 1998 when she moved to the United States, becoming a nurse in the Philadelphia area. "I got so frustrated that I walk out of the business and get a nine-to-five. That made me so grounded, 'cause it mek mi realize that there is life after music," she said.[15] It's not that Junie didn't still have a connection to music, and in fact she did return to recording in recent years, but for women it can be so extraordinarily difficult that it is just not possible to support oneself. "I eat, sleep and breathe music, but I do have to make a living and have another career," she says.[16]

Lady Saw

Since 1993, Reggae Sumfest has been the premier live music event in Jamaica, taking place each year in Montego Bay with an all-star lineup. It was at this event in 2010 that Lady Saw was crowned "Queen of the Dancehall." There are few who would dispute her reign.

Lady Saw was born Marion Hall on July 12, 1972, in Galina, St. Mary, where she grew up with four brothers and four sisters. She started her career in dancehall the same as the others, by deejaying on sound systems, but her love of music, she says, came from her religious upbringing. "I started singing in church, when I was about seven, eight years old. When I was a girl, my father started taking us to a Seventh Day Adventist church; he and my mother raised six of us.... I used to go up and sing in church every Saturday ... and people there used to say I had a very good voice. And then I used to listen to the radio, to Barry G—he was the radio disc jockey on JBC who was very popular at the time—and listen to all the singers on there. People like Sister Nancy, who I really admired," she says.[17] Her knowledge of music also came from the nearby sound system dances. She explains, "I also started going to the dance hall when I was young. Sometimes when my mother and father would go night-fishing, we'd sneak out and go the place where everyone danced. I had an older sister who'd sneak us up by the window. The dance hall was very close to where we were living. And I used to hide and look in the window and see my grandmother dancing there to all those old songs—shaking her legs like that, you know—and I used to try to dance like her."[18]

Lady Saw knew from early on that she wanted to become a deejay. "I heard all that old reggae when I was a girl. There was that sound system, always played it across the street. But then when the music started changing, King Toyan came out with 'Spar Wid Me' and Barry G started playing it on the radio—and Sister Nancy came back with her version. When that new music came out, that new style—that's when I decided I really wanted to be a deejay."[19]

Lady Saw, a pioneer in dancehall, in 2009 (copyright The Gleaner Company [Media] Limited).

When Lady Saw moved to Kingston and began recording in 1991 for producers Castro Brown and Derrick Barnett on their New Name Muzik label, she took the name Lady Saw to honor one of her favorite dancehall artists, Tenor Saw. She gained attention right away for her lyrics, which were "slack," or "x-rated." In 1993, one columnist at the *Jamaica Gleaner* seemed to take offense at Lady Saw's lyrics, and he begrudgingly allowed the new star to be interviewed by him, writing from an angle more of a father than a journalist. He wrote, "Had Lady Saw not recognized and accepted the fact that she would have to change her lyrics, if not her ways, then she could not have qualified for an interview with this writer. She, as one of the leading acts in the dance hall today, deserves an interview."[20] The writer,

Howard McGowen, seemed to forget that men had been performing in the same style as Lady Saw for years, even since the days of mento, but when a woman turned the tables, it was big talk. He insinuated that her choice of expression was out of desperation. "A talented singer as well as a D.J. Lady Saw decided that singing love songs and dying of hunger is not what she wanted, so she went X-Rated. A close listen to her two smash songs will show that she went more like Triple X-Rated," McGowen wrote. The two offending songs were "If a Man Lef" and "Stab Out Mi Meat."

As Norman Stolzoff pointed out in his book on dancehall culture, *Wake the Town and Tell the People*, there was a "notion that a double standard was being employed in the treatment of Lady Saw."[21] Certainly there was. Buju Banton's songs from the year prior to Lady Saw's offending tunes were equally "triple x-rated," with lyrics referring to women grabbing his genitals, women who wear short shorts and have "ripe fruits," not to mention calling for the murder of homosexuals. Others also had employed slackness, as journalist Balford Henry pointed out in the *Jamaica Gleaner*, calling outrage over Lady Saw hypocrisy:

> I can't see what in her lyrics makes her so much more the object of these people's venom than Shabba Ranks, whose motto "sex sells," is the basis of his tremendous success; or, Terror Fabulous, whose "Position" suggests that the woman "ole up yu 'ead and cock up yu bottom" and who is now reaping success of an international label in the United States; or, Spragga Benz, who suggested that the woman "cock it up, jack it up dig out the red." I have not heard one word of objection to any of these songs. When it was suggested that the women "siddung pon it" or "lay dung pon it," it became quite popular from the most sultry downtown dancehall to the most posh uptown club. Nobody thought it offensive enough and, probably, overtly sexist to have demanded that they be banned. For years, the women have quietly digested numerous servings of the most abusive lyrics, like they have done in soca-popular countries without even a squeal. Now, a woman, Lady Saw, emerges putting her own spin on all this sexual amusement and everybody wants to crucify her.[22]

But Howard McGowen stood firmly on his soapbox, writing again of performances where Lady Saw performed on the same bill of stars as Buju Banton and Bounty Killer, and the parallels, not to mention the classicism and sexism, were still lost on him. "As impressive as Buju was, Lady Saw was vulgar," wrote McGowen in his review of the 1993 Reggae Sunsplash festival. "With a nice song sitting in the charts, the talented Lady Saw went to the bottom of the pit and came up with slack and vulgar lyrics that made the average patron cringe. She should know that we have long passed this sort of performance."[23]

Stolzoff points out that Lady Saw's song "What Is Slackness?" is a way to "hit back against her critics and the double standards they employ." Lady Saw attributed the attacks to a "syndicate of man" who wanted to "flop me career," but really it was much deeper than that. Lady Saw gave voice to the female, and perhaps some saw that as a threat. She was not the object of the male gaze, she was the voice of the female expression. Her song "Freedom of Speech" also addressed this fact, noting the double standard and the right for women to also have a voice.

Stolzoff ends with a tone of hope for what Lady Saw brought to the genre of dancehall. "It is my hope that in the future dancehall culture will become a space where Jamaicans will be able to challenge these oppressive orthodoxies and a place that fights for women's rights and gay rights, just as it has historically come to fight for the rights of the poor, of blacks, and of Rastafarians."[24]

In 2004, Lady Saw won a Grammy award for the song "Underneath It All," with the band No Doubt, for best pop performance by a duo or group, a full decade after the release of her first album, *Lover Girl*. She has also recorded with such stars as Missy Elliott, Beres Hammond, Flo Rida, Eve, Beenie Man, and Shabba Ranks. She has sung about sex and sexuality, yes, but also about safe sex and infidelity and miscarriage and infertility. Her devotion to women's issues is so deep that in 2014 she even founded the Lady Saw Foundation to help impoverished women. In more recent years she has also recorded in the gospel genre under her real name, Marion Hall, and she practices her religious roots in ministry. But Marion "Lady Saw" Hall has always been the same individual as she was as a child singing in church—albeit one with many facets and many talents.

Lady Saw's love of Jamaican music, and as a result her musical expression, is all tied together and comes full circle. "I grew up listening to ska, merengue, old-time music. I'd go to 'nine nights'—which is what they set up when people died—and people used to use graters, the graters they used to grate coconuts, to make music. We'd call it 'dinky minny.' The music's different now. But every time it starts changing, I change with it. Like now: I'm [nearly] forty now—I never hide my age—and the music's even faster. But I'm kicking asses harder than any of these young chicks coming up. They can't stand beside me. I spit like a real deejay. Like the best men—I can spit harder than most of them. I spit from way down here [motioning to gut]; I can work for hours. I don't have competition, because that's how good I am. I love it."[25]

CHAPTER TEN

Dance

Open any Kingston newspaper from the early 1960s and you are bound to find advertisements galore for musical performances. Venues throughout Kingston and the north coast—clubs, hotels and cinemas—hosted spectacular live performances to attract tourists and locals looking for an "evening of unlimited enjoyment."[1] To sweeten the pot, club owners hired rhumba dancers to headline or as special attractions for the shows as they accented the rhythms of the orchestras. Largely forgotten today, it is essential to reintroduce to the stage the rhumba dancers who literally and figuratively drew the spotlight to the music performed by Jamaican musicians.

The rhumba began in Cuba in the late 1800s as a conglomeration of several dances with African roots. This wild and frenetic dance became popular in the United States as early as 1913, and when recordings of Cuban music started to spread in North America, so too did the rhumba. In 1930, the song "Peanut Vendor," or "El Manisero," was recorded by Don Azpiazú and his Havana Casino Orchestra, inspiring a rhumba craze. As early as 1934, the *Daily Gleaner* advertised for venues hosting rhumba dancers—some from Jamaica, some from Cuba, some even from New York and Paris. Issa's department store even advertised fashions in 1935 that were inspired by the dance.[2]

The rhumba was banned in Cuba by President Gerardo Machado in 1925, though it was reestablished by the government of Fidel Castro, the president some years later. From the start, like many dances or art forms of African origin in colonized countries, the rhumba was divisive. One of the very first reports of the rhumba in Jamaica was journalistic coverage of a London court case involving indecency with dancers, though the reporter defended the dance and noted that the dance's association with indecency may have had more to do with politics than social norms. The report in the *Daily Gleaner* on October 26, 1934, stated:

> The rhumba, the dance invented by Cuba, which has popularised itself throughout the world, has been recently the subject of grave judicial debate. Those of us who have witnessed this dance, and like the rhythm and the movements of it, who believe that it is distinctively an addition to any dance repertoire, cannot but feel interested in the case now being tried before a London magistrate. This is known as the Caravan club case, in connection with which numerous arrests were recently made of persons staging or present at what was described as "Obscene dances." In these alleged obscene dances the rhumba figured prominently; Cuba, having attracted the world's attention by her repeated revolutions, was, as it were, indirectly indicted for obscenity before a British Court of Law. The barrister for the defence tried to counter the charge against his clients by offering to have the rhumba danced in Court before the learned judge. But the judge would have none of it. He refused

to see the rhumba performed within the sacred precincts. He may have felt that this offer was quite as bad as would be a suggestion that the rhumba should be danced within the confines of a cathedral!

The reporter argued that the rhumba itself was not obscene, no more so than a polka or a waltz was obscene, but that some dancers may perform in an obscene way.

In the 1960s, the rhumba was once again seen as scandalous, although this time, admittedly, dancers may have been pushing some social boundaries. On August 26, 1961, the *Star* newspaper reported on one dancer who was banned for her lewd performance. The dancer, Adina Bellamy, an eighteen-year-old from Barbados better known as Madam Eve Temptation, was sent back to her home country by Jamaican immigration authorities after "the nature of her performances was considered immoral and she would be barred from further engagements." Earlier that week the *Star* had carried a front-page picture of Madam Eve Temptation in her act, though they subsequently received complaints about the photo. On August 31, 1961, the *Star* ran the headline "Ban on Dancer Lifted." The article stated that the proprietor of Club Havana, Conrad Chin, assured the minister of Home Affairs that Madame Eve Temptation would "cover up" and that she had modified her costume, though Chin likened her original outfit to one worn by Brigitte Bardot in a film popularly shown in Jamaican cinemas. Chin argued that his dancer never performed a "striptease" and was clad in a bikini, the "same as worn on beaches and at bathing beauty contests." Evidently, the fine line between provocative and profane was as thin as a thread on a shimmying, shaking ruffle, though it was far from modern-day slackness.

Despite the castigation of female sensuality and sexuality from the establishment, by the 1950s and 1960s, rhumba was, well, in full swing in Jamaica. There were advertisements for dancers with names such as Madame Sugar Hips (Sonia Hylton), Madame Peppersex, Madame Provocation, Madam Loleta, Madame Bridgette, Madam Bibsy, Madam Pussycat, Madame Delores, Madam Rubena, Madame Domirez, Madame B, Madame P, Senorita Esmerine, Shalimar, La Chatte, Shirleena, Chanela, Audita, Sayonara, Zandra, and Pancho and Rena. They were billed as "vivacious," "torrid," "sensuous," "exotic," "exciting," and they were "bombshells" and "balls of fire."[3] The following three rhumba queens were arguably the most pioneering in Jamaica during the 1940s to the 1960s. These are the sirens of Jamaican music.

Daisy Riley

On March 5, 1912, Daisy Veronica Riley was born to Thomasina Cunningham, a butleress, in Kingston, Jamaica. She began her career as an entertainer by winning a beauty competition, then became a prominent member of Pantomime while transitioning to the stages of local clubs as Jamaica's first "Rhumba Queen." Before she received that moniker, she was called a "sepia star." The first time her name appeared in print was in 1932 when, as a member of the Edelweiss Concert Choir, she soloed on a song called "Rumbo."[4]

In 1936, Daisy Riley won the Black Beauty bathing contest, as well as the song and dance portion of the competition. In 1939 she was cast in the film *Devil's Daughter* (the working title was "Daughters of the Island") in a scene shot at the Glass Bucket Club and Manor House. The scene, a Jamaican market, featured "Daisy Riley, a local entertainer, in one of the principal roles in this market scene. She falls in love with a Kingston chappie who is coming to market leading a donkey and accompanied by his wife, and she decides to nab him by hook or by crook. She sings and she dances, first alone, and then with him, for she does nab him in the end."[5]

In June 1934, Riley returned to film when she was cast as a "native dancer" in the film *White Sails*, though in the U.S. it was released as *Obeah!* and in the UK as *The Mystery Ship*. Riley performed with a number of other locals in a bar scene that was shot in Kingston for the film, which starred Jean Brooks and was directed by F. Herrick Herrick of Arcturus Pictures in New York. Over the decade, Riley continued her screen work by appearing in a number of film shorts for Jamaican advertisements, including some with Errol Flynn.[6]

Riley's talents took her to any stage where there was song and dance. She performed in shows with Mrs. Vere Johns as early as 1942, and that same year Riley began to step onto the stage as a dancer accompanying orchestras. She was a draw, an attraction, to entice audiences and add to the value of the music. The *Daily Gleaner* on September 26, 1943, announced a show at Edelweiss Park by promoting "Daisy Riley with her ripping hips and wonderful voice. Redver Cooke's Orchestra in attendance." Though the announcement did not mention the rhumba, it was about as close as one could get. The first mention of Daisy Riley dancing the rhumba comes in the *Daily Gleaner* on December 31, 1943. Riley, the article stated, would be entertaining at a New Year's dance at the Springfield Beach Club with music by Baby O'Brien and his Springfield Club Orchestra. She was billed as the "Rhumba Queen and her troupe." She also danced with the George Moxey's Orchestra and Val Bennett's Rhythm Aces that same holiday season, and in March 1943 her performance of the rhumba at St George's Church hall during "Variety Nite" was called a "refreshing exhibition."[7] She continued to headline her own group of dancers in 1944 at the Springfield Beach Club in February during a "Colossal Floor Show" featuring "Daisy Riley (Ja. Rhumba Queen) and her group" performing to the music of the Springfield Club Orchestra.[8] Bands comprising Jamaican musicians played swing music, some with Cuban and Latin rhythms, as Daisy drew audiences to the Springfield club, which was located "on the sea" and hosted periodic fundraisers for the Alpha Boys' School, as well as other schools.[9]

At the same time, Riley was involved in Pantomime, always sharing the stages with the same performers, including Ranny Williams and Louise Bennett. Williams had previously appeared in the film *Devil's Daughter* with Riley. On Christmas Day 1943, Daisy Riley costarred with Miss Lou in *Anancy Goes to Town* at the Ward Theatre. Only a few days later, Riley performed again with Miss Lou and Ranny Williams at the Ward Theatre in *Soliday and the Wicked Bird*. Perhaps her most popular performance came in July 1943 with the show *Hot Chocolate*, which the *Daily Gleaner* called a "Who's who of the local stage … absolute tops in entertainment."[10] Another reviewer commented, "The girls were hotcha—hot-hipped Daisy Riley singing and swaying the torrid music of the Peanut Vendor, the dark, dimpled, limbed girls of the chorus cavorting to crazy boogie, legs flashing from teasing costumes." Yet another reviewer called her "a sensation."[11] Another on August 30, 1943, wrote, "Once again Daisy Riley stole the show with her dancing in the 'Afro-Cubano' number, the enthusiastic jam-packed audience going wild over her torrid 'Peanut Vendor.' Best feature of 'Hot Chocolate,' in the opinion of many, is the dancing."[12] Edna Manley herself in the *Daily Gleaner*, September 21, 1943, stated, "Daisy Riley seems to be a find. There is a sort of barbaric strength in her dancing that lifts it right above the ordinary."

Riley continued to shake her hips on Pantomime stages and beyond. The *Daily Gleaner* on December 27, 1945, reviewed Riley's performance during a Ranny Williams Christmas show at the Ward with an encore performance on New Year's morning: "It is impossible to pick out individual acts, but Daisy Riley, the Rhumba Queen, has a brand new version of 'Babalu' that sends the blood racing." stated the reporter. Her performances as Carmen Miranda were always sensual, and when performing for more upper-class clubs, such as for the mayor of Kingston at the King's House in July 1945, she was careful to keep her hips in check—after all, she was billed as the "lovely curved dancing sensation" who was "rib rocking."[13] She performed year after year in musicals and holiday shows, all the while attracting audiences as the "Rhumba Queen." She danced to the Eric Deans Orchestra, Ralph Grant and his one-man orchestra, and Rinaldo's Rhumba Kings. It is also to be noted that many of the clubs where Daisy performed, while though they employed black Jamaican musicians and Daisy Riley herself, who was a black Jamaican, did not permit black patrons. These were whites-only, upper-class clubs. One can rightly assume that the effects of this racism and classism were felt strongly by Daisy, as well as by all black artists who were, in a real sense, exploited for the entertainment of the oppressors; and the impact will forever be part of Jamaica's cultural fabric, as well as the fabric of many cultures built upon colonization, slavery, and oppression.

Kitty Kingston reports in her "Personal Mention" column in the *Daily Gleaner* on December 28, 1951, that Daisy Riley had left the stage behind, as well as Jamaica, though she returned to visit. She wrote, "An old and popular favourite of the local stage, who Eric Coverley says helped to give Christmas morning concerts the popularity they have acquired during the past 11 years, was guest of honour at the concert. She is vivacious Daisy Riley—now Mrs Picquett of Chicago, USA. Daisy has come home on a 3-month vacation." Daisy Riley Picquett had married Henry Picquett. Together they had two sons and two daughters, as well as numerous grandchildren and great grandchildren who called her Mama DD. Daisy Riley Picquett died in New Orleans on February 4, 2005.

Anita Mahfood

Rhumba queen Margarita was born Anita Selema Mahfood on June 14, 1939, to a businessman, Jad Eid Mahfood, and his first wife, Brenda May Virtue, a white woman from Jamaica. Jad had immigrated to Kingston from Beirut, Lebanon, in the 1920s. Together, he and wife Brenda had four daughters: Monira, Conchita, Anita and Janet—in that order. Anita's father, Jad, also had two other children with two other women, neither of whom he married; and one of those children was born while he was still married to Brenda. Jad established a thriving fish shop at a depot on the Torrington Bridge called Mahfood's Fisheries; and he wished for his children to all work there to help grow the business, but Anita had other plans for herself. To escape an abusive home life, and to pursue her natural, self-taught talent, Anita began dancing while very young. In 1952, at the tender age of twelve, Anita won first prize on the *Vere Johns Opportunity Hour* talent show. She won competitions week after week, and she took the stage name Margarita. Her daughter Suzanne Bent explains: "I guess she did that to hide it from the Mahfoods. That I believe, because at that time it was not becoming of a woman. But she wanted to be her own person."[14] And hide her dancing she did, until Anita's father found out from his friends. When Anita won a competition at the Glass Bucket, her father was there to see it, unbeknownst to her. She was found out. But there was nothing he could do to stop her. Best friend Faye Chin says, "We danced together. We were in a group on stage. She used to do rhumba; I do creative dancing, limbo dancing. It's Alan Ivanhoe Dance Troupe I was in. She was an individual dancer and whenever they were having performance like pantomimes or the theatre used to have *Opportunity Hour*, she would dance there. She was a terrific dancer and she taught herself to dance. We became friends and we really became close and we were friends for a long, long time until she passed."[15]

Not only did Margarita teach herself to dance the rhumba; she also sewed her own rhumba costumes. Margarita, the ultimate performer, always began her dance the same way with the same

Anita "Margarita" Mahfood, rhumba dancer and pioneer (courtesy Zola Buckland Sergi).

air of anticipation. When the spotlight hit one area on the center of the dance floor, the music began. Margarita was in the corner of the room, out of view. She sauntered to the center, ruffles rushing through the tables of men and women who would turn their heads to watch her passage to the light. When she came into full view, the rhythms of the drums at their height, the audience was fully captivated, fully immersed in her powerful magic. She was auditioning for her dream. One day she wanted to dance on the stages in the United States, but she had to make a name for herself at home first.

Margarita appeared with the same circuit of performers as did most Kingston entertainers of the day. She first met Don Drummond in the 1950s at the Bournemouth Club when they appeared on the same bill. Ads appear in the *Daily Gleaner* in June 1955 for Drummond and "Marguerita (Rhumba Dancer)" together on a lineup with others. Margarita performed at the Ward Theatre, Club Havana, Club Baby Grand, Club Adastra, Carib Theatre, Glass Bucket, Rialto Theatre, Ritz Theatre, and Queens Theatre, and she frequently received top billing. She played the role of a dancer in a club for the documentary *It Can Happen to You*, which was filmed by the Jamaica Film Unit in the 1950s, and she performed regularly during holiday shows.

Margarita not only brought patrons into venues to hear music performed by Jamaican musicians, but also, more importantly, encouraged the introduction of downtown music to uptown audiences. Margarita, more specifically, brought the drums of Count Ossie and his group from the hills into the clubs with her when she danced. She took the drums from where they hid in the hills. She advocated for drum playing, otherwise relegated to marginal spaces of Jamaican society, into the clubs in these exclusive settings where barristers and tourists came to wine and dine. Though Prince Buster may have recorded these drums on the Folkes Brothers' "Oh Carolina," it was Margarita who took the drums of Count Ossie across the class divide, since she was from the upper classes and danced in clubs where members of the upper classes attended. She helped to introduce the music to these patrons. It was historian Verena Reckord who first made this argument for Margarita as ambassador for Count Ossie and his drummers, and thereby for Rastafari music. She writes, "The group got its first legitimate stage break in the late fifties. It was an occasion when the late, famous rhumba queen Marguerita [Mahfood] insisted that she would not appear on a Vere Johns variety show [*Opportunity Hour*] at the Ward Theatre on Christmas morning unless Ossie's group was on the bill. Johns was wary then about using Rastas on his show, but Marguerita was his star attraction. He had no choice. Count Ossie and his drummers were hired. They were a hit. They soon became regulars on Vere Johns' show and other functions."[16]

The Star newspaper on August 22, 1961, mentions one of these performances when Margarita danced with Count Ossie, accentuating their rhythms with her hips. The article reads, "African Drums at Palace Hour. Fans who attend the Palace Theatre tomorrow night will see and hear for the first time on a stage Count Ossie and his African Drums, the band whose sounds have taken Jamaica by storm. They will also hear the famous 'Carolina' which held the Number One spot on the Hit Parade for so long.… For variety there will also be Creative Dancer Margarita." A review of the show in the *Star* on August 28, 1961, called it "A Big Hit." The article stated, "Upwards of 2,000 eager fans thronged the Palace Theatre last Wednesday night to witness the first appearance of Count Ossie and His African Drums, with some of the island's top entertainers. Scores had to stand and hundreds were turned away. The show was good to the last drop and every item was a winner.… Hit of the evening was the dance done by the curvesome Margarita to the beat of the African drums in colourful costume. She received an ovation."

In 1965, Margarita recorded the song "Woman a Come" at Treasure Isle with Baba Brooks, Tommy McCook and Lloyd Knibb. The song reached number seven on the Jamaican charts and was one of the very few songs written and sung by a solo female artist. Most songs that featured female vocalists, up to that point, were duets with other prominent male artists. Marcia Griffiths re-recorded Margarita's song in 1981, which is also a testament to its worth. The lyrics of the song are a sweet but painful love poem to Don Drummond. Margarita Anita Mahfood died in the early hours of January 2, 1965, at the hand of Don Drummond, her lover, who stabbed her four times in the chest, likely as a result of mental illness that was not properly treated. She had been previously married to boxer Rudolph Bent (who died in November 2016), and together they had two children,

Anita "Margarita" Mahfood, the "Rhumba Queen," in 1959 (copyright The Gleaner Company [Media] Limited).

Christopher and Suzanne Bent, who survive. Christopher passed away in mid–January 2017, while Suzanne lives in the Bronx, New York.

Madame Wasp

Born Elizabeth Cespedes, the stage performer better known as Madame Wasp was the great-granddaughter of Cuban revolutionary Carlos Manuel de Céspedes, who led the Ten Years' War, the conflict from 1868 to 1878 seeking Cuban independence from Spain and the emancipation of all the enslaved. He was ultimately successful and today is a Cuban national hero. Elizabeth's daughter, Nadine Taylor, says that Elizabeth was born in St. Catherine, Jamaica, to a Cuban father and Indian mother: "That mixture went with her fluidity in dance and music," says Taylor.[17] Madame Wasp was "good friends with Margarita," Taylor asserts, adding that she "loved her dance and her music." Though Madame Wasp is still alive and well today in Toronto, Canada, her daughter admits says that she does not talk about her days as a dancer as "she wants to bury that part of her life"—a comment that has been also made by other dancers of this era, including Jannette Phillips, who taught dancers step-by-step how to dance the ska. She too said that she doesn't "want to relive that part of her past. It was a long long time ago."[18] But in her day, Madame Wasp was a successful, classy, beautiful dancer and model. In fact, she modeled for a number of album covers for popular musicians, including for guitarist Dennis Sindrey, who remembers. "I knew her quite well," says Sindrey, "because we used to run a floor show on Fridays and sometimes Saturdays as well at the Sheraton Hotel, and we used to have a dance troupe. It's wasn't her troupe, but it was Joan Seaga's, and she had three women and one guy. We'd start with the music and then in the middle we'd let the drummer carry on drumming. The dancers would be dancing. It was a version of the rhumba. They picked out a particular song and we as a band would do a chorus or two and then in the middle the drummer would keep drumming."[19]

Sindrey says that Madame Wasp's performances commanded respect. "Elizabeth always had a lot of poise and pride. She was a great girl and I always liked her. She was very talented but also very humble…. It's hard being a dancer like that and classy at the same time. It was a step above the rhumba dancing because we were at the Sheraton. The real rhumba dancers we had when I used to play with Byron's band and some of them could be pretty rough. But Joan [Seaga] had a good reputation for putting on a pretty good show. It was always a big hit with the tourists. They had a good selection of costumes and would do different dances, like the limbo."

That "Joan" that Sindrey references is Joan Seaga, who had her own troupe of dancers, including Madame Wasp and Madam Sugar Hips. Seaga recalls, "I discovered this girl, her name was Elizabeth, and I called her Madame Wasp because I said when she dances it's like she sting people. I got this other girl called Sonia [Hylton], and when she dance she could vibrate her whole body and I called her Madam Sugar Hips because she shake like sugar in a can. Madame Wasp was a very attractive girl, like Lena Horne, that's the look she had. When she started to dance, the rhumba became very popular, the Jamaican rhumba which was taken from Cuba. They travelled all over the world and perform, and at the same time they were performing, there was this girl performing, Mahfood [Anita Mahfood, Margarita]. She was a very very good dancer. That's how the rhumba in Jamaica started. It was very exciting, very sexy, and it became extremely popular."[20]

In April 1969, Madame Wasp travelled with a delegation to North America for *Springboard to Jamaica*, hosted by the Jamaica Tourist Board.[21] The delegation also included Ken Maxwell as comedian and master of ceremonies, and the Tower Tornadoes, a calypso band from the Tower Isle Hotel. They visited thirteen cities in North America, including New York, where they were joined by Danny Slue, a former member of the Ticklers Calypso Band from Tower Isle who had immigrated to the U.S. They performed for television, press, and functions with travel agents in order to promote Jamaica as a destination.

Madame Wasp left her stage days behind when she married Carl Brady, one of the original members of Byron Lee and the Dragonaires. Together Elizabeth and Carl had three children, two daughters and a son. "She surprised the hell out of everybody when she married Carl!" says Dennis Sindrey. Though the couple divorced, Madame Wasp lives in Toronto, where she is retired from a career as a dance instructor. Her children are also involved in the entertainment industry. Carl Brady died in December 2019.

Ivy Baxter

Where to place a person like Ivy Baxter in the Jamaican cultural canon? With one foot in folk music and another in dance, Ivy Baxter sought to bring together the folk customs of Jamaica through choreographing folk songs and folk ceremonies to celebrate the identity of the Jamaica during the time before, during, and after Independence.

Ivy Baxter was born on March 3, 1923, as the youngest of six daughters. Her father, Edward Baxter, worked for the Jamaican Railway, and her mother, Arabel Baxter, died when Ivy was very young. She was then raised by her aunt. All of the girls received exceptional educations. Ivy studied at Toronto University in Canada as well as at the Sigurd Leeder School of Modern European Ballet in England. She returned to Jamaica to take a position teaching physical education at the YWCA. There was no such entity as the performing arts, at this time, but movement and physical education were related. Seeing the need for a school of dance, Baxter founded her own school, called the Ivy Baxter Modern Creative Dance Group, in 1950.[22] It was at this school that Baxter taught Jamaican dance, rooted in Jamaican folk culture, since students only received training in English dances during this time. In the foreword for Baxter's book, *The Arts of an Island*, Philip Sherlock says of the Jamaican cultural identity, "The first stirrings came through those who, like Ivy Baxter, found a world of music and meaning in the old dance forms and Jamaica rhythms.... Ivy Baxter created new dance forms out of the old and made the dance a part of Jamaican life, preparing the way for the rich flowering of today."[23]

Folk dances go back to the Taíno and cacique Anacaona, who was famed for her choreography. The Eboes, Ashanti, Fanti, Akim, Mandingues, Coromantee and others from Africa kept their cultural dances unique to their tribes. The revivalist cultures—Pukkumina, Myal, and Kumina from the Congo—also featured dance as a way of spiritual connectivity. And many of these cultures were influenced by or molested by the European cultures of colonizers, producing further dances in the John Canoe masquerades or carnival or quadrille. But what was the result of that mélange? What was the identity of Jamaican dance at the time of Independence, when Jamaicans were finally free, in a sense, of their centuries of bondage? That was Ivy Baxter's mission. As she writes in her book, "Now, after 300 years of cultural incubation … the bird of Jamaican folk culture is trying to fly, or rather to be set in flight in a cultural race of eagles and swans of the larger and more communicative countries which did not have such a complicated nesting."[24]

Ivy Baxter brought folk dance back to the folk. Her students were referred to as the "barefoot dancers"[25] since they removed their ballet slippers in exchange for getting back in touch with the earth. "Foot is the root of the human from on which the corpus relies to stand tall and to maintain balance," said Alma Mock Yen, of the University of West Indies at Mona, of Baxter's method of dance.[26] Baxter also introduced dance into the rituals and customs of the folk to enhance the celebration. One article from 1956 revealed that she had choreographed dances to the "laying of ghosts" ceremony, and her dance group was learning the "Yanga," which was described as a Jamaican dance. Additionally, they performed a dance based on "native road-diggers, one based on village life, one with 'religious fervour,' and another involving 'a vignette of Kingston life with a policeman as central figure.'"[27] Ivy Baxter was a dance scholar, choreographer, cultural interpreter, and a dancer herself.

Baxter's dance group toured the United States and Latin America, bringing Jamaican folk dance to thousands of curious people. When her dance school closed in 1967, she had already inspired many other dancers and dance instructors who went on to establish their own dance companies, including the National Dance Theatre Company. Baxter continued her teaching at the Excelsior Education Centre in 1969. It was no light undertaking. She became head of the community college at the school, teaching dance and drumming, and founding a program for the elderly. She retired in 1982.

Ivy Baxter recognized that Jamaican folk culture was Jamaican identity, and dance was an integral expression of that identity, especially in the 1950s and 1960s. "She was an integral part of the awakening of national consciousness and self-confidence which marked the era prior to Independence. She bequeathed to us the appreciation of the dignity, the beauty and the authenticity of our Jamaican spirit and culture through the dance," said P.J. Patterson, then prime minister of Jamaica, in a tribute after Baxter's death on January 9, 1993.[28]

Hazel Johnston

Though her chosen form of dance was a European form, Hazel Johnston was a pioneer in Jamaican dance because she was a black Jamaican mastering and teaching what was, up until that time, a white dance form: "Although at first, dance was taught only to light-skinned islanders, one Jamaican girl, Hazel Johnston, would change all that. Johnston went to England to learn music and returned to Jamaica to become the first dancer to build her own studio—no one would rent studio space to her. She began working toward dance theater based on Jamaica's own culture."[29] It was the 1930s, a time of deep class and racial segregation in Jamaica, but Johnston had the determination to break through these barriers.

Hazel Carmen Seaton Johnston was born on July 30, 1909, to father Charles Edward Johnson and mother Martha Mahala Romans Seaton. Hazel was the middle of five children. Her father was a merchant who had periodically immigrated to Pennsylvania, living there for a number of years each time. He married Martha when he was 47 years old and she was 38. All five of their children were long ago born by the time they married. Martha was a dressmaker and her sister, Lucille, became a well-known pianist.

With a merchant as a father, Hazel was afforded a decent upbringing. She attended Wolmer's Girls School, a prestigious school founded in 1729; it is the oldest school in the Caribbean, with notable alumni such as Edward Seaga, Harry Belafonte, Marlon James, and Sean Paul in the boys' school. After graduation, Hazel attended schools in Leeds and Derbyshire in England, where she further studied music and movement. She returned to England for further training in 1935 at the McLaren School of Dancing, but she again returned to Jamaica to pursue her calling—teaching dance.[30]

In 1938, Johnston had arranged her own version of Disney's *Snow White* featuring the minuet and gavotte. This sort of fairy tale became a frequent part of Johnston's repertoire, likely because her school catered to young girls. Performances included *The Sleeping Beauty* and *Little Red Riding Hood,* using music from Chopin and Schubert. The young students, some as young as three years old, danced as dolls, sailors, ice skaters, and puppets. One of her most notable recitals was a performance of *A Midsummer Night's Dream,* which was a massive success. Newspaper reviews show that all of Johnston's students' performances were well received. One such review bore the headline, "Hazel Johnston Ballet Delightful." The journalist wrote, "Dancing is essentially an aristocratic art. The tradition in its purest form is being promoted, preserved and furthered by Hazel Johnston…. The Hazel Johnston Ballet was a three-item sequence wherein each action, whether by an individual or by the corps, was flexible as steel, intense yet delicate as a gossamer, bound together by the unmistakable signature of constant genius."[31] Another stated, "Hazel Johnston scored a popular success in the most ambitious ballet ever attempted in Jamaica, the moonlight scene from Chopin's 'Les Sylphides' which she included in the recital of her studio at the Ward Theatre on Saturday…. Perhaps, first place must be given to Miss Johnston's skillful choreography. She showed the great departure the modern ballet has taken from the old. The old masters might scarcely have recognized the new dances in which the stiffness so much a 'sine qua non' of the old days had shaded off into suppleness and 'flowingness' of movement."[32]

All seemed to be going well for Johnston, but she had been suffering from a long illness when she died on April 8, 1944. The cause of death stated on her death certificate was "mesenteric sarcoma," or cancer of the bowel. She was just 34 years old. Though her years may have been short, her legacy was firmly entrenched in the world of Jamaican dance. One of her star pupils, Phyllis Cardoza, went on to study at Johnston's alma mater in England, McLaren's School of Dancing, and she returned to Jamaica to continue the teaching methods employed by Johnston.[33] Another one of Johnston's star pupils also continued this legacy of technique and skill for all Jamaicans, not just those who were members of the aristocracy—Ivy Baxter.

Chapter Eleven

Champions

It is bewildering, and likely even futile, to imagine the lives of musicians in isolation of the support of others. This is true for any person of importance. Who would Plato be without Socrates? Who would Helen Keller be without Anne Sullivan? Who would Luke Skywalker be without Obi-wan Kenobi? Mentors, leaders, and teachers are crucial to the success not only of individuals but also of entire movements. For women, it is especially important to serve in this capacity, to other women and to the cultural collective. These are a few of the female champions of Jamaican music.

Sister Mary Ignatius Davies

Without the life of Sister Ignatius, Jamaican music wouldn't be the same. In fact, it is arguable that without Sister Iggy, as she was affectionately known by her students, reggae, rocksteady, even ska might not have seen their genesis through the horns and drums of the boys in her care. The world owes a great debt to Sister Mary Ignatius Davies—a nun, a leader, a mother of sorts who embodies the spirit behind the Jamaican phrase "likkle but tallawa," small but mighty. It's not that Sister Iggy was small. In fact, she was tall, as the Alpha Boys remember her, shrinking a bit later in life due to her age. But she was always skinny, delicate, bird-like even—so thin that Johnny "Dizzy" Moore and other boys referred to her affectionately as "Bones."

Sister Mary Ignatius Davies was born in Jamaica on November 18, 1921, in Innswood, St. Catherine. She was born Marjorie Agnes Davies to John Robert Davies and Ethel Davies, née Starege. Her mother, Ethel, a native of Demerara, Guyana, died in 1935, so father John was left to raise the three children alone, two boys and Marjorie, who was the youngest. John seemed unable to raise a 14-year-old girl and called on Marjorie's aunt, Ivy, to care for her. Marjorie was enrolled at the high school run by the Sisters of Mercy at Convent of Mercy Academy, which was the girls' section of Alpha. According to Sister of Mercy Mary Bernadette Little of Alpha, Marjorie excelled at business classes while in high school—classes such as shorthand, accounting, and typing.[1]

Shortly after graduation from school, Marjorie became a member of the Sisters of Mercy, or a nun, in 1939. She said she felt a calling to the convent after she visited Mother Magdalen, the superior at her high school, who encouraged her life of dedication. Marjorie was only 17 years old when she started her life at Alpha Boys' School, and she stayed

Sister Mary Ignatius Davies of Alpha Boys' School congratulating members of the school's soccer team at the National Stadium on November 7, 1968, after they won a match in the Private Secondary School competition. Sister Ignatius was dedicated to all sports and vocations taught to her boys, especially music, the program for which she helped to build and sustain (copyright The Gleaner Company [Media] Limited).

there her entire life (except for a couple of years when she helped to establish the St. John Bosco Children's Home in Manchester, opened by the sisters at Alpha Boys' School). When Marjorie joined the sisterhood, she adopted the religious name Ignatius after Saint Ignatius Loyola, who founded the Jesuits, a congregation of the Catholic Church. "To all outward appearances, there was nothing dramatic about that time or her involvement in ministry; hers was the humdrum experience of supervising dormitories at night, every one of her charges was provided with the attire that was appropriate for each occasion that presented itself, and that each young boy and/or teenager had the required nourishment for his wellbeing and development," writes Sister Little of Sister Ignatius's quiet devotion to her tasks.

But Sister Ignatius had services, vision, and expertise beyond these day-to-day responsibilities as she rose through the ranks with her quiet commitment to her boys. Always skilled in sports, having played cricket and soccer in high school and having a natural love for competition, Sister Ignatius encouraged her boys to play sports at Alpha. She even played alongside them on the field, showing them how to kick the ball and swing a bat. "Ignatius was the one who train you, tell you how to play, what to play, and at that time she was a young, beautiful person and she used to teach the boys a lot. She wanted them to be the best," remembers Winston "Sparrow" Martin, band director at Alpha Boys' School and former student.[2] Martin says,

> She would teach them how to box because she loved boxing. She would have movies of boxers and she would take us down to the convent and show us these movies of great boxers, Rocky Marciano and Sugar Ray Robinson and all these guys. The guys who do boxing, she would tell them, "When you look at the movie, you should watch his foot and see his hand how he punches." She would tell us about the great English cricketers. She would show us how to bat and all this. She like games. She could play table tennis. She would come around and we'd say, "Sister, can you play a game?" and she'd say okay and she'd play table tennis and we'd try to beat her. She'd smash everything, she always beat the ball, always beat the ball. She would go to football. She show you how to shoot the ball. Everything she would do. If we sit down, she always sit with us, the boys. For spiritualness, she would sit with them.

Sister Mary Bernadette Little says in her book that part of the reason that Sister Ignatius taught the boys about sports was for character building. "It was an interesting and awesome experience to see this nun, fully clothed in habit, don boxing gloves to demonstrate to the boys how this sport could be more deftly or skillfully performed.... And she could play cricket, football [soccer], hockey, baseball, and she was also a swimmer. With the game, there naturally came the qualities of discipline and good sportsmanship and these fundamental elements of good character building were ever in the forefront of her instruction to the boys," writes Little.

Charles Simpson, a student at Alpha Boys' School from 1953 to 1960 and a trombonist in the band, recalls Sister Ignatius and her love for sports, which she passed on to the boys. "The ability about her, and maybe why she is loved by all the boys, is that if boxing is going on, she'll be a part of it. She would put on her gloves while in her habit. She was never in any other thing but her habit. Earlier in the day it was black and white, full black all the way down to the ankles and shoes. They had a white breast plate that ran across the chest. She was always playing. She was a complete sports person. She was a fan of the great Sugar Ray Robinson and they were pen pals. She was a tremendous cricket fan. She loved Collie Smith and love Garry Sobers, but when it came to cricket, Collie Smith was her favorite," says Simpson.[3] He says that as a result, the school excelled at cricket, boxing, soccer, and baseball, winning many national championships. She nurtured a number of Jamaican boxing champions that came from Alpha including Alan Harmon, Roy Lee, and Kid Bassey and soccer player Owen "Ital Stew" Stewart. She founded baseball and cricket associations for the private school league. "The boys know me because I talk to them a lot about sports and other things," said Sister Ignatius.[4] She also had a love for world affairs, reading, and history, and she was especially fond of Nelson Mandela, Martin Luther King, Jr., and Jomo Kenyatta.

Sister Ignatius is perhaps most well-known by those aside from her boys for her great love for music. It was because of her passion for all kinds of music that the band program prospered. The band program at Alpha Boys' School had long been established back in 1892 as a drum and fife corps. It was bolstered in 1908 when a Roman Catholic bishop in Jamaica donated a number of brass instruments to the school. The same year, Walter S. Harrison became a drill sergeant at the school, appointed by the Jamaica Defence Force. He even served as the inaugural bandmaster for one year but continued on as drill sergeant through the mid–1960s. As a result, there was a strong connection between Alpha and the military; after graduation from Alpha, boys frequently took positions in the West Indian Regiment, which became the Jamaican Military Band after independence. Music taught during these times was solely classical. But under the leadership of Sister Ignatius the band program grew, since she saw the opportunities in music for her boys after they left Alpha. The band program also grew in Sister Ignatius's years, because music was her passion.

It is quite a sight to imagine "Bones" in her full habit, spinning records at a DJ's turntables, music pumping from the huge speakers for the boys who danced to the hits, but that's exactly what Sister Ignatius did on many occasions at Alpha Boys' School. "She build a sound system, we call it Mutt and Jeff. The reason for that, the people who used to play the music, one man was very tall, the other one is very short, so we call it Mutt and Jeff," says Martin. Sister Ignatius bought her sound system from Mutt and Jeff, who were sound system operators, modern-day DJs. Mutt was Kenneth Davy; naming his sound system Mutt and Jeff was a reference to a popular comic strip of the day that featured a very tall character, Mutt, and a "half-pint" named Jeff. The comic strip was carried in the *Jamaica Star*, one of the island's newspapers. Davy, who was over six feet tall, held the Mutt moniker, and Jeff was better known as Leighton Geoff, a short fellow with an appropriate last name.

Davy attended Alpha Boys' School and was a skilled public speaker and debater. After he graduated, Sister Ignatius asked Davy to return to emcee various school events and presentations such as plays, concerts, and sporting competitions. He did this all without the aid of any amplification, but around 1956 he purchased a microphone, a small amplifier, and two 12-inch speakers. He quickly moved into providing background music at these events and started hosting sound system dances at Alpha. As word of his entertainment skill spread, Davy began organizing dances outside of Alpha, and he soon found the need to upgrade his equipment to meet demand. Davy worked his full-time day job in the Alpha Boys' School printery, directing the boys in the trade of setting type, inking presses, and printing books that were then bound in the school's bindery. With the blessing of Sister Ignatius, Davy's sound system upgrade was a project handled by the school's woodshop. The boys learned to produce a custom item under the watchful eye of Davy, whose printery was adjacent to the woodshop. He frequently left his shop to help supervise the boys with their table saws, sanders, and hammers. The woodshop, like the printery and the pottery shop and the garden and the shoe shop, were not only areas of trade instruction for the boys; they were also revenue makers, as they still are today, helping to offset the operational costs of the school. Making custom items for customers was part of the school's operation, and part of training for the boys.

Davy was able to generate a decent amount of revenue from the sound system. When he decided in 1964 to leave the life of the sound system behind to spend more time with his wife and their eleven children, he sold his entire set, equipment and music, to Sister Ignatius, who added the records to her already-large collection. Sister Ignatius had hundreds of 78 and 45 records in her collection—everything from classical music to speeches by Malcolm X. This collection was built from not only Davy's additions; Sister Ignatius would regularly send her students, such as Floyd Lloyd Seivright, to purchase records from local record shops, giving them money for the acquisition and a list of her selections.

Sparrow Martin recalls his days as a student when they all listened to her tunes:

> She would come on Saturdays and she would have a whole lot of record, you name it, classical, jazz record, pop record, all kind, Latin, American, European music, Cuban music, and mento music. She would say, "Okay, today we are going to listen to classical music," and she would take out Beethoven, Bach, and she says, especially to the band boys, "Listen to your classical music." Then she'd say, "Okay, I'm going to play jazz for you today," and she'd play jazz music. Then she'd play Cuban music. Now, we don't speak Spanish, but she would take Spanish music from Cuba and she'd say, "Listen to the drums, listen to the bass, listen to how they play saxophone." She would sit down with you so you have the interest.[5]

Sister Ignatius even took up her instrument from time to time. Vocalist Owen Grey says, "Our teacher, Sister Ignatius, she was a musician herself because she could play the saxophone, she could play the flute, and she was very strict."[6]

Why did Sister Ignatius spend so much time and effort on training boys in music? Obviously, she had a great love for music—that is undeniable—but she also recognized the potential of the music for her boys. Music was an occupation. It was a way of earning an income. Sister Ignatius had the vision to see that music was a viable living, a fruitful living, and one that would grow. Of the music that would soon develop in Jamaica and take over the world, largely the result of the talent at Alpha Boys' School, Sister Ignatius once said that she knew it was not going to stay in Jamaica only.

Sister Ignatius helped her boys get employment with the popular orchestras in Kingston after they left Alpha. Orchestras that employed Alpha boys included the Eric Deans Orchestra, a 12-piece group led by Eric Deans, who enjoyed a middle and upper-class clientele, at the Colony Club up on Half-Way Tree Road. Deans had been directing his orchestra since 1944. He attracted crowds because of his repertoire of jazz standards. World-renowned guitar player Ernest Ranglin recruited boys directly from Alpha by working with Sister Ignatius. One of those boys was genius trombonist Don Drummond. Ranglin says, "I have permission for him [Drummond] to come out of Alpha School for Eric Deans band. I had to go to Sister [Ignatius] to get permission for him to play in the band. We were all young fellows and I took four of them out of Alpha. I took one saxophone player, which is Reuben Alexander, he's not alive now, he's passed; Edward Thornton [Tan Tan] who used to play with Aswad and all those bands from England; Blue Bogey [Wilton Gaynair] who is somewhere in Germany; and Don Drummond. I was a member of the group; we all were young fellows in the group."[7]

It was common for bandleaders at the time to source Alpha Boys' School for talent for their bands. Just two years earlier, Sister Ignatius had endorsed the placement of saxophonist Joe Harriott in a position with the Sonny Bradshaw Orchestra. Alpha was a prime source of talent for bandleaders for a number of reasons. Mark Williams writes, "In assessing why so many talented musicians emerged from Alpha in a relatively short period of time, one must probably look beyond merely the quality and nature of the teaching being given. Instead, it could be a function of supply and demand, and the demand was coming from throughout the island, where past Alpha graduates were finding work playing music in various settings…. The hotel and society club's circuit system may have been an active arm of colonial rule, but it also provided a setting for professional, big band swing and Latin music orchestras as well as well-rehearsed jazz ensembles to flourish."[8]

Eric Deans, one of the bandleaders of the time scouting Alpha, was known to groom young musicians into professionals. He immediately secured Drummond, who was joined a few months later by Alpha boy Eddie "Tan Tan" Thornton, who played trumpet and was Drummond's classmate. Tan Tan recalls, "Eric Deans' was society. No poor people could come there. It's just the lawyer, barrister, and tourist, mostly tourist. It's an exclusive club. You have to have money to go in it. We used to play six nights a week—Monday, Tuesday, Wednesday, Thursday, Friday, Saturday. A lot of American tourist used to come there, every night. In those days a lot of American tourist used to come. It's the club they come to first, they go to Glass Bucket after. Eric Deans was the best band in Jamaica, and we play the same music that was played in America—Count Basie, Duke Ellington, Benny Goodman, Artie Shaw, Harry James, everything. The music we played is America music. There was no ska in those days. Nobody know what was ska or reggae."[9]

Other bands that employed Alpha boys through Sister Ignatius's tutelage and cultivation were orchestras led by Sonny Bradshaw, Val Bennett, Baba Motta, Lester Hall, Roy Coburn, Vivian Hall, Tony Brown, and Kenny Williams at clubs such as Colony Club, Bournemouth Beach Club, Glass Bucket Club, and Silver Slipper. They performed at movie theaters between features or on live entertainment nights at places including the Ward Theatre, Carib Theatre, Palace Theatre, Little Theatre, Regal Theatre, Tropical Theatre, Queens Theatre, and Majestic Theatre. These venues had feature nights, especially on holidays, with a lineup of Jamaican jazz musicians, or a headlining act from America, such as Sarah Vaughan or Dave Brubeck, for which Alpha boys played. They performed on the hotel circuit at the Myrtle Bank Hotel in Kingston, the Tower Isle Hotel in Ocho Rios, and others. They took positions in the Jamaican Military Band, the Jamaica Regiment Band, and the Jamaica Constabulary Band. Many left the island to perform worldwide, in London, Toronto, Germany, and the United States.

Alpha boys were not only employable; they were also innovators. The education they received at Alpha, and the possibilities they were shown by Sister Mary Ignatius Davies, who exposed them to a worldwide repertoire of music, allowed them to create, to expand the boundaries of Jamaican music. They weren't just performing the standards in the clubs—they were generating their own form, their own genre, by blending what they learned with what they loved. And so when the rhythm and blues of America combined with the calypso and mento of the Caribbean islands and the jazz of the clubs, it was Alpha, and more specifically Sister Iggy, who made that combination possible. She was the cook stirring the pot to produce a delicious blend known as ska, without which there would have been no rocksteady and no reggae. They entered the studio when the recording industry ignited, performing the instrumentals behind the vocalists who would propel the island to fame. Alpha boys launched the careers of Bob Marley, Jimmy Cliff, Desmond Dekker, Millie Small. Alpha boys launched and sustained the recording industry by producing hit after hit for Coxsone Dodd, Duke Reid, King Edwards, Prince Buster, Leslie Kong, Vincent Chin, Justin Yap, and Sonia Pottinger. Through their recordings, Alpha boys reached the people of the island who flocked to the dancehalls and yards to dance to the sound systems that played their compositions, and reached the people of the world as their music spread to other countries through immigration and inspired countless others to create their own versions. In short, Alpha boys gave all who listened the joy of their imagination and talent, none of which would have been possible without Sister Iggy. To conceive how Jamaican music would be changed without the impact of Sister Ignatius, Charles Simpson says it is "Impossible. It could not be."

Musicians who got their start at Alpha, thanks to the guidance of Sister Mary Ignatius Davies, include Don Drummond, Lester Sterling, Tommy McCook, Johnny "Dizzy" Moore, "Deadly Headley" Bennett, Joseph "Jo-Jo" Bennett, Eddie "Tan-Tan" Thornton, Cedric "IM" Brooks, Glen DaCosta, Bobby Ellis, Winston "Yellowman" Foster, Vin Gordon, Owen Grey, Tony Greene, Tony Gregory, Joe Harriott, Lennie Hibbert, Bertie King, David Madden, Vincent Tulloch, Raymond Harper, Johnny Osbourne, Dizzy Reece, Rico Rodriguez, Floyd Lloyd Seivright, Leroy Smart, Leroy "Horsemouth" Wallace, Wilton "Blue Bogey" Gaynair, Bobby Gaynair, Harold "Little G" McNair, Dr. Leslie Thompson, and more.

The reach of Sister Mary Ignatius Davies goes beyond music. She gave thousands of boys not only a means of employment through learning a trade at Alpha Boys' School—gardening and agriculture, tailoring, printmaking and binding, brickmaking, and woodworking; but also a roof over their heads, food on their plates, clothes on their backs, character skills, and love. She truly cared for her boys, and she was even able to reach the tough ones. Simpson says, "She is one of the greatest persons, to take what you would call a troublemaker, and she fall in love with that troublemaker and she had a means, a way, of getting to them and to like them. She would give them a special little pet name. We had a fella one time, she gave him the name 'Sly Fox' because he was tricky. There was a fellow that played with Byron Lee, Uriah Johnson was his name, and he was the split image of Sammy Davis Jr. and she named him 'Little Sammy.'" Sparrow Martin got his nickname this way, given to him by Sister Ignatius. He recalls,

> We were told in school not to go out in the rain cause of the cold that you would catch, and we like to play in the rain. But Sister always come down when the rain starting. She would come down with her umbrella and she walk and she look to see who is in the rain. So one day, I was in junior home and I didn't see the sister was coming up. I was playing in the rain. So I climb up in a tree and when I climb up, it start to rain some more. And she come under the tree and said, "Come out of the tree, you naughty little sparrow. What would your mother do, if you stayed here and drown?" The boys now heard her so they start singing, "Sparrow in the treetop, Sparrow in the treetop, la la la la la." From that come my name. When I left Alpha, I wanted a name as a musician, so I used the name and I became world famous.

She was a teacher, a leader, a mother to her boys. Sister Little says, "When they were ill, she nursed them back to health. The band boys would always know that their uniforms would be ready for an engagement, nor would they have to be anxious about transportation, since this was also a given at the Alpha Boys School; their meals would be reserved for them when they returned from an engagement and Sister, good listener that she was, would willingly share in their success as they recounted them."[10] She gave them vocational support, emotional and psychological support, spiritual support and, most of all, love.

Sister Mary Ignatius stayed in touch with her boys all through their lives. She grew them into young men, she sent them off into the world, and she stayed with them every step of the way. Sparrow Martin tells the story of when some of the musicians went overseas to try to find success in Europe. "She try to arrange for them to go to England to stay at somebody's house. They live in England ten years and come back with their wife and children. She used to say, 'How many children you make?' and you'd say, 'Four, sister,' and she'd say, 'And those that you don't know about?' [laughs]. She would treat you like a human," says Martin.

It is well known that Sister Ignatius cared deeply for Don Drummond. She saw his potential and ushered him into the band, and she helped him to grow into a successful musician. She also loved the music he produced, and "Eastern Standard Time" was her favorite. But Charles Simpson says that she also had such a connection with Drummond that after he murdered Margarita and died in Bellevue Mental Hospital, Sister Ignatius felt a responsibility. Simpson recalls, "She told me one day after Don Drummond died, she said, 'I feel like I am supposed to be blamed for Don Drummond.' I'm telling you straight, you're getting it from the horse's mouth. She told me that because she said, 'I think I send him out to the wolves too early.' In other words, she let him leave school too early, and she send him out into a big man world. And I never forget the way in which she said it, like she was taking blame for what happen to him." He adds that Drummond's brilliant talent made it easy for Sister Ignatius to think he was ready:

> The military band always play at Victoria Park in downtown, the last Sunday of each month, and there was a discussion. Mr. Delgado, the bandmaster, went down there and told the bandmaster of

the military band, "I have a little boy at Alpha who can play better than all of them." And he thought he was just boasting about it. So they decided to send Don Drummond down there one Sunday when the military band was playing. A likkle boy at Alpha, he went there and stole the show! Stole the show! And that was when everybody start to be aware of him, from that time, and his name start to spread across Jamaica, while he was still a little boy at Alpha. So his name start to become a household name before he even left school. And he was in demand. And I think that is why Sister Ignatius blame herself because she said she send him out before time, she send him to the wolves that aim to destroy. So she took it personally. If you listen to her you could see she was emotional about it because she did love her boys.

Drummond left Alpha Boys' School on October 31, 1950, six weeks before graduation. He returned frequently to visit with Sister Ignatius.

"She loved them like they were her child," says Simpson. "There was a gift she had there because she could respond to them in a loving way. She was just a beautiful sweet human being. If you talk to one hundred Alpha Boys, 95 percent of them would refer to her as their mother. And that speaks volumes. When you leave the school, she never leave you. She know where you are. She keep on top of all her children. Leaving school wasn't the end of it. She know where they were and the boys would keep in touch with her. I think she was a living saint, you know? Maybe we could not detect, but she was just a living saint," says Simpson.

Sister Mary Ignatius Davies died on February 9, 2003, of a heart attack at the age of 81, after ailing from heart disease for three years. Her funeral was held at Holy Trinity Cathedral on North Street in Kingston, and she is interred at Dovecot in St. Catherine. She has not been awarded the Order of Distinction, although she certainly had earned it. She was awarded the *Jamaica Observer* Award for Outstanding Community Service on February 25, 1997. "Sister Ignatius never wants to be in the spotlight, preferring to be in the supporting role, yet being the strongest pillar of the foundation," wrote Dr. George Phillip, CEO of the newspaper. Perhaps the most poignant statement of her impact comes from *Jamaica Gleaner* columnist Gordon Robinson, who wrote, "If Clement Dodd is the father of Jamaican popular music, Sister Ignatius is the mother."[11] Upward and onward.

Marjorie Whylie, OD

"Marjorie Whylie not only exemplifies the essence of artistic expression," says musicologist Herbie Miller, "she embodies it. As performer, actor, writer, composer, presenter, administrator and teacher, Whylie has shown that art at its best comes not from natural talent alone, but, perhaps, more importantly, through thrusting oneself fully into the rigorous mental and physical preparation necessary to better ensure the kind of performances she often achieves, which have provided artistic fulfilment, audience satisfaction and scholarly achievement."[12] Such an accolade is not off target. Whylie has performed a variety of roles in the entertainment industry, in music and theater and dance, and she has done so for decades. She has that mental and physical preparation that Miller lauds and the years of work to follow that establish her as a "national treasure," a term that Miller has aptly assigned to this legendary woman.

Marjorie Whylie was born in October of 1944, and she grew up in Kingston's Collins Green neighborhood, just southwest of Emancipation Park. "My parents were both pharmacists, and I had one brother and one sister,"[13] she says. According to journalist Marcia Erskine, "Several stories are told about her entree into the music world. For her own part, she remembers trotting off to Miss Ena Helps' Music Studio for classes in pianoforte and theory of music at the tender age of seven. She had always been told by her parents that she actually began playing the piano at two and a half years old. But her brother tells an amazing story of being left to babysit a twenty-two-month-old Marjorie only to hear the strains of a piano being played in the house. Knowing there was only the two of them in the house, he quietly entered the sitting room only to see baby Marjorie at the piano."[14] Marjorie confirms this story and says, "I was 2½ years old, I'm told, but I have no recollection of it. I was too young to remember but I don't know of a time that I was not playing the piano. I couldn't get away from music. Music was always there."

Marjorie's musical debut came on a popular radio show called *Lannaman's Children's Hour*, which featured the talent of Jamaica's young performers. "It was a program for children where they'd show off their various talents on radio. I first played when I was about six. I lived very close to the radio station so I was invited to play fairly often, and very often when they didn't have participants they'd call up and ask my mother if she'd send me down, so that was it and I end up playing very often," she says.

Marjorie Whylie, pianist, educator, and champion of music, in 1968 (copyright The Gleaner Company [Media] Limited).

Marjorie attended Saint Andrew High School, a boarding school, at age nine, which was difficult for her at first because she had never been away from home. She was a creative child, and she lived in a dormitory with three other girls. She credits her schooling with developing her creativity through participation in competitions, drawing and painting, theater productions, cooking, dance, and fashion. She took ballet and piano lessons outside of school.

At the young age of 14, Marjorie was the featured artist for the Institute of Jamaica's lunch hour series, which Erskine says was "then regarded as 'The Debut Venue for young performers.'"[15] She performed the works of Bach, Beethoven, Chopin, and Debussy on piano. She then attended the University of the West Indies, where she received her bachelor's degree in Spanish in 1965. She subsequently pursued a diploma in music education from the Jamaica School of Music, which is now part of the prestigious Edna Manley College for the Visual and Performing Arts. Marjorie says, "At the University of the West Indies I studied Spanish, so I taught Spanish at Kingston College for nine years. While I was there I also headed the Kingston College Chapel Choir, and I taught music—that would have been singing and musical appreciation—for first and second formers. After that I worked with a social development commission as part of Olive Lewin's cultural work for about a year and a half, and after that I went to Edna Manley; I was head of their Folk Music Research Department."

Marjorie also became involved with the National Dance Theatre Company during its founding days. She says,

> In my very late teens the National Dance Theatre Company was formed, and I was with them playing piano for classes, and that's where I learned to play the drums—with Ronan Critchlow. It was 1962 when Jamaica got independence, and I was invited to play for a show that was done for independence called *Roots and Rhythms*. Some of the dancers in that show formed the nucleus of the dance company, which formed immediately afterwards. When I left school I also did some classes in modern dance with Eddie Thomas, who was a co-founder of the dance company with Rex Nettleford. I used to play for practices, play for rehearsals in the orchestra—which was led by Mapletoft Poule—and then after the company toured Britain during the Commonwealth Festival of 1965, on my return, Maple gave up as head of the orchestra, and I led the orchestra and was formally named musical director early in 1966.

Marjorie served in this post for 45 years, retiring in 2013 and becoming musical director emerita. "She is a multitalented musicologist, pianist, percussionist, jazz singer and academician," said Rex Nettleford, late artistic director of the NDTC.[16] Some of Marjorie's well-known musical compositions include "Mountain Women," "Ni Woman of Destiny," "I Not I," "Blood Canticles," "Drumscore," "Caribbean Canvas," "The Black Widow," and "Journeys Beyond Survival."

In her early years, Marjorie also studied music with a prestigious overseas school. "I'm a trained classical musician. I did all the exams at the Royal School of Music in theory and piano, so I have a classical background, and I also did a four-year program in two years of music education, which prepared me to become director of music at UWI Mona campus," she says. She became director of studies at the University of the West Indies in 1982, and she currently holds the position of director of music there. "For a short time in my late teens and early 20s I also played vibraphone and did some work at the Jazz Workshop and was taught vibes by Taddy Mowatt. I was about 15 at the time and did some work with the Jazz Workshop, which was led by Sonny Bradshaw. There were a number of others that taught youngsters. We did repertoire and learned harmony and so on."

Marjorie says that she also performed with other drummers outside of the theater and dance arenas, including at Count Ossie's camp in Rockfort near the Wareika Hills. "A couple of times we used to go over and play some drums there, once with Count Ossie himself; and after he pass on, Brother Sam invited me over. I've done one or two lectures there for the community. I've jammed and I used to do some drumming with Cedric Brooks," she says.

She describes her process as one that is interactive with the other variables in the piece, such as the dancers, the medium, and the choreographer. She pushes herself to her fullest potential to realize her strength. She explains,

> I'm always amazed at people who sit at a piano and compose. I compose at a desk. I hear it all in my head and I put it on paper. I am a channel for the music. That is not to say that when I have an assignment to do, it doesn't become a chore. There are times when I leave what I have to do until I get to very last minute and I get to panic stage and it comes. There's a lot of inspiration that fuels me, and it gets to a point where it dries up, and then somebody challenges me to finish it and says, "You can't do it, you can't write in the same style again," and that's one thing—don't challenge me! I am going to get in there and do it! That's how some larger works have come through. At other times

it just flows. In writing music for dance, it was always a good process working with somebody like Rex Nettleford, because he had an idea of the kind of rhythms he wanted. I would take it all down and work with it, come up with melodic lines. When I worked with Sheila Barnett, I would go and observe the choreographing process, and I would notate the rhythm patterns, write notes about areas where it needed to be lyrical, things that were particularly rhythmic, and I would go away and sometimes I would go ahead of where she was in her scenario and push her in a direction, so in most instances it was a hand-in-glove situation, working with different choreographers.

Marjorie has also worked with youth community centers and with institutions using music in rehabilitation: "It's been a very interesting life. When I was with Olive Lewin's group and part of her Cultural Department of the Social Development Commission, they used music in rehabilitation, both at the Bellevue Mental Hospital, and also in the prisons. They did a lot of work with the prisoners, so that was very very interesting," she says. Her dedication in working with the physically and mentally challenged extended to voluntary service at the Lister Mair Gilby School for the deaf, working with the blind in Jamaica, and a short project with special needs children in London, England.

Marjorie has taken Jamaican music to many parts of the world. In the Caribbean, she has conducted workshops on traditional folk material and rhythms in Trinidad, Dominica, and the Cayman Islands and has been a featured performer in jazz festivals in St. Lucia, Antigua, Barbados, Trinidad, and Jamaica, as well as in London, Birmingham, The Hague, Berlin, Hamburg, Montreux, Miami, Washington, Viennes in the south of France, and Paris. Her one-woman show, *From the Cradle to the Grave: Jamaican Rhythm and Music in the Stages of Life*, has been presented at Carib Expo in Trinidad and Tobago, as well as in England, Canada, the USA and Germany. She has been a visiting artist in high schools in Canada, the UK and U.S. and has been artist in residence at Camden Arts College in London; she has also delivered several lectures in that city as well as in Birmingham and Nottingham. Whylie has served as a consultant to the BBC on a television documentary on Jamaican independence.

While in England, Marjorie devised a program for six- to eleven-year-old students using an Anansi story as the basis for developing performance skills in acting, singing, basic instrumental accompanying, and dance, culminating in a performance at the Royal Festival Hall. She has also performed at Commonwealth in Concert in Edinburgh, Scotland, hosted by Prince Charles for the Commonwealth Prime Ministers' Conference; with Jazz Jamaica in London and Paris; with Monty Alexander at New York's Blue Note and in Europe; and satisfied a two-week residency with her trio Whylie Wrhythm at Ronnie Scott's in London. "It's been all kinds of layers. I've been in entertainment and what I like to call edutainment. I've been in the formal education system and I've worked in the tourism industry, done cultural work, testing for groups and schools, and training for teachers," she says.

Never married, Marjorie says that over the years she has nurtured several children in her home, namely those of her family members or friends. "At various periods I had children living in my house. I had a girlfriend who went off to the states, and she left one of her sons with me. He spent almost a year. And my mother's goddaughter lived with us for about two years, and it sort of fell to my lot to look after her. There also was a year when my sister-in-law was away, my brother was terribly busy, and so my niece lived with me for a little over a year," she says.

"I think I'm a fun person," she says when asked to describe her personality.

> I'm very sociable, but I think there are certain lines which I like to be drawn. There are some people who step across the line, and I don't suffer that. I would think I'm a fun person, easygoing. When it comes to professional situations, I think I'm very disciplined, and I like to work in a situation where everything is clear, your roles are clearly defined. People would say I am a workaholic. I've been going through some old papers and I've looked at some things I've written and composed, and I thought, "My God, that was me?" I can't believe some things. But I think I'm fairly easygoing, but there are some people who like to push my buttons, and I will put up with it and put up with it, but there comes a time when I explode. I am a Scorpio!

She received the Order of Distinction for her contributions to Jamaican culture, and in 1997 she was inducted into the Jamaica Jazz Hall of Fame. In 2004, she received the Prime Minister's award for Excellence in Theatre and Music. She has performed at Carnegie Hall, the Montreal Jazz Festival, the Caribbean Jazz Festival, and the British Commonwealth Festival. Through it all she says she has never suffered the same tribulations as other women in other parts of the music industry:

> I really never had any problems at all. There was the same sort of lack of respect as you'd find in any profession, but I can't say that with any strength to it because very often I was in a role of leading a group and at that time, most of the active musicians in the area that I was working with were men, so I had no problem at all. When I was a student at UWI, there was a small steel band that had ten members, and there was a point where I was the only woman with nine men. I have played consistently with men. When I performed with the Pantomime orchestra, we had a flautist and a violinist who were women; the rest of them were men, and I was there as leader of the orchestra, and that's how it has been. I taught drumming at Edna Manley, I've taught at UWI and various other areas, tourist training for the tourist board and for a product development company and so on, and I've worked with a lot of men. I've not had a problem.

Today Marjorie is working on her health and serving in an advisory capacity for groups with which she has been involved over the years, and she still performs on occasion. She says,

> I had a stroke last year [2013] which robbed me of a lot of energy. It hasn't affected my movement, but the energy is just not there. If Myrna Hague is doing her show, she still insists that I play songs with her. I teach some voice, percussion, and piano at home. I have a very few students because I just don't have the energy. Every so often I work with a church group and do a workshop on Caribbean music for worship and how to use the drum in service. I have written a lot of church music, and that was some part of my development. I've written a mass and I've written canticles. I am musical director emerita of the NDTC, and they ask me to come by rehearsals and see how it is going. Also I am asked to speak particularly to the newer dancers on traditional works that are a part of the repertoire, so I set them in an historical context and talk about the dance forms, how the body is used and that kind of thing. But I am just trying to bring back my strength and hope I gain full health. I am very careful about how I use my time. I really don't have anything in front of me, but there are some things I would like to have published that need some work, some papers I've presented over the years.

What is it about Marjorie Whylie that sets her apart? Aside from her nurturing other performers, educating the next generation, and fostering her country's cultural heritage of music, Herbie Miller says,

> As quick as a wink, she can change a straight-ahead jazz piece into a mento riff, interjecting along the way a figure or two borrowed from kumina or ragtime, by simply changing emphasis and directing her band into expressing both the Jamaican and American antecedents of popular music that emerged as independent indigenous forms here on the island as well as on the northern mainland, respectively.... Miss Whylie performs music with the élan of someone who would have been much more appreciated and celebrated in a world where acknowledgement and reward by organisations,

critics, fans and peer alike, is more forthcoming and generous…. Her performances reveal diversity, eclecticism and are specifically peer and audience focused.[17]

Edna Manley

Though she is known more for her visual art than music, Edna Manley still deserves recognition for her dedication to all visual and performing arts. Born in 1900 in Bournemouth, England, Edna Swithenbank was one of nine children. Her father, a Methodist minister, died when she was just nine years old. Edna had a love for art even as a child, and she attended art school in England. She married her cousin, Norman Manley, who was eight years her senior. They met after he traveled from Jamaica to England to study law at Oxford as a Rhodes Scholar. Moving to Jamaica in 1922, Edna continued her study of the arts as a sculptor, working in bronze, mahogany, and later clay. Her sculptures expressed the Jamaican people's desire for progress, and the culture of Jamaica. She also produced paintings and drawings.

In order to help her work and inspire her art, Edna Manley regularly listened to music, along with her husband Norman Manley. Norman was founder of the People's National Party, played a crucial role in Jamaican independence, served as premier of Jamaica from 1959 to 1962, and today is a national hero. The couple held two-hour-long musical performances in their home, according to journalist Michael Reckord.[18] Edna believed that all people should be able to express themselves through all forms of art, and so in 1950 she co-founded the Jamaica School of Art, which then became the Cultural Training Centre in 1976 and eventually the Edna Manley College of the Visual and Performing Arts in 1995. The college comprises four schools: drama, dance, visual arts, and music. The music school was founded in 1961, and shortly thereafter, according to the college website, the school "established a Folk Music Research Department on the recommendation of the Most Hon. Edward Seaga, then Minister of Culture…. A Music Education Division was established to train teachers in schools and the Folk Music Research Department established in 1976, under the direction of Marjorie Whylie."[19]

For her devotion to Jamaican independence, Jamaican culture, and Jamaican arts in all forms, Edna Manley is a champion of her nation's people. Her contributions allowed many artists, both visual and performing, to develop and realize their potential and others to enjoy those fruits. Edna Manley died in 1987.

Olive Lewin

In the foreword to Olive Lewin's book *Rock It Come Over: The Folk Music of Jamaica*, the late former Prime Minister Edward Seaga begins, "Jamaica is one of the few countries which have made the transition from a folk-based culture to a popular international music form."[20] Central to the preservation of that folk-based culture has been Olive Lewin, who recorded mento, ring play songs, Maroon drumming and abeng, Burru rhythms, emancipation celebration songs, revivalist ceremony songs, the drumming of Count Ossie, songs for dinki-mini, and songs for loading bananas and boiling sugar and hoisting utility poles.

Lewin was born in 1927. Writer Chris Salewicz says she was born into a household that encouraged education and curiosity. "She was born in Vere in Clarendon, to teachers—her father had a reputation as one of the finest historians in Jamaica. She enjoyed an intellectual upbringing, with the family sitting and reading together every night," he says.[21] Surely being cultivated in such a family encouraged Lewin to experience Jamaican culture with a deeper appreciation, and as she grew and explored her own academic interests, she was naturally drawn to history, anthropology, and music. She and her sister studied at an elite private school for girls, Hampton School, on scholarships funded by slaveowners. She further won a scholarship to study at the Royal Academy of Music in 1943, where she was the only black student. There she studied classical composers but soon realized her calling to "work towards the understanding, study and appreciation of Jamaica's music."[22]

Lewin performed in London, at Royal Festival Hall and on BBC, as a skilled concert pianist; then she soon returned to Jamaica, where she taught at Mico College. In 1966, Seaga appointed her to the position of folk music research officer, having just completed studies of Jamaica's folk music and traditions himself a few years earlier. One year later, in 1967, Lewin established the Jamaican Folk Singers, a group of performers who brought Jamaican folk music to audiences all over the country.

Jake Homiak of the Smithsonian wrote that Lewin was a "renowned Jamaican musicologist, folklorist, singer, actress, and community servant.... She was a tireless advocate for Jamaican culture and folk music and is perhaps best known for the founding of three major organizations related to these interests: The Jamaican Folk Singers, the Jamaica Youth Orchestra, and the Memory Bank Project. The latter project ... added to over twenty years of work that Dr. Lewin had already done in collecting songs and oral histories around the island. Presently, the African-Caribbean Institute of Jamaica holds more than 1,500 audio recordings of traditional Jamaican songs she made from 1966 through the term of the Memory Bank Project."[23]

Olive Lewin died in 2013 at the age of 85. Minister of Culture, Gender, Entertainment and Sport Olivia "Babsy" Grange said of Lewin, "She gave of herself fully, and Jamaica owes her a lot for how much she did in preserving and promoting Jamaican culture."[24]

Olive Lewin, founder of the Jamaican Folk Singers and champion of Jamaican folk music, in 1969 (copyright The Gleaner Company [Media] Limited).

Dr. Carolyn Cooper

Dr. Carolyn Cooper was born in 1950 as one of three children to George Cooper, a tailor, and Modesto Cooper, a teacher. She studied at the University of West Indies Mona, where she eventually taught for 36 years. She helped to begin the Institute of Gender and Development Studies at UWI Mona in 1980, and in 1992, Cooper established the International Reggae Studies Centre to bring an intellectual and academic approach to all forms of reggae culture—music, literature, and expression. Two years later, in 1994, this became the Reggae Studies Unit at the University of the West Indies Mona. In 1997, Cooper established the annual Bob Marley Lecture as a community event to discuss the importance of Marley's music and message. Speakers have included Lady Saw, Buju Banton, Tony Rebel, Queen Ifrica, Luciano, Capleton, Ninjaman, Alan "Skill" Cole, Cindy Breakspeare, and Marlon James, to name a few. She has written numerous journal articles and has spoken all over the world on such topics as dancehall culture, slackness, gender, racial identity, politics, tourism, folklore, and the African diaspora. She has also written two books, *Noises in the Blood: Orality, Gender, and the "Vulgar" Body of Jamaican Popular Culture* and *Sound Clash: Jamaican Dancehall Culture at Large*. She has been called the surrogate mother to dancehall artists Vybz Kartel and Ninjaman, both of whom are currently serving life sentences for murder.

Cooper believes that music education should be part of public school curriculums, and she has been a fierce advocate of the Jamaican dialect/patois, writing columns for the newspaper and her own blog that appear in both patois and formal English. Her recognition of the culture of the Jamaican people by creating a place for its research, study, and preservation to further the growth of these forms of human expression has been crucial. She has helped to give validity and authenticity to music and culture that many others deemed unworthy.

Chapter Twelve

Studio

Who ran the microphone cords for the Staple Singers on "Respect Yourself" and the guitar cord for Pops at Stax Records? Who tested the guitars for Prince at the Kiowa Trail Home Studio for "Little Red Corvette?" And who set up the cymbal stands for Keith Moon at Olympic for "Baba O'Riley?" As cliché as "behind the scenes" may sound, that is exactly what many studio staff were; but without them, these iconic songs would not exist. Those who ran the electrical cords, pushed the levers, pointed their fingers to begin, and even chose who would be permitted into the studio to record at all, were for decades frequently men in Jamaica, the United States, and elsewhere. A few women in Kingston were able to make their marks in the studio—running cords, signing artists, and entering people's homes through the airwaves. These are the women of the studio.

Enid Cumberland

Her name rarely appears on the lips without the name of her duo partner preceding it, but Enid Cumberland is much more than one half of Keith and Enid. Raised in a humble home from humble beginnings, you'd never have expected that this woman would go on to record as both a duo and solo act, and would also go on to work for Studio One for over 40 years, supporting others with their careers and aspirations.

Enid Cumberland lives today in Stony Hill, and she remembers her childhood with a sense of humor. Born on December 11, 1930, Enid is still whip smart, active, and filled with love. "My mom had eleven of us—can you imagine?" she recalls.[1] "My daddy was a soldier in the army, and at that time it was King Edward the Eighth. When my mommy used to go out, she had to leave some of us with grandma or she had to share us with somebody because we were so plenty. My mother was part African and my daddy was Jamaican and part Jewish, and we have a mixture, some darker than some."

It was a strict household, with so many kids needing support and resources, which were tight. "My mother was very cross," she says, "and my daddy was the saint." She continues,

> My mother, you can't do any wrong even when you're right. She would slap you for it. She's say, "What you learn you must remember," every time she slap you…. She don't beat us often, but we sin at times, like we take away money and she don't know, for something that we want. Sometimes she make something for lunch and we don't want it, or we come home from school and we don't want to

eat it and we give it to each other, and we have to go into the pan to take something to buy for school to eat, and we don't open the pan until the end of the year when she open it and say you can buy what you want because we have to buy things for ourselves, you know. She says, "Well you won't be getting anything because you don't have some," and she slap you. "You must tell me when you're taking out." Yes, she's a governess.

Even though her mother was severe with the children, it was from her mother that Enid learned to sing. She says, "My mommy could sing. Sometimes when she's washing, because in those times mommy didn't have a washing machine, she wash with her hands, you know? A lot of scrubbing and she was singing. Mommy was a good singer, but her diction was a little foreign to us because she was part African, and when she was singing we just have to watch her mouth as to what she is singing. I had a sister, Gloria, who was going to sing with a band. She was a very good girl but she died when she was 18. She was the first person to take me outdoors to sing. We were always singing. I had a brother whose voice could go high up in the air. I started to sing when I was in school. Three of us girls could sing, but I was the one who loved to sing. I was about six."

Enid Cumberland at Studio One in the 1990s (photograph by Ron Vester).

It is important to know that Enid's surname, Cumberland, was not a common one in Jamaica, then nor now. The name likely originates from the English county of Cumberland. Many times, when people left their village or county, they were given a surname that reflected their land of origin. Cumberland was such a name and likely came from Enid's paternal ancestors, who were originally British natives—hence her father's employment with the British military. But it was this last name that brought attention, a good kind of attention, to Enid and her siblings as a young child. "The school where we went, it was a Catholic school. We were spotted in school because my daddy was brought up in Alpha. The same teachers that taught him in Alpha came to our school and started to teach. So when they see we were Cumberland they said, 'What was your daddy's name?' and we had so much advantage in everything," she says, noting that even when she married later in life she chose to keep her family surname. "My husband, Allan Campbell, is gone a good while now, but my name is Cumberland. I never change my name. We have too many Campbells all over the place, and mine was a real name, so I keep it!" she says with a laugh.

Enid was given special opportunities in school—opportunities like singing for the school choir. She also sang in church, her own and others. "We grow up Roman Catholic but I never understood much of that, to be frank. It was in Latin and there's a lot of Latin. I always go to all churches because I can sing, and my friends would have a concert and ask me if I could come and sing, and I say you have to ask my mommy and daddy, so they give information and come and take me. And I wasn't a person that was scared. I show off when I'm singing! [laughs]. And they say, 'Oh this little girl! She can sing like a big woman!'" But it wasn't until after graduation from school that Enid really got her start. It was at the *Vere Johns Opportunity Hour*, that musical launch pad, that Enid Cumberland also got her big break into the world of show business. "I sing for *Vere Johns* when I was 20 or 22, something like that, but I found a partner. His name was Keith Stewart, and we did a few hits and we were recognized in Jamaica over time," she says.

Keith Stewart, born Altamont Stewart on July 1, 1938, was a graduate of Kingston Senior School. In addition to being a smooth singer, he was an excellent cricketer and commercial artist. He began work for an advertising agency just out of school. At the same time, he began singing with Enid. After they appeared on the *Vere Johns Opportunity Hour*, they were an immediate hit. The duo was together for three years, joining together in 1958 (which would have made Enid 28 instead of 20 or 22, and eight years Keith's senior). They hit the stage for all of the big shows in Kingston during that time, such as performing with Byron Lee and the Dragonaires for the American soul singer Jerry Butler on one of his visits to Jamaica at the Ritz Theatre; with Higgs and Wilson and Owen Grey at the *Rock & Mash* show, also at the Ritz Theatre; at the *Pre-Independence Jump Up* with Jimmy Cliff and Derrick Harriott at the Carib Theatre; and dozens of others.

Keith and Enid's first recordings were for Simeon Smith, known as Hi-Lite. Hi-Lite had a record shop at the corner of Spanish Town Road and Harris Street; it was also a hat shop, hardware store, and a business he had in common with so many other producers—a liquor store. He began the Smith's label and started working with musicians such as Keith and Enid, who recorded three songs for Hi-Lite in 1960—"Send Me," "Everything Will Be Alright," and the classic tune "Worried Over You." All three songs were also released in the UK on the Blue Beat label, although no monies from these deals were ever realized by the artists. The duo recorded again for Hi-Lite in 1962 and 1963 with the songs "It's True Love," "When It's Spring," "Yield Not to Temptation," and "Just a Closer Walk." Again, these songs were released overseas in England. But before recording those songs, in 1961 Stewart and Cumberland recorded for another producer distributing records in the UK as well as Jamaica: Chris Blackwell, the producer who launched the careers of Millie Small and Bob Marley, among numerous others on his Island Records label. "It's Only a Pity," "Never Leave My Throne," "Return to Me," "What Have I Done," and "You're Gonna Break My Heart" were all recorded for Blackwell in 1961, a prolific year, and "It's Only a Pity" and "Leave My Throne" featured The Caribs as backing band (they had also performed on "Worried Over You"). The Caribs, consisting of Lowell Morris, Peter Stoddart, and Dennis Sindrey, all of Australia, had been a house band at the Glass Bucket and Myrtle Hotel before becoming the studio band at Federal Records and for numerous local producers. Keith and Enid were also backed by Sonny Bradshaw and His Orchestra on these early recordings.

But in 1963, Keith and Enid broke up. Keith performed solo on the club circuit, especially on the north shore in places like Club 35 in Montego Bay. He also performed in the U.S., in clubs in Texas, and he recorded for Byron Lee, who produced the song "You Don't Have to Cry" with the B side "Play It One More Time" by Keith Stewart and the Dragonettes. Keith's most popular solo recording was the album *Yellowbird* for WIRL (West Indies Records Ltd.), which featured twelve calypso and mento tunes, including the classic Jamaican folk song "Linstead Market." On November 10, 2010, Keith Stewart died at the age of 72 from kidney cancer in his home in Montego Bay on the same day as legendary producer Sonia Pottinger.

Enid continued to record, primarily as a duo artist, performing songs with Lord Creator at Studio One. Lord Creator, whose real name was Kentrick Patrick, was a calypsonian made popular by his hit song "Independent Jamaica" in 1962. With Enid he recorded "Simple Things," "Love Lost (Lost My Love)," "I Cried a Lie (I Cried a Tear)," and "Beyond," all at Studio One in 1963 and 1964. She also partnered with other artists over the years as they came into the studio, such as Roy Richards and Larry Marshall, but it was all done at Studio One after the Keith-and-Enid breakup. She explains why:

> I wanted to have children. Show business I had to leave, because you don't get much. Whatever we did get, it helped us, but that was years ago and it's whatever they offer you. You cannot survive on it, you know? And I got married and started to have my children, and I didn't bother with the singing outdoors on stage and so on. I started to work at Studio One for Coxsone. Why I did that was because I was sure of my salary and don't have to wait until someone call me to come do a job. I did supervision. People would come in, and backup artists, so I show them where they stand and get the microphones and move them up and down. I did that for Studio One for about 40 years. Everybody come here, and some invite me to England, but I think you're not really suited to that when you have children.

Enid Cumberland had four children of her own—two girls and two boys who are now grown—and she has six grandchildren. But Enid was mother to more than just her own. "I raise a lot of children because my sister want to leave six of them with me. At that time I didn't have my four and I took care of her six and then my four. I really love my siblings, even though sometimes they didn't show the love that I want them to show. But children are something I hold in the bosom. I had my children last—I was the last one to get pregnant. I had my first child at 30. So children are always asking for me and I love kids. People call me granny even though they are not my grandchildren," says Enid.

Enid took care of her children, her sibling's children, and those in the studio. She was, in short, a caretaker. Later in life, Enid became involved in her church. She had always been a spiritual person, growing up in the Catholic Church, singing in churches as a child, and recording a number of religious and gospel tunes, even for Coxsone's Tabernacle label, which was devoted to gospel. She recorded three songs of a religious nature for this label under the name "Sister Enid," or "Sister Enid and the Soul Blenders." She became a part of the congregation at Bethel New Testament Church of God and has been a member for nearly four decades, even becoming a deacon there at one point, but she had to retire from her post. "I was a deacon, but I give that up because you have to be in church always. I'm 83 years old, you know! But they adore me at that place. They adore me. If there is something that is special and I can't make it, everybody call me and three or four of them come running for me up in Stony Hill. Yes, that's how I am!" she says.

Enid Cumberland did sing from time to time over the years, as backup for whoever came into the studio and needed a little extra vocal; and on stage, such as for King Omar's (Kingsley Goodison's) Tribute to the Greats annual concert series. Kingsley and Enid are close friends, having worked together for many years at Studio One. "I am really particular to who I sing for. Sometimes the theatre is expensive [to rent] or they have to pay different people, and you don't get anything much when you're coming away. And if you're coming to a gig you have to doll up yourself to make yourself look nice, buy a new dress or new shoes so when you go on stage your shoes don't flop and you look like a fool. So sometimes you don't get anything much," she says.

Still, the impact that Enid Cumberland has had on the music industry is meaningful. She showed women that it was possible to have a hit record and be a featured singer on the biggest stages of Jamaica during a time when it was a man's world. Her talent allowed her to overcome those obstacles, and she never compromised her values, her personality, or her family in order to achieve. She had to choose between being a mother and being a singer, and she chose not only to be a mother, to her own children and her sister's children, but also to keep one foot solidly planted in the music industry where it could be more stable—from the inside. Today, even though she doesn't receive any kind of royalties or a pension from her decades of work in the industry, Enid Cumberland is proud of her accomplishments, as she should be. "I have five awards—one from King Omar, one from [Edward] Seaga when he was in the entertainment business, and I have one from Stars R Us, and I got one in the USA, so there are a few things here to look at, you know?" she says. Perhaps even greater than a few awards to hang on the wall is the legacy she has left to others. "One of my granddaughters does music but she is still in school and she sings beautifully, and another granddaughter plays the guitar," she says. And then there are those she influenced in ways she doesn't even know.

Sonia Pottinger, OD

Sonia Pottinger was born Sonia Eloise Durrant in Leith Hall, Jamaica, on June 21, 1931. At a young age, she and her family moved to Kingston, where she attended St. George's Girls School. After graduation, she studied accounting and secretarial skills, and she married Lindon O. Pottinger, a businessman. Lindon had graduated in 1948 from the Jamaica School of Commerce, receiving a certificate in bookkeeping, or accounting, according to a *Daily Gleaner* article in 1948.[2] He was an entrepreneur, and he and Sonia set up a variety of businesses, such as a bicycle shop and a store that sold Sonia's homemade patties.

According to writer David Katz, "Lindon began to produce records in 1961, recording local acts such as the Mellow Larks and Jimmy James. Founding the labels Gaydisc, Golden Arrow and SEP (his wife's initials), he opened a small recording studio at the family home. It was the first such facility in Jamaica to be owned and operated by a black person. There, he recorded artists including the Maytals, Derrick Harriott and Lord Tanamo. The material was sold at the Tip Top record shop and distribution centre, established by the Pottingers on Orange Street, then the centre of the Kingston music scene."[3]

When Lindon left the music business in 1964, he sold his equipment to family friend Duke Reid. It was at this time, in the mid-1960s, that Sonia and Lindon parted ways. Some writers have claimed that Lindon died in the mid-1960s, but in fact, Sonia and Lindon were separated for a number of years and then divorced in a final decree absolute in January 1971.[4] Sonia had to build her studio and pressing plant behind the Tip Top shop out of necessity, to raise and support her three children and a fourth child born in the early 1970s. But more than simple financial need, Sonia had a heart for the music, a feel and intuition that brought her recording and production company to new heights for her artists.

Going solo in 1965, Sonia Pottinger decided to try her hand at production, and she recorded "Every Night" by Joe White and Chuck Josephs, backed by the Baba Brooks Band. "It was such a big hit, I knew it would be a big kick off for the label,"[5] said Federal Recording Engineer Graeme Goodall. She established her own labels—Gay Feet, Excel, Pep, and High Note, and then later an imprint called Glory, which released gospel titles.

Goodall says that Sonia's direction was shaped by Holford Plummer, who was a senior producer at the time at RJR. Goodall explains, "Sonia was very vague with where she wanted the label to go. She was very close with a man named Holford Plummer, or Hal, who also went by the name Andy Capp. He was at RJR and later produced for Gay Feet. He found the spirit of upper-class ska and could play it on RJR and feel out the media there. Sonia would see what tested well and would then pursue that sound. She was a very sharp business lady."

Sonia recorded fellow female Millicent "Patsy" Todd, one of the few solo females recording at the time. Two of the solo songs that Sonia produced for Patsy were "Fire in Mi Wire" and "Pata Pata Rock Steady," which were unique in their content. "Fire in Mi Wire" is a soca tune originally written by Calypso Rose of Tobago, another pioneering woman, whose lyrics are the typical sexual innuendo of calypso and soca but are certainly not typical of those sung by a female up to this point. "Pata Pata Rock Steady" was also a song written by a female artist, this one in 1957 by Dorothy Masuka for singer Miriam Makeba, both South African artists. Sonia had an affinity for African music, especially African drums, and so she brought in Count Ossie's drummers for the track. Patsy remembers, "That was a weird night! We climbed up on our hands and knees going up in the Wareika Hills. It was one o'clock in the morning, in the dark. Pitch black. Me, Sonia, and Hal Plummer."[6] Hal was the father of Sonia's fourth child, David.

It was during the rocksteady era, 1967 to 1968, when Sonia Pottinger's career really began to thrive. Not only did she produce and promote female artists like Patsy, but she also added Stranger Cole to the mix for some of the best duo tunes Jamaica has ever heard. Stranger and Patsy were incredibly prolific, recording such rocksteady classics for Sonia as "Down the Train Line," "Satisfy My Love," "Tonight," and "Give Me the Right," among many others. Their sound was sweet and soulful, high and deep, the perfect combination of yin and yang. Sonia's ear was able to shape this sound. She brought her creative intuition to countless artists during this time, establishing herself as a producer that many sought to support their own artistry. Stranger Cole recorded for Sonia as a solo artist, as did other male artists including Eric "Monty" Morris, Ken Boothe, and Alton Ellis. Rocksteady groups also found a home with Sonia's studio, including The Gaylads, The Ethiopians, and The Melodians.

As the 1970s arrived and reggae left rocksteady and ska behind, Sonia continued her support for strong women artists who many times offered their versions of songs originally recorded or written by other female artists. For example, Sonia produced Judy Mowatt's version of the Fontella Bass song "Rescue Me." Lorna Bennett offered her take on Diana Ross's "It's My House," a statement of feminine power and sexuality. She produced and recorded Phyllis Dillon, Carlene Davis, and Sonya Spence. Her list of male artists and groups is long with names like U-Roy, Big Youth, and of course, Culture, as well as others. She supported her clients' careers by taking them to tour other continents and countries, such as Africa and Belize. Stranger Cole says, "She was very fair, and in the early days of the recording industry it wasn't always like that. She was a very nice lady."[7] They came to Mrs. P, as they called her, because she was honest and didn't exploit them. They came to her because she paid more than others. They came to her because she brought something no one else had—woman's intuition.

She had a direct hand in their lyrics, she had a direct hand in the melodies and harmonies, and she even occasionally sang backup herself. But even though Sonia Pottinger was a record producer on par with others of the day, she was not given the same respect;

one would assume this was because the industry and culture were so male dominated. Even though newspaper coverage of the recording industry in the 1950s, 1960s, and 1970s was rare because mento, ska, rocksteady, and reggae were seen as music of the streets, downtown music, this successful businesswoman, Sonia Pottinger, received plenty of newspaper attention—for her fashions. Not one article, not one review or column or editorial or public opinion story, appeared on trailblazing Sonia Pottinger's business. Instead, her name, accompanied by a description and an artist's sketch, appeared time after time with accounts of her wardrobe. "Tangerine linen featuring cutwork embroidery with white accessories." "Evening dress of white satin with diamante to one side and detachable stole lined in red." "Black and white satin evening gown with elegant butterfly sleeves." There were dozens of sightings, dozens of ensemble descriptions. On only two occasions was she even referred to as a "record producer." Instead of an entrepreneur, an essential hands-on producer of world-renowned artists, a singer, and a hugely successful label owner, decade after decade, the newspaper, that medium of society's measure, relegated her value, her worth, to the clothing she wore.

Patsy, all these years later, remembers Sonia for more than her fashion sense, more than her records and albums, more than her paychecks. For Patsy, Sonia was a mentor, especially during a time when the industry was so cruel. Patsy says, "Sonia Pottinger, this woman, it was not about the money with her and me. Because right now where I'm standing, I think without her I wouldn't be here, because she showed me what it was to be a lady. She showed me what to do in this world, how to go about things, and what she gave me, money couldn't buy it." Patsy told journalist Basil Walters, "This woman was the wind beneath my wings. And everything that I learned and applied to myself now, she showed me the way. And she made me understand that I could do whatever I want to do." Marcia Griffiths also has shared a strong bond with Sonia, who has herself said that it was if the two were related. They were sistren. Could any other producer claim such connections with their clients? Certainly not. Rather than a businesswoman, she was a womanbusiness. She went on to acquire and manage the Treasure Isle catalog and was awarded the prestigious Order of Distinction in October 2004. Upon her desk she had a sign that read, "Heaven will protect the working girl." She died in November 2010 but leaves behind a lasting contribution to world music that will forever be felt.

Marie Garth

Marie Garth was a disc jockey for 17 years for Radio Jamaica Rediffusion during a time when there were virtually no other female disc jockeys on the island. She had a great passion for her job. "It was the satisfaction I got from making so many people happy. I realized that just by playing a song or speaking cheerfully to somebody, I was able to help. So I felt I was really serving a purpose. When I am on the air, I put my problems behind me and concentrate on the people who are listening," she said.[8]

Marie Beverly Garth was born an only child in Kingston and went to St. Hugh's High School, where she participated in drama and read science scripts for the school's broadcasting programs. "I got three guineas per script, and that helped me to buy books. It was my first introduction to radio and I was taught how to use the microphones properly. This was so closely related to drama," she said. After she graduated, Marie went to the Eastern School of Accountancy and studied shorthand and typing. She secured a job as a secretary and a stenographer but didn't find the work fulfilling, so she left Jamaica for New York to attend the Announcers Training School. After she graduated nine months later, she returned to Jamaica and took a position as junior announcer at Radio Jamaica Rediffusion (RJR). Marie began on a program called *The Busy Bee Club*, which was a show for children. She said, "I tried to get the children to use their imagination to create different things." Over the years she hosted many other shows including *Swap Shop*, *Woman's World*, *Jamaica Today*, *The Best by Request*, *The M.G. Special*, *Afternoon Special*, *Sunday Magazine*, and *Top Ten Music*. As a radio host she emceed a number of holiday concerts and stage shows throughout Jamaica.

Being a woman in a male-dominated industry was not easy for Marie. "Along the way Marie has met several obstacles to her progress. There have been people who have been less than kind and even hostile to her. She has, however, kept her cool. Her determination and commitment to the audience that she loves has also kept her afloat some stormy waters," stated an article.[9] Marie also served as public relations officer for the Friends of the Kingston Public Hospital, and she was a member of the Friendly Darts League. She left Jamaica and RJR in 1985 to pursue a more lucrative career in the U.S. and became host on Radio Waves, a station in Miami, Florida, but she soon changed careers completely. She married Neville Sharpe, became Marie Garth Sharpe, and joined with her husband to sell real estate in Florida. In 2003, Prime Minister P.J. Patterson honored Marie with a Medal of Appreciation for Service to Jamaica.

Chapter Thirteen

Mothers and Wives

In 1945, athlete Meryll Frost once said, "Although I am not a great man, there is a great woman behind me,"[1] thus coining the phrase used for years to come, especially during the feminist movement, that behind every great man is a great woman. The music industry during the 1940s through the current day may have been a man's world, but behind many of these great producers, vocalists, and musicians stood strong women with just as much talent and business acumen, if not more.

Lucille Reid

One of the first men to enter the music industry as a sound system operator was Duke Reid, born Arthur Stanley Reid in Black Rock, Portland. The date of his birth is by most accounts July 21, 1915, and by others May 14, 1923. His mother was named Catherine Pearce, but no father is listed on his birth certificate. After he graduated from school he moved to Kingston and joined the police force. He served as a police officer for ten years and during this time met and married Lucille Homil. When officials and administration in the police department discovered that he had moved in with his mother-in-law, Susan Blagrove, and was helping to run their grocery story, Pink's Grocery on the corner of Beeston and Pink Lane (the name later changed to Treasure Isle), he was dismissed but given a sum of £30 as a sort of severance pay. Reid used this money to purchase speaker boxes to play music at the front of the grocery store to attract customers. It was his first foray into the music business.

The customers at the grocery store and his friends encouraged Reid to continue his musical adventure, so he began taking his sound system to the streets, setting up his equipment at places such as Forrester's Hall and Chocomo Lawn in his Trojan van. Lucille recalls her husband's growth as a sound system operator. She says,

> He eventually got a little sound system at the time and some box, and he started to play about four hours each day. And you know you have a lot of people around, they like the sound and they like the records. So he decided to go all out in the sound system. And so he bought some boxes [speakers]. The first time he played was at Drummond Street, matinee dance. People loved the music and they loved the sound, and he was a very nice man. They would actually lift him out of his car like a king. The whole hall would pack up when Duke came. And after his sound is set up and he is about to play, everybody would start to clap and really make a lotta noise. They would say, "Duke, Duke is on now! He's the king of the sound."[2]

Lucille Reid adds that he carried his gun around "as protection" from his days as a police officer. After dethroning his competitors in sound system clashes, including Tom "the Great Sebastian" Wong, who left downtown to play at the Silver Slipper, and Coxsone Dodd, who Reid flopped by playing "Mr. Berry" by Roscoe Brown, Reid decided to enter a new business endeavor—construction. After losing out on a contract to assist construction of the Norman Manley Airport, Reid's company went bankrupt. "He lost everything, including his sound system," Duke's son Anthony Reid told *Jamaica Gleaner* reporter Balford Henry in 1995.[3]

Lucille Reid owned a home on Mountain View Avenue. By taking out a loan against the house, Duke Reid was able to put his feet back on the ground. In 1962, using the funds from the loan, Duke Reid bought back property he lost at 33 Bond Street, rebuilt the liquor store, built a studio upstairs, and founded the Treasure Isle record label. It was because of Lucille that her husband was able to reestablish himself and bring himself back from failure. Treasure Isle went on to leave a musical legacy, and without Lucille Reid, that fortune would never have been realized. Lucille Reid was critical to Duke Reid's growth as a businessman, both when he had success and when he failed.

Lucille loved her husband tremendously. Every year for many years after Duke Reid died from cancer on September 26, 1976, Lucille would take out a memorial ad in the *Daily Gleaner* which featured a photo of Duke Reid and reminded him of her love. One memorial read, "In memoriam, Reid—Arthur Stanley: Late of Treasure Isle Recording Co. and Liquor Store. In loving memory of my dear husband who departed this life on the 26th of September, 1976. Two sad and lonely years today. Lives of great men all remind us, / We can make our lives sublime / And departing leave behind us / footprints on the sands of time. Sadly missed by your loving wife Lucille (Reidie)."[4] The following year, the text was the same but the poem had changed: "Beautiful memories are wonderful things / They last till the longest day / They never wear out / They never get lost / And can never be given away / To some, you may be forgotten / To others a part of the past / But to me who loved and lost you / Your memory will always last," read the verse.[5] The next year, four years after his death, the ad was again the same but this time Lucille's poem read, "No morning dawns, no night returns / But that I think of you. / Those left behind are very good / But none replaces you / Many a silent tear is shed / When I am all alone / The one I love so very much / The one I called my own."[6] Even in 1995, Lucille wrote a poem in a memoriam ad for Duke Reid, this one also signed by Anthony. "Your stay on this earth though brief changed history. / Your life was a shining example whose light will never be dimmed. / We love you and will keep your memory alive till the end of time," read the verse.[7] Duke must have greatly loved Lucille too, naming the label imprint "Duchess" after her, though this was a common custom among producers.

Graeme Goodall, engineer at Federal Records, remembers that the couple had a strong partnership, despite rumors that Anthony was not Duke's son and that Duke fathered a number of other children outside of the marriage. Goodall says,

> She was very very quiet, particularly when Duke was around. I never ever saw her when Duke wasn't there. She was always with Duke as a strong right hand. I don't want to say she wasn't communicative, because she was, but he was the main man and she was there, as a fantastic back up. But they loved each other dearly. She never said, "I think you should, I think you should," so people who didn't know better might this she's complacent, but she wasn't. She was just a good third hand for Duke Reid. Reidie was Duke's first love. His second love was his Pontiac car. It was a "boat," maroon and grey, two door. Big American cars were very desirable; however, driving on the left side of the road mean that you had to "profile" to judge width, which gave you the look of "attitude."[8]

After Duke Reid died in 1976, Lucille ran the Treasure Isle label and catalog. The decades that followed were marked by lawsuits and court decrees that saw a number of different interested parties seeking control over the catalog. After Lucille's death the fight over the catalog only worsened. Rights ultimately ended up going to Sonia Pottinger. After Sonia's death, her daughter, Sharon Gibson, took legal and physical possession of the Treasure Isle masters and rights.

Doris Darlington

Coxsone Dodd, Duke Reid's biggest competitor both in the sound system yards and in the studio, perhaps acquired his tenacity and business acumen from his strong mother, Doris Darlington. Doris Darlington was born near Buff Bay in Portland on July 1, 1914, and she moved to Kingston when she was 17 years old to help her sister Edith run her grocery store. She had one other sister, Ruth, who remained in Portland. Doris then opened and ran her own grocery store located on Beeston Street and Love Lane, which is likely how she knew both Duke and Lucille Reid. In fact, she was friends with them. Doris's grocery store was just ten blocks away from Reid's store. Doris was a Maroon, a descendant of the slaves who escaped in the 18th century, established communities in the mountains, and fought the British in a number of wars. They were tough and respected, like Doris, and so Doris was given the nickname of the female leader of the Maroons, Nanny. Her store, first a food shop, then a liquor store, was called Nanny's Korner. She was also respectfully called "Miss D."

Kingsley Goodison, who worked at Studio One for many years remembers Doris at the studio:

> She's the matriarch. She was the matriarch of the team because Sir Dodd was the only child for her— the only child of Doris Darlington. Downbeat was the only child for her, although he had several other brothers and sisters. She was the first woman. There was really nobody else but her. She started a cold supper shop, a night shop on Water Street where you could get meals. At the time, Mr. Dodd was going to the farm work, the program in the states—you pick apple and cut cane—those things, and he would bring back the rhythm and blues, the black American music, the Fats Domino, Roscoe Gordon, Smiley Lewis, Joe Liggins, Louis Jordan, Joe Turner, those people. When he went into a full-fledged sound system operator in about 1955, prior to that in the cold supper shop with his mom he used to play the records that were current in a box in the food shop. And his friends encourage him to go into the sound system. His mother was the first female disc jockey, the selector, the first female selector, because when the sound started out, Sir Dodd was still on the farm overseas doing the work. She started to take his jobs, to go out and play, and she was the one who was playing the music, putting on the records and playing them. Yea mon, she was a powerful woman, powerful. Very very very strong. And up until her death it was like that with her. She was the boss. She was the boss. He chose no other one but her. They call her Nanny because she was a Maroon and Coxsone was a Maroon. They are from Portland, the section the Maroons are from. And that's how she got the name, from Nanny of the Maroons, and she was very strong like Nanny.[9]

Coxsone even had the words "Nanny's Korner" painted on the bottom of his "houses of joy," his speaker boxes.

Coxsone Dodd himself said of his mother, "She is the founding mother of everything, for without her nothing would've happened."[10] When Coxsone was in the U.S. working in the farm program, he sent money back to his mother so she could have the sound systems built for him. When he returned home, he hit the ground running—he contacted a school friend of his, Winston Cooper, also known as Count Matchuki, and he was rolling. Not only did Doris help to set up and run Coxsone's sound systems while he was away, but she also was a fixture around Studio One, which Coxsone founded at 13 Brentford Road in October 1963, and she ran her own music shop, Music Land in Spanish Town, five days a week. She brought the records from Studio One to the shop in Spanish Town at 10 Cumberland Road. "I supply his people," Doris stated.[11] "People come from as far as Montego Bay to stock up their shops," she adds. She was also factory manager for the pressing plant at Studio One in later years. Coxsone Dodd's father was in the construction industry and, in fact, he helped to build the structure that houses Studio One. He died in 1969. Doris, who was active even at age 83 in running the record shop, died on June 28, 1998. Numerous musicians and dignitaries attended her funeral service, and there was a musical tribute given by Sparrow Martin, Myrna Hague-Bradshaw, and Jimmy Tucker.

Norma Dodd

If Doris Darlington was the matriarch of Studio One then Norma Dodd, Coxsone's wife, was something of a big sister. She not only fulfilled an administrative role at Studio One, but also was a caretaker of sorts for the artists, an important job when times could get a little rough and tough.

Norma Dodd was born in 1943. She and Coxsone met and Kingsley Goodison remembers the married couple as strong, at least in the beginning. "They were tight. When they started out they were like peas in a pod. She was a beautiful woman. The young guys used to go to the record shop on Orange Street, what they call Musik City. The sailors go in there, not to buy record, but to just look at her, this beautiful woman, yes, a lot of young sailors go in there and instead of buying records they just sit and have a look at her. She was a pretty girl, a pretty woman," says Goodison.[12]

Norma didn't only help out in the store selling the records; she also helped to run the business and the studio. "In the early stages she did administrative work. She was a good administrator. She was really the backbone then in the early part, the start of Studio One, she was the backbone there. She ran the shop before she went up to the studio. And she was a good cover notes writer, liner notes writer. Yea mon, for some of the early recordings she was a good liner notes writer," Goodison says.

Perhaps one of her most important roles was one of mediator. Coxsone could be a tough guy. When he liked you, he called you "Jackson," but when he saw no need for you he told you to come back in a year or two or, in the case of Don Drummond, threatened to take away the trombone he had provided to Drummond if he didn't play what was demanded. Norma was the soft touch. She simply managed the relationship between Coxsone and the artists. "She was like a mother to most of them. A mother or big sister. When the artists and Mr. Dodd were not getting along, they and her would speak and they'd be friends with her and she advise them on this and that, so she really played a good role in it, played a great role. She was a counselor and administrator. She was a diplomat, very skilled in diplomacy, and no man could have done that. She was a beautiful girl, bright," says Goodison.

Jamaican talk show host Barbara Gloudon said, "Her marriage to a man who was a celebrated visionary in the development of Jamaica's popular music offered her a special role to play. Life at Studio One was not always smooth sailing. No business ever is. But

Coxsone Dodd and Norma Dodd at Studio One in the 1990s (photograph by Ron Vester).

Norma Dodd was there with her husband taking the rough with the smooth, the sour with the sweet. Creative artistes are never easy to deal with. The music industry is not for the faint of heart. But the Dodds, Norma and Clement, Sir Clement and Lady Norma, did what they had to do."[13]

Norma and Coxsone Dodd had eight children—Carol, Sandra, Tanya, Courtney, Junior, Claudia, Morna, and Paulette. It is well known that Coxsone also had a number of children outside of the marriage. Myrna Hague-Bradshaw says, "I know Norma had many emotional issues. There was a lot of infidelity on the part of the men and they had to deal with that, cope with that, so I'm sure their lives were fraught with complex emotional issues and cultural issues."[14]

Coxsone and Norma Dodd immigrated to the United States in the 1980s and set up an office for Studio One in Brooklyn, New York, where they continued to manage the label. "When they left for the states, there was a lull. There was nothing going on," says Goodison. "This was in the '80s and it came to a standstill. It was a time of turmoil, political violence, and it wasn't conducive to doing anything there. Both of them went together, and the whole family went."

Part of the reason why the Dodds left Jamaica for the United States, as many other producers did during this time, was the clampdown on the market. In the 1970s the Jamaican government began to fix prices in the recording industry, which made record producers uncomfortable—not just because they had a ceiling on their profits, controlled by someone else, but because of the political climate. Jamaica geographically is located close to Cuba, and so many worried that the communist system in Cuba would stretch its wings to their little island. The Jamaican government during this time seemed to be showing signs of controlling business, business folk thought, and so they set their sights on freer markets, such as the U.S. The Ministry on Trade and Industry went so far as to set a limit on the price of 45s at 75 cents each. This was done in response to the Jamaica Record Producers Association's attempt to set the limit at one dollar due to rising manufacturing costs. "The big producers/manufacturers will not feel it much if any at all, but the little producers are being run out of business," said the *Daily Gleaner's* "Merry-Go-Round" column on April 20, 1971. It was still early, but such legislation and lack of bargaining power set the climate. It only got worse. Patricia Chin recalls, "At one time we couldn't export any records because the government banned exportation of music. Politics in the country was unstable and we thought we were going communist, so we moved to have a better life. We left and a lot of businesspeople left. Most of the recording companies left. Beverley's left, KG left, Prince Buster left, Byron Lee left."[15]

In 1998 Norma and Coxsone returned from New York to their original studio in Kingston to continue recording and manage distribution. Norma continued her role in assisting the family business until Coxsone died in 2004, and then she kept the business alive and distributed the catalog internationally until her own death on August 31, 2010. At her funeral, Minister of Youth, Sports, and Culture Olivia "Babsy" Grange eulogized Norma by saying, "Norma was humble, gentle, polite; almost reticent and a great and supportive wife to Coxsone. But she was also a shrewd businesswoman whose contribution helped to establish Studio One as, arguably, the leading producer of reggae music."[16]

Patricia Chin

Like Chris Blackwell, Vincent Chin, patriarch of the Randy's label, got his start in the music industry through jukeboxes. But Chin, unlike Blackwell, didn't have the money to own his own machines and charge establishments rent. Instead, he worked for the jukebox owner, Isaac Issa, placing new records into the jukeboxes each week, and removing the old ones. All the while, right by his side, typewriter in her lap making the song title cards to place into the jukebox slots, was his wife and partner, Patricia Chin.

"I grew up in Kingston, right in the heart of Kingston. I was born at Jubilee Hospital, from a Chinese mother and an Indian father," says Patricia, who also had a sister and a brother.[17] She continues, "I grew up in Greenwich Town, Greenwich Farm they call it. My father ... used to be a manager at a haberdashery store that also sold a lot of dry goods, like salt fish, right up to anything that can be sold. It was owned by a rich Indian. My mother's side, they owned stores also. All the Chinese, they go into a neighborhood, the poorest neighborhood, and they service the community; they can grow there, and then you have a community that is loyal to you, and you make friends."

It was through this bakery that Patricia met Vincent. She says, "My grandmother mother's side had a bakery and my husband got a job to drive the bread van, and that's how we met. And it's funny, his parents and my grandparents came from China at the same time. And they both had the name Chin. My mother's name was Chin and then she married a Williams, and I was Williams and then I married back Chin [laughs]. When he left the bread company he got a job at Issa's. They had a lot of businesses in Jamaica, and one of them was jukeboxes. You drop the money in and then the record comes out and play. You get five songs for a quarter. It was just American records. I used to go with him around the country areas to change the records. So I used to take a typewriter and would write up the little slot."

But then Vincent Chin got an idea that would see him no longer working for a boss, but for himself. "After my husband worked there [Issa's] for maybe three or four years, they didn't know what to do with these old records. There was a stockpile of them. So we bought them out and we sell them. So we selling jukebox records because after a time you could not get old records in the store. People were so happy to get Little Richard or Fats Domino, or The Drifters, Temptations, all those American records.... They were happy to buy used records. We did very well with those. And we bought a little place in an ice cream parlor at 17 North Parade in Kingston one block from Ward Theatre.... We were selling all used records and 78 records and we imported a lot of vinyl, the old 12 inch records. That's how we started business," says Patricia.

The store was called Randy's Records, named after a location in Tennessee that Vincent heard advertised on the Nashville radio broadcasts that could be picked up in Jamaica on a clear night. But Vincent hadn't yet made enough money to give up his day job. Patricia states,

> When we started up the store, I used to stay in the store because he was still working. Part of the store was a little space that sold records, the rest was an ice cream parlor that we rented out, and we bought and expanded the little shop into a big store. We were selling candies and ice cream. Artists like Bob Marley would come by and hang out, because where we have our store at 17 North Parade was a very popular area where the higglers would sit on the sidewalks and sell their fruits. There was a corner store called Idler's Rest. A lot of people come there to meet people, to buy, to sell, just congregate. It's a resting place, and if you want to know what's going on, you come. The artists used to hang around, and we started a wholesale business because we realized that people from the country want to buy music and they come to talk about what's new and artists and so on, so my husband said, you know, it's a good idea to build a studio upstairs.

The Chins built a four-track studio and entered the recording industry. Patricia continues:

> We bought 17 North Parade and 18 North Parade so we have two buildings now, so we build a studio upstairs because the young singers did not have the money to go to the big studios to record. So my husband build the studio. We give them the studio time for them to do what they have to do, and we help them to master the record and press it, and then I would sell it and pay them. They would earn a living that way, and we create a business where they can be part of the business, and we were both happy. When they are recording upstairs, you have a lot of people gather on the sidewalk because they are looking for jobs. They could be a pianist, a chorus singer, anything, and then they go right up and you have a musician. That's where we have Rita Marley, Bob Marley, Peter Tosh, all of them just hang out. It was really a meeting spot for everybody. People from England, record companies, meet right there too to see what artist was new, and you could sign a contract right on the sidewalk. Exciting times. Everything was happening right there—all the artist and higglers—all one big happy family. It was a big melting pot of business, a place of congregation.

But balancing the family business with raising a family had its challenges. Patricia and Randy had three children of their own, as well as Patricia's stepson Clive, who runs the business today. But they were all young when the business was thriving, and fortunately, Patricia says she had assistance. She says, "I was blessed because I had some good helpers at home. Although I don't know how my daughter grow up to tell you the truth, because the business was growing so fast! In the mornings I would bathe her and put on her porridge or whatever, but I had a good helper that really grew her up for me. On Fridays she would always bring her down to the store or took her to the park where there were other kids to play with. It was a lot of juggling—a house and a business. But I think the business is what kept me going. I wasn't so good at housekeeping, because in the morning at 9 o'clock I leave and I don't get back until 7 o'clock. My whole life was in the business."

In many ways, the artists were Patricia's extended family. She took care of them. She nurtured them. She understood them. Clive Chin says,

> She balanced it well. My memories are that she was always busy. The only time we really had together as a family with my other siblings was on a Sunday, but from Monday to Saturday, it was just all business. I remember seeing her over the record counter putting records on the turntable and taking them off when the customers would want that record. She was a very straight-up person. She was very sociable and also very kindhearted to the customers. That's why they loved her and keep coming back. I think one of the most important things they remember, even Lee Perry talked about this, was that Miss Pat would give him free studio time to record his music because at that time when he started out he had no money. When he made the music, whether it was Dennis Brown or John Holt or Bob Marley, he would press the records and come back, and Miss Pat would take out the money for the studio time when he had enough earnings from the records. She was always for these guys that became big legendary producers and artists.[18]

It was work, but it was also a labor of love for Patricia and soon even her father got involved. She says, "We had so many sound systems and jukeboxes.... The music played a big part in the politics. Every time there's an election going along, they would use the music to draw the crowd. If they have a meeting on a corner, my father would drive the truck ... and on the loud speaker, 'come to this avenue.'... So the politicians do their piece and then to keep the people focused they would play the music and have the deejays dee-jaying and rapping and everything like that. So the music and the sound system has a big part in politics. My father was very involved in that. I had just started in business at that time. It was a good time."

Patricia says that helping musicians, connecting with them, supporting them was an important part of her job and her life. "I've enjoyed seeing the artists, how they can grow and develop. Sometimes the artist come to you, not even sure what they want to do, and sometimes they're not very successful, but you give them a little hope and try. Try and try and try. Encouraging people. I like to give them hope," she says. But times got tough in the 1980s when the Jamaican government set restrictions on exporting music, she says. "We moved to the U.S. and started to do the same thing here. We continued doing what we were doing, helping artists to sell their product. I've often had them come and tell me, 'Miss Pat, you are the first person who ever buy my music,' and they remember." Vincent first moved and set up a store in Queens, New York, in 1977, and Pat sent records from Kingston. She stayed until 1979, when she joined Vincent. They changed the name of the business to VP Records, since Randy's Records was already an established business in Tennessee. The V represented Vincent; the P represented Patricia.

From the first tracks produced in the early years, such as Lord Creator's "Independent Jamaica" and classics from The Skatalites and Toots and the Maytals, to hit reggae from Augustus Pablo and Lee "Scratch" Perry's work with Bob Marley and the Wailers, to Sean Paul and Shabba Ranks, Patricia Chin has been at the center of Randy's Records and VP Records. When Vincent died on February 2, 2003, Patricia continued the business with her stepson Clive, who runs the New York location and the Randy's catalog that he helped his dad to build. Clive's son, Joel Chin, who served in A&R for the Kingston location of VP Records, was tragically murdered just outside of his Stony Hill home in August 2011.

Joel joined the family business in 1990 and was responsible for signing Sean Paul and Beenie Man. Patricia's daughter Angela and Angela's husband Howard opened a branch of VP in Miramar, Florida. In addition, Patricia oversees the daily operations for Riddim Driven, VP's clothing line. "We continue to do what we do best. I still go on weekends to the retail store to meet and greet my customers and talk about music and what's going on," she says.

Miss Pat, as she is called, "played a very vital role" in the business and Jamaican music, Clive Chin explains: "You didn't have that many women who were involved with their husbands or partners, but she stood right by my dad and stood right beside the business and made it happen, you know? Even though she wasn't physically a producer herself, she had good ideas of what would make a record a hit record. She had a very good ear for talent. She played a very important role in the development of the business itself from a small record shop to a musical empire. We came from a very small middle-class family. I would say that she played a major role in the development of both the record store to the recording studio to distribution, the label and she is also involved in our clothing line. She has been around a long time."

Gloria Khouri

Ken Khouri, owner of Federal Records, once claimed that he was the "complete pioneer of everything."[19] He had a point. As founder, owner, and operator of the only real pressing plant on the island, Khouri was the man who took Jamaican music and turned it into a commodity that could be sold and exported, which was critical to its spread both locally and internationally. But one woman was always by his side, from the beginning through to the end, the dynamo behind the family business. Gloria Khouri led many aspects of the business, as well as played host to business functions at the family home and raised the family who went on to evolve the business into its modern incarnation. Without Gloria Khouri, there would be no Federal Records and no Jamaican music as we know it today.

Gloria Khouri was married to Ken for 55 years before he died on September 20, 2003. They had six children, three boys and three girls. One of those boys, Paul Khouri, says that his mother and father both came from Middle Eastern families with a business background, and both shared a love for music:

> My mother's [Gloria's] dad was from Damascus, Syria. Her mother was half Spanish and half English. Her father left Syria at the age of 15 and worked on a ship and worked his way to New York. From New York he got on another ship and worked his way down to Jamaica. He was a trader. He traded, and then he moved to a town called Black River, where he worked and traded and bought a whole lot of buildings and a whole lot of property, and he did well for himself. Her mother, Cathleen Baracat, and father, Alfred Khouri, eloped because her mother's family felt her father wasn't good enough. Her father was a character. He never trusted the banks, and he hid all of his money underground in a big safe. It's a different mentality. My mother was brought up in the town called Black River that's on the southwestern side of Jamaica, and that was where the only shipping port was in Jamaica. Now it's in Kingston. My mother was one girl with two brothers, David and Carlton. They lived in a big guesthouse that had six rooms, and her mother rent it as a bed and breakfast. When my mother grew up to the age of needing further schooling, she had to go to Kingston with her aunt. That's where my father met her.[20]

Ken Khouri's mother was born in Jamaica but of Cuban decent, and his father was from Lebanon and came to Jamaica when he was just 12 years old. Paul says that the English pronunciation of the family name is not correct. "It's not 'Koor-ee.' 'Koor-ee' is English. 'Who-de' is how it's pronounced. But when our grandparents and parents came here, 'Koor-ee' is what the English-speaking tongue understood," he says. Ken was born in 1917 and had three older sisters. His father owned a store and was a businessman. Paul says, "The Middle Eastern people were businesspeople. My grandfather owned a store that was like a miniature Wal-Mart with furniture and toys and a variety of goods." Even though Ken worked for Joseph Issa, a family friend and owner of multiple stores, hotels, and other enterprises throughout the island, Ken wasn't interested in continuing the family business. He had other pursuits in mind.

"My dad had always loved music," says Paul:

> I don't know where it came from because his mother and his father thought he was looney tunes wanting to go into the music business. He wanted him to take the business, make money, sell furniture.... But he was adamant. His father got ill and he had to go to Florida to take him to the hospital. Now, my dad had no money. He worked in a store called Issa's. Issa's was like the Macy's of the U.S. He worked in there and when they sold something they would say, "wrap here".... He would take the thing and he would wrap it in brown paper because they never had bags, and tape it and give it to you in a wrapped situation. He was just a wrapper because he had not much education. He barely finished high school and went to no university. He came out of school and he went and worked in Issa's, earning God knows, pinochle money. And his father said, "come in the business," and he wouldn't. He was proud and he wanted to be on his own. When he went to the U.S. of A. he rented a car. Now, the car had to have a radio.... So he took off with his dad, and when he was going up to the hospital, the radio quit. So he took his dad to the hospital, settled him in and said, "Dad, I'm going back to have them do something for the radio." So he once again thought he was a little bit off his rocker. When he went back to the rental car place, they said "We don't have another car with a radio, but take this car to the shop that repairs all of the radios and electronics in our cars." So he went there, and he found this man who was there trying to sell a cutting machine. When you finish in the studio, you have to go and master the disc, make a lacquer, and the lacquer makes a metal mold, and the metal mold goes in the press and presses the records. In those days, this cutting machine was used for people sending birthday greetings, so you would talk in the microphone and they would cut the record, cut the wax and that wax you could play, so instead of sending a birthday card, you would have a wax with a little label that you wrote on it, "Best wishes." Well, this man had a hard luck story. He said his family is in problems, he has to sell his cutting machine. My dad said to him, "Look, I don't have any money with me now, I'm coming back for the radio; can you meet me back here and I'll see if I can get the money from my dad." He went back to the hospital and said to his father, ... "Pa, I need some money.... I need to buy a disc machine that you can speak into it and I can cut a disc and sell the disc and make some money." Once again his dad said, you know what—"You're a crazy guy." But he was the only son. He was the last child of four children, three girls, and all the Middle Eastern guys want sons, not a girl, because that's what carries the name. So he was spoiled rotten. So he gave him the money.

That cutting machine cost $350 U.S., which was not a small sum, especially at that time, and $50 for 100 lacquers. "He went back and the guy sold him the cutting machine," says Paul. He continues:

> He sold him the lacquers, and [Ken] took that back to Jamaica after his dad was taken care of. He left Issa's and he started to travel the whole of Jamaica, cutting these lacquers for birthday wishes and greetings and this and that. We had a lot of migrants that went to London, and they would send these discs that had wishes and greetings so they could play it on the dog and horn—remember RCA with the dog and horn? But then he met this group—two calypsonians—one was called Lord Flea, one was called Lord Fly, and they are the ones that initially took calypso to the U.S. He then

cut this record, "This Little Flea." It was kind of smutty with a little cover-up. He sent that to London to have that processed in London with Decca Records. He would produce and he would get a hundred records manufactured. These were 78s, the ones that if they drop they broke. And now he had no money to get this processed. He went to this gentleman who was called Alec Durie, who owned the chain of Time Stores, like a Sears Roebuck where you had a soda fountain upstairs that sold hamburgers, but a massive chain store that sold lawnmowers, bicycles, tools, everything. Alec Durie was an heir to a multimillionaire who owned 600 prime acres in the hills, and he went to Alec Durie, who had an English background, who was very considerate, very understanding. He listened to his argument when he said, "Here is a new project in Jamaica and nobody has ever done this. I want to send this over to England to have these records manufactured, come back to Jamaica. Will you sell it in your soda fountain?" He said, "Not a problem, let's do it. Let's try it. If it fails, it fails." He gave him the money to send it away and have it done, and when the records came back, those hundred records were the first ever records recorded in Jamaica and sold off in about a day. People lined up and it was gone. So Alec Durie said, "Ken, let's send back and get some more." He sent back and got 250 because they were cagey, which sold off in another day. So Alec said to him, "Ken, this is crazy. We are sending away to get records and the cost of it selling." It wasn't good for the profit margin. He said, "Why don't you investigate and see if there is some way of manufacturing the stuff so we can make the molds in England, they can send the molds and we can press the records here," which he did. Two or three storefronts away from where Alec Durie owned the Times Store, he got this building, and he went to the U.S. of A. and he met with some people in the U.S. of A. who set him up, sold him a record press and a boiler and whatever it took to manufacture the records, and he was his own pressman. He pressed the records, he manufactured it. Once the boiler actually exploded and nearly killed him, but he went back because he was in the process of trying to figure out how to do everything correctly.

Ken Khouri's plant was started, and although the boiler exploding was not the only problem he encountered at first, he continued. Another problem he had was how to properly remove the disc from the die without it sticking, and in fact the first few times when the record stuck, he actually used a penknife to pry the vinyl from the die. He also had to manage where to procure the vinyl and had a few snafus along the way. Paul explains how the plant expanded:

> Alec Durie said to him, "Ken, why don't you go now and see if you can get a franchise of some other label—not only press the ones you are recording, but the ones in the states." So he went to Mercury Records. The first song he got from them was "I Saw You Crying in the Chapel," and the second was by the Crew Cuts, called "Sheboom." It went on and on and on, and he went and got Capital Records. Alec said, "Ken, you cannot press all of this with one press." My dad started making money, and Alec was a prince, because he gave my old man the majority shares and gave him a contract that said under no circumstances can he, Alec Durie or any other partner that comes in, remove Ken Khouri from the controlling partner, even though he had the least amount of money involved. So he protected him, and he said, "Okay, let's go and find more property in an industrial estate," which he went and bought—something like 15 acres and built a new factory—a new this, and new that, and had six or seven presses. This was all with Alec Durie's money. Alec Durie made a fortune, and my old man went and got other partners, different investors, and he grew and grew and grew, and we became self-contained where we had our own art department, our own printing department that was fully mechanized with Heidelberg presses. We manufactured our own sleeves for the 45s, we printed and folded it and made our own jackets, everything. You could go into the studio at 8 o'clock in the morning and have a record at 5 o'clock in the evening. The only plant of that nature in the world—there was no other plant in the world. Even CBS Records came down to Jamaica and was so impressed that they joined us—not as a franchise, but as CBS Jamaica Limited. They invested in our business and became partner with us. So we had every label—Capitol Records, Mercury Records, Atlantic Records, Motown Records—you name it, we took care of every person who wanted to produce in Jamaica.

But always at his side, during the entire process, was Ken's wife Gloria. In fact, she was part of the business. An article entitled "Disc-Making Plant Here" states,

> Increased productivity in the islands' rapidly expanding industrialization pattern was marked this week by the opening of Federal Record Manufacturing Co. Ltd., an important factory for record pressing which provides clear evidence of the phenomenal growth of the Industrial Development Corporation's Industrial Estate says an IDC release. Directors of the new record manufacturing factory are Messrs Alec Durie, Anthony Hart and Kenneth Khouri, Mr. Khouri being the Managing Director. Mrs. Gloria Khouri has been appointed Secretary of the Company.[21]

Of his mother's involvement, Paul says that she not only became part of the business at Federal, but also was the one who supported the family while Federal was getting a foothold:

> My mother was the financial controller. She graduated with her LSR in music, she played classical music, and she used to give recitals. She was the musician in the family, not my dad. He was a music lover. He knew what was saleable, which was the perfect combination. She had been so schooled that she was a financier for a company called Soap and Edible, a massive corporation, when my dad grew with Alec Durie. We have a saying, "While the grass is growing, the house has to be fed," so she was the one who was bringing in the big bucks while my dad was developing with his business. He got to a stage where he now needed someone with a little financial intelligence. She left Soap and Edible and came and joined him, her husband. She was the one who manipulated everything he did into this magnitude. She took this money and invested some of it in a different business. While we had the cash, she said money is not the answer to everything, you need to have income, you need to have investments. She did this and did that, and our company grew to a magnitude. They wanted us to go on the stock exchange and we never did. We kept it in the family. It grew and grew.

Federal Records grew to the point that they decided to enter other areas of the entertainment industry, and Gloria Khouri was right there at the helm of the ship. In an article titled "Jamaica's First Independent TV Studio," Gloria Khouri features prominently as a spokeswoman for the story.

> Along Marcus Garvey Drive [previously named Foreshore Road], among the busy factories that give evidence of Jamaica's industrial growth, there is a prosaic looking door that opens on a little bit of Hollywood.... This is Jamaica's first independent television studio. Only commercials are filmed there now but the company, Federal Record Manufacturing Company Limited, expects the studio to be used soon for fall-length shows, perhaps even for plays. The studio is brand new. It is not even completely finished, although it is in use. "The customers just couldn't wait," explains Mrs. Gloria Khouri, wife of Federal Records Managing Director Kenneth Khouri. "So we are fixing it up as we go along.... We started in a little place on King Street," Mrs. Khouri recalls, "There was a press man, a man to wipe the record and take them out in a little buggy, and Ken and I. At first we used to make about 30 records a day and sometimes when we put them on the spindle they would break and all of our work would have been for nothing." But it didn't take the Khouris long to become experts in the techniques of stamping records. By the end of six months they were whisking off the press at the rate of thousands a week. The company now has five record stamping presses and two soundproof studios are used by most local "sound system" bands as well as other groups. "Jamaican composers and artists are producing music here which become hits not only in Jamaica but all over the Caribbean," says Mrs. Khouri.... Their plant exports to almost every Caribbean country as well as producing for the local market. During Independence Week alone, Federal presses turned out around 20,000 records.[22]

Graeme Goodall, studio engineer at Federal Records who also helped to build the studio, confirms that Gloria was an integral part of the business:

> She never took part in the actual production of music, as such, but she ran the office. She was the lynchpin, no doubt about it. Ken Khouri had the vision and was the one who started it all, regardless, I mean he was the one who went into the recording business. He was the one who started pressing records, the first person in Jamaica. And he often took part in the production, particularly with calypso or mento. But this goes back further, when Gloria was part and parcel of the furniture store

on King Street. He started off selling scrap leather, believe it or not, and then he went into furniture and Gloria was there with him. She ran the actual financial side, the bookkeeping, to use an old word. Ken Khouri, I never saw him put down anything except working out what a food bill was worth. She was the one who kept a very strict eye on the day-to-day running of the business. When they went home at night, I'm sure Ken and Gloria went and sat down and talked about whether or not they could afford for him to buy a piece of equipment, a new press, a stamper plate, a cutting head, and if it would be viable. Later on when there was a government restriction put on the importation of phonograph records, she would often attend the Board of Trade meetings because she knew what the market would bear, and if somebody came in with records that she had or somebody was trying to buy something that she had a contract for the distribution of that particular label, particularly from the U.S., then she would contest it and say, "I don't want that record brought in," and of course the government would say, "Certainly, by all means."[23]

Like any good businessman or businesswoman, cultivating the business relationship is part of the song and dance. Gloria and Ken Khouri were skilled in the finesse of the business relationship. Goodall remembers, "The house up at Cherry Gardens, Ken was the one who said, 'This is the piece of land,' and Gloria said, 'This is the house I want.' Ken arranged the contractors and Gloria said, 'I want the hand basin here, I want the windows there, I want the doorway here,' and Ken said, 'You hear what the lady says, this is where she wants the door.' That's the sort of relationship they had between the two of them. The house was four bedrooms and five bathrooms. This house was a beautiful house. The Lebanese mentality, I saw it over and over again. If Ken wanted a favor from you, you would be invited up to Cherry Gardens and you would have kibbeh and roti daal and all the beautiful dishes that Gloria would have the maid cook, and he'd convince you to do a favor. The old theory though is you've eaten with me so guess what—I'm not going to pay you for anything [laughs]."

Gloria and Ken raised a family together and brought the children into the family business. They had six children—Richard, Robert, Paul, Jennifer, Patricia and Gina. "On school vacations, Richard and Paul were there helping the family out and occasionally I saw the eldest daughter, although I can't remember their names. Paul and Richard were very much involved with the actual operation and helped their father, and they were a good help to him too, there's no two ways about that. It's a Middle Eastern family concept," says Goodall.

Paul says that the home was used for a lot of entertaining in those days and that his mother was a wonderful host to many famous artists. "That house in Kingston, at the top of the hill in Russell Heights, entertained movie stars—Paul Anka, Dionne Warwick, Marvin Gaye, Lionel Hampton, you name it, they came and stayed with us, because we were accustomed to them. We never fussed around them. Maybe you could have been my sister. It meant nothing to me. Paul Anka lived with us and we took him out in our boat —because we had a 31-foot Bertram—and went fishing and had a wonderful time in that house. That house had its fill of all these top-notch guys, names I can't even remember. She was the perfect hostess," he says of his mother.

Graeme Goodall was very fond of Gloria and says she had the perfect personality for business. "Gloria was very very funny, but when she was not funny with a person, when she was angry with a person, it was very transparent. She could be very tough when it came to paying the bills for stuff you had pressed there or mastered there, and she was a no-nonsense person when it came to that. She was always very friendly," he says.

When Michael Manley took office in 1972 and served as prime minister until 1980, the business climate in Jamaica changed, says Paul Khouri, and so his mother and father left the island. As he tells it,

> When Michael Manley, with this whole ordeal of communism and Castro and Cuba, it frightened us to death. My sister-in-law was a Cuban who had experience of this take over with Che Guevara with Castro, so she was telling us all of this. We had only heard about Castro and Che Guevara as we would read, but she was telling us by living it. Reading it was one thing, but living it was another disaster, and so we all thought we had to flee. So my mother said, "Look, we have to disappear because we are going to lose everything. Let's try to get everything sold off, let's get rid of everything," so they did, and they got money. They had money and so we all left. He made so much money, we were living in a 12,000 square-foot home that had, you name it, the butler, everything. We took the [mixing] boards with me, took the cutting machine with me.

Graeme Goodall remembers that there was fire at Federal Records around this time. "Later on after the fire, Paul lived in Miami for a long time, and all of the disc cutting equipment that he had at Federal all of a sudden mysteriously appeared in Miami, and Paul was cutting masters in Miami. To quote Sergeant Schultz, 'I know nothing!' But Lee Perry bought a lot of the equipment and that's how he started his recording operation," Goodall says.

Paul says that his parents retired and despite cashing out, found themselves in dire straits later in life. "My mother had retired with my dad, they had cash. He now and then was a torrential gambler, but he had built this massive house which she still lives in. She's 94 years old and has all her faculties—can do mathematics in her head today at 94. Your calculator can't do it as fast as she can. He gambled it all away except for the house, and no cash. When he died he had a lot of debts. She had to mortgage the house to bury him and get rid of his debts and bills. So now my baby sister, who is 50, is living with her, and they are migrating back to the U.S. She's an American citizen, and she is selling her house to get the cash and leave with her baby daughter to go to Florida and live out the rest of her days," says Paul. Gloria Khouri died in Jamaica on October 30, 2016.

Paul Khouri and Graeme Goodall both agree that Gloria Khouri was the foundation of Federal Records and the family. Goodall says, "Like a lot of the ladies in Jamaica at the time—Pat Chin, Sonia Pottinger, Lucille Reid, Coxsone's wife—there always seemed to be a lady around there somewhere, assisting, and they always had their finger on the cash register, and this is where they shine. They never took the limelight, but they were a very very strong part of the whole industry. On the surface, I really don't think any of these men would have been as successful because the men were so involved in the business, they didn't take care of the business. So when you think of these ladies and look at the areas they had to work in, it was a pretty rough area."

Paul says,

> She was the Rock of Gibraltar. She was the one that controlled everything. She was the one that made all of us what we are. She was the one that gave all of us the self-esteem and made us all feel we were numero uno, but at the same time, never letting us lose respect for everyone. I thought I was number one, but you also were number one, so I had to give you that respect. If you come to my house you will be treated royally. She made that clear with everybody, even with the helper. That's how we were brought up. My dad was a silent guy who just went along in business. He wanted to earn his money, take care of the family, but my mother was the one that taught us moral values. And that's what I taught all of my kids. She was the stalwart of the family, not because she's my mother—I would have told you if she wasn't. She was not a stay-at-home mom. And she never ever get recognition for it, like my dad. My dad was the winner, but he was the winner because he had the best trainer.

Sheila Khouri Lee and Jean Benson

Born to Michael Francois Khouri and Lily Khouri, Sheila Khouri was the eldest of five girls. Her father would go on to marry again and have five boys. It was a comfortable childhood in the Barbican area of Kingston. Her father was related to Ken Khouri, but the two never mixed business. "My father and Ken's father were two brothers," Sheila says.[24] Instead, Sheila grew up to cross paths with another man in the music industry, one who would found his own record studio, pressing plant, and band—Byron Lee.

Sheila Khouri came to know Byron Lee through the same circle of friends. She remembers, "Eddie Seaga was a childhood friend before I even knew Byron Lee. We were a very tight community in the 50s and so on. I knew Eddie as a child. He was friendly with my parents. He was younger than they were, but all the young men loved my parents. My dad was a captain in the British army, so of course we were British subjects. Eddie was a friend of mine and we were always on a first name basis. Peter Stoddart lived next door and Max Wildman [both of the Caribs] married my mother's best friend, who used to live with us in a house on Liguanea Avenue."

It was through Eddie Seaga that Sheila came to meet Byron Lee, but it didn't happen as children, or by way of introduction—it was by being a dancer of the ska in America. Sheila says,

> My dad left Jamaica in 1961 to go to England because things weren't working out financially for him here [Jamaica], and I went along with him because he and I were very close. I had a job with Martin's Tours on the north coast, and I expected to come back to Jamaica, but I couldn't leave him alone in England, so that was the end of me in Jamaica. I left when I was 18 and I didn't come back until after Byron and I were married. England didn't work out for my dad, so we went to live in America. At that time, British subjects were non-quota. Anybody could migrate to America without any red tape. So we went to New York at the end of 1962. Now, we didn't realize with the Jamaican independence that you would have to choose if you wanted to be British or you wanted to be Jamaican, which posed a problem for my dad because I was born here, [Jamaica] so it didn't matter—I could automatically get my Jamaican citizenship—but later on in the early 70s I had to apply for him to be a Jamaican and be able to live here [Jamaica]. So we went into America and when we were in America, Ronnie Nasralla was one of those friends of my parents, and Eddie Seaga, and we kept in touch. And that was when Jamaican music was trying to find a footing in the worldwide market. So Eddie Seaga had this lawyer in New York, Paul Marshall, and Paul used to gather together the West Indians that he could find, and I was one of them because my parents had a nightclub in Queens and I was found through Ronnie. And so I was one of six. There were three couples who used to go all around the place demonstrating the ska. We even appeared on American Bandstand. Paul had a gold Rolls Royce and he used to drive us in his Rolls Royce, to Philadelphia and New Jersey. It was a lot of fun. And he made costumes for us to wear that were very sexy but looked a bit Caribbean, calypso type of thing, a one-shoulder thing. So now comes along the World's Fair, 1964 in New York, and Byron Lee is coming to perform. He wanted to have a frontline of dancers, so obviously, we—the persons who for many months, demonstrating the ska all over the eastern seaboard—were invited to perform at the World's Fair in front of the band. So Ronnie Nasralla made me his partner. I had another partner who lived in New York. Ronnie partnered with me and six of us, three couples, performed the ska at the World's Fair in front of the band. Basically, they really wanted Jannette Phillips, who is now Jannette Miles. She was in Florida at the Peppermint Lounge, so she could not come to the New York set up, and they chose to take the six of us who were doing it. She was really Ronnie's partner. There is a film where Tony Verity is talking and they're talking and demonstrating how to do the ska, that would be Ronnie and Jannette.

Sheila Khouri Lee says teaching people how to dance the ska was an enjoyable part of her history, especially since it led her to her husband Byron Lee:

Eddie [Seaga], who was a family friend, needed this done, and Ronnie [Nasralla], who is a family friend—there was no money passing. We weren't paid for what we did, and to be honest, I really wasn't very patriotic—to me, Jamaica wasn't anything special, but I did it because of my connection with Ronnie and Eddie. I worked with a lawyer, and I was his secretary in a legal firm in Massapequa, New York, and eventually I gave that up so I could be free to travel. I was a fan of Byron's. I used to go with Ronnie to their sets. I loved to dance, and Ronnie was a dancer, and because he was a friend of the family, I was allowed to go with him to these dances that they used to have at Emmett Park—but I personally never met Byron at any of them. My first interaction with Byron was at the World's Fair. Then he wanted to get his musicians' union card for America, and so the band decided to stay in New York while they applied for their cards. As I said, my parents had a nightclub in Queens, and what they did was to have Byron work there on weekends for little and no money, but it enabled them [Byron and the band] to pay their expenses while they were waiting for their Local 802 cards. That's how his and my relationship started, from that point, when he was working there, in 1964, right after the World's Fair. But we didn't get married until 1967.

Sheila explains why it took three years before the two were married. She says,

[Byron] met this gentleman, William Wilson, who owned a hotel, among other things, upstate on Lake George, the Lake George Inn. We had the band performing there. He was instrumental in our gaining our 802 cards. 802 is the musician's union card. So for several years after that we would do an annual stint at the Lake George Inn, much like the *Dirty Dancing* movie, the same type of scene. Then I started to come back to Jamaica on visits, but I still lived in New York, and it wasn't until 1966—we had a difference of opinion with my dad, who was very Lebanese and did not approve of intermarriages, so Byron being Chinese did not sit well with him in the early days—so that's when I moved back to Jamaica. Byron bought us a home in Trafalgar Park. Funny enough, we eventually sold that home to Sonia Pottinger—very small world.

Byron Lee had been married previously. Graeme Goodall says, "His first wife, we knew her as Bibi. She was a Chinese girl, Bibi. The two sons and Byron's daughter, Deanna, were children of his first marriage." Sheila had a child before she married Byron as well.

Sheila explains how Byron took his band and together they built a business:

Byron was under contract with Federal Records. He left Federal Records and went independent. He did not have a desire to be part of the manufacturing portion of the industry. He signed up with West Indies Records. Eddie was no longer part of West Indies Records. It was now British American Insurance Company. Bunny Rae, Clifford Rae, in partnership with Ronnie [Nasralla], they build the studio which was formed by Byron—25 percent by Byron, 25 percent by Ronnie, 25 percent by West Indies Records Jamaica, and 25 percent by British American Insurance Company, so they were now distributing. Somehow or the other, the Ertegun Brothers [Ahmet and Nesuhi] from Atlantic Records met Byron when Eddie was trying to promote West Indian music in America. And we joined forces with George Benson, at Record Specialists. Byron and I went to Nashville and we bought a press, but of course the press had to be hooked up to a boiler, blah blah blah. We have none of this and no means to secure this. So we went into an agreement with George Benson where we went to his place at number one Torrington and hooked up to his press. Byron said he didn't want to have anything to do with it, he was only interested in being a musician, he wanted nothing to do with that aspect of music, so I ran it.

George Benson's wife, Jean Benson, was also an integral part of her husband's business at Record Specialists. A *Daily Gleaner* article states:

The phonograph records manufacturing business today is big business. And one of the biggest persons in Jamaica's record-making business is a woman—Mrs. Jean Benson, Director/Secretary of Record Specialists Limited. Mrs. Benson, whose company won the Prime Minister's Cup for champion manufacturer/exporter in 1969 and 1970, is a Canadian who fell in love with Jamaica and decided to make it her home. Record Specialists also employ what Mrs. Benson says must be the first female record press operator in the Caribbean, Miss Tina Bailey. Record Specialists do not manufacture "stampers," (so called master copies). They press records from imported stampers brought to them by local artists. And they print labels for the locally-pressed records.

The company also holds the local franchise to press records owned by some of the major overseas companies and individuals in the business with names and labels including CBS, Mercury, Philips, Stax (Isaac Hayes), Staple Singers, Booker T., Liberty, United Artists and Pickwick, among others. Record Specialists started business at 1 Torrington Road in May 1967 with seven people including Mrs. Benson and her husband, Mr. George Benson, who is Managing Director. They now employ some 28 people and have six interchangeable presses each of which can produce 350–400 LP's per 8-hour shift or 1,000 45 r.p.m. over the same period. Sixty-five percent of their production—including their own franchise labels and a number of local records—is exported to some 300–350 regular retail outlets in Carifta and other areas including British Honduras, Panama, Bermuda, and the Bahamas. As Director/Secretary, Mrs. Benson's job includes looking after accounts and supervising the payment of royalties. She is also Production Manager and responsible for billing for custom (non-franchise) pressing. She does some correspondence—virtually all when her husband is away, as he often is on regular, sales promotion trips. Music for recording and release is chosen by the Managing Director, to whom Mrs. Benson is directly responsible. Mrs. Benson, who came to Jamaica permanently in 1960, has been in the record-producing business since 1962 when she and her husband formed part of a group which took over, West Indies Records. Mr. Benson had been in a similar business for five years previously in Trinidad. Mrs. Benson first came to Jamaica from Toronto in 1951.... The Bensons have two children—a daughter who works at Record Specialists and a 17-year-old son studying in Toronto. Mrs. Benson says she likes her job despite its many demands because she loves working with people in general, her staff in particular.[25]

Sheila Khouri Lee says that securing the help of those like Jean Benson and others in the industry were crucial to the success of Dynamic Sounds:

I had Tommy Cowan working for me, Sir Lord Comic, and a friend of Byron's, Victor Sampson, and we brought in brother Neville [Lee] from England to join us as well, and we ran that, our company, Lee Enterprises Holdings Limited. Because the Ertegun Brothers, who fell in love with Byron, told him that when their contract with Ken Khouri expired, they were going to give it to him, and they did that, even though he was only a musician. He had nothing to do with the manufacturing part or the distribution of product. And so that kind of forced us to get into that aspect of the business, and it was mine. It was mine. I bought a piece of land on Hagley Park Road, drew to scale how I wanted to see the factory and studios, and in the interim we had the fire at West Indies Records. We feel it was deliberately done, and they owed us so much money that we put them into receivership. This was in 1968 or 1967, and at this time I'm operating out of Torrington Road, Record Specialists, but this man now, I had a hit and I couldn't get him to put the stamp on the press because according to him, he is doing a run and it wouldn't be cost effective for him to pull the press down. That became a nightmare, and so when the fire was at 13 Bell Road, we decided we were going to make an offer to the receiver to purchase that, because the studio that Byron loved so much was already there. But another thing was Bunny Rae, as the managing director of West Indies Records Limited, was supposed to collect the rental from the studio, and as a 25 percent shareholder, he cheated the whole thing so that we went into arrears and he legally took over. It was a really nasty controlled business in those days.

Meanwhile, Byron Lee and the Dragonaires were experiencing success as a band. So too did the studio.

So Byron is going on with his band and becoming more and more popular overseas. So we decided to put in a bid for the burnt-out West Indies Records. None of the stamper plant or the studio had been destroyed, and Federal was trying to buy it, and Eddie [Seaga] stepped in and he said, "We cannot have a monopoly in the country so you have to absolutely accept our bid," and that's when we took possession of that property at 13 Bell Road. Byron said, "I do not want that number. We should call it 15 Bell Road," and that is how Dynamic Sounds was formed. We opened the doors the first of May, 1969. And we actually built a second studio because we were having so much interest from abroad. We had so many artists—like the Rolling Stones album *Goats Head Soup* was recorded in our studio, and tons of stuff. Cat Stevens came down here and spend a long time with us doing *Wild World*. It was just amazing.

It was all because of the Ertegun Brothers. They had faith in Byron, who was nothing but a musician. They said, "You are going to be a thing to be reckoned with in the Caribbean." They saw his potential and all on a handshake gave him the label [Atlantic Records] that was the hottest label of the day. People like Aretha Franklin, you name it—those artists that were in their heyday in the 60s—and they gave it to Byron, and he had no company, he was just a musician! They were awesome, they were really awesome.

Not only did Sheila Khouri Lee establish a business and support her husband's band, but she also began and maintained a family:

I had a child before, but our first child was born in January of 1969 and the company opened in May of 1969. I was pregnant and working down at Torrington Road. His two boys came to live with us, and I had to take them to school. They went to George's [school] and I would drive them to school in the morning, and then I would go to Torrington Road and I would do my business there. Byron was married before and had three children, two boys and a girl, and the girl stayed with her mama, she was in boarding school here in Kingston. The two boys came to live with me from 1968 up until they became young men and moved out on their own. They always lived with us, and it was wonderful. Our children traveled; they drank wine instead of water as young kids because that's how the Europeans were. We used to put them in a hotel in Nice, and we would leave them and drive into Cannes every morning to do our business. Byron loved Europe. And we loved the sea. Byron bought a small boat, and every weekend we went out. Over the years we bought a bigger one and bigger one until eventually he had a large Hateras, which we used to go marlin fishing; and we could go snorkeling. Cat Stevens was on out on the boat with us. The Stones had their own boat. Keith Richards brought his own boat down. It was a magical time. A magical time.

Byron Lee may have built his band because of his talent and personality, but he built his company because of his wife Sheila. They were a team. At his funeral, then–prime-minister Bruce Golding said, "What is so profound about Byron Lee is that Byron Lee and the Dragonaires never left the stage and can be said to be the most enduring of the musical bands that have come on the stage in Jamaican history. Byron Lee and the Dragonaires today is more than just a band, it is an institution, it is a part of our culture and a part of our heritage."

Lillian Johns

Ask any vocalist from the 1950s and 1960s where they got their start, and they will often tell you that they either participated in or attended the *Vere Johns Opportunity Hour*. This talent show was responsible for launching the careers of a great percentage of Jamaican vocalists during the time when studios were looking for talent. It was a test, a rehearsal, a springboard for further success. The show began not in Jamaica, but in the United States, as Colby Graham writes in his blog, Vintage Boss. Graham finds that Vere Johns migrated to the United States in 1929 after he was married to his first wife, Dorice Constance Lucas of Linstead. It was here in New York that Vere Johns began working as a journalist. But when his marriage ended in 1934, according to Graham, he found his second wife, Lillian Margaret May of Brooklyn, while performing in a Harlem theater, as he had a love for acting and producing. Graham states:

The Johns eventually moved to Savannah, Georgia where Vere became the editor of the *Savannah Tribune Newspaper*. He quickly became a central figure in the Savannah area and gained a lot of respect from many. One such person was the owner of the Savannah Star Cinema, a Mr. Thomas, who asked Vere to give him an idea in order to boost the attendance at the cinema. Vere took the matter to his wife and she suggested the implementation of the "Opportunity Hour" talent show. Wasting no time, Lillian organized the very first "Opportunity Hour" in 1937, in which she auditioned the contestants, emceed and performed. The contest ran until 1939 when the family relocated to Jamaica and where the then manager of the Palace Amusement Company, Audley Morais, asked the Johns to continue the contest at the Palace Theatre. Hence, the first Jamaican "Opportunity Hour" took place at the Palace Theatre in 1939 with the first winner being Denzil Laing.[26]

After the first show, Lillian told a reporter, "Everybody wishes to be a singer," and she was nicknamed "Lady Luck." The reviews of that first season were promising: "At the close of Friday night's finals of the popular all-Island 'Opportunity Hour' at the Palace Theater, Mr. Vere Johns and his popular wife 'Lady Luck' received tremendous compliment for their very laudable efforts of unearthing the talent of Jamaica in the entertainment world and for the undoubted success achieved.... With the close of the 'Opportunity Hour' we say to Mr. and Mrs. Johns 'THANK YOU!'... We hope that with Friday night's close the work of unearthing Jamaica's talent will continue by this pair, and we hope that by their effort bigger and greater things will be achieved for Jamaica in this respect."[27] If ever there was a statement of prophecy, this was one.

Music historian and journalist Roy Black said of the *Vere Johns Opportunity Hour*,

> It goes without saying that stars such as Millie Small, John Holt, Bob Marley, Jimmy Cliff, Alton Ellis, Hortense Ellis, The Blues Busters, Derrick Harriott, Derrick Morgan, Lascelles Perkins, Higgs and Wilson, Bunny and Scully, Laurel Aitken, Wilfred "Jackie" Edwards, Jimmy Tucker, Girl Satchmo, Lloyd "Sparrow" Clarke, and musicians Roy Richards, Charlie [sic] Organaire, and Rico Rodriguez, who all came under his wing, played significant roles in shaping Jamaica's popular music. They came in droves—hopeful actors, dancers, tricksters, singers, kneeling at his feet for an opportunity to become popular entertainers. There was hardly a performer who grew up in Kingston who didn't come into his fold. To them it seemed that only one man held the key to the door of success. The city's famous theatres—The Palace, at the corner of East Queen Street and South Camp Road; The Majestic, which faces Maxfield Avenue from the Spanish Town Road intersection; and The Ambassador, along Seventh Street in Trench Town—were the venues that Johns found logistically convenient to host these shows. The events took on a carnival atmosphere following auditions held mainly in the hometown of the aspirants. With the winners being decided by crowd reaction, competition was fierce and intense.[28]

Vere and Lillian Johns in 1955. Lillian was crucial to the creation of the *Vere Johns Opportunity Hour*—a talent show that launched the careers of dozens of Jamaican artists (copyright The Gleaner Company [Media] Limited).

Black also describes how the idea for the talent show came about. It was a team effort with his wife, who also acted as emcee of the events alongside her husband. Black states,

According to Colby Graham, who did extensive research on Johns, the idea for a Vere Johns talent show was born out of a request by the boss of the *Savannah Journal* newspaper with whom Johns worked, to devise a strategy to boost attendance at cinemas. With the help of his wife, Lillian, they came up with the idea for the show which began in Savannah, Georgia, in 1937, before the couple moved the event to Jamaica in 1939. In the late 1940s, he began a long-running *STAR* newspaper column "Vere Johns Says," mainly on the topic of music. But half the story has never been told as, in the 1950s, Johns added another dimension to his already illustrious career where he was a talent scout, impresario, journalist, radio personality, elocutionist and war veteran, by venturing into the world of movies. He played roles in the 1955 adventure thriller *Man Fish*, which also featured Eric Coverly, and returned a year later in the 26-minute documentary, *It Can Happen to You*, in which he played the role of a father of two sons who had syphilis.[29]

That film was the same documentary in which Margarita (Anita Mahfood) portrayed a rhumba dancer who performed in a club as patrons watched and caroused with one another. It is available through the National Library of Jamaica, which has now posted it on YouTube (www.youtube.com).

Not only did Vere Johns encourage other performers to have a career through his talent show but he also was a performer on stage and screen. He even dressed up as Santa Claus at some of his holiday shows. He and Lillian performed a comedy radio show in 1943 called *Razzle Dazzle*. Lillian was also a stage actress, "Lady Luck," who conducted the talent show band and sang at the talent performances. In 1940 on New Year's Day, Lillian danced in a troupe that performed a production of *Show Boat*, which was described as a vaudevillian presentation. The newspaper also touted another show: "The cast of 'Pagan Fire' stage presentation at popular Majestic tomorrow night is hard at work and will be ready to give of their best. They comprise the following: Mrs. Vere Johns (Jungle girl)—returns to the Jamaica stage and will be seen in two dance specialties…. Vere Johns (Chief Crandall)—veteran actor and director in a stirring dramatic role…. 'Pagan Fire' is an original playlet by Mr. Vere Johns. Place: Kango Isle in the South Seas. Production and direction by Mr. Johns, dance sequences by Mrs. Johns."[30] In 1943 Lillian Johns wrote a play called *Fool's Paradise* that was directed by Vere Johns. It was performed at the Ward Theatre and was billed as "A Rich Action Packed Drama of Our Every Day Life in 3 Acts."[31]

Another article from 1939, with the headline "Play at Palace," detailed another one of the plays presented by the Johns that Lillian herself had written:

> "When a Heat Wave Hit Breadnut Bottom," a one-act comedy written by Mrs. Vere Johns and directed by her husband, and in which both took leading parts, was presented, at the Palace Theatre last night to a very appreciative audience. Like their "Opportunity Hour" progammes, this presentation was a further endeavour of Mr. and Mrs. Vere Johns to present to the Jamaica public, Jamaica talent, and they succeeded in no uncertain way in this respect. Throughout its 40 minutes duration, the presentation was followed with interest, interspersed with the applause of the audience. Apart from Mr. and Mrs. Johns, outstanding performers in the play were little golden-voiced Frederick Stanley, who sang three very delightful songs, little Lester Johns (son of Mr. and Mrs. Vere Johns), and Ranny Williams, who as Tom, the headman of Mass Charlie's (Mr. Vere Johns) plantation did justice to his part.[32]

Lillian and Vere also had at least one other son, Vere Johns Jr., who went on to emcee in 1984 for the *Vere Johns Opportunity Hour* when Bunny and Scully performed. This event took place at the Odeon Theater, and Vere Johns Jr. was billed as the "Ace from Outa Space."

Lillian and Vere Johns had served as supporters, mentors, and directors to the

Caribbean Thespians, a group of actors from various theaters around the city. An August 5, 1941, a *Daily Gleaner* article stated, "Vere Johns, well known locally for his many talents, has been heard only too infrequently in the one role in which he excels as a truly great artist. Vere Johns is a Shakespearian actor of extraordinary power. His grip and understanding of the dramatic possibilities of the Shakespearian tradition will amaze and delight his audience, sustaining at the same time the lyrical beauty of the Elizabethan English," showing that both Vere and Lillian were greatly involved in the theater community.

In November 1960, Lillian and Vere Johns brought this sense of the theatrical directly into their lives when they renewed their wedding vows. The newspaper stated, "Vere and Lillian Johns join hands and renew the marital vows they made 25 years ago at a silver wedding anniversary celebration at their home in Mona Heights, St. Andrew. Rev. Canon R.O.C. King officiates; William Seivright acts as 'Father of the bride,' Russell Lewars as 'bestman' and Maisie Thompson as 'maid of honour.' Also present is Alexander Bustamante, Mayor Frank Spaulding and other dignitaries. Following the cutting of their silver wedding anniversary cake, a small floor show featuring artists from the Johns' 'Opportunity show' is presented."[33] Six years later, Vere Everette Johns died on September 10, 1966, at the age of 73, from an aneurysm.

Chapter Fourteen

Female Representation in Song Lyrics

When Virginia Woolf was tasked with delivering a lecture on the topic of "Women and Fiction," which then became the extended essay "A Room of One's Own," she wrote about the difficulty in tackling such subject matter. "I soon saw that it had one fatal drawback. I should never be able to fulfil what is, I understand, the first duty of a lecturer—to hand you after an hour's discourse a nugget of pure truth to wrap up between the pages of your notebooks and keep on the mantel-piece for ever. All I could do was to offer you an opinion upon one minor point," she wrote in this treatise of feminism, going on to talk about the room, the space, the agency.[1] And here too is a task with a "fatal drawback," in that it can never be fulfilled by this writer, or certainly not in a single chapter or even a book, neatly wrapped up for the library shelf forever. The subject of women and Jamaican song lyrics is too massive. It is like trying to describe the ocean while looking at a single drop of water. But what follows is an attempt, an opinion, based in as much truth as this writer can offer. It is a start.

Relationships and failed relationships are frequent subjects of song, in any culture. However, when the majority of music writers, vocalists, performers, and producers are men, the male perspective dominates. Such is the case in Jamaica, where the number of Jamaican songs about men is small in comparison to the bounty of songs concerning women, and it is rarely the female at the microphone. She is the subject of song, yet rarely involved in any way in the song itself. The number of female vocalists at the onset of the recording industry in Jamaica, the late 1950s and early 1960s, one can count on one, maybe two, hands. And these women were frequently combined with a male voice during this era for a duet, as was the popular style in American rhythm and blues music, which is what early performers and producers in Jamaica tried to emulate. Before the duet, too, mento music featured the female as the subject of song.

Jamaica's first original genre of music was mento, and as writer David V. Moskowitz states, it was a "folk music that combined sacred and secular elements."[2] He continues about mento lyrics that they "run the gamut from rural themes of food preparation to more cosmopolitan images of relationship issues and even bawdy topics." Only one female mento vocalist, Lady Earle, is known to have performed during mento's golden era in the 1950s, but she never recorded. Though sometimes people cite Louise Lamb as a mento performer, she was more of a jazz singer and an entertainer. Therefore, mento lyrics were essentially all sung by the male about or to the female, unless they concerned other topics altogether. Mento, like calypso, commonly chronicled real-life events or provided social commentary, as singers served as troubadours and storytellers. Topics ranged from the beauty of the island's sea and shore to the obeah in rural communities.

One quality of mento is that it featured innuendo and double entendre with a ribald sense of humor. Some of these songs contained lyrics that boasted of the sexual prowess of either party. Count Lasher's "The Ole Man's Drive," for example, uses a car as a euphemism for the virility of the "ole man" that the "young gal" should not "under rate." Count Owen's "Old Lady's Taxi" is similar in content, and some versions of this song feature the woman as the rider, while others feature the man as the rider. Euphemisms abound in mento, including Count Lasher's "Man with the Tool" who cannot be stopped; "Robusta Banana," which is fairly self-explanatory; Lord Kitchener's needle, which was too big; Mighty Sparrow's "big bamboo"; and of course, wood and fruits of all varieties. Women were gossips, as in "Mother Bad Mine" by Count Lasher, who "su su" and talk about "your business." Some girls were admirable, like Sally Brown in Count Lasher's "Island Gal Sally," who is "cross-bred but yet so kind" and "believes in brotherhood." Sometimes women were duppies (spirits), as in "Woman Ghost Fool Man" by Chin's Calypso Sextet. Lord Flea sings of woman in "It All Began with Adam and Eve" as "out to trap a man," saying that when they get married, "the woman she start to wear the pants." This is just a very small sample of some of the ways in which women were represented by men in mento, though each song seems to offer its own perspective and variation. Further examples are offered later in this chapter.

Songs performed as a duet in ska and rocksteady were typically sweet love songs from boy to girl and girl to boy. The vocals either responded to each other, mirrored each other, or were sung in unison, further demonstrating the partnership. "Housewife's Choice" by Derrick Morgan and Patsy Todd in 1962 features ample instrumentals punctuated by the male appeal to the female for her love, to which Todd, in the female role, replies innocently and reciprocates the love. While the mento song with the title "Look Before You Leap," featuring vocalist Alerth Bedasse, cautions young girls to listen to their mothers or else they will "have nine months to weep, because you didn't look before you leaped," the duet song of the same name by Morgan and Todd is completely different. Todd provides vocal harmonies on the refrain, while Morgan tells of the dangers of rushing into a new relationship after an old one has broken up. It is sweet and innocent in style.

"When You Call My Name" by Stranger and Patsy in 1962 is also indicative of this style of sweet love duet. Stranger Cole sings his stanza to Patsy, who responds in her stanza with virtually the same lyrics and only a slight modification; the sentiment is the same. "Yeah Yeah Baby" from the same duo in 1964 is performed in unison, with a breakout stanza from Stranger Cole, but the lyrics remain virtually unchanged from the main refrain. Their entire repertoire of songs was performed in this same style.

Keith and Enid's "Everything Will Be Alright" from 1960 is also vocalized in unison with lyrics about love and marriage. "Worried Over You" from the same year is also a sweet love song, or a breakup song as it were, with the lyrics sung in unison by Keith Stewart and Enid Cumberland in beautiful harmony. In 1961 they recorded another breakup song, "What Have I Done," but in this one they reconcile, singing each word of the lyrics in unison, in partnership. Their other songs, of which there are roughly a dozen, are all in the same vein.

"We'll Meet," by Roy Panton and Millie Small in 1961, features Panton in the role of the male appealing to Small, the female, saying that he loves her, but she rebukes his love for a life of independence. The following year in 1962, Millie recorded with Owen Gray for the song "Do You Know," in which the male asks the female to forgive him; she responds in her stanza that she was hurt, but still loves him, and will take him back if he will promise to be true. "Sit and Cry" is another reconciliation song where Owen and Millie sing in unison. In "Sugar Plum," performed by Millie Small and Owen Gray in 1963, each line of the love song is also voiced at the same time in harmony.

Roy Panton also recorded a number of songs with Yvonne Harrison, who later became his wife. "Two Roads" from 1964 featured the same lyrics performed by the male, Roy, that are then performed by the female, Yvonne. That same year, "No More" featured the male, Roy, rejoicing that his love has returned to him and the female, Yvonne, singing harmonies on the refrain, with a stellar bridge from Charley Organnaire on harmonica. Yvonne also recorded the classic "Meekly Wait" with Derrick Morgan in 1961, which featured Yvonne in the role of a spirit or mother, singing the Biblical phrase and telling her son to "go on," though from what trouble it is not certain.

Hortense Ellis and her brother Alton Ellis had a string of duets in the 1960s that also fit neatly into this model, including "Breaking Up Is Hard to Do" which features the female and male singing exactly the same stanza at different times and coming together for harmonies on the refrain. "Easy Squeeze" is performed together straight through in harmony. "Don't Gamble with Love" is somewhat unique in this form of duet songs in that the two vocalists, male and female, do not seem to be singing to each other, but rather offering their advice to the listener. Hortense Ellis also performed duets with Derrick Morgan through the 1970s.

There were dozens more songs with many other combinations of male and female singers, including those with Jackie Edwards, Jackie Opel, Prince Buster, Delroy Wilson, and others using virtually the same handful of female vocalists. The themes and style were very much the same as already outlined.

But not every song with women as the subject or part of the subject was so harmonious. When woman sang solo in songs, which was rare, the lyrics were typically not disparaging toward woman, as might be expected. And it should be pointed out that in any genre of music, emoting displeasure at the opposite sex after being wounded emotionally is common. Therefore, because most of the musical artists in Jamaica (and in many other countries) during the 1950s to the 1980s were male, much of this frustration and angst was aimed at the female. These are classified as conflict songs, and they form a large body of work in Jamaican music.

Perhaps a good place to start with analysis of conflict songs is with the work of noted anthropologist and author Jacob Delworth Elder of Trinidad and Tobago, whose research on conflict in calypso lyrics provides insight into Jamaica's music. Elder utilized a scientific approach to analyzing the male/female conflict in popular calypso music of Trinidad through the use of the Cantometics coding system established by ethnomusicologist Alan Lomax. The lyrics analyzed in Elder's work in Trinidadian calypsos, and the lyrics and analysis that follow here for Jamaican music, are, as Elder states, a reflection of "a complex sociological phenomenon common to all known cultures." Therefore, one should be careful about assuming anything about the Jamaican male perspective of the female as anything uniquely Jamaican. It is not so simple.

Elder's work examines Trinidadian calypso lyrics for 107 popular songs, from the earliest work songs through contemporary calypsos over a period of 50 years. He codes these lyrics with a male/female conflict classification and observes that there was a lack of female participation in singing and writing calypsos, and perhaps as a result, the "female theme occurs four times as often as the male theme."[3] This is similar to the occurrence in Jamaican music, where the male vocalist or lyricist offers his judgment or advice on female behavior much more often than the converse, as well as much more often than the male vocalist or lyricist offers his judgment or advice on male behavior—as a male counseling a male (as in the rude boy songs). Elder says that the female as subject of Trinidadian calypsos is "a subject of male preoccupation as much as the victim of his condemnation."[4]

He continues his analysis by putting these lyrics into nine different categories, which are also helpful in looking at Jamaican lyrics. These categories include separation anxiety, sexual jealousy, female rejection, fear of female magic, conquest tales (seduction), derision, admonition, pejorative accounts (of female deviance), and disgust. It is not possible to perform the in-depth analysis of Jamaican lyrics that Elder performs, simply because of the amount of songs that reference the female subject. According to the online Roots Knotty Roots Discography of Jamaican Music, there are some 2,411 songs with the word "girl" in the title, 1,143 songs with the word "woman," 835 with the word "gal," 338 with the word "lady," 263 with the word "mother," 266 with the word "mama" or "momma," 130 with the word "wife," 150 with the word "miss," 158 with the word "queen," 57 with the word "princess," 52 with the word "grandma," and 24 with the word "Mrs."[5] (Note that a large majority of these songs feature "girl" in the title, as opposed to another way to refer to the female. Because the early days of the Jamaican recording industry drew upon Jamaicans' affinity for American rhythm and blues, much of the lyrical content in Jamaican songs mirrored that of American music. As a result, songs in the Jamaica in the 1960s more frequently called the female a "girl" rather than a "woman" in the title or lyrics, as did American music. The reasons for this may be best left to the work of an anthropologist, sociologist, or certainly a feminist, but as a way of example, a few of these titles include "Little Bitty Girl," "School Girl," "Girl Next Door," "Tripe Girl," "Back Street Girl," "Happy Go Lucky Girl," and "Girls Like Dirt," just to name a few.) With no scientific data available from analysis of the music as a whole, obtained through a similar codification that Elder used, it is helpful to look at a few examples as insight into this phenomenon. Though this is by no means comprehensive or conclusive, it is still fascinating.

A derision song, as Elder describes, "includes events which are out-right use of denigrative stereotypes to negatively categorize as deviants, the female-figure in her several forms—mother, wife, sister, daughter, niece, girl-friend, mistress, concubine and prostitute. Women are declared to be bad, superstitious, scheming, tricky, unfaithful, thievish, wayward, pretentious, hypocritical, immoral, over-sexed, perverts, deviants, etc."[6] One example of a derision song in Jamaican music is Prince Buster's "Girl Answer Your Name," which tells of a "sweet girl like you telling me lies" and misrepresenting her identity to him after he approached her at a party. He responds in scorn, "to every man you give a one-night stand." In some songs, the male is permitted to take another woman, and if the wife calls attention to it, she is the one called out, as in Boris Gardiner's song "My Commanding Wife." This song begins with his wife yelling at him, setting the tone for the rest of the song as he sings about her wanting to destroy his life after she catches him lying about being out with his friends despite having lipstick on him. He chastises her for criticizing him and calling him names. Marriage must be particularly difficult for

Gardiner, who also recorded about the "Vicious Mother-In-Law" who moved in with him after her husband "died with a smile on his face," snores, makes a mess "all over the place," ruins his life, and even makes the devil rebel. She too makes an appearance as a character in the end, bellowing. Gardiner's is but one of a number of mother-in-law songs that paint this female family member in a negative light.

Pejorative accounts of female deviance feature lyrics with the male in the role of the witness and judge of the female, who suffers exposure of her immoral or anti-social deeds, as classified by Elder. One such example is the Kingstonians' song "Make You a Woman." They sing, "I'll make you to be a woman, a woman as you were meant to be." Another such song is Black Uhuru's "Shine Eye Gal," based on a folk tale of the same name, which tells of a girl who is never satisfied (shine eye), who is a "trouble to a man," doesn't appreciate the things the narrator does for her, and even goes out to talk to her friends without making her bed. The latter is not a metaphor; it is meant literally to show that she has frivolous priorities over keeping house. Kelling Beckford's "Samfy Girl" portrays an untrustworthy partner who is "nothing but a samfy girl, you take my money and you run away." Justin Hinds sings a number of songs about gossiping women, including "Cock Mouth Kill Cock," meaning be careful of what you say or your words will come back to haunt you. "Carry Go, Bring Come" tells the story of a woman who is a gossip. She carries gossip and goes, and gathers gossip and brings it back, as the title indicates, which "brings misery." Hinds comments, "You're going from town to town making disturbances. It's time you stopped doing those things, you old Jezebel." Hinds suggests in "Mount Zion High" that this "Jezebel" gossiper turn to a sacred life rather than oppressing man. Freddie McGregor's version of Hinds' song has him commenting to the woman directly, "Shut your blabber mouth."

The "Jezebel" is a black female stereotype frequently used in Jamaican lyrics by such artists as Derrick Morgan, Owen Gray, Clint Eastwood, Eric "Monty" Morris, and, as previously indicated, Justin Hinds. This stereotype originates from biblical texts and depicts the female as seductive and promiscuous. Similarly, the "Delilah" stereotype also originates from the biblical and is used throughout Jamaican music, including in songs by Horace Andy, Inner Circle, Ranking Joe, and Laurel Aitken. Alerth Bedasse and Chin's Calypso Sextet's "Samson and Delilah," written by Everard Williams, was "a lesson for one and all, men never trust a pretty face." Dr. Donna Hope writes of the "Delilah complex," citing the work of anthropologist Barry Chevannes, that the "female/feminine is treated as dangerous, with the power to weaken or betray men/male," and that the complex is "rife in Jamaican gender and folk culture."[7]

Admonition songs may also serve as a warning to women to stay away from some men, like sailors, and not become deviant in behavior, as in Junior Reid's song, "Don't Stray," or they may command women about how to behave, as is evident in Prince Buster's "Ten Commandments." This song is also a fine example of Elder's classification of sexual jealousy, and any reciprocal sexual jealousy is given admonishment, and even worse. The commandments detail that the woman essentially belongs to Prince Buster and she should not anger him or be jealous of the possessions that other women have, like dresses or shoes, because she will only be supplied with necessities by him. Additionally, he will not stand for bad habits, such as smoking, drinking, and foul language. He also tells her that she is to provide him with sex every day and twice on Sunday, because he is insatiable and she is to "obey" him. If these commands were not shocking enough, the jealousy becomes sadistic in the latter half of the song. Commandment six admonishes the woman that she should not search his pockets or "annoy me" with her "hearsays," while commandment seven addresses the infidelity head-on. Prince Buster admonishes that if his woman sees him in the street with another woman, she is not to yell at him there, but to "wait intelligently" until he returns home to "both have it out decently." However, if she commits adultery, according to commandment nine, the lyrics take a serious turn from admonishment to violence. "For the world will not hold me guilty if I commit murder," he states.

The female response to this song by "Princess Buster," which was actually Patsy Todd on vocals posing as the woman married to "your royal highness, Prince Buster," is credited to Prince Buster as writer. Though Princess Buster admits she too is jealous, she comments that she is jealous "like any other woman" and even more jealous now that she is married to him. While he commands sex every day, and twice on Sunday, she prefers that he takes her out every day and twice on Sunday to shop for fine clothes and fine foods. She comments that because she is married to him, she refuses to go out "shaggy," so she is concerned with her appearance only as it relates to his satisfaction, not her own. And though this song was likely produced as an equal response, forced sex is hardly equivalent to shopping and dining. Additionally, she wants Prince Buster to allow her to search his pockets at night—not because she is a "thief," but because she wants to find phone numbers he "forgot to dispose of," as if his absentmindedness is the crime, not the infidelity. In commandment six, she admonishes him not to commit adultery, and in a threat parallel to Prince Buster's murder of her in his song, Princess Buster responds, "The world cannot hold me guilty if, for spite, I date your best friend." In commandment nine Princess Buster commands that he is not to hit or slap her, tear her dress, pull her hair, or scare her, and commandment ten states that Prince Buster should honor her name so that "every other man shall honor it," and if he obeys her, she will obey him. Another response to this song has been recorded using the rhythm of Dawn Penn's "You Don't Love Me (No, No, No)." This 2019 song, "10 Commandments," by The Specials, features Birmingham activist Saffiyah Kahn voicing a feminist response to male oppression.

The Two Kings' "Hit You Let You Feel It," whose B side is perplexingly "Honey I Love You," also encourages violence against women. The lyrics, performed in off-key harmonies by George Murphy and Maurice Johnson in a 1965 recording produced by Theo Beckford, state the title, followed by "then you will know I mean it," because the female "tried to make a fool of" the male.

Desmond Dekker's "Dracula" is fine example of a song classified as fear of female magic. According to Elder, this classification "includes episodes in which the female reverts to sorcery (obeah, voodoo, etc.) and supernatural acts in order to acquire marriage or the attentions of the unwilling male. These accounts, while concealing the concept of the powerful male whose love can be gained only with the aid of supernatural forces, project a deviant image of the female and a rationalization of the female's real superior and compulsive power over males."[8] Dekker's "Dracula" tells the tale of a girl who was "fabulous," had an angelic face, and "eyes like blazing fire." However, when the object of his desire smiled, she had gruesome teeth "ready to stick your veins," so he warns the listener not to fall in love with her, even though she is "pretty smart," since "believe me folks, she is a Dracula." He runs to bleed in a tree but is called down by her like Jesus to Zacchaeus, so an added layer of the spiritual or biblical on top of the supernatural renders the male powerless against the female's powers.

Though a conquest song typically tells of an event in which the female is won through the power of the man, according to Elder, one Jamaican song that falls into this category reduces the conquest not to the woman herself but to her body parts. The singer admits he does not care if she is ugly, because it is not her face in which he is interested. Prince Buster's "Wreck a Pum Pum" uses the term "pum pum," Jamaican patois for a woman's genitalia, and in the course of the song, he fully describes the stiff state of his own. This song was later covered by Lord Creator and Yellowman. Many songs in the mento tradition, especially those written by Everard Williams, used innuendo to describe carnal longing and activities. Most representative of this is the song "Night Food," which was banned for being vulgar, though the lyrics are somewhat hidden by innuendo, as was "Red Tomato," rife with double entendre. Both of these songs, however, feature the woman in the position of power over the male. In "Night Food," it is the female protagonist who invites the innocent male in so she can "tell him" why night food is so good. And in "Red Tomato," the woman says that the male can "pick my tomato," but only if he has "the right stick." No such lyrical humor is evident in "Wreck a Pum Pum." Also lacking in ribaldry is Leo Graham's "Greedy Gal" who will "kill you wit her pum pum" because the "more she get it, the more she want it."

Prince Buster's "Rough Rider" is also a conquest song and is a reworking of the mento version by Everard Williams. These tunes bear the same name, same sentiment, but different lyrics—Williams's is a tale told by an omniscient narrator, Prince Buster's places himself in the narrative as the beneficiary. The mento version tells of a man who "showed his fullest length" to the "rough rider," named Miss Ida, who ended up putting him in the hospital. In Prince Buster's version, he is the recipient of the rough rider, the "strong whiner," the "cool stroker" who made him "feel so bruk up today."

It should also be noted that Prince Buster in "Wreck a Pum Pum" identifies the object of his desire as a "fat girl." A "fat girl" was the object of desire in many Jamaican songs, from the 1960s forward. Carol Turpin of St. Catherine, Jamaica, interviewed on NPR's *All Things Considered*, explains, "'I don't want a meager woman,' that's how the men would speak.... They're figuring if you look meager, you look poor, in the sense that you're not being taken care of."[9] Sonjah Stanley Niaah, director of the Institute of Caribbean Studies and Reggae Studies Unit at the University of the West Indies at Mona, further clarifies, "If you have no meat on your bones, the society can't see your wealth, your progress, your being."[10]

Songs that demonstrate the "fat girl" persona include Clancy Eccles's classic "Fattie Fattie," recorded in 1969, which was covered more than a decade later by Bad Manners in England as a parody for the then-hefty vocalist Buster Bloodvessel. In Eccles's version, the "fattie fattie" was the object of desire for her body. The Slickers' "Run Fattie" was recorded for Beverley's in 1969 and, once again, this woman was the object of desire as she "run all over town," and the vocalist observed, "I know them want to feel you up," revealing his sexual jealousy. Trevor Blair released "That Fat Girl," in which he sang, frequently off tune, about a fat girl "from down the street" that he watched for years, though he does not seem to distinguish any other characteristics of her as a person, including her name.

Derrick Howard, also known as Maga Man, recorded "Fat Girl" with the flipside "Fatty Bum Bum" in 1975. The Heptones recorded "Fattie Fattie," and Leroy Sibbles recorded his dancehall version in 1991. The same title was recorded by Roland Burrell in 1979, who also recorded "Fatty Fay" in 1985. The Mighty Avengers released "Fatty Shirley" in 1985, a soca-tinged tune whose vocalist felt "like a total wreck" the morning after Shirley "squeeze" and "bounce" him. Other songs include "Fat Girl, Sexy Girl," by

John Holt, and the catchy tune "Fat Girl in Red," by The Mellotones. There was "Fattie Bum Bum" by Carl Malcolm in 1975, with versions by Jah Woosh; The Diversions; and Skin, Flesh, and Bones. Laurel Aitken responded that same year with his take on Malcolm's hit song, followed by "Fatty Bum Bum Gone to Jail," which talked of "woman's liberation" causing a "very big sensation." The Trojans offered their dub version of "Fatty Bum Bum Gone to Jail" two years later, in 1977. These tunes inspired the Fattie Bum Bum rhythm, which was used by female vocalist Barbara Jones in 1976 for her response song, "Slim Boy." The subject of the song was a male, boasting and bragging, but he "couldn't cool a dumpling."

In "Ease Up Fattie," by The Meditations in 1983, the vocalist tells that his grandmother warned him about carrying too heavy of a load, though it is doubtful that the vocalist's interpretation of that sage wisdom is what she meant. He sings that his female partner is "too fat to be on top" and that he loves to see "his woman in her miniskirt" but that she is "too fat, you can't wear miniskirt." Those who were too skinny, as in "Skinny Leg Girl" by Hopeton and Glen, or "Skinny Legs and All" by Joe Tex, were also not desirable. Peter Tosh's "Maga Dog," with a beautiful female vocal backup, talks about a woman who came from the country; he helped her, and she took advantage of him and left. "Maga," a patois version of "meager," meaning skinny or homely looking, is Tosh's description of the dog, or female.

Carl Malcolm seemed to like to describe the female physique in his songs, as he had another hit in 1975 with "Miss Wire Waist." Malcolm sang that he was "trying very hard to capture and control" the woman who he invites to take a short walk and to give her a small talk. Female vocalist Yvonne Harrison responded with her version called "Knotty Screw Face," in which she sang of the dreads in town who, when she "wine my waist," or dance, they "start to screw them face," or get upset or angry, likely because she does not succumb to their advances. Additionally, Everard Williams describes a woman with a waist that is "wiry" in his mento tune "Jamaica Gal." Malcolm's song may be classified as a derision song, as Elder described above. Another example of a derision song in Jamaican music is Steel Pulse's "Leggo Beast," which refers to a woman as "leggo," meaning wild, as well as a "vulture." The male vocalist says that she is a "lady of easy virtue" who lies and cheats and lays traps for men.

Another form of derision song is one that might be classified by the stereotype of a gold digger. Culture's "Money Girl" features the male singer who tells of a girl who only wants the singer's money and only shows up on payday. Similarly, Freddie McGregor's "Miserable Woman" describes a woman to whom he has given everything she wants while he is living his "humble life" and "working hard day and night"; but she is not happy and she wants to ruin his plan. All he wants, he says, is peace and love. He ends by telling her to "settle down" and get used to his "humble" way of life. John Holt's "Fancy Make Up" warns men to resist the lure of pretty dresses, sparkly jewelry, and, as the title suggests, fancy makeup, because "they will make you want to cry." The Meditations also warn men in their song "Woman Is Like a Shadow" that men should be careful because women want to hurt them.

In Peter Tosh's "Brand New Second Hand," he chastises a woman for her "painted face," saying that underneath she is "just a disgrace," and for her "hidy-tidy [hoity-toity]" ways, saying, "you very nasty" and "wicked." Harold Richardson and the Ticklers' "Glamour Gal," a mento tune from the 1950s, is similar. The lyrics, written by Everard Williams, recount the tale of a girl who dresses stylishly with expenses tastes and powder on her nose, so she is the "kind of gal that always make you mad." The Ticklers' song "Country Gal," on the other hand, features a woman without the "glamour" style. The country gal is carefree, wears a scarf and basket on her head when she goes to the market to shop for food, has her "own peculiar style, and dem make yuh happy all de while." In "Parish Gal," which predates the Beach Boys' "California Girls" with a like approach, each different parish in Jamaica is featured, including "Clarendon gal, some of dem is rude," Trelawny girls are "big and fat," and Westmoreland gal "dem love to sing."

A similar version of this same sentiment is portrayed in Jimmy Cliff's "Roots Woman," who does not worship diamonds, pearls, silver, or gold, but instead is happy with life and will give him "plenty lovin.'" She will "cook that country porridge" and "keep a lookin' smashin.'" "Queen of the Ghetto" by John Holt admires the strength of the title woman, who lives "down where there is no pity" and "she don't wear no fancy make up, she don't wear no fancy dress."

A song of disgust, as Elder clarifies, features a male singer who "assumes the role of the father-figure—moralistic, long-suffering and concerned over the questionable life the female leads. Finally, he gives up and in disgust over his task, deserts the evil female.... The male boasts that he is independent." Desmond Dekker's "Get Up Edina" falls into this category perfectly, as the male sings that he tried to teach "Edina, girl," by sending her to school and church, but she refused to learn or hear and so he is going to send her back to her mama and papa. "Only a Smile" by The Paragons is another example of disgust, as the male vocalist tells of a woman whose smile seduces any man, but that is all she has to offer. The male vocalist was a victim of this woman's smile and he left her, like all men will, he sings. It is a lyrical attack as a defense mechanism, a method of self-preservation for the male artist.

Sang Hugh, a roots reggae vocalist, condemns women's acting in ways equal to a man in his disgust song, "Woman a Follow Man." These women, as clarified by Hugh, are Babylon women, which resonates in content, culturally, to Fela Kuti's "Lady." Hugh sings that women cut their hair, wear pants, walk with a gun, drive a bus and truck, "just like a man." He condemns seeing women every time he goes into the barber shop or tailor shop, and he enlists the support of his "bredren" in this disapproval. Hugh's song, "No Portion a Gal" (on some copies spelled "No Potion a Gal") condemns a "gal" who comes "from nowhere," meaning the country, but now she dresses up in a mini skirt, high heeled shoes, big hair, and red lipstick, in a "pop style." He sings that she should "pop it pon rascal" but "nuh pop it pon rasta," meaning that some men, rascals, may accept her style but the Rasta community will not accept her.

Female rejection songs feature "overt masochistic acts in which the male despises the once haughty and beautiful female in retribution for her past refusal of his love" and are "fundamentally aggressive in character." "Don't Try to Use Me" by Horace Andy falls into this category. It tells of a girl who wants to leave him and take all of his money. Bobby Aitken's "Devil Woman," recorded in 1963, and Leslie Levy and the Tendertones' song of the same title, recorded in 1969, are both excellent examples of this category. Lord Lebby's mento "Dr. Kinsey" hints at sexual rejection of a different kind. He sings of the Kinsey Report and how it has studied sexual behavior to take the world's attention by storm, relegating other news, such as the "Russian H-Bomb," to page nine in the newspaper. But his own experience with women, sings the vocalist, is that "you just get them cooking and they stub their toes or got some kind of blockage in their libido." For Justin Hinds and the Dominoes, the woman who was wrong now comes back around to apologize, in a way, in the song "Rub Up Push Up," but the male will not be tempted.

Additional versions of female rejection come in the form of infidelity tales. "Boogu Yagga Gal," a mento written by Everard Williams and performed by Alerth Bedasse and Chin's Calypso Sextet, describes a gal who was sad her boyfriend had migrated to England to work, earn money, and send for her to migrate as well. However, she soon found another paramour, and when her boyfriend returned home, he came with a gun in hand, shooting when he found her bedded by another. She blamed him for making her wait, as she had sexual needs. The classic mento song "Talking Parrot" also tells a story of infidelity that is revealed to the married man through the words of his pet parrot.

Plenty of Jamaican artists, especially during the rocksteady era, sang of love without scorn toward women in all genres of Jamaican music. Carlton and the Shoes' "Love Me Forever" is a beautiful creative take on the Casinos' hit song "Then You Can Tell Me Goodbye." Many love songs were actually redemption songs, apologizing for mistreating the woman, as is The Clarendonians' song "I Am Sorry" and The Silvertones' "True Confession." Others bemoaned a lost love, like Derrick Harriott's classic "The Loser," without vilifying the female and instead presented a character with self-pity or self-preservation, as in Harriott's song "I Won't Cry."

Bob Marley is known for his political lyrics, but perhaps equally so for his love songs in which he tries to win the woman's love. This sense of a woman being wooed, being courted, and that the male must earn the right to her admiration, is perhaps one reason why women, and all human beings, find his lyrics admirable and respectable. Eminent writer and scholar Kwame Dawes writes that there are three categories of Marley love songs: "Marley's persona in his early love songs was almost always that of a man who was trying to win the affection of a woman who was decidedly hard to win. If this was not the scenario used, it would almost always be the other standard scenario: Marley reproaching a woman for having abandoned him for someone else. The third category of Marley love song was the decidedly sexual song—the song of seduction that relished the idea of sex and found joy in telling stories about the sweetness of sex.... Marley seemed to prefer songs that allowed sexual innuendo to guide the seduction process."[11] Marley portrays himself as lonely, vulnerable, in need of love and affection.

Jamaican music scholars (*left to right*) **Dr. Donna Hope, Dr. Carolyn Cooper,** and **Dr. Sonjah Stanley Niaah** at the University of the West Indies at Mona in 2015 (photograph by Heather Augustyn).

Not all of Marley's songs are so. "Pimper's Paradise" is a classic admonition song, or as Dr. Carolyn Cooper calls it, a "fallen woman" song. Cooper writes, "The song opens with the man's indictment of the fashion-conscious, pleasure-seeking, drug-addicted woman." She notes, however, that Marley still shows care for the woman, and the "song moves toward a clear statement of sympathy.... The woman becomes more than exploited commodity; she is challenged to reclaim her humanity."[12]

A number of artists performed songs in Marley's sweet seduction style, including Gregory Isaacs in his classic "Night Nurse," where he is ailing, in need, suffering, and only attention "around the clock" will "satisfy this thirst." Marley's "No Water" is perhaps the inspiration for this tune. The entire subgenre of lovers' rock in the 1980s and 1990s featured romantic content in the same fashion, as opposed to lyrics that were derogatory and offensive toward females. It also so happens that female vocalists were more prevalent; therefore, the lyrics were less sexist in this subgenre. This category of Jamaican music, however, was more of a diasporic genre that originated in the United Kingdom and then grew in popularity in Jamaica. Suddenly Boris Gardiner was singing "I Want to Wake Up with You," which featured no nagging wife or mother-in-law as part of the audio; Dennis Brown declared, "Love Has Found Its Way"; Sugar Minott proclaimed, "My Heart Is True"; and Freddie McGregor now put his miserable blabbermouth woman aside and professed he encountered "First Sight Loving." Dennis Brown's "I Am the Conqueror," recorded in 1974, even calls for men to treat women with respect, telling them that they should never call sisters "leggo beast" and treat them "rough."

The roots reggae subgenre in the mid- to late–1970s featured lyrics that depicted females in a more spiritual light, perhaps inspired by the Black Is Beautiful movement, but more so the Rastafari culture. There are songs such as "African Daughter" by Big Youth, "Beautiful Daughter of Zion" by Giddeon Jah Rubbaal, "African Princess" by Frankie Paul, "Daughter of Zion" by Bagga, Augustus Pablo's "African Queen," and "Queen of the Universe" by Ras Clifton, to name a few that are emblematic of these respectful and celebratory songs. But as Maureen Rowe, a Rastafari woman, points out, "Once redeemed, the Rastawoman becomes Queen/Empress, occupying a pedestal which precludes sexuality. She is separated from her sexual nature and becomes almost a religious icon and cultural role model."[13]

Female representation in the dancehall has been studied extensively by such eminent scholars as Dr. Sonja Stanley Niaah, Dr. Donna Hope, and Dr. Carolyn Cooper at the University of the West Indies Mona, as well as Norman Stolzoff and Garth White. Cooper writes about the female represented as the "virgin" in a number of dancehall lyrics and the converse, "leftover food."[14] Hope writes about the female as "gold-digger" in the context of the masculine monetization-as-power culture. She also writes substantially about the masculine in dancehall culture, as it relates to a number of other subjects, including the female. She discusses dancehall lyrics that present the female as the subject of the masculine sexual discourse, which is rife with innuendo and portrays the "role of women as sexual objects."[15] She says that the "mythologized narrations of the sex act in dancehall culture" have resulted in a number of different euphemisms for male and female genitalia in dancehall lyrics, and she discusses the use of the male character as an "Ole Dawg," in whose nature it is to "engage in multiple sexual liaison[s]" in order to "legitimize their status."

Sociologist R.W. Connell writes that dancehall can present two facets of the female as represented in lyrics. "A thin, contemptuous misogyny, in which women are treated basically as disposable receptacles for semen, coexists with a much more respectful, even admiring view of women's strength. Sometimes these views coexist in the same head."[16] This coexistence is portrayed, albeit mildly, in a dancehall song by Macka B recorded in 1992. The song, "Sex Machine," features lyrics that state, "She's more than a sex machine, the woman is a human being," as he recognizes the woman who has a science degree, runs a company, is a trained nurse, a soldier, a teacher. He says he knows men who want an "idiot gal, might as well go and get a rubber doll."

Other dancehall songs are not as gentle. They do not present two facets of women at all. Beenie Man sings that he has women in twos and threes and that it is common knowledge that an "Ole Dawg" like him is promiscuous. Hope analyzes this song in terms of Jamaican culture, including the race, class, and regional applications of his lyrics and concludes, "The role of the feminine remains critical to the upliftment of heterosexual masculinity."[17] This Beenie Man song was a far cry from a tune like Alton Ellis's "Girl I've Got a Date," where the male "just can't stay late" with her because he has a date with another girl. Ellis in the role of the male had previously warned her, the lyrics state, that he was as "free as the birds in the trees." Really, though, is this meaning any different from Beanie Man's, though not as overt? The male is presented as promiscuous and polygamous, with the female as the subject of that action. This act is a form of masculine power making. The female is subjugated, argues Hope, in order to elevate the male. For more on masculinities and femininities in dancehall, Dr. Hope's extensive work is a valuable resource.

Jamaican music lyrics have, as in many other cultures, demonstrated the battle of the sexes. This battle, however, has hardly been fair. There is little parity in these lyrics. There are essentially no songs calling for a virtuous man. No songs feature a woman looking for a man who is a virgin. No songs can be found where a woman sings about a young schoolboy and tells him she wants to show him the way. One would be hard pressed to locate lyrics where a woman commands that her man should wear particular shoes or respectable clothes or how to keep his face clean. Few Jamaican songs, and few songs in most cultures and genres, feature a woman singing about working all day to provide for her man who just spends it on watches and expensive clothing, while the man refuses to cook and clean for her and just runs around town; or that her country man is now acting hoity-toity and flashing his glamorous style around the city to lure other women. Lyrical representation of the female in Jamaican music does reflect, as Elder argues, a "complex sociological phenomenon common to all known cultures," and as the biographies of the women in this book reveal, it was one that required a monumental level of stamina, power, and talent to break through.

Chapter Notes

Introduction

1. Page and Reason, "Playing Like a Girl."

Chapter One

1. Auld, "Anansi and the Yam Hills."
2. Gottlieb, *A History of Queen Nanny*, 10.
3. Gottlieb, 15.
4. "Obeah and Myal," people.vcu.edu/~wchan/poco/624/harris_south/Obeah%20and%20Myal.htm.
5. "Obeah and Myal."
6. Gottlieb, 44.
7. Gottlieb, 46.
8. Gottlieb, 24.
9. "Nanny of the Maroons," Jamaica Information Service, jis.gov.jm/information/heroes/nanny-of-the-maroons/.
10. Ibid.
11. Gottlieb, 40.
12. Ibid.
13. Lewin, *Rock It Come Over*, 255.
14. *Jamaica Gleaner*, Mar. 13, 1998.
15. Lewin, 269.
16. Lewin, 297.
17. Comments by Christine Levy are from a personal interview with the author, June 3, 2013.
18. Morris, *Miss Lou*, p. 4.
19. Morris, introduction to *Selected Poems*, xv.
20. Bailey, "A Chat with Louise Bennett," *Bluebeard*, n.p.

Chapter Two

1. *Daily Gleaner*, May 8, 1974.
2. *Daily Gleaner*, Aug. 26, 1922.
3. *Daily Gleaner*, Dec. 29, 1931.
4. *Daily Gleaner*, Sept. 10, 1977.
5. *Daily Gleaner*, May 21, 1937.
6. *Daily Gleaner*, May 22, 1937.
7. *Daily Gleaner*, May 29, 1937.
8. *Daily Gleaner*, Nov. 1, 1938.
9. *Daily Gleaner*, Jun. 19, 1939.
10. *Daily Gleaner*, Oct. 1, 1943.
11. *Daily Gleaner*, Apr. 28, 1945.
12. *Daily Gleaner*, Feb. 1, 1940.
13. "At the Sunset Lodge in Montego Bay," *Daily Gleaner*, Mar. 23, 1948.
14. *Daily Gleaner*, Aug. 16, 1946.
15. *Daily Gleaner*, Sept. 10, 1977.
16. Ken Jones, *Daily Gleaner*, Dec. 5, 1977.
17. "Building at St. Ann's Bay Hospital Named in Honour of Dr. Wilson," Jamaica Information Service, Feb. 13, 2005, https://jis.gov.jm/building-at-st-anns-bay-hospital-named-in-honour-of-dr-wilson/.
18. Aldene Shillingford, notes delivered at Ivy Graydon's funeral, provided to author July 16, 2019.
19. Shillingford, funeral notes.
20. familysearch.org.
21. *Daily Gleaner*, May 9, 1928.
22. *Daily Gleaner*, Nov. 19, 1935.
23. *Daily Gleaner*, Mar. 29, 1937.
24. Shillingford, funeral notes.
25. Comments by Gloria Phillipps are from a personal interview with the author, July 19, 2019.
26. Comments by Aldene Shillingford are from a personal interview with the author, July 16, 2019.
27. Shillingford, funeral notes.
28. *Daily Gleaner*, Nov. 3, 1952.
29. *Daily Gleaner*, Jan. 5, 1973.
30. Shillingford, interview.
31. *Daily Gleaner*, May 25, 2010.
32. Comments by Myrna Hague Bradshaw are from personal interviews with the author, Oct. 11, 2013, and May 28, 2014.
33. Comments by Janet Enright are from a personal interview with the author, June 24, 2013.
34. *Daily Gleaner*, Feb. 20, 1957.
35. Hartley Neita, *Jamaica Gleaner*, May 11, 1995.
36. *Daily Gleaner*, Sept. 20, 1954.
37. *Daily Gleaner*, Mar. 17, 1959.
38. *Daily Gleaner*, Mar. 17, 1959.
39. *Daily Gleaner*, Mar. 4, 1963.
40. *Daily Gleaner*, Dec. 18, 1934.
41. *Daily Gleaner*, Dec. 13, 1939.

42. *Daily Gleaner*, July 18, 1946.
43. *Jamaica Gleaner*, Jan. 1, 2003.
44. *The Gleaner*, Aug. 25, 2006.
45. *Jamaica Gleaner*, May 27, 2012.
46. *Daily Gleaner*, Mar. 18, 1974.
47. *Jamaica Gleaner*, Jun. 4, 2000.
48. *Jamaica Gleaner*, Mar. 30, 2001.
49. *Jamaica Gleaner*, May 13, 2001.
50. Comments by Christine Levy are from a personal interview with the author, Jun. 3, 2013.
51. Comments by Richard Chin are from a personal interview with the author, Jun. 17, 2013.
52. Comments by Margaret Wong are from a personal interview with the author, Jun. 20, 2013.
53. Comments by Marie Crompton-Nichols are from a personal interview with the author, Jun. 14, 2013.
54. *Daily Gleaner*, Oct. 21, 1968.
55. *Daily Gleaner*, Feb. 2, 1969.

Chapter Three

1. *Star*, June 15, 1956, p. 6.
2. "Lord Tanamo," Trojan Records, Aug. 30, 2019, http://trojanrecords.com/artist/lord-tanamo/.
3. *Ibid.*
4. *Ibid.*
5. Daniel T. Neely, personal correspondence with the author, July 1, 2019.
6. "Mento Music," MentoMusic.com, http://www.mentomusic.com/2scans.htm.
7. *Star*, Feb. 8, 1956.
8. *Jamaica Gleaner*, Jul. 7, 1997.
9. *Daily Gleaner*, Apr. 22, 1949.
10. *Jamaica Gleaner*, May 19, 2008.
11. *Jamaica Gleaner*, May 19, 2008.
12. *Jamaica Gleaner*, Oct. 25, 2002.
13. *Daily Gleaner*, May 28, 1957.
14. *Jamaica Gleaner*, Jul. 7, 1997.
15. Unless otherwise noted, comments by Calypso Rose are from a personal interview with the author, May 15, 2013.
16. Interview with Marco Werman, *The World*, Public Radio International, Dec. 22, 2009, https://www.pri.org/stories/2009-12-22/calypso-rose.
17. "Calypso Rose: The Woman Behind the Music," caribbearnbelle.com/interviews/calypso-rose.php. Accessed Oct. 17, 2013.
18. Anna S. Gottriech, "Whe' She Go Do": Women's Participation in Trinidad Calypso," UF: George A. Smathers Libraries, ufdc.ufl.edu/CA00400129/0000.1.
19. Gottriech.
20. Obolo, dir., *Calypso Rose: The Lioness of the Jungle*.
21. Obolo, *Calypso Rose*.
22. Obolo, *Calypso Rose*.
23. Obolo, *Calypso Rose*.
24. Obolo, *Calypso Rose*.
25. Obolo, *Calypso Rose*.
26. Obolo, *Calypso Rose*.
27. Obolo, *Calypso Rose*.

Chapter Four

1. Hague, "Totlyn Jackson," p. 42.
2. Hartley Neita, "But Totlyn Doesn't Get the Breaks," *Star*, Feb. 4, 1954.
3. Hague, p. 47.
4. Hague, p. 43.
5. *Ibid.*
6. Hague, 49.
7. Hartley Neita, "But Totlyn Doesn't Get the Breaks."
8. *Daily Gleaner*, Oct. 6, 1968.
9. Comments by Sheila Rickards are from a personal interview with the author, Aug. 18, 2019.
10. *Sunday Gleaner*, Jan. 18, 1998.
11. Comments by Dennis Sindrey are from a personal interview with the author, Aug. 20, 2019.
12. *Sunday Gleaner*, Jan. 18, 1998.
13. *Daily Gleaner*, Mar. 31, 1963.
14. Comments by Chris Flanagan are from a personal interview with the author, July 25, 2019.
15. *Jamaica Gleaner*, Oct. 16, 2018.
16. Unless otherwise noted, comments by Myrna Hague are from personal interviews with the author, Oct. 11, 2013, and May 28, 2014.
17. *Flair Magazine*, Oct. 15, 1985, p. 8.
18. *Daily Gleaner*, June 15, 1979, p. 4.
19. *Jamaica Gleaner*, June 26, 2002.
20. *Flair Magazine*, Dec. 21, 1998, p. 2.
21. *Jamaica Gleaner*, Apr. 24, 2014.
22. Garfield L. Angus, *Good News Jamaica*, Jan. 6, 2016.

Chapter Five

1. Comments by Millicent Todd are from a personal interview with the author, March 3, 2009.
2. Comments by Graeme Goodall are from personal interviews with the author, June 13, 2011, Dec. 11, 2013, and Aug. 12, 2013.
3. Comments by Stranger Cole are from a personal interview with the author, Dec. 21, 2012.
4. Comments by Doreen Shaffer are from a personal interview with the author, Feb. 21, 2014.
5. Comments by Yvonne Harrison are from a personal interview with the author, June 26, 2013.
6. *Daily Gleaner*, Nov. 27, 1959.
7. *Daily Gleaner*, Feb. 24, 1976.
8. *Daily Gleaner*, Aug. 1, 1971.
9. *Daily Gleaner*, July 11, 1974.
10. *Daily Gleaner*, Aug. 14, 1975.
11. *Jamaica Gleaner*, Nov. 5, 1998.
12. *Daily Gleaner*, Jan. 9, 1956.
13. Steffens, "Beverly Kelso," p. 26.
14. *Ibid.*
15. White, "Songbird of Simmer Down," p. 49.
16. Steffens, p. 26.
17. White, p. 49.
18. Steffens, p. 27.
19. *Ibid.*
20. White, p. 50.

21. *Ibid.*
22. Steffens, p. 28.
23. Steffens, p. 29.
24. *Ibid.*
25. Steffens, "First Fruits: Original Wailer Cherry Green," *The Beat* 23: 3, 2004, 38.
26. David Katz, Cherry Green obituary, *The Guardian*, Nov. 19, 2008.

Chapter Six

1. *The History of Blue Beat: The Birth of Ska.* Liner notes. Trojan Records, 2011.
2. Comments by Millie Small are from personal interviews with the author, Dec. 9, 2013, and July 18, 2018.
3. Comments by Roy Panton are from a personal interview with the author, Dec. 11, 2013.
4. Comments by Graeme Goodall are from personal interviews with the author, Dec. 11, 2013, and Aug. 12, 2013.
5. *Daily Gleaner*, Mar. 17, 1964, p. 7.
6. Finnis, liner notes, *You Heard It Here First*.
7. Webb, *100 Greatest Cover Versions*.
8. Comments by Chris Blackwell are from a personal interview with the author, Aug. 16, 2013.
9. "Spectro Pop Welcomes Millie Small." Spectropop.com/MillieSmall/, accessed Feb. 19, 2020.
10. *Ibid.*
11. *New Amsterdam News*, Aug. 1, 1964, 47.
12. *Daily Gleaner*, July 27, 1964, p. 6.
13. *Daily Gleaner*, July 31, 1964, p. 8D.
14. Comments by Ronnie Nasralla are from a personal interview with the author, Aug. 16, 2013.
15. According to her son, Raymond Miles Jr., in a phone conversation, Aug. 11, 2013.
16. *Daily Gleaner*, Aug. 12, 1964, p. 2.
17. *New York Amsterdam News*, Aug. 16, 1964.
18. Grant, *The Natural Mystics*, p. 91.
19. *Jamaica Gleaner*, Oct. 12, 2011, p. D6.
20. *Jamaica Gleaner*, Mar. 13, 2016, p. D4.
21. Daily Gleaner, Apr. 10, 1970, p. 6.
22. "The Blue Beat," Getty Images, https://www.gettyimages.com/detail/news-photo/singer-dancers-beverly-mills-and-boysie-grant-do-the-blue-news-photo/3269585.
23. Roots Knotty Roots—The Discography of Jamaican Music, s.v. "Blue Beat," accessed Feb. 19, 2020, www.reggaefever.ch/rkr/.

Chapter Seven

1. *Jamaica Gleaner*, July 6, 1997.
2. Comments by Owen Ellis are from a personal interview with the author, Sept. 9, 2013.
3. Comments by Christel Reid are from a personal interview with the author, Jan. 11, 2014.
4. David Katz, Hortense Ellis obituary, *The Guardian*, Nov. 10, 2000.
5. *Jamaica Gleaner*, July 6, 1997.
6. Comments by Myrna Hague are from a personal interview with the author, May 28, 2014.
7. Comments by Lorna Goodison are from a personal interview with the author, Jan. 12, 2014.
8. Katz, Hortense Ellis obituary.
9. Comments by Winston Jones are from a personal interview with the author, May 21, 2013.
10. Comments by Merlene Webber and Cynthia Webber are from personal interviews with the author, June 15, 2013.
11. Walter Jekyll and Lucy Etheldred Broadwood. *Jamaican Song and Story: Annancy Stories, Digging Sings, Ring Tunes, and Dancing Tunes*, Volume 55. Folk-lore Society, 1907, pp 219-220.
12. *Jamaica Gleaner*, Nov. 1, 2000.
13. Comments by Roy Panton are from a personal interview with the author, Dec. 12, 2013.
14. *Jamaica Gleaner*, Dec. 18, 2005.
15. *Daily Gleaner*, Apr. 20, 1995.

Chapter Eight

1. Comments by Norma Fraser are from a personal interview with the author, July 16, 2013.
2. Vanessa Salvia, *Eugene Weekly*, May 26, 2005.
3. "Merry-Go-Round," *Daily Gleaner*, Sept. 15, 1967.
4. Abzug, *Bella!*, inside flap, front cover.
5. Comments by Marcia Griffiths are from a personal interview with the author, Jan. 15, 2014.
6. Comments by Judy Mowatt are from an interview with Roger Steffens, Aug. 2, 1981 at the Sunsplash Festival, used courtesy of Steffens.
7. *Jamaica Observer*, May 8, 2011.
8. *Jamaica Gleaner*, July 21, 2002.
9. "Merry-Go-Round," *Daily Gleaner*, June 16, 1971.
10. Penn, *Story of My Life*, p. 9.
11. Penn, p. 13.
12. Unless otherwise specified, comments by Dawn Penn are from personal interviews with the author, Mar. 21, Apr. 4, and Apr. 21, 2014.
13. Penn, *Story of My Life*, pp. 31–32.
14. Penn, p. 34.
15. Comments by Susan Cadogan are from a personal interview with the author, Jul. 2, 2014.
16. *Sunday Gleaner Magazine*, Mar. 21, 1976.
17. Barrow and Dalton, *Rough Guide to Reggae*, p. 394.
18. Comments by Althea Forrest and Donna Reid are from personal interviews with the author, Aug 12, 2014.
19. *Daily Gleaner*, Sept. 21, 1947.
20. *Daily Gleaner*, Feb. 26, 1978.
21. *Daily Gleaner*, Nov. 20, 1977.
22. *Sunday Gleaner*, Oct. 19, 1970.
23. *Daily Gleaner*, Apr. 11, 1977.
24. *Sunday Gleaner*, Jan. 18, 1998, p. 2E.
25. *Ibid.*
26. *Sunday Gleaner Magazine*, Nov. 9, 1975.
27. *Daily Gleaner*, Aug. 13, 1985.
28. *Daily Gleaner*, Oct. 6, 1992.
29. *Outlook Magazine*, Apr. 20, 2008.

30. *Daily Gleaner*, Aug. 13, 1978.
31. *Jamaica Observer*, Aug. 20, 2017.
32. *Sunday Gleaner*, Mar. 14, 1998, p. 82.
33. *Ibid.*
34. *Ibid.*
35. *Daily Gleaner*, Oct. 18, 1969, p. 6.
36. *Daily Gleaner*, Mar. 7, 1968.

Chapter Nine

1. *Sunday Gleaner*, Feb. 20, 2005.
2. Kenner, "Sister Nancy and Producer Winston Riley's Son Talk," *Billboard Magazine*, Feb. 16, 2016. Billboard.com, accessed Feb. 20, 2020.
3. *Sunday Gleaner*, Feb. 20, 2005.
4. Kocchar, "Ain't No Stopping Sister Nancy Now," *The Fader*, June 4, 2017.
5. Blais-Billie, "Sister Nancy," *Pitchfork*, March 14, 2018.
6. Battan, "Song of the Summer," New Yorker, Aug. 19, 2016. www.newyorker.com, accessed Feb. 20, 2020.
7. Kenner, "The 30-Year Journey," *Genius*, Jan. 4, 2017. www.genius.com, acccessed Feb. 20, 2020.
8. *Ibid.*
9. "Interview with Junie Ranks," Penthouse Records, Oct. 2008, http://penthouserecords.free.fr/Interview_Junie_Ranks.htm.
10. *Ibid.*
11. *Ibid.*
12. *Ibid.*
13. *Ibid.*
14. *Sunday Gleaner*, Feb. 20, 2005.
15. Campbell, "Give You My Loving by Junie Ranks," n.p.
16. "Interview with Junie Ranks."
17. Jelly-Schapiro, "An Interview with Lady Saw," *Believer*, July 1, 2010, n.p. believermag.com, accessed Feb. 20, 2020.
18. *Ibid.*
19. *Ibid.*
20. Howard McGowen, "Lady Saw—The New Dance Hall Sensation," *Jamaica Gleaner*, Jun. 4, 1993.
21. Stolzoff, *Wake the Town*, p. 240.
22. Henry Balford, "Kulcha' and Hypocrisy," *Jamaica Gleaner*, Aug. 22, 1994.
23. Howard McGowen, "Splash Draws Big Crowd at Dance Hall Night," *Jamaica Gleaner*, Aug. 7, 1993.
24. Stolzoff, *Wake the Town and Tell the People*, p. 246.
25. Jelly-Schapiro, "An Interview with Lady Saw."

Chapter Ten

1. *Daily Gleaner*, May 7, 1948, p. 4.
2. *Daily Gleaner*, Sept. 2, 1935.
3. "Vivacious," *Daily Gleaner*, Mar. 3, 1945, 8; "torrid," *Daily Gleaner*, Aug. 16, 1961, 7; "sensuous," *Daily Gleaner*, Feb. 25, 1935, 11; "exotic," *Daily Gleaner*, July 10, 1966, 7; "exciting," *Daily Gleaner*, Sept. 4, 1965, 7; "bombshells," *Daily Gleaner*, Oct. 26, 1946, 4; "ball of fire," *Daily Gleaner*, Sept. 11, 1965, 7.
4. *Daily Gleaner*, May 18, 1932.
5. *Daily Gleaner*, Aug. 18, 1939.
6. *Daily Gleaner*, Sept. 12, 1948.
7. *Daily Gleaner*, Mar. 12, 1943.
8. *Daily Gleaner*, Feb. 8, 1944.
9. *Daily Gleaner*, July 18, 1948.
10. *Daily Gleaner*, July 24, 1943.
11. *Daily Gleaner*, Aug. 6, 1943.
12. *Daily Gleaner*, Aug. 30, 1943.
13. *Daily Gleaner*, Feb. 15, 1947.
14. Comments by Suzanne Bent are from a personal interview with the author, Mar. 3, 2011.
15. Comments by Faye Chin are from a personal interview with the author, Mar. 21, 2011.
16. Reckord, "Reggae, Rastafarianism and Cultural Identity," p. 10.
17. Comments by Nadine Taylor are from a personal interview with the author, Oct. 28, 2016.
18. According to her son, Raymond Miles Jr., in a phone conversation on Aug. 11, 2013.
19. Comments by Dennis Sindrey are from a personal interview with the author, Jan. 4, 2017.
20. Comments by Joan Seaga are from a personal interview with the author, Feb. 18, 2016.
21. *Daily Gleaner*, Apr. 12, 1969.
22. Yen, "Remembering Ivy Baxter," p. 10.
23. Baxter, *Arts of an Island*, p. vii.
24. Baxter, p. 32.
25. Yen, p. 14–15.
26. Yen, p. 15.
27. *Daily Gleaner*, Sept. 8, 1956.
28. *Daily Gleaner*, Jan. 11, 1993.
29. "Dance," Caribya!, http://caribya.com/jamaica/culture/dance/.
30. *Daily Gleaner*, Apr. 11, 1944.
31. *Daily Gleaner*, Dec. 15, 1943.
32. *Daily Gleaner*, Dec. 18, 1942.
33. *Daily Gleaner*, Apr. 15, 1944.

Chapter Eleven

1. Little, *"You Did It Unto Me,"* p. 196.
2. Comments by Winston Martin are from a personal interview with the author, June 15, 2011.
3. Comments by Charles Simpson are from a personal interview with the author, Jan. 6, 2014.
4. Little, p. 197.
5. Comments by Winston Martin are from a personal interview with the author, June 15, 2011.
6. Comments by Owen Grey are from personal inerveiw with the author, Jan. 11, 2011.
7. Comments by Ernest Ranglin are from a personal interview with the author, Sept. 8, 2011.
8. Williams, liner notes.
9. Comments by Eddie "Tan Tan" Thornton are from personal interviews with the author, Feb. 22, Feb. 26, and Feb. 27, 2011.
10. Little, p. 198.
11. *Daily Gleaner*, Aug. 5, 2012.
12. *Daily Gleaner*, Apr. 5, 2009.

13. Comments by Marjorie Whylie are from a personal interview with the author, Jul. 14, 2014.
14. Marcia Erskine, *Daily Gleaner*, Sept. 27, 1990.
15. Erskine, *Daily Gleaner*, Sept. 27, 1990.
16. *Jamaica Gleaner*, Apr. 19, 2013, C2.
17. *Sunday Gleaner*, Apr. 5, 2009, E8.
18. *Daily Gleaner*, June 15, 1990.
19. Edna Manley College, https://emc.edu.jm/schoolofmusic/about-us/.
20. Lewin, *Rock It Come Over*, p. ix.
21. *The Independent*, Jul. 14, 2013.
22. *The Independent*, Jul. 14, 2013.
23. Jake Homiak, "Olive Lewin (1927–2013): A Life of Service," Smithsonian, Apr. 23, 2013, https://festival.si.edu/blog/2013/olive-lewin-1927-2013-a-life-of-service/.
24. *Jamaica Observer*, Apr. 11, 2013.

Chapter Twelve

1. Comments by Enid Cumberland are from a personal interview with the author, Jan. 12, 2014.
2. *Daily Gleaner*, Aug. 30, 1948.
3. David Katz, Sonia Pottinger obituary, *The Guardian*, Nov. 18, 2010.
4. *Daily Gleaner*, Jan. 19, 1971.
5. Comments by Graeme Goodall are from a personal interview with the author, Aug. 12, 2013.
6. Comments by Millicent "Patsy" Todd are from a personal interview with the author, Mar. 3, 2009.
7. Comments by Stranger Cole are from a personal interview with the author, Dec. 21, 2012.
8. *Flair Magazine*, Mar. 12, 1985.
9. Ibid.

Chapter Thirteen

1. *Shreveport Times*, May 9, 2015.
2. Johnson and Pines, *Reggae*, p. 67.
3. *Jamaica Gleaner*, Apr. 23, 1995.
4. *Daily Gleaner*, Sept. 26, 1978.
5. *Daily Gleaner*, Sept. 26, 1979.
6. *Daily Gleaner*, Sept. 26, 1980.
7. *The Jamaican Weekly Gleaner*, Sept. 29–Oct. 5, 1995.
8. Comments by Graeme Goodall are from a personal interview with the author, Aug. 12, 2013.
9. Comments by Kingsley Goodison are from a personal interview with the author, Jan. 12, 2014.
10. *Jamaica Gleaner*, Jul. 12, 1998.
11. *Jamaica Gleaner*, Nov. 9, 1997.
12. Comments by Kingsley Goodison are from a personal interview with the author, Jan. 12, 2014.
13. *Jamaica Observer*, Sept. 20, 2010.
14. Comments by Myrna Hague-Bradshaw are from a personal interview with the author, May 28, 2014.
15. Comments by Patricia Chin are from a personal interview with the author, Aug. 30, 2013.
16. *Jamaica Observer*, Sept. 5, 2010.
17. Comments by Patricia Chin are from a personal interview with the author, Aug. 30, 2013.
18. Comments by Clive Chin are from a personal interview with the author, Aug. 16, 2013.
19. David Katz, "Ken Khouri: 'I am the Complete pioneer of Everything,'" *Caribbearn Beat*, Issue 67 (May/June 2004)caribbearn-beat.com, accesed Feb. 20, 2020.
20. Comments by Paul Khouri are from a personal interview with the author, Aug. 27, 2013.
21. *Daily Gleaner*, Oct. 18, 1957.
22. *Daily Gleaner*, Nov. 2, 1963.
23. Comments by Graeme Goodall are from a personal interview with the author, Dec. 11, 2013.
24. Comments by Sheila Khouri are from a personal interview with the author, Aug. 7, 2013.
25. *Daily Gleaner*, Aug. 29, 1971.
26. Colby Graham, "Remembering Vere Johns Pt. 2," Vintage Boss Blog, June 3, 2007, http://vintageboss.blogspot.com/2007/06/remembering-vere-johns-pt2.html.
27. *Daily Gleaner*, July 25, 1939.
28. *Sunday Gleaner*, May 27, 2012.
29. *Sunday Gleaner*, Dec. 30, 2012.
30. *Daily Gleaner*, Feb. 18, 1941.
31. *Daily Gleaner*, July 31, 1943.
32. *Daily Gleaner*, Jun. 22, 1939.
33. *Daily Gleaner*, Nov. 3, 2000.

Chapter Fourteen

1. Virginia Woolf, *A Room of One's Own*, ed. Mark Hussey (Boston: Mariner Books, 2005f), p. 3.
2. Moskowitz, *Caribbean Popular Music*, p. 205.
3. Elder, "The Male/Female Conflict in Calypso," p. 28.
4. Elder, p. 28.
5. Roots Knotty Roots—The Discography of Jamaican Music," accessed Aug. 30, 2019. www.reggaefever.ch/rkr/.
6. Elder, p. 30.
7. Hope, *Man Vibes*, p. 69.
8. Elder, p. 30.
9. National Public Radio, *All Things Considered*, Mar. 22, 2010.
10. Stanley Niaah, "Taking Surprising Risks."
11. Dawes, *Bob Marley*, 60.
12. Cooper, *Noises in the Blood*, p. 131.
13. Maureen Rowe, "The Woman in Rastafari," Caribbean Quarterly, Vol. 26, No. 2 (1980), p. 14.
14. Cooper, p. 137.
15. Hope, p. 20.
16. R.W. Connell, quoted in Hope, *Man Vibes*, 20.
17. Hope, 25.

Bibliography

Abzug, Bella. *Bella! Ms. Abzug Goes to Washington.* New York: Saturday Review Press, 1972.

Augustyn, Heather. *Don Drummond: The Genius and Tragedy of the World's Greatest Trombonist.* Jefferson, NC: McFarland, 2013.

_____. *Operation Jump Up: Jamaica's Campaign for a National Sound.* Chesterton, IN: Half Pint, 2018.

_____. "Rhumba Queens: Sirens of Jamaican Music." *Jamaica Journal* 37, no. 3 (2019): 28–35.

_____. *Ska: An Oral History.* Jefferson, NC: McFarland, 2010.

_____. *Songbirds: Pioneering Women in Jamaican Music.* Chesterton, IN: Half Pint, 2014.

Augustyn, Heather, and Adam Reeves. *Alpha Boys' School: Cradle of Jamaican Music.* Chesterton, IN: Half Pint, 2017.

Auld, Michael. "Anansi and the Yam Hills." Accessed Aug. 1, 2019. https://archive.org/stream/24961/24961_djvu.txt.

Bailey, Lilieth Lejo. "A Chat with Louise Bennett." *Caribbean Writer* 12 (1992): N.p.

Barrow, Steve, and Peter Dalton. *Rough Guide to Reggae.* London: Rough Guides, 2004.

Battan, Carrie. "Song of the Summer: Sister Nancy's 'Bam Bam.'" *The New Yorker*, Aug. 19, 2016.

Baxter, Ivy. *The Arts of an Island.* Metuchen, NJ: Scarecrow, 1970.

Blais-Billie, Braudie. "Sister Nancy Calls JAY-Z and Kanye's 'Bam Bam' Samples 'a Blessing.'" *Pitchfork*, Mar. 14, 2018.

Campbell, Howard. "Give You My Loving by Junie Ranks." *United Reggae*, July 9, 2018.

Cooper, Carolyn. *Noises in the Blood: Orality, Gender, and the "Vulgar" Body of Jamaican Popular Culture.* Durham, ND: Duke University Press, 2006.

Daily Gleaner. Numerous articles accessed at http://jamaica-gleaner.com/.

Dawes, Kwame. *Bob Marley: Lyrical Genius.* London: Bobcat, 2002.

Elder, J.D. "The Male/Female Conflict in Calypso." In *Caribbean Quarterly,* Calypso Monograph, ed. Kim Walcott (Kingston: UWI, 1968), pp. 73–92.

Finnis, Rob. Liner notes to *You Heard It Here First.* CD. Ace, 2004.

Foster, Chuck. *Roots Rock Reggae: An Oral History of Reggae Music from Ska to Dancehall.* New York: Billboard, 1999.

Gottlieb, Karla. *The Mother of Us All: A History of Queen Nanny, Leader of the Windward Jamaican Maroons.* Trenton, NJ: Africa World, 2000.

Graham, Colby. "Remembering Vere Johns Pt. 2." Vintage Boss blog, June 3, 2007. http://vintageboss.blogspot.com/2007/06/remembering-vere-johns-pt2.html.

Grant, Colin. *The Natural Mystics: Marley, Tosh, and Wailer.* New York: W.W. Norton, June 20, 2011.

Hague, Myrna. "Totlyn Jackson: From Country Girl to World Stage." *Wadabagei,* vol. 12, no. 2 (2009): 40–51.

Hope, Donna P. *Man Vibes: Masculinities in the Jamaican Dancehall.* Kington; Miami: Ian Randle, 2010.

Jelly-Schapiro, Joshua. "An Interview with Lady Saw." *Believer*, July 1, 2010.

Johnson, Howard, and Jim Pines. *Reggae: Deep Roots Music.* London: Proteus, 1982.

Kenner, Rob. "Sister Nancy and Producer Winston Riley's Son Talk 'Bam Bam' Sample on Kanye West's 'The Life of Pablo.'" *Billboard*, Feb. 16, 2006.

_____. "The 30-Year Journey of Sister Nancy, Jamaica's First Female Dancehall Star." *Genius,* Jan. 4, 2017.

Kocchar, Nazuk. "Ain't No Stopping Sister Nancy Now." *Fader,* Jun. 14, 2017.

Lee, Helene. *The First Rasta: Leonard Howell and the Rise of Rastafarianism.* Chicago: Chicago Review, 2004.

Lewin, Olive. *Rock It Come Over: The Folk Music of Jamaica.* Kingston, Jamaica: University of the West Indies Press, 2000.

Little, Mary Bernadette Little, Sister RSM. *"You Did It Unto Me": The Story of Alpha and the Sisters of Mercy in Jamaica.* Cincinnati: Beyond the Trees, 2013.

Miller, Herbie. "Brown Girl in the Ring: Margarita

and Malungu." *Caribbean Quarterly,* Dec. 2007, pp. 47–74.

Morris, Mervyn. Introduction to *Selected Poems,* by Louise Bennett. Kingston, Jamaica: Sangster's, 2005, pp. ix–xxvii.

——. *Miss Lou: Louise Bennett and Jamaican Culture.* Kingston, Jamaica: Ian Randle, 2014.

Moskowitz, David V. *Caribbean Popular Music.* Westport, CT: Greenwood, 2006.

New York Amsterdam News. Numerous articles accessed at https://newspaperarchive.com/.

Obolo, Pascale, dir. *Calypso Rose: Lioness of the Jungle.* Trinidad and Tobago: Maturity Productions, 2011.

Page, Carrie Leigh, and Dana Reason. "Playing Like a Girl: The Problems with Reception of Women in Music." Newmusic USA, July 19, 2018. https://nmbx.newmusicusa.org/playing-like-a-girl-the-problems-with-reception-of-women-in-music/.

Penn, Dawn. *Story of My Life.* London: Da Beat, 2002.

Perrone, Pierre. "Obituary: Sister Mary Ignatius Davies." *The Independent,* Mar. 3, 2003.

Reckord, Verena. "Reggae, Rastafarianism and Cultural Identity." *Jamaica Journal,* Aug. 1982, p. 70.

Roots Knotty Roots database. Numerous songs accessed at reggaefever.ch/rkr.

Salvia, Vanessa. "Norma Fraser." *Eugene Weekly,* May 26, 2005.

Stanley Niaah, Sonjah. "Taking Surprising Risks for the Ideal Body." NPR, Mar. 22, 2010. www.npr.org/templates/story/story.php?storyId=124700865.

Star. Numerous articles accessed at the National Library of Jamaica.

Steffens, Roger. "Beverly Kelso: The 'Lost' Voice of the Wailers." *The Beat* 23, no. 3 (2004).

Stolzoff, Norman. *Wake the Town and Tell the People.* Durham, ND: Duke University Press, 2000.

Webb, Robert. *The 100 Greatest Cover Versions: The Ultimate Playlist.* Carmarthen, UK: McNidder & Grace, 2013.

White, Timothy. "Songbird of Simmer Down." *The Beat* 10, no. 3 (1991).

Williams, Mark. Liner notes for *Alpha Boys' School: Music in Education 1910–2006.* CD. Trojan Records, Jan. 17, 2006.

Yen, Alma Mock. "Remembering Ivy Baxter: Her Life and Legacy." *Caribbean Quarterly* 47, no. 1 (2001): 7–29.

Index

abeng 4–5, 159
Abner, Joe 95
Abrahams, K.R. 68
The Abyssinians 121
Abzug, Bella 102
Acadomusic Publishing 120
Adams, Glen 64–65, 117
Adams, Yvonne see Harrison, Yvonne
Adastra Club 120, 141
Adastra Gardens see Club Adastra
Admiral Bailey 133
African-Caribbean Institute of Jamaica 160
Aitken, Bobby 199
Aitken, Laurel 63, 68, 76, 85, 96, 188, 195, 198
Aitken, Marcia 121
Alan Ivanhoe Dance Troupe 141
Alberga, Gayman 121
Alexander, Monty 157
Alexander, Reuben 151
Allan, Elkan 82
Allen, Roy "Hawkeye" Forbes 120
Alpha Blondy 129
Alpha Boys' Band see Alpha Boys' School
Alpha Boys' School 14, 19, 21, 26, 139, 147–154, 209, 210
Alphonso, Roland 18, 43, 48, 65, 66, 99, 100, 112
Althea and Donna 85, 117, 120–123, 205
Alton and Tthe Flames 90, 113; see also Ellis, Alton
Ambassador Theatre 89, 188
American Federation of Musicians 126
Anacaona 144
Anansi 3, 9, 157, 203, 209

Anderson, Alpharita see Marley, Rita Anderson
Anderson, Gladstone 113
Andy, Bob 54, 103, 105–106, 117
Andy, Horace 131, 196, 199
Anka, Paul 98, 182
Antigua 116, 119, 157
Apollo Theater 123
Ariwa 119
Armstrong, Louis 68, 69, 83
Ashanti 4, 5, 144
Ashbourne, Peter 24
Asher, Peter 86
Asia 81
Aswad 151
Atlantic Records 180, 185, 187
Attila the Hun 37
Audley Williams Combo 28, 44
The Avengers 30–33
Aznavour, Charles 47

The Baby Grand 120, 141
Back O Wall 103
Bad Manners 117, 197
Bagga 201
Bahamas 35, 47, 63, 90, 186
Baker, Josephine 96
Baldwin, Mavis see Lady Baldwin
"Bam Bam" 29, 131–133, 209
Barclay, Owen 66
The Bare Essentials Band 127
Barker, Dave 85, 131
Barnett, Michael 67, 96
Barnett, Sheila 157
Barrett, Aston "Family Man" 117, 129
Barrett, Howard 106
Barrow, Steve 119, 205, 209
Barry G 134
Bass, Fontella 167
Bassey, Shirley 52

Baxter, Ivy 144–145, 146, 206, 209, 210
The Beatles 79, 80, 81, 184
Beck, Jeff 31
Beckford, Kelling 195
Beckford, Theophilus 26, 66, 85, 196
Bedasse, Alerth 192, 195, 200
"The Bed's Too Big Without You" 128
Beenie Man 32, 136, 178, 202
Belafonte, Harry 8, 146
Belize 59, 115, 125, 167
Bellamy, Adina see Madam Eve Temptation
Bellevue Mental Hospital 153, 157
The Beltones 106
Bennett, "Deadly" Headley 101, 152
Bennett, Joseph "Jo Jo" 152
Bennett, Kay 127
Bennett, Kenneth "Toney" 127
Bennett, Lorna 127, 167
Bennett, Louise see Coverley, Louise Bennett
Bennett, Val 25, 113, 139, 152
Benson, George 185–186
Benson, Jean 185–186
Bent, Christopher 142–143
Bent, Rudolph 142
Bent, Rupert 54
Bent, Suzanne 140, 142–143, 206
Benz, Spragga 127, 135
Beverley's see Kong, Leslie
Big Beat Show 48
Big Youth 167, 201
Bim and Bam 120
Birdland 21, 78
Black, Roy 24, 85, 188–189
Black Ark 116; see also Perry, Lee "Scratch"
Black Prince 37

Black Uhuru 73, 77, 195
Blackwell, Chris 77–80, 83–85, 128, 164, 175, 205
Blair, Trevor 197
Blake, Monte 120, 125
Blake, Winston 67, 112, 114, 120, 125
blue beat 50–51, 75, 85, 205
Blue Beat (label) 69, 75, 86–87, 164
The Blues Busters 24, 76, 83, 104, 188
Bob and Marcia 86, 105–106; see also Andy, Bob; Griffiths, Marcia
Bob Marley Lecture 161
The Bodysnatchers 26
Bolt, Usain 32
Bond, Brigitte 87
Bond, Gary 87
Bond, Joyce 87, 130
Bonitto, Frankie 36, 44
Bonnie, Clive 63
Boom, Barry 119
Boothe, Ken 25, 65, 85, 92, 100, 117, 128, 167
Bounty Killer 135
Bournemouth Beach Club 15, 16, 19, 21, 44, 61, 62, 141, 152
Bow, Ben 117
Bowers, Ben "Hi-De-Ho" 120
boxing 149
Boyce, Owen 105
BPR 78
Bradshaw, Sonny 21, 43, 44, 47, 52–54, 70, 91, 151, 152, 156, 164
Brady, Carl 144
Braithwaite, Franklin Delano Alexander "Junior" 70, 73–74
Brammer, Robert "Clint Eastwood" 90, 195
Bramwell, Doc 70
Bramwell, Ermine Ortense see Green, Cherry
Breakspeare, Cindy 73, 161
Brevett, Lloyd 18, 61, 112
Brigadier Jerry 131
British American Insurance Company 185
Brooklyn Fox 80
Brooks, Baba 109, 142, 166
Brooks, Cedric "IM" 152, 156
Brown, Chris 132
Brown, Dennis 25, 119, 121, 126, 128, 177, 201
Brown, Hux 123
Brown, James 80
Brown, Oral 54
Brown, Owen "OB" 120
Brown, Roscoe 171

Brown, Tony 152
Brown Jug 29
Brown Sugar 119
Brubeck, Dave 21–22, 49, 84, 152
Bryan, Rad 123
Brynner, Lloyd 101
Bryson, Peabo 32
The Buccaneers 96
Buckley, Henry 107
Bucknor, Sidney 72
Buena Vista 35
Buju Banton 135, 161
Bunny and Scully 25, 76, 92, 188, 189
Bunny Lee 49, 63, 65, 90, 94, 124
Burgie, Irving 8
Burke, Solomon 66
Burnett, Watty 96
Burning Spear 77
Burrell, Roland 197
Burru 159
Bustamante, Alexander 4, 47, 190
Buster Bloodvessel 197
Butler, Harold 125
Butler, Jerry 164
Butler, Leslie 21–22
Byron Lee and the Dragonaires 28, 30, 31, 59, 82, 83, 84, 90, 104–105, 112, 125, 144, 160, 186, 187

Cadogan, Susan 114–120, 205
Calneck, Blondel see Lack, Ken
calypso 22, 30, 34–42, 59, 64, 101, 120, 127, 144, 152, 164, 165, 167, 179, 181, 184, 192, 193–194, 195, 200, 204, 207, 209, 210
Calypso Rose 36–42, 59, 167, 204, 210
calypso tent 38–41
Campbell, Cecil Bustamante see Prince Buster
Campbell, Cecile 108–124
Campbell, Howard 85, 209
Campbell, Lloyd 104
Canada Dry 82
Capitol Records 180
Capo Records 65
The Caravelles 78, 84
Carib Theatre 11, 44, 48, 53, 82, 98, 100, 104–105, 108, 141, 152, 164
Caribbean Carnival 8
The Caribbean Thespians 190
The Caribs 28, 44, 48, 164, 184
Carifesta 52–53
Carlton and The Shoes 200
The Carnations 10, 26–33, 112
Carnival 22, 37–38, 41–42, 144

The Casinos 200
Castro, Fidel 137, 183
The Cavaliers 101
Caymanas Park 120
CBS Records 106, 180, 186
Cespedes, Elizabeth see Madame Wasp
Chalice sound system 131
Chan, Suzy see Wong, Margaret
Chang, Lloyd 31
chantrels 37–38
Charles, Hubert Raphael see Roaring Lion
Charles, Ray 58, 76
Charlie's Calypso Records 41
Charmers, Lloyd 90
Chen, Colston 31
Chen, Phil 31
Chen, Ray 30
Chevannes, Barry 195
Chin, Clive 90, 129, 177, 178, 207
Chin, Conrad 31, 138
Chin, Faye 140–141, 206
Chin, Ingrid 26–33
Chin, Ivan 30
Chin, Joel 177–178
Chin, Kes 28, 31
Chin, Keyoung 28
Chin, Patricia 175–178, 183, 207
Chin, Patrick 30
Chin, Richard 26–33, 204
Chin, Tessanne 32
Chin, Vincent 30, 66, 77, 99, 124, 129, 152, 175–178
Chinese-Jamaicans 30–31
Chin's Calypso Sextet 30, 192, 195, 200
Chocomo Lawn 71, 82–83, 170
Chung, Geoffrey 127
church 15, 33, 40, 43–44, 46, 50, 56, 61, 69–70, 71, 74, 92, 94, 102–103, 110–111, 115, 124, 129, 134, 136, 139, 148, 158, 163–165, 199
Chynn, Tami 32
Cindy Star and the Rude Boys 87
Clapton, Eric 31
The Clarendonians 90, 110, 200
Clark, Lloyd 66
Clarke, Annette 87
Clarke, Garfield 21–22
Clarke, Johnny 90, 96
Clarke, Lloyd "Sparrow" 76, 188
class 10, 20, 22, 29, 51, 75, 82, 84, 85, 95, 99, 100, 124, 135, 140–142, 145, 151, 167, 168, 171, 175, 178
Clemonson, Merle 107–108

Cliff, Jimmy 32, 48, 52, 76, 83, 87, 94, 110, 124, 129, 152, 164, 188, 199
Club 35 101, 164
Club Baby Grand 120, 141
Club Havana 30, 31, 101, 112, 138, 141
Club Maracas 29, 30
Club Paradise 9
Coburn, Roy 36, 152
Cole, Allan "Skill" 108, 162
Cole, Wilburn Theodore "Stranger" 25, 56–58, 65, 90, 92, 96–97, 167, 192, 204, 207
Collins, Ansel 85, 123, 131
Colony Club 16, 19, 20, 44, 151, 152
Como, Perry 96
Connell, R.W. 201–202, 207
Connor, Pearl 50
The Contours 80
Cooke, Redver 36, 70, 139
Cooke, Sam 48–49, 98
Cooper, Carolyn 160–161, 200–201, 207, 209
Cooper, Winston see Count Matchuki
The Copa 100
Coromantee see Koromantee
Count Basie 48–49, 83, 151
Count Lasher 35, 192
Count Matchuki 172–173
Count Ossie 90, 141–142, 156, 159, 167; see also Wareika Hills
Count Owen 192
Count Shelly 69
Count Suckle 124
Courtleigh Manor Hotel 22, 52
Coverley, Eric 8–9, 141
Coverley, Louise "Miss Lou" Bennett 7–9, 18, 19, 34–35, 48, 70, 120, 139, 203, 209, 210
Cowan, Tommy 24, 25, 120, 121, 126, 186
cricket 15, 47, 54, 148, 149, 164
Cuba 4, 16, 23, 46, 108, 114, 120, 137, 139, 143, 150, 174, 183
Cugat, Xavier 96
Culture 99, 167, 198
Cumberland, Enid 162–166, 192, 207

DaCosta, Glen 21, 152
DaCosta, Tony 62
Dalton, Peter 119, 205, 209
dance 7, 8, 29, 30, 33, 41, 50, 68, 71, 78, 82–83, 87, 93, 107, 109, 112, 125, 137–146, 154, 155, 156, 158, 159, 184–185, 188–189, 198, 205, 206

dancehall 32, 124, 131–136, 161, 197, 201–202, 206, 209
Darin, Bobby 80
Darl 78
Darlington, Doris 172–173
Dave Yuen Show Group 33
Davies, Sister Mary Ignatius 19, 22 144–154, 210
Davis, Carlene 125–127, 167
Davis, Sammy, Jr. 48, 51, 58, 153
Dawes, Kwame 200, 207, 209
Dean, Nora 108, 124–125
Deans, Eric 19–21, 36, 44, 140, 151
Decca 85, 180
deejays/DJs 78, 80, 109, 116, 122, 131–133, 134, 136, 150, 177; see also sound systems
Dekker, Desmond 85, 86, 90, 100, 101, 110, 152, 196, 199
Delgado, Junior 119
Delgado, Reuben 153
The Deltones 26
Denham Town 71, 123
Dennis, Rudolph "Garth" 73
Desmond, Paul 49
Devil's Daughter 138, 139
Dick, Steve 70
Dillinger 90, 131
Dillon, Phyllis 95–97, 113, 167
dinky minny/dinki mini 8, 136, 159
The Diversions 198
Dixon, Jeff 105
Doctor Bird 86; see also Goodall, Graeme
Dodd, Clement Seymour "Coxsone" 52, 54, 61, 63, 65, 66, 71–72, 76–77, 89, 90, 94, 99–100, 104, 105, 106, 108, 112, 113, 123, 124, 152, 154, 165, 171, 172–175, 183
Dodd, Norma 63, 173–175
Domino, Fats 81, 172, 176
"Don't Touch My Tomato" 96
The Doors 83
The Dovells 80
Downbeat see Dodd, Clement Seymour "Coxsone"
The Drifters 66, 176
Drummond, Don 18–23, 29, 43, 44, 64, 68, 70, 95, 109, 122, 141, 142, 151, 153–154, 173, 209
dub 64, 198
duets/duo 11, 38, 56, 58–59, 60, 61, 63, 65, 66, 67, 69, 76, 77, 86, 90, 92, 96, 99, 101, 104, 105, 106, 111, 116, 119, 121, 122, 123, 135, 142, 162, 164, 165, 167, 191, 192, 193

Dunbar, Sly 123, 131; see also Sly and Robbie
duppies 192; see also obeah
Durie, Alec 180–181
Dylan, Bob 106
Dynamic Sounds 24–25, 31, 126, 184–187

"Eastern Standard Time" 153
"Easy Snappin'" 85
The Ebony Sisters 124
The Ebonys 128
Eccles, Clancy 66, 123, 197
Eddie Thomas Group 125, 156
Eddy, Duane 29
Edelweiss Concert Choir 128
Edna Manley College for the Visual and Performing Arts 155, 159, 207
Edwards, Adina 10, 24–26
Edwards, George see King Edwards
Edwards, Roy 15
Edwards, Wilfred "Jackie" 25, 76, 77, 85, 90, 110, 128, 188, 193
Elder, Jacob Delworth 193–202
"Electric Boogie" 109
"Electric Slide" see "Electric Boogie"
Ellington, Duke 83, 151
Elliott, Missy 136
Ellis, Alton 30, 71, 74, 76, 88, 89, 90, 92, 96, 113, 121, 131, 167, 188, 193, 202
Ellis, Bobby 152
Ellis, Hortense 1, 30, 48, 58, 71, 74, 76, 88–92, 100, 188, 193, 205
Ellis, Owen "Blakka" 88–92, 205
Elvis D 128
The Emotions 128
Enright, Janet 10, 18–24, 203
Epiphany Night Club 127
Eric Deans All-Girl Orchestra see Deans, Eric
Eric Deans Orchestra see Deans, Eric
Erskine, Marcia 154–155, 206
Ertegun Brothers 185–186
Estraleta Dancers 197
ET sound system 133
The Ethiopians 167
Europe 12, 18, 47, 51, 52, 54, 65, 70, 80, 84, 106, 110, 144, 153, 157, 187
Evans, June see Junie Ranks
Evans, Tyrone (Don) 106, 112
Excelsior Education Centre 145
Ezz Reco and The Launchers 87, 93

Fab 69
Fagan, Kendris 68–70, 76, 188
Federal Records 58, 77, 79, 107, 125, 164, 166, 171, 178–183, 185, 186
"Feel Like Jumping" 105
Festival Song Competition 29, 65, 121, 131
The Ferry Club 108
50/50 32
Finian's Rainbow 48
Finnis, Rob 78, 205
"Fire in Mi Wire" 41, 59, 167
Fitzgerald, Ella 18, 21, 51
The Five Dimensions 79
Flamingo Hotel 29
Flanagan, Chris 49, 204
Flynn, Errol 139
folk 3–9, 53, 95, 125, 144–145, 156–161, 164, 191, 195, 209
Folkes Brothers 141
Fong, Neville Cha 30–31
Fontana 78–80, 83, 85
Forester, Joseph 65
Forrest, Althea *see* Althea and Donna
Forreste, Sharon 119
Forrester, Dawn 24
Forrester's Hall 170
Foster, May 36
Foster, Winston "Yellowman" *see* Yellowman
Foulds, Howard 54
Foxx, Inez 82
Francis, Connie 96
Francis, Francisca 70
Francis, Hugh 46
Franklin, Aretha 101, 105, 187
Franklin, Gloria 58
Fraser, Neil *see* Mad Professor
Fraser, Norma 98–102, 205, 210
Freed, Alan 78

Gabbidon, Basil 66
Galleon Club 19
Gamble, Rollo 82
Gardiner, Boris 24, 113, 117, 194–195, 201
Garth, Marie 58, 168–169
Gay Feet 41, 59, 166, 167; *see also* Pottinger, Sonia
gay rights 102–135
Gaye, Barbie 78
Gaye, Marvin 80, 182
The Gaylads 25, 90, 167
The Gaylettes 102, 106–108
Gaynair, Bobby 21, 22, 101, 152
Gaynair, Wilton 18, 19, 20, 21, 151, 152
General Echo 133
General Smiley 23

Germain, Donovan 133
Gibbs, Joe 121
Gibson, Sharon 172
Gifford, Marlene 72, 108
Gilberto, Astrud 127
Gillespie, Gilly 120
Gilmore, Sydney Fitzgerald 13–14
Girl Satchmo *see* Fagan, Kendris
Girl Wonder *see* Marley, Rita Anderson
The Gladiators 93
Glascow, Deborahe 119
Glass Bucket 15, 16, 36, 44, 45, 47, 93, 95, 96, 138, 140, 141, 151, 152, 164
"Glass Thief" 38
Gloria and the Dreamlets *see* Franklin, Gloria
Gloudon, Barbara 173
Goday, Joe "Happy" 47
The Golden Dragon 31
Golding, Bruce 187
Goldman, Vivien 117
Goodall, Graeme 58, 77–82, 84, 86, 166–167, 171, 181–183, 185, 204, 205, 207
Goodison, Kingsley 73, 165, 172–174, 207
Goodison, Lorna 91, 205
Goodman, Benny 83, 151
Gordon, Roscoe 172
Gordon, Vin 122, 128, 152
Gore, Lesley 81
gospel 24–26, 40–42, 69–70, 107, 111, 124–125, 126, 127, 136, 165, 166
The Gospelaires *see* Fagan, Kendris
Gottlieb, Karla 4–6, 203, 209
Graham, Colby 187, 189, 207
Graham, Leo 197
Grandison, Errol 93
Grange, Olivia "Babsy" 126, 160, 175
Grant, Boysie 15, 87, 93, 205
Grant, Olive "Senya" 129
Grant, Ralph 140
Graydon, Dudley 14
Graydon, Ivy 1, 10, 12–18, 87, 203
Green, Cherry 74, 205
Greene, Tony 152
Greenwich Town 35, 47, 175
Gregory, Tony 48, 63, 72, 94, 105, 126, 152
Grennan, Winston 96
Griffiths, Albert 93
Griffiths, Marcia 1, 25, 90, 92, 102–110, 142, 168, 205
Guyana 13, 114, 147
Gyftt Records *see* Fraser, Norma

Hague-Bradshaw, Myrna 17, 45, 50–55, 91, 158, 173, 174, 203, 204, 205, 207, 209
Hall, Lester 44, 152
Hall, Marion *see* Lady Saw
Hall, Pam 96, 119
Hall, Vivian 18, 152
Hammond, Beres 105, 136
Hammond, Orville 23
Hampton, Lionel 182
Hannah Town 103
"The Harder They Come" 77
Harlem 8, 187
Harper, Raymond 120, 152
Harriott, Derrick 25, 76, 90, 92, 97, 100, 121, 164, 166, 188, 200
Harriott, Joe 18, 151, 152
Harris, Arthur 120
Harris, Earl 124
Harrison, Walter S. 149
Harrison, Yvonne 58, 64–68, 193, 198, 204
Harry J *see* Johnson, Harry
Harvey, Bernard "Touter" 122
Heineken Startime 67, 96, 127
Hendrix, Jimi 83
Henriques, Sean Paul Ryan Francis *see* Sean Paul
Henry, Adrian 54
Henry, Balford 135, 177, 206
The Heptones 25, 65, 197
Herman, Bongo 128
Hi-Hat 68
Hi-Lite 164
Hibbert, Lennie 21–22, 48, 152
higglers 89, 95, 176
Higgs, Joe 24, 74
Higgs and Wilson 76, 164, 188; *see also* Higgs, Joe; Wilson, Roy
High Note 43, 106, 166; *see also* Pottinger, Sonia
Hill, Lauryn 132
Hilton Hotel 52, 53, 126
Hinds, Justin 195, 199–200
The Hippy Boys 65
Hitchman, Don 120
Hogman, Pete 78
Hoken, Elsa 78
Holding, Ralph 52–53
Holiday, Billie 49, 127
Holt, John 76, 97, 106, 177, 188, 198, 199
Hope, Donna 195, 200, 201, 202, 207, 209
Hope, Johnny 87
Hope Gardens 54
Hopeton and Glen 198
Horne, Lena 50–51, 143
Hot Chocolate 8, 36, 70, 139
Hotel Casa Blanca 11, 12

House of Chen 108
"Housewife's Choice" 58, 192
Howard, Derrick 197
Hugh, Sang 199
Hurricane Flora 40
"Hurt So Good" 116–119
Hyatt, Charles 52
Hyatt, Leon 63
Hylton, Sheila 127–128
Hylton, Sonia see Madam Sugar Hips

The I-Threes 94, 102, 106, 108–109, 113
immigrants/immigration 58, 69, 73, 87, 94, 96, 128, 131, 138, 140, 144, 145, 152, 174
Imperial Hotel 35
improvisation 18, 21, 23, 37
independence 23, 26, 43, 144, 149, 156, 157, 181, 184
Independence celebrations 81–82, 83, 90, 111, 112
Independence Jump Up show 69, 164
Ingrid Chin and the Mighty Avengers 30
Inner Circle 102, 121, 195
Institute of Jamaica 5, 51, 55, 155, 160
International Reggae Studies Centre 161
Iron Curtain 46; see also Soviet Union
Isaacs, Gregory 99, 201
Island Records 58, 77, 84, 128, 164; see also Blackwell, Chris
Issa, Isaac 175
Issa, Joseph 44, 179
Issa's 44, 137, 175–176, 179; see also Issa, Joseph
It Can Happen to You 141, 189
The Itals 63, 99
Ivanhoe, Martin 77

Jackson, Jackie 123
Jackson, Sigmund "Siggy" 75
Jackson, Totlyn 43–46, 48, 68, 88, 204, 209
Jah Woosh 198
Jamaica Bandstand 27
Jamaica Big Band 52
Jamaica Constabulary Band 152
Jamaica Defence Force 17, 149
Jamaica Philharmonic Group 116, 125
Jamaica School of Music 53, 155
Jamaican dialect/patois 8, 119, 161, 197, 198
Jamaican Federation of Musicians 53, 66, 92, 126

Jamaican Folk Singers 125, 160
"Jamaican Fruit" 49
Jamaican Hit Parade 107
Jamaican Musicians Union 16
The Jamaicans 90, 112, 113, 126
James, Jimmy 166
James, Phillip 104
Janet Enright Combo 21; see also Enright, Janet
Jarrett, Donald 15, 21
Jay and the Americans 80
Jay-Z 132, 209
jazz 11, 16, 18–23, 28, 31, 36, 43–55, 56, 64, 68, 70, 83, 88, 91, 95, 101, 108, 112, 127, 150–152, 156–159, 191
Jazz Hall of Fame 54, 158
Jazz Jamaica 157
JBC 9, 52, 53, 76, 107, 112, 116, 118, 126, 134
Jennifer and the Mohawks see Jones, Jennifer
Jethro Tull 77
"Jikele Maweni" 59
The Jiving Juniors 68, 83
John, Elton 106
John Mouse 133
Johns, Lester 189
Johns, Lillian 187–190
Johns, Vere 34, 46, 69, 93, 187–190, 207, 209; see also Vere Johns Opportunity Hour
Johnson, Cluett 20–21
Johnson, Harry 106, 127, 128
Johnson, Joseph 61, 62
Johnson, Maurice 196
Johnson, Nicky 78
Johnson, Uriah 153
Johnson's Drive Inn 68, 101, 112
Johnston, Hazel 145–146
Jolly Boys 34
Jones, Barbara 198
Jones, Desi 54
Jones, Jack 21
Jones, Jackson 65
Jones, Jennifer 58
Jones, Quincy 81
Jones, Winston 92–93, 205
Jones Town 74
Jordon, Louis 172
Josephs, Chuck 166
Judah Recording Studio 126
jukebox/jukeboxes 77, 175, 176, 177
Junie Ranks 132–133, 206, 209

Kangaroo 69
Katz, David 74, 89, 166, 205, 207
Kaufman, Murray "the K" 80
Kay, Janet 119
Kay, Shirley see Dillon, Phyllis

Keith and Tex 67, 92
Kelly, Pat 96, 131
Kelso, Beverly 70–74, 204, 210
Kennedy, Imogene "Queenie" 6–7
Kes Chin and the Souvenirs 28–31
KG's Records 31
Khan, Chaka 127
Khan, Saffiyah 196
Khouri, Gloria 178–183
Khouri, Ken 69, 79, 107, 179–183, 186, 207
Khouri, Paul 178, 183, 207
Kid, Gloria 25
King, Ben E. 58, 105, 116
King, Bertie 12, 18, 152
King, Martin Luther, Jr. 36, 83
King Edwards 66, 99, 152
King Jammys 133
King Pharaoh 37
King Radio 37
King Stitt 25, 71
King Toyan 134
Kinsey Report 199
The Kingstonians 195
Kitty Kingston 140
Knibb, Lloyd 18, 61, 62, 96, 101, 142
Knight, Gladys 32, 105
Kong, Jeanette 30
Kong, Leslie 30, 58, 77, 99, 104, 110, 112, 152, 175, 197
Koromantee 4, 144
Kumina 6–7, 144, 158

Labelle, Patti 32, 71, 82, 90, 103–104, 105
Lack, Ken 66, 90
Lady Ann 133
Lady Baldwin 39
Lady Earle 34–35, 191
Lady G 133
Lady Iere 38–39
Lady MacDonald 39
Lady Saw 26, 32, 133–136, 161, 206, 209
Lady Trinidad 39
Lake George Inn 185
Lamb, Blossom 35–36, 108
Lamb, Louise 35–36, 70, 108, 191
Lane, Thelma see Lady Trinidad
Lannaman's Children's Hour 46, 155
Lawson, Beryl 107–108
Lebanese-Jamaicans 140–143, 178–187
LeBlanc, Norman see Richard the Lion Heart
Led Zeppelin 83

Lee, Byron 24–26, 28, 29, 30, 31, 48, 59, 63, 66, 67, 82–84, 90, 95, 104–105, 112, 125, 143, 144, 153, 164, 175, 184–187
Lee, Errol 94, 127
Lee, Neville 25
Lee, Sheila Khouri 184–187, 207
Lee, Winston 31
Lennon, Julian 36
Leslie Levy and the Tendertones 199
Lester Hall's Orchestra 44, 152
Levy, Christine 26–33, 203, 204
Levy, Jeanne 27
Levy, Michael 117–118
Levy, Morris *see* Levy, Moishe
Lewin, Olive 6, 156, 157, 159–160, 207
Lewis, Aubrey 40–41
Lewis, Herman 44
Lewis, Hopeton 96, 100
Lewis, Hortense 108, 124
Lewis, Jerry 116, 117
Lewis, Jerry Lee 80
Lewis, Pat 23
Lewis, Roger 121
Lewis, Smiley 172
The Liberators 19
The Lido Club 11
Liggins, Joe 172
Lightbourne, Robert 70
"Linstead Market" 95, 126, 164
Little, Sister Mary Bernadette 147, 149, 209
Little Anthony and the Imperials 80
Little Richard 78, 176
Little Theatre Movement 9; *see also* Pantomime
Livingston, Neville O'Riley "Bunny" 70, 73
Llewelyn, Barry 65
Lloyd, Cecil 22
Lodge, J.C. 119
Lomax, Alan 193
London 8, 18, 35, 45, 46, 50, 52, 63, 69, 77, 78, 79, 81, 84, 85, 86, 87, 93, 97, 117, 118, 119, 123, 128, 129, 130, 137, 152, 157, 160, 179, 180
Lopez, Jennifer 32
Lord Comic 25, 186
Lord Creator 99, 100, 165, 177, 197
Lord Executor 37
Lord Flea 179, 192
Lord Fly 179
Lord Iere 38
Lord Inventor 37
Lord Jellicoe 48
Lord Kitchener 35, 41, 120, 192

Lord Koos 90
Lord Lebby 35, 96, 199
Lord Superior 39
Lord Tanamo 35, 62, 166, 204
Lou and Ranny 9, 139; *see also* Coverley, Louise "Miss Lou" Bennett; Williams, Ranny
Love, Dawn *see* Ellis, Hortense
"Love Forever" 125
lovers' rock 119, 125, 201
Loy, Herman Chin 65
Lucas, Dorice Constance 187
Lyceum Ballroom 124
Lyn, Keith 31
Lyn, Warwick 121
Lynn, Barbara 29
Lynn Taitt and the Jets 58, 113; *see also* Taitt, Lynn

MacDonald, Doris *see* Lady MacDonald
Macka B 202
Macka Diamond 133
MacLean, Ranchie 123
Mad Professor 119–120
Madam Eve Temptation 138
Madam Sugar Hips 143
Madame Wasp 30, 143, 144
Madden, David 152
Madison Square Garden 124
Maga Man *see* Howard, Derrick
Magnet Records 117, 118
Mahfood, Anita 30, 68, 76, 109, 140–143, 153, 189, 209
Majestic Theatre 93, 100, 152
Makeba, Miriam 45, 59, 167
Malcolm, Carl 198
Malcolm, Carlos 18, 48, 112
"A Man Is a Two Face" 58
Manley, Edna 18, 139, 159, 207
Manley, Michael 182
Manley, Norman 4, 18–19, 44, 159
Margarita *see* Mahfood, Anita
Marks, Louisa 119
Marley, Bob 1, 2, 31, 54, 70–74, 76, 77, 84, 94, 98, 100, 102, 105–106, 108–109, 113, 116, 124, 126, 152, 161, 164, 176–177, 188, 200–201, 207, 209
Marley, Damian 132
Marley, Rita Anderson 72, 88, 98, 100, 102, 106, 108, 124, 176
Marley, Ziggy 98
Maroons 3–6, 159, 172, 203, 209
Marquis, Herman 122
Marshall, Larry 165
Marshall, Paul 184
Marshall, Wayne 32
Martha and the Vandellas 80
Martin, Winston "Sparrow" 148, 150, 153, 173, 206

Mason, Norma 69–70
Masuka, Dorothy 59, 167
McCook, Denise 62
McCook, Tommy 18, 25, 30, 43, 62, 69, 96, 112, 120, 122, 142, 152
McDonald, Christopher 54
McDonald, Larry 21, 23
McGann, Connie *see* Penn, Dawn
McGowen, Howard 135, 206
McGregor, Freddie 107, 195, 198, 201
McKay, Claude 8
McKay, Freddie 128
McMillan, Dudley 20 *see also* Colony Club
McNair, Harold 18, 152
McPherson, Milton 11, 70
McRae, Carmen 21
The Meditations 198
The Mellotones 198
The Mellow Larks 166
The Melodians 113, 167
"Melody Life" 52, 54, 55, 105
Memory Bank Project 160
mento 8, 19, 22–23, 34–42, 56, 108, 129, 150, 152, 158, 159, 164, 168, 181, 191–192, 197–200, 204
Mercury Records 80, 180, 186
merengue 19, 136
Merritone *see* Blake, Winston
Messado, Karley 23
The Mighty Avengers 197
The Mighty Diamonds 117
Mighty Duke 37
Mighty Sparrow 37, 40, 41, 66, 90, 192
The Mighty Spoiler 37
The Mighty Vikings 28, 31
Miller, Hugh 21
Miller, Jacob 121, 122
Millie in Jamaica 82
Mills, Beverly 87, 93, 205
Minnelli, Liza 47
Minott, Sugar 201
The Miracles 80
Miss Lou *see* Coverley, Louise "Miss Lou" Bennett
Mittoo, Jackie 18, 61, 100, 101, 105, 112
The Moderniques Orchestra 11–12
money/pay 59, 66, 90–91, 93–94, 95, 96, 99–100, 107, 112, 113–114, 117, 123, 124, 128–129, 132, 164, 165, 168
Montego Bay 10, 11, 12, 34, 46, 49, 54, 72, 76, 82, 95, 100, 101, 107, 115, 133, 164, 173, 203
The Moon Invaders 63

Moore, Johnny "Dizzy" 18, 23, 112, 113, 147, 152
Moore Town 6
Morais, Althea 27
Morgan, Derrick 25, 48, 56–58, 60, 63, 64, 66, 67, 76, 90, 92, 96, 188, 192,193, 195
Morgan, Earl 65
Morgan, Paulette 58
Morris, Eric "Monty" 57, 76, 167, 196
Morris, Lowell 28, 164
Morris, Mervyn 8, 9, 203, 209
Mosely, Pam 27
Moskowitz, David V. 191, 207, 210
Mossip, Leila Doris see Wilson, Leila
motherhood 6, 8, 15–16, 17, 18, 26, 29, 31, 36, 42, 44–45, 47, 48–49, 50–51, 60–62, 64, 74, 75, 88, 91–92, 94, 103, 107, 109, 115, 119, 131, 132, 134, 157, 162–163, 165–166, 172–173, 176–177, 179, 183, 194–195
Motown Records 80, 180
Motta, Baba 21, 44, 46, 47, 152
Motta, Stanley 12, 34, 35, 36
Mowatt, Judy 106–108, 126, 167, 205
Moxey, George 11, 70, 139
Mullings, Foggy 21, 36
Murphy, George 196
Murray, Arthur 83
Murvin, Junior 85
Music Land 173
Musik City 110, 173; see also Dodd, Clement Seymour "Coxsone"
Mutt and Jeff 150
"My Boy Lollipop" 75, 77–80, 83–85
myal 6, 144, 203
Myrtle Bank Hotel 12, 15, 29, 47, 68, 152, 164
The Mystery Ship 139

Nanny of the Maroons 3–6, 172, 203
Nanny's Korner 172
Narcisse, Iverlin 69
Nash, Johnny 106, 113
Nasralla, Ronnie 82, 84, 184–185, 205
National Dance Theatre Company (NDTC) 145, 156, 158
National Labour Congress 16
National Stadium/Arena 25, 29, 76, 86, 96, 148
"Natty Dread" 108
Nectar Records 106; see also Andy, Bob

Neely, Daniel 35, 204
Neita, Hartley 16, 19, 35, 44–45, 203, 204
Nelson, Ezekiel 21
Nettleford, Rex 156
The New Beats 80
New Kids on the Block 32
New Name Muzik 134
New Orleans 68, 140
New York 8, 10, 17, 32, 33, 45, 49, 59, 65, 66, 67, 73, 78, 80–84, 96, 97, 102, 123, 124, 125, 128, 137, 139, 143, 144, 157, 169, 174–175, 177, 178, 184, 185, 186
New York World's Fair 1964–1965 28, 82–84, 184–185
Niaah, Sonjah Stanley 197, 200, 210
Nichols, Marie Crompton 27, 29, 30, 32, 204
Nicodemus 131
"Night Food" 34, 197
nine night 136
Noblett, Richard 34–35

obeah 4–5, 6, 192, 196, 203
Obeah! 139
O'Brien, Baby "Babe" 15, 139
O'Brien, Captain "Chappy" 15
The Ocean View Club 100
Ocho Rios 19, 21, 29, 30, 43, 46, 50, 52, 53, 54, 95, 107, 112, 120, 152
Ocho Rios International Jazz Festival 53–54
Oliver St. Patrick and the Diamonds 96
Olympic Studios 78
Opel, Jackie 61, 62, 72, 90, 193
Orange Street 56, 110, 112, 166, 173
Order of Distinction (O.D.) 49–50, 75, 86, 97, 115, 154, 158, 168
Organaire, Charley 76, 188
Osbourne, Johnny 131, 152
Our Gang 9
Ozou'ne 54

Pablo, Augustus 177, 201
Page, Patti 64, 96
Palace Theatre 68, 112, 142, 152, 188, 189
Palmer, Robert 77
Pam Pam 25
Pama 111, 129
Pantomime 9, 48, 66, 84, 86, 89, 112, 120, 138, 139, 140, 141, 158
Panton, Roy 56, 66, 67, 76–77, 82, 84, 95, 193, 205
Papa Michigan 23

Papa San 21, 126
The Paragons 90, 103, 106, 112, 199
Parker, Charlie 18, 78
Parker, Ken 94
Parker, Man 6
Parker, Ole 6
Parks, Lloyd 96, 123
Patrick, Kentrick see Lord Creator
"Pata Pata Rock Steady" 59, 167
Patterson, P.J. 66, 145, 169
Paul, Donna 26
Paul, Frankie 201
Paul, Sean 32, 146, 177, 178
payola 78, 116
"Peanut Vendor" 137, 139
Pearl White 38
Penn, Dawn 110–114, 125, 196, 205, 210
People's National Party 159
Peppermint Lounge 184
The Pepperpot 19
"Perfidia" 96
Perkins, Lascelles 25, 66, 74, 76, 89, 188
Perry, Lee "Scratch" 65, 90, 108, 116–117, 120, 124, 176
Peterson, Pete 78
Peyton Place 120
Philips Records 79, 186
Phillip, Theophilus see The Mighty Spoiler
Phillipps, Gloria 15–17, 203
Phillips, Jannette 82–83, 143, 184
Phillips, Naomi 58, 63
"Pied Piper" 106
Pinkney, Dwight 99
Pink's Grocery 170
The Pioneers 86
The Pipers see The Wailing Souls
Plummer, Holford 167
Pocomania see Pukkumina
The Police 127, 128
Pottinger, Lindon O. 66, 77, 108, 166
Pottinger, Sonia 41, 58–59, 66, 96, 106, 108, 124, 152, 164, 166–168, 172, 183, 185, 207
Poulle, Mapletoft 11, 12, 34
Pouyatt, Buddy 52
Powder, Ted 124
Presley, Elvis 81
Prince Buster 56, 66, 77, 85, 90, 93, 94, 99, 110, 113, 141, 152, 175, 193–197
Protoje 127
Pukkumina 6, 144
The Pyramids 86

Quakers 110
Queen Elizabeth 47, 71
Queen Tiney *see* Ellis, Hortense
Queenie *see* Kennedy, Imogene "Queenie"
Queens Theatre 141, 152
Quevedo, Raymond *see* Attila the Hun

Rainbow Orchestra 36
Rainbow Room 81
Randy's *see* Chin, Vincent
Ranglin, Ernest 18–19, 31, 71, 78, 83, 100, 151, 206
Ranking Joe 195
Ranks, Lushy 128
Ras Clifton 201
Rastafari 23, 135, 142, 201, 206, 207, 209, 210
Ready, Steady, Go! 82
Reckord, Verena 142, 206, 210
Record Specialists 185–186; *see also* Benson, George; Benson, Jean
recording industry 22, 31, 34, 41, 61, 69–70, 72, 77–79, 93, 99–100, 105, 166–168, 170–187
Redding, Otis 82, 129–130
Reece, Dizzy 18, 152
Regal Theatre 68
reggae 49, 52–55, 69, 73, 94, 98–130, 134, 161, 167, 197, 199, 201, 205, 206, 207, 209, 210
Reggae Studies Unit 161, 197
Reggae Sumfest 133
Reggae Sumfest 54; *see also* Reggae Sunsplash
Reggae Sunsplash 53–54, 129, 132, 135
Reid, Anthony 171
Reid, Arthur Stanley "Duke" 57–58, 69, 74, 95–96, 99, 104, 106, 109, 113, 124, 152, 166
Reid, Christel 89–92, 205
Reid, Clifford 120
Reid, Donna *see* Althea and Donna
Reid, Ezzard *see* Ezz Reco and the Launchers
Reid, Junior 195
Reid, Lucille 170–172, 183
The Renegades *see* The Wailing Souls
revivalist religions 6–7, 131, 144, 159
The Revolutionaries 96, 123
Rhooms, Uriah "Bad Move" 125–126
rhumba 30, 68, 137–144, 189, 209
rhumba box 34

rhythm and blues/R&B 52, 56, 58, 75, 78, 88, 107, 111, 152, 172, 191, 194
Rialto Theatre 141
Richard Organization *see* Goday, Joe "Happy"
Richard the Lion Heart 37
Richards, Cynthia 123–124
Richards, Keith 31, 187
Richards, Roy 76, 90, 165, 188
Richardson, Harold 198
Rickards, Sheila 1, 21, 46–50, 88, 204
Rihanna 132
Riley, Daisy 8, 138–140
Riley, Jimmy 105
Riley, Winston 131, 132, 133, 206, 209
Rinaldo's Rhumba Kings 140
Ring Ding 9
Ritz Theatre 141, 164
RJR (Radio Jamaica Rediffusion) 17, 47, 76, 107, 116, 167
Roaring Lion 37
Roberts, Johnny 78
Robin and the Nightingales 65
Robinson, Roy 77
Rockfort 103, 105, 109, 120, 156
rocksteady 29, 58, 59, 88–97, 102, 105, 111, 113, 120, 147, 167, 192, 200
Rodriguez, Rico 18, 76, 152, 188
The Rolling Stones 79, 186–187
The Roots Radics 99
Ross, Diana 127, 167
Roulette Records 78
Rouse, Michael 45
Rowe, Karl 69
Rowe, Keith *see* Keith and Tex
Rowe, Maureen 201, 207
Roy Coburn Orchestra 36, 152
Royal Academy of Music 160
Royal Festival Hall 157, 160
The Royal Jamaicans 11
Rubbaal, Giddeon Jah 201
Ruby and The Romantics 29, 109
rude boy 87, 194
Rugs, Bunny 117
Russell, Ophlin *see* Sister Nancy
Russell, Robert *see* Brigadier Jerry

St. Peters, Crispian 106
Salvation Army 24, 110, 111
Sampson, Victor 186
Samuels, Winston 90
Sandy-Lewis, McArtha Linda *see* Calypso Rose
Sang, Herman 31
Saunders, Mahalia *see* Ellis, Hortense

sca 84
Schloss, Cynthia 114, 125
Seaga, Edward 7, 65, 82, 84, 103, 146, 159, 160, 166, 184–186
Seaga, Joan 143, 206
The Searchers 80
Seivright, Floyd Lloyd 150, 152
Selassie, Haile 182
sexual exploitation 94, 100, 118–119, 123
Shabba Ranks 133, 135, 136, 177
Shaffer, Doreen 2, 58, 60–64, 112, 204
Shaggy 32
Shakespeare, Robbie *see* Sly and Robbie
Shalit, Emil 69, 75
The Shangri-Las 80
The Sharks 99
Shaw, Marlena 88
The Sheiks 101
Shelly Thunder 133
Sheraton Hotel 48, 127, 143
Sherlock, Philip 144
Shillingford, Aldene 12–15, 203
Shirley and Lee 76, 94
Shurland, Roy 22
Sibbles, Leroy 96, 197
Silver, Ric 109
Silver Seas Hotel 15, 35, 43
Silver Slipper Club 15, 152, 171
Silvera, Larry 23
"Simmer Down" 71, 73, 204, 210
Simmonds, Beverley 111, 129–130
Simms, Noel "Scully" 25, 76, 92, 122, 188, 189
Simone, Nina 106
Simpson, Charles 149, 152–154, 206
Sinatra, Frank 44, 96
Sinclair, Carlene *see* Davis, Carlene
Sindrey, Dennis 28, 48, 143–144, 164, 204, 206
The Singer Bowl 83
Sir Lord Comic *see* Lord Comic
Sister Charmaine 133
Sister Enid *see* Cumberland, Enid
Sister Ignatius *see* Davies, Sister Mary Ignatius
Sister Nancy 131–132, 133, 134, 206, 209
Sisters of Mercy 147, 209
ska 23, 26–33, 56–87, 91, 92, 95, 102, 113, 136, 151, 152, 167, 184, 192, 205, 209
ska dance 82–83
The Skatalites 23, 28, 61–64, 66, 71, 72, 73, 84, 85, 100, 101, 105, 112, 177

Index

Skin, Flesh, and Bones 123, 198
slack/slackness 96, 124, 134, 135, 138, 161
slavery 3, 4, 8, 34, 49, 124, 140, 143, 160, 172
The Slickers 197
Sly and Robbie 77, 122, 127, 128
Small, Jaelee 86
Small, Millie 75–86, 94, 110, 152, 164, 188, 193, 205
Smart, Leroy 152
Smash Records 78, 80
Smith, Byron 124
Smith, Cherry see Green, Cherry
Smith, Denver 54
Smith, Earl "Chinna" 54, 122
Smith, Ernie 126
Smith, Germaine 131
Smith, Simeon see Hi-Lite
Smith, Slim 63
Smithsonian 7, 160, 207
Smitty's Record Shop 124
soca 41, 59, 135, 167, 197
soccer/football 26, 108, 148–149
The Sombrero Club 29, 108, 112
soul 52, 88, 106, 107, 129, 132, 164
The Soul Brothers 100
The Soul Sisters 108, 124
The Soulettes 72, 102, 108, 124
sound systems 31, 57, 71, 98–99, 104, 131, 133–134, 150, 152, 170–173, 177, 181
Soviet Union 46
Span, Norman see King Radio
The Spanishtonians see The Webber Sisters
Spanishtown 124
The Specials 196
Spence, Hugh 69
Spence, Lloyd 101
Spence, Sonya 128, 167
Spence, Trenton 12
Spencer, Robert 78
Spencer Davis Group 85
Springfield, Dusty 80, 81, 127
Springfield Beach Club 12, 19, 139
Stag 111
Staple Singers 162, 186
Starline 69
State Theatre 90, 100
Stax 162, 186
Steel Pulse 66, 198
Steffens, Roger 1, 73, 204, 205, 210
Stephenson, Pauline 70
Sterling, Lester 28, 64, 68, 101, 152
Stevens, Cat 77, 101, 187

Stewart, Keith 48, 164, 192
Stewart, Ken 66
Stewart, Rod 31, 78–79, 106
Stills, Stephen 96
Stoddart, Peter 28, 164, 184
Stolzoff, Norman 135, 201, 206, 210
Stony Hill 82, 162, 165, 177
"Stop That Train" 92–93
Studio One 54, 61, 71–73, 76, 89, 93–94, 99, 100, 104, 105, 106, 108, 112, 113, 123, 162–166, 172–175; see also Dodd, Clement Seymour "Coxsone"
The Sugar Hill Club 16, 120
"Sugar Plum" 76, 193
"Sugar Sugar" 62
Sunset Orchestra 12
Super Cat 133
Supernova Ska Festival 60, 63
The Supremes 80, 116
Suzette see Penn, Dawn
Symonette, George 96

Taino 144
Talent Corporation 121
Tarzan 123
Taylor, Nadine 143, 206
Technique Disco 133
The Techniques 90, 131
The Temptations 80, 176
Tenor Saw 134
Terror Fabulous 135
Tex, Joe 198
Third World 77, 117, 121, 128
Thomas, Carla 104, 105, 109
Thomas, Edna see Lady Iere
Thomas, Ruddy 119
Thompson, Carroll 119
Thompson, Errol (DJ with JBC) 109
Thompson, Errol (producer) 109, 121
Thompson, Leslie 152
Thornton, Edward "Tan Tan" 18, 151, 152, 206
The Thunderbirds 128
The Ticklers 144, 198, 199
Time Store see Durie, Alec
Time Will Tell 86
Tip Top 166
Tivoli Gardens 103
Tobago 36, 37, 38, 39, 40, 157, 167, 193, 210
Tobias, Charles 114
Todd, Millicent "Patsy" 2, 41, 56–60, 67, 88, 90, 167–168, 192, 196, 204, 207
Tommy Dorsey Orchestra 44
Tommy McCook and the Supersonics 30, 69, 96

The Tonettes see The Webber Sisters
Toni Marie see Harrison, Yvonne
Tony Liquidator 67
Toots and the Maytals 25, 29, 77, 84, 86, 126, 131, 177
Top of the Pops 106, 118, 122
Toronto 7, 9, 49, 59, 126, 143, 144, 152, 186
Tosh, Peter 70, 101, 126, 176, 198
Tower Isle Hotel 21, 22, 144, 152
Townsend, Pete 31
Treasure Isle 69, 95, 142, 168, 170–172; see also Reid, Arthur Stanley "Duke"
Treasure Isle Time 74; see also Reid, Arthur Stanley "Duke"
Trench Town 70–74, 88–89, 103, 108, 125, 188
Trinidad 37–41, 90, 101, 120, 157, 186, 193–194, 204, 210
Trinity 121
Trojan Records 69, 86, 117, 205, 210
The Trojans 198
Truth 23
Tucker, Jimmy 46, 74, 76, 173, 188
Tucker, Junior 126
Tuff Gong 113, 129
Tulloch, Vincent 152
Turner, Joe 172
Turpin, Carol 197
The Two Kings 196

U-Roy 25, 96, 167
U2 77
UK 50, 51, 52, 65, 69, 75, 77, 78, 79, 80, 82, 86, 94, 106, 114, 121, 122, 128, 139, 157, 164; see also London
United Artists 186
United Fruit Company 110
Universal Records 117
University of the West Indies Mona 42, 54, 115, 127, 128, 156, 161, 197, 200, 202, 209
Up Park Camp 15
The Upsetters 65
"Uptown Top Ranking" 85, 121–122

The Vagabonds 31
Valli, Frankie 80
Vaughan, Sarah 21, 51, 54, 95, 96, 152
Vere Johns Opportunity Hour 24, 34, 44, 46, 65, 68, 76, 89, 90, 92, 93, 112, 140, 141, 164, 187–189

Verity, Tony 105, 184
The Version Band 30
Vester, Ron 89, 163, 174
Vineyard Town 64, 127
The VIPs 123
Vishawadia, Shay 66
The Voice 32, 68
VP Records 177–178; *see also* Chin, Patricia; Chin, Vincent
The Vulcans 95

The Wailers 65, 70–74, 96, 99, 100, 108, 124, 129, 177, 210
The Wailing Souls 73, 108
The Wailing Wailers 70, 72–74
Waits, Tom 77
Walker, Constantine 72, 108
Wallace, Leroy "Horsemouth" 152
Walters, Basil 168
Walters, Maxine 23
Ward Theatre 24, 36, 44, 48, 66, 98, 101, 104, 111, 112, 139, 140, 141, 142, 146, 152, 176, 189
Wareika Hills 104, 156, 167
Warwick, Dee Dee 123
Warwick, Dionne 80, 90, 96, 109, 182
Washington, Dinah 51, 61, 70
Waterman, Pete 117–118
Webber, Cynthia *see* The Webber Sisters
Webber, David 93
Webber, Merlene *see* The Webber Sisters
The Webber Sisters 92–95, 205
Webster, Bob 95
Webster, Lloyd 128

"We'll Meet" 76–77, 193
West, Kanye 132, 209
West Indian Regiment *see* Jamaica Military Band
The Western Standard Time Ska Orchestra 63
White, Bruce 120
White, Garth 202
White, Joe 166
White, Poppy 45
White, Roy 70
White, Timothy
White Sails 139
The Who 83
Whylie, Marjorie 24, 125, 154–159, 206
Wildman, Max 184
Williams, Audley 28, 44
Williams, Bertie 120
Williams, Eric 38, 40
Williams, Everard 34, 35, 195, 198, 200
Williams, Ken 120, 152
Williams, Mark 151, 206, 210
Williams, Noel *see* Lord Lebby
Williams, Oswald *see* Count Ossie
Williams, Ranny 9, 48, 120, 124, 139–140, 189
Wilson, Delroy 25, 63, 90, 100, 193
Wilson, Ernest 105
Wilson, Jackie 66
Wilson, Leila 10–12
Wilson, Nancy 109, 127
Wilson, Roy 24, 74; *see also* Higgs and Wilson
WINS-FM 78, 80
Winston and The Tonettes 92–94; *see also* Jones, Winston; The Webber Sisters
Winwood, Steve 77
WIRL 44, 164, 185, 186
Wiz Khalifa 132
Wolfram, Eddie 86
Wolmer's School 146
"Woman a Come" 109, 142
"Woman of the Ghetto" 88
Wonder, Wayne 133
Wong, Florence 28
Wong, Margaret 27, 28, 32–33, 204
Wong, Sonny 28, 31
Wong, Tom, "the Great Sebastian" 31, 171
Wong, Victor 28, 31
Wood, Ron 31
World Disc 89; *see also* Dodd, Clement Seymour "Coxsone"
Wright, Hazel 94

Xhosa 59
Xu, Christina 30

Yap, Justin 30, 99, 152
Yap, Stanley 31
"Yellow Bird" 44, 53
Yellowman 99, 102, 132, 152, 197
Yen, Alma Mock 145, 206, 210
Yen, Iggy Fong 15
Young, Cecil Moo 31
Young, Desmond 92
"Young, Gifted and Black" 106

Zap Pow 99
Zion 6
The Zodiacs 44
ZQI 8

www.ingramcontent.com/pod-product-compliance
Lightning Source LLC
Chambersburg PA
CBHW060342010526
44117CB00017B/2931